# THE TUDOR LAW OF TREASON

# STUDIES IN SOCIAL HISTORY

*Editor:* **HAROLD PERKIN**

Professor of Social History, University of Lancaster

*Assistant Editor:* **ERIC J. EVANS**

Lecturer in History, University of Lancaster

*For a list of books in the series see back end paper*

# THE TUDOR LAW OF TREASON

## An Introduction

### John Bellamy

*Professor of History*
*Carleton University, Ottawa*

LONDON: Routledge & Kegan Paul

TORONTO AND BUFFALO: University of Toronto Press

First published in 1979
in Great Britain
by Routledge & Kegan Paul Ltd
and in Canada and the United States of America by
University of Toronto Press
Toronto and Buffalo
Printed in Great Britain by
Redwood Burn Limited
Trowbridge and Esher

British Library Cataloguing in Publication Data

Bellamy, John
The Tudor law of treason. – (Studies in social
history)
1. Treason – England – History
I. Title    II. Series
345' .42'023/          KD8022

RKP ISBN 0 7100 8729 2
UTP ISBN 0 8020 2266 9

This book has been published
with the help of a grant from the
Social Science Federation of Canada,
using funds provided by the Social Sciences and
Humanities Research Council of Canada

# Contents

# Introduction

The historians who in the last century and a half have
addressed themselves to studying the complex Tudor law of
treason and how it operated have been few in number although there has been a large amount of writing concerned
with the political, religious and economic features of the
many conspiracies, insurrections and traitorous expres-
sions of dissent occurring in that period.    Only with
J.F. Stephen's 'History of the Criminal Law of England'
published in 1883 was there a serious attempt to break
away from reliance on the writings of Coke and Hale and
to place the law of treason in a proper historical setting, albeit in a way which was extremely rudimentary. (1)
In regard to the scope of the treason law the important
issue for Stephen was why the act of 1352 was found insufficient in the years 1533-1603 and how it was supplemented.    He divided the treason legislation of Henry
VIII's reign into those acts aimed at securing this 'great
religious and political revolution' by maintaining the
king's position against the pope and the statutes that
were intended to protect the king's plans for the succession.    Rightly he fixed on the use made of the treason
act of 1352 from the Henrician reformation to the death of
Elizabeth, drawing attention to periods when he thought
the statute was interpreted narrowly and others when it
seemed a wider interpretation prevailed.    The former he
identified with the later years of Henry VIII, the latter
with the reign of Elizabeth.    Stephen was acute enough to
notice how unsatisfactory were the comments of Coke and
Hale on conspiracy to levy war.    He pointed out that the
act of 1352 omitted the offence, and argued that the de-
fect could only be remedied by special legislation.    He
also drew attention to the medieval statute's failure to
make treason out of forming an intent to depose or incap-
acitate the king.    In his comments on the scope of

1

treason Stephen was in fact doing little more than review-
ing critically the writings of famous law treatise writers
of earlier centuries, relying for the most part on his
professional knowledge as a judge.  The same is largely
true of his treatment of treason trials, although there he
did utilize printed extracts of the arraignments of some
of the more famous sixteenth-century traitors and Cobbett's 'State Trials'. (2)  If the materials were thin,
Stephen's comments were shrewd and indeed seminal.  In
only a few lines he got close to the heart of the Tudor
treason trial, an achievement which, considering the lack
of historical research to that time, was quite remarkable.
    W.S. Holdsworth, in his 'History of English Law', fol-
lowed Stephen in identifying three types of addition to
the treason law by the Tudors. (3)  He devoted a relatively large amount of space to the statutes which expan-
ded the act of 1352 (and were thus 'of more permanent interest'), quoting and offering some sort of explanation of
the terminology of each and showing that they 'clearly
brought within the law of treason' the two great omissions
of the medieval statute 'conspiracies to levy war which
had for their object the deposition or coercion of the
sovereign'.  He was particularly eager to emphasize that
in Elizabeth's reign, in contrast with those of her
father, brother and sister, new statutes on treason ceased
to be promulgated because of the judges' use of 'construction', that is to say the interpreting of an existing act
(usually that of 1352) so that it covered a greater variety of treasons than had originally been supposed or intended.  Constructive treason, he argued with some cogency, derived primarily from the clauses in the 1352 act
which made it treason to compass or imagine the king's
death or to levy war against him. (4)  However, he did
not notice, as did Miss Thornley a few years later, that
examples of constructive treason could be found before the
Tudor period. (5)  Little of Holdsworth's contribution to
the history of the Tudor law of treason was original.
Where he did not follow Stephen he used Coke and Hale,
other treatise writers like Fitzherbert, and the report of
the trial of Roger Casement.  He utilized almost no ar-
chival material and provided little historical background.
Where Holdsworth did advance Tudor-treason scholarship was
in attempting a comprehensive survey of treason legislation through considering, in addition to the acts dealing
with central themes, such less important aspects as counterfeiting and forgery, the statutes making reference to
witnesses and 'offences cognate to treason'.  Yet, when
all is considered, his comments on treason cannot be said
to be among the better sections of his work.

In 1922 there appeared J.R. Tanner's 'Tudor Constitutional Documents A.D. 1485-1603 with an Historical Commentary'. In his introduction to the section devoted to the law of treason, Tanner gave some historical background to the statute of 1352 and endeavoured to show that constructive treason developed during the fifteenth century. In dealing with the Tudor treason statutes he adopted in essence the divisions proposed by Stephen and briefly commented on those acts he thought important. He demonstrated the alternating severity and moderation of the law in the middle years of the century. (6) He recognized that because of Miss Thornley's work it could no longer be held against Henry VIII that he or his minister was the inventor of treason by words. In his introduction to documents relating to treason trials, Tanner largely followed Stephen once more, but he was careful to list the sixteenth-century statutes which in some way affected the form of those trials by, for example, making stipulation as to witnesses or depriving the accused of benefit of clergy or of sanctuary. Tanner also had comment to make on two neglected, yet important, aspects of treason, namely acts of attainder and trial before the court of the lord high steward, although for both of these subjects he relied considerably on L.W. Vernon Harcourt's 'His Grace the Steward and Trial by Peers'. (7) Another useful part of Tanner's book, although again without claim to originality or depth, was a few remarks on the punishment of treason and the forfeiture of traitors' possessions. The book set the law of treason better in its historical, particularly its constitutional, setting than previously and it provided easier access to a number of relevant statutes, (8) yet it is clear that, apart from attempting to precis and clarify the work of the great commentators Coke and Hale and provide historical background, Tanner and the other modern writers on Tudor treason law had to this point achieved very little.

The next study in chronological sequence of the Tudor treason law was that of S. Rezneck, who was by training a political scientist. (9) It was he who first saw in the large amount of sixteenth-century treason legislation proof of modernity, the solving of problems by means of parliamentary acts. He drew attention to several distinctive features of the operation of the laws against traitors which had not been emphasized hitherto. He pointed out that the chief Tudor contribution to treason legislation was through statutes dealing with traitorously written or spoken words. He noted the way in which the Tudor kings extended the concept of treason to embrace the powers, titles and dignities of the sovereign as well as

his person, and also to the opposition against existing or
proposed treason legislation which manifested itself in
1547, 1571 and 1584.   He sought to show in addition that
the law could not make a valid distinction between religious and political obedience, since the two were so en-
tangled.   Did not parliament and the courts hold that
popery and treason went automatically together?   The end
of the sixteenth century, so he argued, provided example
of almost any attack on the state being construed as an
attack on the sovereign and therefore treason which, if it
was an oversimplification, rightly drew attention to the
odd attitudes the crown lawyers took to rebellion at that
time.   In regard to trials for treason Rezneck advanced
the important argument, drawn apparently from the report
of Nicholas Throckmorton's trial,  that during Mary and
Elizabeth's reigns the crown took to prosecuting traitors
under the act of 1352 once more because it offered procedural advantages, such as no time limit within which the
prosecution should be begun, which assisted conviction.
He suggested also, though with less foundation, that the
Tudor judges discovered in the 'common law' a bottomless
reservoir from which they might dredge vast numbers of
ancient treasons and treason cases profitable to the government.   Despite these advantages for the prosecution
Rezneck thought he could detect 'a broad movement toward
moderation' in the arraignment of Tudor traitors, and this
regardless of his asseveration that the council performed
tirelessly 'an inquisitorial function' for such trials.
Where perhaps Rezneck made his greatest contribution to
treason scholarship was in his brief analysis of the
trials of traitors as a vehicle for governmental propaganda.   He noted the open nature of these arraignments,
the giving of evidence by the crown lawyers even when the
accused had confessed the charge, the use of judges on
circuit and preachers to give the official account of the
traitor's misdeeds and his conviction, and the publishing
of pamphlets for the same purpose.   Thus Rezneck's account of the Tudor treason law was a valuable one, although because of its brevity, and perhaps because insufficient consideration was given to legal technicalities,
it was of necessity superficial in many aspects. (10)
Several of the more stimulating and provocative ideas
which he drew  from contemporary writers turn out on inspection to be exceptional in reflecting no general trend.
At the present time it might occur to historians to criticize the study because it takes examples in each section
from all parts of the Tudor period, yet it seems to me
that as long as the examples are comparable and not different in kind, and particularly where the theme is the
history of legal notions, it is no bad thing.

The most recent study of the Tudor law of treason of
any size has been by Professor G.R. Elton and it is a most
important one. (11)   The contribution is in two parts
namely the section devoted to treason in his 'The Tudor
Constitution.   Documents and Commentary' (1962) and the
major part of his 'Policy and Police' (1972).   The first
covers the whole of the Tudor period, although only in the
form of short introductions to various documents, the
second only the years when Thomas Cromwell was Henry
VIII's chief adviser (1532-40).   Here the detail is ex-
haustive, but the 'enforcement of the reformation' is the
main theme even if treason figures on most pages of the
book.   In 'The Tudor Constitution' Elton took up a position quite distinct from earlier writings on the law of
treason.   The Tudors, he argued, relied on statute to
extend the scope of treason as set in 1352 rather than
accept judicial construction, and thereby drew limits
where there had been none previously.   In the case of
treason by words the Tudors through legislation merely co-
dified common law precedents.   There was, he avowed, no
truth in the charge that the Tudors made treason out of
any heinous crime.   Elton was much closer to previous
historians in his brief comments on procedure in treason
trials.   He found the advantages which the crown enjoyed
were substantial:   'the court could be rigged against the
accused and he was deprived of normal privilege in the
conduct of his defence', though there was nothing improper
in this.   Furthermore in the course of the sixteenth century this 'unbalance' increased and therefore it was not
surprising that 'very few men accused of treason ever escaped the net'.   Even attainder became more severe, being
used to dispose of persons who had not yet been tried,
whereas 'originally, and nearly always, attainder was used
to supplement a conviction in a court of law'. (12)   This
was written, I think it is fair to say, before Elton had
embarked on any thorough investigation of the Tudor law of
treason and related subjects, an investigation which was
undertaken only later as a necessary part of his study of
how the Reformation was enforced, and thus, although at
least one major new interpretation was forthcoming, the
factual basis was traditional.
   In 'Policy and Police', on the other hand, the search
for factual examples was very wide and almost every type
of treason and restiveness against the regime in the 1530s
was subjected to close scrutiny;   so was the way in which
these problems were handled by the government.   The origins and political background of the treason legislation,
actual and planned, of that period were examined in exemplary fashion and the earlier work of Miss Thornley super-

seded almost entirely.   From the many separate cases reviewed a strong argument was made that traitorous and
seditious talk and activity was reported spontaneously to
the government (even if sometimes with malicious intent
towards the accused), and that the ascendant minister did
not need to operate a system of spies.   All he needed,
and he had it, was the co-operation of the gentry and the
use of the traditional methods of prosecution.   If there
was a Tudor revolution in government, it did not extend as
far as the police methods used to preserve public
order. (13)   In regard to trial procedure Elton moved
somewhat from his earlier position so as to argue that the
crown, or Cromwell at least, was intent on bringing virtually all legal proceedings against treason suspects
under the rules of the common law, unless the offence was
that of open insurrection, and that 'due process' nearly
always prevailed.   His examples tended to demonstrate
that the investigation of suspected treason was usually
directed from the centre, by king, minister, or the king's
council, and that no cases were brought to trial unless
the evidence against the suspect had been looked at thoroughly and accusations maliciously inspired weeded out.
At the actual trials convictions were by no means automatic, the reason being that the petty jurors were sometimes 'overfriendly' to the accused.   Even when a man was
convicted of treason he had a good chance of excaping the
penalty of death unless he had committed his crime 'in
open rebellion or unquestioned conspiracy to rebel' or
'had got caught up in the high politics of a violent age'.
A man denounced for 'words' 'stood approximately three
times as good a chance of being dismissed without any consequences as of being brought to his death'.   Overall the
enforcement of the Reformation was a triumph for legalism.
There was a 'rigid regard for the forms of trial and conviction at common law' and 'no intention to do more than
punish real guilt as defined by law' save for a few exceptional cases where there was a 'savage lashing out' at
opponents because of politics or personal feelings. (14)
Even in such cases, Elton endeavoured to show, closer investigation could reveal that the crown kept to the law
much better than had hitherto been supposed.
    Elton's interpretation of the law of treason and its
operation like the other parts of his study, although most
enlightening and valuable, was essentially a political
one.   This was because the work was based largely on
Cromwell's own correspondence, happily preserved by his
attainder, which does not take very much notice of legal
factors, often tending, as statesmen and their correspon-
dents do, to simplify important criminal law matters and

reduce them to lay terms.   Surviving court records relating to treason for this period, as Elton pointed out, are
few.   Thus, in his study the legal side was played down.
There are few examples of, or comments upon, the actual
indictments, few identifications of the acts under which
they were drawn and little detail about the outcome of
cases decided in the courts.   The lack of attention to
legal detail does not always matter very much but occasionally it can cause concern, as for example in the failure to make a distinction between disruptive talk, which
came under three medieval statutes and was punishable by
the authority of the council, (15) and talk actually traitorous.   Two other comments are provoked by this study.
Could not a government keep to the letter of the law but
arrest, examine, and try treason suspects in a ruthless
and tyrannical manner, seeing that some parts of the judicial process were unregulated by either statute or common
law?   There was nothing, for example, to limit the length
or duress of a pre-trial sojourn in gaol, severe examination utilizing torture was not forbidden, and the crown
might make out of the execution either a quick and relatively clean death or a lingering one.   Second, is a government which has acted brutally and unfairly to be immune
from criticism because it has done so under a brutal and
unfair act of parliament?   If the statute was without
precedent and did not follow the norms of earlier legislation, and if its application seemed excessive to moderate
men of the time, then surely not.   Earlier practice must
be the key in both cases.
   The present book is intended only as an introduction to
the complexities of the Tudor treason law.   It covers all
the Tudor period but there can be no suggestion that it
does so exhaustively.   It will be some years, I think,
before that task can be put in hand.   If there is one
overriding theme it is the development of legal notions
touching treason, and I have endeavoured wherever possible
to demonstrate the medieval antecedents because they often
tell us a great deal.   For the chapters dealing with the
scope of treason I have relied on that much under-studied
source, the statute book;   the vocabulary and its etymo-
logy alone is a major archive for the study of the history
of English law.   The other prime component is the indictments.   I have made full use of the indictments in the
file known as the *Baga de Secretis*, which although they
sometimes concern important men and women are in no way
legal freaks as has sometimes been implied.   As Elton has
remarked, there is a paucity of other court records of
relevance.   There are almost no treason indictments in
the few quarter session files which survive from before

1550 and they are rare in those of the second half of the sixteenth century. This we might expect, since few types of treason could come before the quarter sessions. A more serious loss is the entire disappearance (save for Wales) of gaol delivery records before the late 1550s and of oyer and terminer ones (under which commission important cases were often handled) throughout the whole period. Where the records are fairly full, as for example in the case of the gaol delivery files for the south-eastern counties for the reign of Elizabeth, treason indictments are rare. There are, it is true, a number in the rolls of king's bench but a thorough search has yet to be conducted. With such great deficiencies in record material the value of any quantitative analysis of indictments, trial verdicts, and such would be of doubtful value.

For the chapters which deal with the fate of the accused from the time when he or she first aroused suspicion until acquittal or punishment, I have relied on a variety of sources, some official or legal, others literary, many casual. I have not hesitated to use accounts which are plainly partisan when incidentally or accidentally they illuminate legal procedure, and where the bias is not relevant or allowance can be properly made for it. There is, for example, quite a mine of detail about pre-trial procedure to be worked with care in descriptions by co-religionists of the lives of Jesuits, seminary priests and catholic traitors. In the second half of the book I have undoubtedly been guilty of abandoning a strictly chronological approach where I have thought the establishment of the theme would benefit by it. I can only say I have always tried to compare or connect like with like. As to the topics I have selected for consideration in these chapters, while a few have been touched on by earlier investigators concerned primarily with other matters, the majority have been almost entirely neglected, for despite the work of the historians mentioned above, and a good deal of writing on rebellions and traitorous conspiracies by others, the law of treason over the Tudor period as a whole has never been given close examination. It is surprising that there has been so very little written on, for example, martial law, attempts to extradite treason suspects, gaol conditions pre- and post-trial, the use of torture, the manner of punishment, and forfeiture. Perhaps the reason has been a fear that such topics might tend to emphasize too heavily the darker side of the Tudor criminal law.

# 1

## The Scope of Treason: 1

When Henry VII ascended the English throne, the crime of
high treason rested largely for its definition on the
statute of 1352, 25 Edw. III st. 5 c. 2.   There it was
clearly separated from petty treason, which was the slay-
ing of a master by his servant, husband by his wife or
prelate by a lesser cleric.   High treason, although the
adjective high did not appear regularly before the end of
the fourteenth century, was to include only offences
against the king's person and his regality.   These were
listed as:  to compass or imagine the death of the king,
his queen or the royal heir;  to violate the king's con-
sort, his eldest daughter or the wife of his eldest son;
to levy war against the king in his realm or adhere to
the king's enemies and be provably attaint of it by men
of the offender's own condition;  to counterfeit the great
or privy seal or the king's coin, to introduce counterfeit
money into England knowing it to be false;  also to kill
the chancellor, treasurer, or a justice of either bench,
of eyre, of assize or of oyer and terminer while executing
his office.   Why the statute took the shape it did is to
be discovered in the way treason had been defined in previous cases under the common law and also in the course of
mid-fourteenth-century English politics.   In enunciating
the definition of 1352, Edward III was prompted chiefly
by demand in recent parliaments that he should declare exactly what treason was, since royal justices had of late
been holding as such crimes which had never been so interpreted in the past.   These justices, and through them
juries, so it seems, had been over zealous in their interpretations, calling felonies treasons and afforcing indictments by talk of accroachment of the royal power.
Either they or King Edward may have been affected by new
knowledge of continental law, but whatever the inspiration
the purpose was clear enough.   They hoped by extending

the category of treason, and thereby inflicting heavier
and more certain punishment, to suppress local lawless-
ness;  no doubt they also hoped to replenish their master's coffers by the forfeitures incurred.   Another
reason, though perhaps of less import, for the new act may
have been supplication by the magnates that Edward should
annul the convictions against a small group of men who had
been condemned for treason over twenty years before.
There is however no indication that the baronage brought
any strong pressure to bear.

     In parliament the act was passed subsequent to a re-
quest by the commons simply for remedial legislation:   no
detail was given as to what the new law should say.
There was no suggestion of a political confrontation between Edward and a bitter baronage, and for this reason
the 1352 act of treason was more likely to be long-lasting, since Edward had no humiliation to revenge.   The new
law when passed gave a decidedly narrow interpretation to
treason.   Seriously diminished were the king's chances of
obtaining forfeitures, and on the face of it royal power
suffered a decline.   Perhaps the king and his advisers
accepted the fact that the nebulous periphery of treason
often used to their advantage in the past was an unavoid-
able casualty in an age of increasing legal definition
and, viewed politically, at a point when popular support
was very necessary for the war with France.   Whatever his
feelings; Edward himself made no subsequent effort to restore the royal position and this, together with the lack
of internal dissension until the last years of his reign,
seems to have allowed the 1352 statute to become hallowed
by time.

     There is no doubt that at heart Edward III's treason
act was founded on the crimes which were customarily held
as treason under the common law.   True, kings had not
been absolutely consistent in what hitherto they had
called treason but thirteenth- and early-fourteenth-cen-
tury precedents can be found for nearly every category of
traitorous offence which was included in the act.   This
close correlation may have been the reason why lawyers of
the later fourteenth and the fifteenth centuries did not
refer like their Tudor counterparts to 'common law' treasons, although it was accepted that unless a statute con-
travened the common law that law remained standing.   For
them there was no need to look for treason categories
beyond the 1352 act. (1)

     The most important development in the interpretation of
the law of treason between 1352 and 1485 concerned the
clause in the Edwardian act about imagining and compassing
the king's death.   Apart from those based on the offence

of levying war against the king, a fairly frequent offence
in the political upheavals from Richard II's reign onward,
indictments concerned with 'imagining' were dominant.
The reason for this was the discovery by kings and their
judges that the category could be extended to embrace a
wide variety of offences.    Words and writings which commented on the king and his behaviour in what was regarded
as a malicious manner were often the basis of these indictments.    If the words did not suggest a direct intent
to bring about the king's demise then they were held to do
so indirectly and the accused found guilty of treason just
the same.    Commenting on some words from a sermon with
approval led to one accusation of treason, repeating
gossip, crying out in the street damaging comments about
the king's personal characteristics and using the magic
arts to make predictions about his future, led to others.
This wide interpretation of the treason law was being justified by the king's lawyers in the second half of the
fifteenth century on the grounds that these deeds were intended to destroy the cordial love which his people had
for the king and thereby shorten his life by sadness.

The crown seems to have used this wide interpretation
of 'imagining and compassing the king's death' which has
often gone under the name 'constructive treason' in pref-
erence to a procedural device which the 1352 statute
thoughtfully provided.    This was that when 'doubtful'
cases of treason arose the justices were to delay giving
judgment until the issue was brought before the king in
parliament and it was declared whether it should be held
treason or felony.    It was the judges and the king who
decided if in fact the case was a doubtful one.    If the
situation was novel but they had no doubts about what to
do then they 'constructed', and they do not seem to have
been brought to task for their interpretations.    Parliamentary declaration of treason, despite its unpopularity
with the king, may have survived into the fifteenth century, but only as an element in the act of attainder.
Such acts were intended to affirm and supplement convictions made outside parliament, to serve sometimes as a
form of exaction and outlawry and to set penalties which
were beyond the power of the common law courts to inflict.
In the matter of the definition of treason for all their
extra-legal appearance they played only a small role,
nearly always following the act of 1352.

The Edwardian statute was not the only treason act of
the later Middle Ages;   there were others in the fifteenth
century although much less important.    A statute of 1414,
which owed much to contemporary continental conventions,
decreed that those who ignored truces the king had made

with his enemies and the safe conducts he had granted
should be judged for high treason. (2)   An act of 1416,
in dealing with the clipping, washing and filing of coins,
consciously supplemented the 1352 statute, as did the statute made in the parliament of 1423-4 concerning escape
from gaol by those committed on suspicion of high treason. (3)   Other legislation extended treason to include
extortion by threat of arson (1429-30), the seizure of
goods in three English border counties by Welshmen (1442)
and compassing the death of Richard, duke of York
(1460). (4)   In addition to new laws there were in the
fifteenth century a number of occasions when the penalties
for treason were awarded by parliament in suspension, so
to speak, so as to force particular miscreants to appear
before a court. (5)   Here again we have the phenomenon of
certain crimes being classified as treason so as better to
maintain public order.   Since parliament legislated these
devices they cannot be viewed as illegal, although the departure from general principle in order to benefit a
single suppliant must be decried.   Yet speaking in general terms it seems that even when the quality of government was poor, as for example in the middle of the fifteenth century, there were very few occasions when a
charge of treason was legally unwarranted.   The English
kings of the period, with perhaps one exception, seem to
have been happy to abide by the law, feeling no doubt that
the use of judicial construction made it quite favourable
to their interests.

In contrast to the later medieval period the Tudor era
is remarkable in the history of treason for the large
amount of legislation which concerned itself with that
subject.   Between 1485 and 1603, according to one calcu-
lation, there were no fewer than sixty-eight treason statutes enacted, though there had been less than ten in the
period 1352-1485. (6)   This proliferation is explained by
the fact that many Tudor acts were the by-product of royal
concern over the succession to the crown and the king's
ecclesiastical supremacy, problems previous kings did not
face in the same form, and also by the reluctance of the
Tudor monarchs to put their trust in judicial construction
based on existing statutes.   The large number of acts
should not be taken automatically as an indication of the
king's success in expanding the scope of the treason laws.
The history of treason in the fifteenth century demonstrates that how the law was interpreted was sometimes
more important than the bald statute, and indeed the later
Middle Ages as a whole suggest that to define treason more
exactly was in general to the king's disadvantage, serving
to reduce his ancient prerogative powers.   This issue of

how wide the scope of treason extended is the central one
in this chapter, but it cannot be studied simply through
examination of the statutes alone, important as they are.
Indictments and how they were drawn tell us much, and so
do the comments about treason made formally or informally
by judges, justices, ministers and even the monarch himself.

Together with the width of the treason law must be considered the general fairness of that law.   Did the Tudors
adhere to the principles which had guided past legislators
and were the rules made in harmony with the tenor of the
English common law?   Most of the comments of those historians who have dealt with the matter directly have been
unfavourable.   Tanner said of Henry VIII's treason legislation that it 'abandons any logical principle and con-
verts treason into a crime which has no character except
heinousness'. (7)   Pickthorn drew attention to the device
utilized by the king and his ministers in 1531 'of denoun-
cing and punishing as high treason whatever was especially
disagreeable to the government' and reflected it was 'an
expedient several times repeated in the course of the
reign'. (8)   Rezneck, concurring with Tanner, referred to
the 'amazingly novel character' of the addition to the
treason law by Henry VIII and regarded the general trend
of Elizabethan legislation on the subject as being towards
increased severity 'even exceeding Henry VIII's harsh-
ness'.   A.F. Pollard remarked on the 'ferociousness' of
Henry VIII's treason laws and thought one promulgated in
Queen Mary's reign (1 & 2 Ph. & M. c. 9) even worse. (9)
The only categorical denial of these opinions has come
from G.R. Elton, who has sought to refute the argument
that the Tudors 'fudged the whole meaning of treason by
turning the supreme political offence into an emotional
term for any heinous crime' by proposing instead that
'typically Tudor legislation extended treason to cover new
aspects of the fundamental offence against king and
realm'. (10)   Lawyers have been less willing to damn than
historians, although they have been loth to defend.
Holdsworth, quite remarkably, seems to have avoided any
comment at all.   Stephen, clearly on the defensive, wrote
that he thought the impression which Henry VIII's treason
laws 'have created of tyranny is somewhat exaggerated
though it is not unnatural'.   He argued that they were a
necessary outcome of the war between Henry and the pope
and that they were not intended to last for an indefinite
time or to apply to a normal state of society:   to believe
otherwise 'is to misunderstand them pedantically'.   Less
restrained was the earlier legal historian Reeves, who was
prompted by the Henrician laws to write that this repres-

sive legislation ordained for law 'the strangest inven-
tions that ever were thought worthy to become the objects
of penal jurisdiction'. (11)

Alongside the generally derogatory remarks of historians and lawyers of a later period may be cited the comments of contemporaries.   Here we find some occasional
and scattered complaint but no loud or general outcry
about the scope of the treason laws.   One grievance was
the accounting as treason of seditious words used in
everyday speech.   Bishop Fisher's brother Robert is reputed to have said in February 1535 that 'speaking is made
high treason which was never heard of before'. (12)   In
1540, at the time of Thomas Cromwell's fall, there was a
complaint that by sanguinary laws he had made into treason
inadvertent words spoken in good intent. (13)   Yet in
fact among the large number of seditious speeches which
came to the government's attention between 1532 and 1540,
the time when the offence was probably most common, very
few indeed criticized the law defining treason even indirectly. (14)   Later in the century there were one or two
occasions when protest was made in parliament against the
extension of the scope of the treason law.   When in 1571
the commons were discussing a proposed new treason act
one member, Snagg, showed his opposition by arguing that
he thought the statute of 1352 was itself sufficient.
In the parliamentary session of 1585 Dr Parry was seques-
tered for saying that the treason bill against Jesuits,
seminary priests and 'such like disobedient subjects' was
'full of blood, danger, despair and terror' to the people
of the realm and further that it was 'full of confisca-
tions'. (15)   One obvious target of criticism, at least
from the wealthier classes, were the rules about forfeiture yet surprisingly the only contemporary complaint
seems to have come from a governmental source.   Reginald
Pole in Starkey's 'Dialogue between Reginald Pole and
Thomas Lupset' is made to say that the law was 'over-
strait' because the innocent heir and the stock of the
convicted traitor could not inherit his lands and creditors were deprived thereby of their chance of payment. (16)   To these few criticisms about the content of
the treason statutes should perhaps be added complaints
concerning how the crown interpreted them.   Robert Fisher
is supposed to have said that the government was going to
expound the treason act of 1534 according to its pleasure,
regardless of the inclusion of the word 'maliciously'. (17)   In 1554 Sir Nicholas Throckmorton, when on
trial for his life, saw fit to criticize the way judges
were able to construe the laws of treason to the king's
advantage. (18)   The Yorkshire insurgents of 1536, when

referring to the malpractices of two of Cromwell's min-
ions, claimed that 'what so ever thay will have doyne must
be lawfull and who contrarys theym shall be accusyd off
tresun'. (19)
    This criticism of the scope of treason stemmed largely
from individuals who were aggrieved at one particular proviso of the treason acts.    A general and substantial complaint about the scope of treason only showed itself on
Henry VIII's death, when there was a widespread though
temporary desire to make the law more narrow.    Even then
there were outspoken critics of the change.    The return
to the statute of 1352 was called the worst deed done in
that generation and the western rebels of 1549 sought a
return to 'the statute that made words treason'. (20)
The Tudor monarchs benefited greatly from the fact that
the opposition to their policies, political or religious,
rarely came from the same quarter for more than a few
years at a time.    There was no constant source of opposition until well on in Elizabeth's reign.    Thus there was
no contrary philosophy about the scope of treason as for
example the baronage of the early fourteenth century had.
Even the transmarine English catholics of the 1580s and
1590s, who had plenty of time to philosophize, showed
neither the ability nor the inclination to expose the
legal weaknesses in the laws deciding the scope of treason.    The Tudor kings and queens had it virtually all
their own way.
    Any study of the scope of the Tudor treason laws is
best divided around 1530, four years before the most important of the relevant statutes was enacted.    Until that
year the pre-eminence of the act of 1352 was unchallenged,
yet the twenty-four years of Henry VII's reign and the
first twenty-five of his son's were by no means devoid of
events significant to the law of treason.    There was legislation on treason in 1487-8 and 1495, important declarations by the judges in 1485, 1517 and 1525, new trends in
the formulation of indictments and two remarkable constructions of treason by Henry VIII and his advisers.    In
Henry VII's second parliament it was enacted that if any
servant in the royal household should compass to destroy
or murder the king or a lord of the realm or other coun-
sellors of the king or the steward, treasurer or comptrol-
ler of the household, it was to be held felony.    Hitherto
conspiring, as distinct from achieving, the death of anyone other than the king was not a crime at all.    To imagine the king's death, on the other hand, was high treason.    The aspect of the act which attracts our attention
most is its actual diminution of the scope of treason in
one area.    The principle, we must admit, was reasonable

enough, for the 1352 act stated that any servant who imagined his master's death was to be held guilty of petty
treason, and for that crime the penalty was the same as
for felony.   Very likely the reason for the act was no
delight in legistic principles but lay, as one usually
discovers when changes occurred in definitions of crimes,
in actual offences committed or attempted in the recent
past.   In this case it was apparently the behaviour of
one John Spynell, a yeoman of the crown, and some eighty
disorderly followers, who on 15 December 1487, while parliament was sitting, assembled together for the purpose of
murdering several of the king's chief officers and members
of his council. (21)

The so-called 'de facto' act of 1495 (11 Hen. VII c. 1)
should also be read with recent circumstances very much in
mind.   Late in 1494 or early in 1495 it was revealed by
Sir Robert Clifford, who was either a defector from Warbeck's cause or a royal spy, that the chamberlain of the
royal household, Sir William Stanley, brother of the earl
of Derby who had played such a vital role at Bosworth, was
a traitor.   According to Polydore Vergil, Stanley's treason amounted to nothing more than saying that if Warbeck
was indeed the son of Edward IV as claimed he would not
fight against him. (22)   Stanley and other suspects, who
included Lord Fitzwalter, Sir Simon Mountford, several
ecclesiastics and men of lower rank, were arrested and put
on trial.   Stanley was indicted of imagining the king's
death through an intent to levy war against him, and
through communication with Warbeck, and of adhering to the
king's enemies.   Clifford was similarly indicted but
whereas Stanley was tried, convicted and later executed,
Clifford failed to appear even to plead a pardon known to
have been granted to him. (23)

That Henry was much disturbed by the revelations is obvious.   Oyer and terminer commissions of great size were
appointed to investigate offences south of the Trent, from
the Welsh border to the North Sea, and the king made a
progress in the summer with what has been described as
'the obvious object of awing Stanley's tenants and retain-
ers'. (24)   A contingent of Warbeck's forces landed at
Deal in July 1495 and, though they were all killed or captured, the king must have felt his throne was most inse-
cure.   The parliament which he summoned to meet in October was used to legislate an attainder act which provided
for the forfeiture of lands held to the use of Stanley,
Mountford, and two outlawed traitors in sanctuary. (25)
These measures of repression  were accompanied by one of
inducement.   To retain the loyalty and ease the fears of
men who had been Yorkist partisans and sympathizers in the

past Henry saw to it there was promulgated a statute which promised that 'no manner of person ... that attend upon the king and sovereign lord of this land for the time being in his person and do him true and faithful service of allegiance' within the realm or without, was to be convicted by act of parliament or process of law to the loss of his life or the forfeiture of his possessions.  This meant, as Pollard said, that there would be no future proceedings against Yorkists who had so far escaped attainder and forfeiture on the grounds of what they had done before Henry came to the throne. (26)   Suspending the legal principle *nullum tempus occurrit regi* in this way was not new:  in an earlier and very important example Edward III had done the same thing in 1361 with regard to those who, living in the northern shires, had been guilty years before of adhering to the king's Scottish enemy. (27)

There is no suggestion in the act that Henry was anything less than king de jure or that the question of the succession was other than closed.   Henry and his parliament were merely recognizing facts:  that there had been kings with, as they saw it, no proper claim to the throne, but they were ruling monarchs and loyal service to them should not be punished, not at least at that distance from Bosworth, unless they committed another offence.   The kings who had ruled from 1461 to 1485 had not questioned the validity of laws enacted by those they supplanted, and there is even to be found example of treason against Henry VI being tried in the courts of the king who usurped him, Edward IV. (28)   In 1495 Henry VII was extending this acceptance from legislation and judicial decision to political circumstance, that is to service to the de facto king in war.   The act set down no new principle for the future, it merely made a rule about behaviour at a time in the past.   Nor should anything novel be seen in the use of the phrase 'prince ... for the time being'.   Those lawyers who pleaded in the courts of common law had used the de facto concept from at least 1470, (29) and if we take into account the parallel political idea of a separation between the king's person and his office then the origins are to be found in the earlier fourteenth rather than the fifteenth century.   In the reign of Edward II the notion was popular among the baronial opposition. (30) After 1495 the phrase disappeared for more than forty years, reappearing only in the proclamation act of 1539 (31 Hen. VIII c. 8).   The section of the act of 1495 which made void any subsequent act or process of law which contradicted it was largely propaganda to make the offer doubly attractive to erstwhile Yorkists by seeming to, although of course it could not, provide continuous protec-

tion in an age of sudden turnabout in political fortune.
Again the device was not entirely novel.    Richard II's
treason statute of 1397-8 provided the penalties of treason against those who later sought and were convicted of
annulling any of the proceedings of the present parliament. (31)    The act of 1495 was not referred to at all
during the subsequent century.    It was a temporary expedient and in the history of the scope of treason has
only a minor place despite the many comments made about it
by historians.

As well as by new act, the scope of treason was affected by judicial interpretation of treason laws already on
the statute roll.    Sometimes this construction, as it is
often called, was the result of formal consultation among
the legal advisers of the king.    At other times there is
no reference to any confering together:    there simply
appeared a new type of indictment.    There were at least
two important judicial conferences concerned with the definition of treason in the period 1485-1530, the first in
Henry VII's first year as king.    The judges of the two
benches, when asked about the attainder of treason which
the new monarch had incurred whilst in exile during the
previous reign, affirmed there was no legal problem.
There was no need for an act to annul the earlier act, was
the general opinion, since by becoming king Henry had
automatically discharged himself of his attainder. (32)
One judge pointed out that at the time of his re-adeption
Henry VI, who likewise had been attainted by an earlier
act, did not have that act reversed.    The other judges
said the present king was not under attainder at all but
merely disabled and when he seized the crown was enabled
automatically.    The judges, we may suspect, were really
playing with words so they would not have to make a judgment about the king's right to the throne.    They were
also evading having to admit openly that a de facto king
was king de jure the moment he seized the crown and that
the acts governing the succession counted for little.

The other notable judicial conference which concerned
treason was in 1517.    The occasion was the riots in London directed against foreigners on the eve of 'evil May
day'.    When order had been restored 'the justices with
all the king's councell learned in the lawes' assembled at
the house of the chief justice of the king's bench, Sir
John Fineux.    The intent was to decide how the riots
should be treated in law.    Having told us this, Holinshed
adds enigmatically 'and first there was read the statute
of the third yeare of Henry the fift'.    This act dealt in
fact not with riotous behaviour but with treason.    It decreed that those of the king's subjects who ignored safe

conducts issued by the crown and its truces made with enemies and those who killed and robbed men travelling under
such protection were committing high treason.   The statute was thought to be applicable in 1517 because at that
time Henry VIII had truces with France, Burgundy and Spain
'all the which truces were violated by the said insurrection', that is to say the nationals of those countries
suffered in the rioting.   Then it was decided 'by the
whole councell there assembled that the king's sergeants
and attournies should go to the chancellor to have a sight
of all the said leagues and charters of truces to the intent they might frame their indictments according to the
matter'. (33)   Chief Justice Fineux told the gathering
that all the trouble-makers were guilty of high treason
whether they had robbed or not 'bicause that the insurrection in it selfe was high treason as a thing practised
against the regall honour of our sovereigne lord the
king'.   This interpretation Fineux supported with the
statement that 'the same law holdeth of an insurrection
made against the statute of labourers', saying it had been
applied against those who had once risen in Kent against
that statute.

At first sight these tactics for the prosecution of the
king's case seem to be bad law based on worse history.
It is remarkable that the judges should have held the
London riots as treason.   We must assume that it was King
Henry or Wolsey or some other minister on their command
who told the judges that treason was to be the charge.
Whoever had the idea of using the statute of 1414 was certainly not well informed historically.   The act had been
used against piratical seamen, that is against infractions
of truces at sea, but probably not since the mid-fifteenth
century in any case.   There had, it is true, been a case
where the murder in London of a Genoese ambassador travelling under safe conduct was declared treason, but that was
thirty-five years before the 1414 act. (34)   Fineux may
have known the weakness of the crown's case.   This is
suggested by his reference to an insurrection in Kent
'made against the statute of labourers'.   He may have
been thinking of the act of 1381 (5 Ric. II st. 1 c. 6)
which made it treason to recommence *the* riot, that is to
say the peasants' revolt of the previous June.   This law
had been referred to at the time of John of Northampton's
rising in London in 1384 and again in 1394, but does not
seem to have been used as a basis for indictments beyond
the end of the fourteenth century. (35)   More likely he
was thinking of the misdeeds of June 1381 when the rebels
broke into London and turned to destruction and pillage.
On that occasion, when the king's authority was restored

and trials began, the misdoers were indicted in a way
which demonstrated that the crown at that time lacked both
a clear judicial policy on popular insurrection as well as
control over the indicting juries.   There was no consistency in the presentments.   The same offence might be
treason to one jury and felony to another.   Juries called
as treason what seemed to them to be treason, not what actually was.   The list included the murder of men loyal to
the king, destroying loyal men's houses, royal records and
buildings and giving the rebels something more than modest
assistance. (36)

In the fifteenth century disturbances of the type which
occurred in 1517 would probably have been dealt with as
riot (which was trespass), or if the miscreants had been
well armed and armoured and displayed some form of military discipline then as the treason of levying war against
the king.   Less likely, but a possibility none the less,
was that the riot would be construed as in some way compassing or imagining the king's death.   That there was
some consideration of this form of indictment in 1517 is
suggested by Grafton, who says that 'upon examination it
could never be proved of any meetyng, gatheryng, talkyng
or conventicle at any day or tyme before that day but that
the chaunce so happened without any matter prepensed of
any creature savyng Lincoln'. (37)   This, if true, meant
the crown was seeking evidence of men conspiring together,
which in turn indicates a charge of imagining the king's
death was in mind.   The judges' discussions were not
merely academic:   thirteen rioters were later found guilty
and sentenced to the normal penalty for treason, to be
drawn to the gallows, hanged, disembowelled and their
bodies quartered.

The lack of clear legal provision for riots that were
not merely part of a private feud as were usually those
involving the magnates and the gentry, but directed
against a general grievance, was demonstrated again in
1525 when the cloth workers of Suffolk assembled in harness to resist collection of the 'amicable' grant.   The
dukes of Norfolk and Suffolk persuaded them to disperse.
Later the rebels, in token of repentance, went to Bury St
Edmunds in their shirts with halters about their necks in
order to seek pardon. (38)   There was then some debate
between the two dukes and Cardinal Wolsey as to what offence should be charged against the ringleaders.   Norfolk
and Suffolk told Wolsey how in the rebels' presence they
had rather unwillingly 'aggravated' the offence, declaring
it to be high treason 'and never made it less'.   Wolsey
may have pressed for the bringing of charges of treason
but the king's 'temporal counsel' and the judges seem to

have reached the conclusion that the crime was only riot
and unlawful assembly. (39)   Eventually a few of the
leading dissidents appeared in the star chamber, which
shows it was the law officers' recommendations that were
accepted by the king.   At the end of the century popular
insurrection of a similar nature was to cause more concern
and produce interpretations of the law as strange as in
1517.

Nowhere is the scope of the treason laws better revealed than in actual indictments.   Acts may have been
passed, and judges have made declaration, but only by
looking at the form of bills of indictment and how grand
juries framed the charges can we be certain of what was
eventually laid against the suspect in court.   Examination of treason cases in the legal records of the period
reveals in general some interesting changes in the phraseology of indictments and more particularly evidence in two
cases of definite sharp practice.   The cases were those
of Sir Richard Empson and Edmund Dudley and occurred soon
after the accession of Henry VIII.   Both men were accused
of planning to govern the new king, and thereby the realm,
against his wishes, using force to do so. (40)   Though
reprehensible, this was not treason.   In the fourteenth
century it would probably have been called 'accroaching
the royal power' but the kings and magnates of that time
had been unable to gain the admission of the offence into
the law of treason or even make it felony.   An accepted
charge of treason was mentioned in both indictments:   it
was that the accused intended to destroy the king, or
rather the king's heir, for the plotting took place when
Henry VII was on his death bed.   What made the indictments so different from previous ones was that the accusations were conditional:   Empson and Dudley intended the
king should be destroyed *if* he and his council should refuse to be ruled and governed by them.   Sir William
Stanley, according to Polydore Vergil, was guilty of saying that he would never bear arms against Perkin Warbeck
*if* he were sure Warbeck was the son of Edward IV.   This
may possibly be true, but when Stanley was put on trial
the indictment, as we have seen already, contained the
quite proper charges of imagining the king's death and
adhering to the king's enemies.   Francis Bacon, whether
he had seen the plea roll or not, was much impressed by
what he took to be the weakness of the charge against
Stanley.   He explained the circumstances thus:   'it seems
the judges of that time (who were learned men and the
chief of them of the privy council) thought it was a dangerous thing to admit ifs and ands to qualifie words of
treason;   whereby every man might express his malice and

blanch his danger'. (41)   If Bacon was correct, if the
charge of imagining the king's death was founded on Stanley's words about Warbeck, the construing of conditional
statements as treason had started before 1509:  if not the
novel nature of the accusations against Empson and Dudley
were probably inspired by Henry VIII.   Someone must have
been aware of the unsatisfactory nature of the indictments
of 1509, since their conditional form never appeared again
in the Tudor era.   Like the question of popular disturbances, the issue of whether seeking to govern or control
the prince was treason arose again at the end of the century, when despite the welter of legislation on treason in
the interim it still seems to have been without statutory
sanction.

These then were the more important acts, declarations
and cases which affected the scope of the treason law in
the period 1485-1530.   There was also a treason act
passed in the parliament of 1488-9, which made treason
the forging of foreign coins current in payment at that
time in the realm, as well as several things of interest
on the procedural side, like judicial declaration on sanctuaries and the last obvious case of that chivalric ano-
maly, trial under the law of arms, but these are better
dealt with in later chapters. (42)   That it was for the
history of treason not a critical period is obvious, yet
there was portent of change to come.   This lay in the
harsh fashion in which the misdeeds of Empson and Dudley
were construed and the decision to make treason out of
popular disturbances in London in 1517.

In the history of the scope of treason, as in the history of the sixteenth century as a whole, the years 1530-
6, that is to say roughly the period of the Reformation
Parliament, can be considered the most crucial.   As well
as the act designed solely to deal with treason of 1534
(26 Hen. VIII c. 13), the first and second acts of succession (25 Hen. VIII c. 22 and 28 Hen. VIII c. 7) and the
act which extinguished the authority of the pope (28 Hen.
VIII c. 10) considerably affected the official definition
of treason.   These acts were intended to defend King
Henry's anti-papal policy, his attack on the liberties of
the church and his matrimonial arrangements.   This revolution, for it was hardly less, having no real parallel in
English medieval history, was bound to create opposition,
and since the question of obedience and to whom it was
owed was at the heart of the king's policies, new categories of treason might be expected.   This did not of necessity mean new laws, although since there had been statutes made in the fifteenth century which consciously supplemented the act of 1352 there was nothing to prohibit

it.   Many attacks on the changes which the government was
accomplishing could perhaps have been dealt with by judicial declaration, as had happened periodically since 1352,
that they were in fact treasonable.   The reason given
might have been that they grieved the king and therefore
were likely to cause his illness and death. (43)   By this
interpretation the offences would have come under the
clause of the 1352 act concerning imagining or compassing
the king's death.   Since judicial interpretation had
played a crucial role in 1509 and 1517, why the king and
his ministers in the 1530s resorted to statutes to rede-
fine the scope of treason is thus an important matter.
    From the king's point of view declaration of treason by
the judges had a serious flaw in it.   The judges could
not always be counted on to see the crime in exactly the
same light as the king and his legal advisers.   On occasion they might show a most independent spirit and Henry
VIII may well have had his attention drawn to the example
of Chief Justice Markham, who is said in 1468 to have
found what Edward IV thought was treason to be misprision
only. (44)   The king therefore had probably begun to take
precautions.   It is very likely that in Tudor times conferences among the judges about points of treason were
prompted by the crown, and that furthermore the judges
were under some pressure to find the offence at issue
traitorous. (45)   Significantly, judicial declaration
operated against the king, perhaps for the first time
under the Tudors, in November 1533.   Henry wished the
crimes of Elizabeth Barton, the Kent prophetess, and her
associates to be declared as high treason, and for that
purpose assembled not merely judges and lawyers but bishops and nobles as well, intending perhaps that they should
overawe any opposition on the part of the legal experts.
Henry seems to have argued that Elizabeth had failed to
reveal traitorous dreams and a knowledge of traitorous
plans,which of course was treason.   The judges, however,
pointed out that a year earlier she had revealed all when
she prophesied before the king in person and they would
not concur. (46)   As a result Elizabeth and her accomplices were proceeded against by bill of attainder in parliament and not by indictment in a court of common law.
    The lack of compliance by the judges in a case which
was of particular political importance helps to explain
why comprehensive legislation on treason could not thereafter be long delayed, but it does not suggest why the
king and his ministers had been toying with drafts of a
new treason act since 1530.   That a new statute took so
long to materialize implies a reluctance to legislate
until positively obliged to do so.   Arguments that the

king and his advisers wanted to perfect their new treason
rules first or that they were incapable of drafting a
reasonable act at an earlier moment are not very compel-
ling.    No doubt the royal lawyers drew Henry's attention
to how any new act would tend ultimately to be to the detriment of the royal prerogative and would limit the king's
room to manoeuvre.    Although it may not have been recognized as such at the time the policy of relying on construction under the 1352 act received a jarring blow early
in 1531.    At that time there was passed an act concerning
treason which is best explained as an occasion when the
king's personal interest overbalanced legal and parliamentary principles, for in every way it was a most unsatisfactory piece of legislation.
      The act was for the attainder of treason of Robert
Roose; his crime was poisoning.    It was alleged he had
put poison in a vessel full of yeast in the bishop of
Rochester's kitchen at 'Lambeth Marsh' which had caused to
be 'mortally enfected' seventeen people, one of whom was
dead already.    A number of poor, who were fed at the
bishop's kitchen, were also poisoned and one of them
died. (47)    We cannot tell who first brought the matter
into parliament but Chapuys gives the information that it
was the king himself who mentioned the subject of poisoning to the house of lords. (48)    The act stated the crime
was high treason and convicted offenders of a later date
were to suffer the same death by boiling that Roose was to
undergo.    Like all attainder acts it awarded the penalties of high treason after the crime had been committed,
but rather differently it awarded them out of context
since poisoning was not treason at common law.    For this
there was some form of precedent, it is true.    In the
mid-fifteenth century several men accused of crimes which
were not traitorous were ordered by act to appear in court
to satisfy certain complainants by a set date or stand
attainted of high treason.    The device was a form of parliamentary outlawry.    It is also true that in the act
which posthumously attainted Jack Cade in 1453 there had
been a declaration as treasonable crimes which were not so
under existing law. (49)    The retroactive nature of the
1531 attainder act was of course usual but its making of
new treason at the same time was an undoubted novelty, and
so so was both the manner of execution, which was boiling,
and the type of forfeiture.    Instead of the attainted
poisoner's possessions being forfeit to the king, as was
the practice in cases of high treason, they were to go to
the lord of the fee, as in crimes of petty treason and
felony.    There was one precedent.    The act of 1424 which
concerned the escape from gaol of suspect traitors made

exactly the same proviso about forfeiture, although, unlike the attainder act of 1531, it omitted to say whether
in escaping the prisoners were guilty of high or petty
treason. (50)   In 1531 by awarding forfeited possessions
to the lord of the fee Henry was perhaps seeking support
for the act from the members of the upper house, although
the move may not have been utterly divorced from legal
principle, since those in general best placed to poison
others were cooks, and for a cook to murder his master was
petty treason.   Fundamentally the act which condemned
Roose was different from earlier attainder acts, yet it
managed to contain all the most obnoxious features of its
varied predecessors.   The inclusion of a provision to
deal with future poisoning suggests it may have been the
half-way stage between construction on the one hand and
comprehensive new legislation on the other.

Even before the issue of poisoning reached parliament
new treasons concerned with the more central themes of the
safety of the king and obedience to him were being considered by the royal advisers for inclusion in an act.   The
unpolished draft, dating possibly from late 1530, contained four ideas. (51)   They were 1 withdrawing contemptuously after a summons to appear before the king, to
any of his castles and maintaining resistance there;   2
departing from the realm contemptuously (if a natural
subject of the crown) and taking an oath to a foreign potentate renouncing allegiance to the English king;   3
activity maliciously contrived by a subject of the king
when in another realm so as to annoy the king, his ambassadors, messengers or servants when they were executing
the king's business;   4   introducing into the kingdom
writings or orders slandering or dishonouring the royal
jurisdiction or the royal person.   Since all earlier laws
touching treason had been largely designed to remedy particular crimes already committed rather than to anticipate
possible offences in the future, it is likely the bill
proposed in 1530 was also.   Identification of the actual
offenders and misdeeds which lay behind the four ideas
would help considerably in explaining the line of legal
thought, but this cannot be done at the moment with any
degree of accuracy.   Perhaps the reference to maintaining
resistance in castles was prompted by the behaviour of
James ap Griffyth ap Howell in South Wales.   On 7 October
1530 a warrant was addressed to Walter, Lord Ferrers as
justice in South Wales to apprehend Griffyth ap Howell,
who had fortified himself in the castle of Emelyn. (52)
Malicious activity in another realm by an English subject
which was annoying to the king, his ambassadors and messengers is suggestive of the complaints in August and

September 1530 by Richard Croke, a diplomatist then en-
gaged in forwarding the king's divorce on the continent,
that the king's packet of letters had been opened and the
contents were known generally. (53)   Any more positive
identification must await future research.

   The draft containing the four ideas for treason may
have been prepared for the parliamentary session of January-March 1531, but it does not seem ever to have been
introduced.   Whatever happened then, we know that another
treason bill was being drawn up from about Michaelmas 1531
and based largely upon the earlier one. (54)   This time
the extensions to the scope of treason were these:  1 the
taking by a natural born subject of the crown of an oath
to a foreign prince or nobleman and agreeing to pay them
money contrary to the king's prerogative;  2 fleeing the
realm after proclamation made in the offender's neighbourhood that he should appear before the king;  3 the forfeiture by a convicted traitor of all the property which
others held to his use in addition to that which he had in
possession.

   Commenting on the seven new treasons intended we may
say that the first, withdrawing to a royal castle after
proclamation and resisting the king was really the old
treason of levying war in the realm, at least it was as
long as some missile was directed at any royal besiegers.
Fleeing after proclamation to appear before the king was
not a treason under any previous act but around 1440, as
we have seen, there were instances of suspended attainder
acts being passed by parliament to enforce appearance in
the courts to answer particular plaintiffs.   In turn
these may have been inspired by the process adopted by
the lords of parliament to ensure the appearance there of
the earl of Northumberland and Lord Bardolf in 1406. (55)
More recently, in 1486, Sir Thomas Broughton, Sir John
Hodylston and their adherents, who had disobeyed various
royal letters and privy seal writs, were commanded by
proclamation to appear before the king in forty days or be
reputed traitors and forfeit lives, lands and goods. (56)
The second and third offences of the first group and the
first of the second were designed to extend one of the
basic treasons of the 1352 act, that of adhering to the
king's enemies, so as to include foreign rulers perhaps
hostile to but not actually at war with the English king
and therefore not as yet his enemy.   The matter of allegiance was important, yet not well covered by law.   Renouncing allegiance, *diffidatio* as it was called, was held
by the magnates in the mid-thirteenth century as excusing
later treasonable conduct. (57)   At the end of the fourteenth century Richard II had made compassing to renounce

liege homage into treason, but the act was annulled two
years later and the issue had not arisen since.  We may
admit that there was room for legislation against those
who took oaths of allegiance to foreign princes if they
had not become denizens of that country previously.   To
make treason out of activity to the annoyance of English
ambassadors, royal messengers and servants abroad was, in
contrast, an unwarranted extension. (58)   In 1379 the
killing of John Imperial, a Genoese ambassador, had been
declared treason by parliament;  to make the mere annoying
the equivalent was extreme.

Introducing into the kingdom writings slandering the
king was a novel treason without close medieval precedent.
Written words about the king's personal qualities and political capacity had been classified as treason in the fifteenth century if they could be construed as in some way
likely to upset his health and thereby endanger his life.
The short distance from this to mere slander is obvious.
Furthermore, although there was a section of the first
statute of Westminster (1275) and its subsequent renewals
which laid down procedures against those who originated
and spread false news or scandal tending to produce discord between the king and his people or the magnates, the
punishment was to be decided by council and thus could not
involve forfeiture of life or estates.   If a provision
about slander of the king was not unexpected, an addition
to the law about the forfeiture of traitors' possessions
was overdue.   Hitherto those convicted of high treason
under the common law had forfeited only lands held in fee
simple and their goods and chattels.   Since the beginning
of the fifteenth century, acts of attainder had generally
been used to reach the property which traitors held in fee
tail or the lands held to their use by others, because at
common law those possessions were not regarded as belonging to the traitor himself. (59)   The labour of getting
an act of attainder passed was often matched by the need
for another act to repeal it at a later date when the
traitor or his descendants had re-established themselves
in royal favour.   Both Henry VII and Henry VIII had been
responsible for acts which enabled them to repeal parliamentary attainder of treason by letters patent but, perhaps because of opposition, they had limited this power to
a term of years. (60)

As a whole the seven proposed treasons followed rather
than went against past interpretations.   Where there was
something quite new it was in order to fill a troublesome
gap in the laws.   We cannot escape the fact, however,
that whoever drafted the proposals - Henry VIII himself,
one adviser or many - did not have quite as good a know-

ledge or appreciation of antecedents as their medieval
predecessors.   Whether this stemmed from lack of concern
or from an inability to interpret legal records accurately
is difficult to discover.   Another noticeable feature was
that the proposals merely added marginally to laws already
standing and were without coherence or an idea common to
all.   This perhaps should not be held against them for,
as the preamble to the act planned for 1531 stated, they
were merely to cover new treasons not thought of in the
fourteenth century as allowed for by the statute of 1352.
The bill which contained them does not seem to have gone
before parliament in 1532, as must have been originally
intended.   Whether it was because of lack of a suitable
parliamentary opportunity or the march of events outside
parliament is uncertain.

The failure of the judges and the other members of the
specially assembled council of 1533 to declare the crimes
of Elizabeth Barton, the 'Nun of Kent', as treason meant,
as we have seen, that the alteration of the scope of treason by a new statute was bound to follow.   Pending general legislation the Nun and her supporters were convicted
by an act of attainder which was markedly different from
other such acts.   The section of it which described
Elizabeth's offences did so in the greatest detail. (61)
The exact relationship between Elizabeth and her handlers
was clearly demonstrated, as was the role they had played
in the scheme for her promotion.   The Nun's chief offence
was her prophecy that if the king continued with the divorce proceedings and married again he would very soon
die:   this piece of prognostication was said to have been
'to the utter reproche and perell of distruccion of the
kynges person'.   The bishop of Rochester and other cler-
ics more closely associated with the Nun were held to have
traitorously believed in their hearts that Henry, after
his recent marriage, was no longer rightful king before
God.   On this account they had, so it was stated, withdrawn from their natural duty of obedience and persuaded
others to do the same, intending to make such a division
and rebelling in the realm that Henry should be in peril
of his life and in jeopardy of losing his crown.   The
circumstances of each misdeed were far more clearly defined than was the usual custom in acts of attainder.
This, together with the general format and the legal phraseology, reminds us forcibly of treason indictments in
the records of the king's bench.   Indeed, it seems likely
the act was based directly on the draft of an indictment,
perhaps the one Cromwell noted he must draw for the offenders in treason and misprision concerning the Nun of
Canterbury'. (62)

The crimes attributed in the act to Elizabeth Barton were probably those which the judges had refused to declare as treason.   For prognosticating the king's death there were precedents good enough.   Roger Bolingbroke, on behalf of Eleanor Cobham, duchess of Gloucester, had in October 1440 predicted the king would soon meet his death, and it was called treason. (63)   In 1477 Doctor Stacey, Thomas Burdet and Thomas Blake were convicted of treason for calculating the nativities of King Edward and the prince of Wales in order to find out when they were going to die, and announcing the prince's death was to occur in the near future. (64)   These crimes were construed as imagining the king's or his heir's death and therefore falling under the 1352 act.   The only way Elizabeth Barton's offence differed was in her predictions being phrased in the conditional sense:   the king would soon die *if* he married again.   This may have been one factor which caused the opposition from the judges.   If it was, then they had changed from the position their predecessors had presumably taken in 1509 when Empson and Dudley were convicted on the grounds they intended to destroy the king *if* he should refuse to be ruled and governed by their faction;   also, if we accept Bacon's account, they had changed from the position the judges of Henry VII had taken over Sir William Stanley's misdeeds.   If this line of reasoning is correct, then Henry VIII and Cromwell were facing opposition from the professional judges of a strength previous kings had not encountered.   Turning the draft of an indictment into a bill of attainder may have been the way Cromwell or the king, or both, showed the judges they would get their way none the less.   The similarity of the act to an indictment and the record of a trial in king's bench was perhaps intended as a demonstration of their power, even if the publicizing of the misdeeds of the Nun and her associates was the largest factor in their design.

The need for an act of attainder against Elizabeth Barton, the need to avoid trial of the Nun in a court of common law, being dependent for conviction on parliament, and the fear of similar crimes arising in the near future are each likely to have played part in the conceiving and drafting of the first act of succession which was promulgated in the spring session of parliament in 1534. (65) The act removed any legal irregularities connected with the Boleyn union and protected it by making into treason deeds or written or printed words imperilling the king's person or prejudicing or slandering his recent marriage, deeds, which if they had not been committed by the Nun, had most certainly been committed by her associates.

Also to be treason was interfering with the arrangements made for government in the case of a later minority.   One clause in the act copied almost exactly a provision in the draft of early 1531.   This was that forfeiture by those convicted of the new treasons was to include all the lands they had in possession or were seised to, which included fee tail, or which were held by others to their use.

While the act was being drawn up it seems that Cromwell's ideas in the matter were criticized by the king's legal advisers more than once.   Of particular interest in its importance to sixteenth-century definitions of treason in general was the learned counsel's comment that 'rebellion is already treason'. (66)   This was a great change from fourteenth- and fifteenth-century ideas.   In the late medieval period 'rebellious' had never been the equivalent of 'traitorous', but meant rather disobedience or refusing commands, usually by a fairly large number of men of the lower classes.   Now the two words apparently meant much the same thing.   Another successful criticism by the lawyers ensured that attacks which endangered the king's person and slandered the Boleyn marriage were not to be treason if made merely by spoken words and not by writing or printing or 'exterior deed'.   Attacks by spoken words only were to be misprision of treason.   This was a novel category of offence unknown in the later Middle Ages, where only misprision *tout court* appears.   The meaning had been at first default and later misbehaviour, usually by officials in regard to their duties.   Only in Henry VII's reign had there been established a connection between misprision and concealment of treason and even then the phrase 'misprision of treason' had not appeared. (67) Even in the first succession act it did not mean concealment, but rather the reverse.   It was probably a creation of Thomas Cromwell and the king's legal advisers, who needed an offence less serious than treason but which contained the word, for purposes of political propaganda. There was no sharp practice really, for misprision had already been drawn into the orbit of treason.   Words spoken traitorously were not the only form of this new crime created by the act.   Failure to take the oath to the succession was similarly defined although the actual oath was not set out in the act in complete form.

If the king and Thomas Cromwell had intended the first act of succession should make traitors of those like Elizabeth Barton, who by words imperilled the king and slandered the Boleyn marriage, they had undoubtedly been thwarted.   By the time of the next parliamentary session in the subsequent autumn there was much greater need to make such words into treason for the future.   If the

king was to continue the revolution now begun and bring it
to a successful conclusion, more universal tools of repression were essential, for incidents involving seditious
speech seem to have been multiplying.    Obviously the penalties for misprision, which were forfeiture of possessions and imprisonment at the king's pleasure, were having
insufficient effect.    Significantly, in March 1534
Chester herald, when writing to Cromwell to inform him
about treasonous words by a prebendary of Southwell, was
moved to state that he had been a servant of the king and
his father for over thirty years and until this recent
occurrence had never heard any subject 'rail upon them'
except one on the day Perkin Warbeck was 'raynyd' in
Cheapside. (68)    Since the details of nine or ten cases
from the summer of 1534 which involved words against the
king's second marriage found their way into Cromwell's ar-
chives, thus showing his concern over them, there may well
have been others similar which were heard in courts of
gaol delivery or assize or before council whose records
are now lost to us. (69)    We may take it that the definition by act of these words as misprision prevented even
the most outrageous being declared by the judges as treason under the act of 1352 through imagining the king's
death.    A new general law of treason was thus inevitable.
    The treason act, 26 Hen. VIII c. 13, passed in the
parliamentary session which began on 3 November 1534,
broke away from the drafts of 1530-2 and the first succession act and contained what events of the previous year
suggested it would contain:    traitorous words were really
the centre-piece.    To wish or attempt bodily harm to the
king, queen or the royal heir or to try to deprive the
king of his title by malicious deeds, writings, and spoken
words, was now laid down as treason, as was pronouncing
the king a heretic, schismatic, tyrant, infidel or usurper
of the crown.    The first category was an extension of the
1352 statute in the sense that attempting bodily harm
against the king, his queen and his heir now supplemented
the compassing of their deaths.    This brought the scope
of treason in England nearer to the versions of continental Europe, where in general any attempt against the
prince and his family was viewed as traitorous. (70)    It
has sometimes been suggested that there was a second extension of the fourteenth-century act;    that the 1534
statute only required words in speech, whereas its predecessor asked for an overt act.    This is based on a mis-
reading of the Edwardian statute where overt act referred
not to imagining or compassing the king's death (the section of the statute relevant to words) but to adhering to
the king's enemies or giving them aid or comfort.    The

1352 act was intended here to stop the king claiming as
forfeit without escaetorial inquest of fact the lands of
northerners who had supported the Scots in their inroads;
the king had been wont, in fact, to make these claims
solely on the authority of his own word that the occupants
of the lands were traitors. (71)   A yearbook case of 19
Hen. VI led to a judicial opinion which was not contradicted, that 'si home ymagyn le mort de Roy et ne fait pluys
il serra traye et pend et disclos', and such interpretations continued. (72)   At the trial of the duke of Buckingham in 1521 Chief Justice Fineux stated that between
felony and treason there was a clear difference:  there
could be no felony without some act done, but merely to
intend the king's death was high treason and such intention was sufficiently proven by words alone.   In such
cases no overt deed was needed beyond, that is, the traitorous statement which revealed the intent in the
mind. (73)   One apparent objection to this argument lies
in the fact that in 1460 the 1352 statute was seemingly
being misinterpreted, for an act of that year made it
treason to imagine the death of the new heir to the
throne, Richard duke of York, by open deed done, not
simply imagine his death *tout court.* (74)   There is, however, a possible explanation.   The 1460 act did not signify that words were not held treason any more, rather
that by then words were given formal recognition as being
the equivalent of any overt deed.   This development was
reflected in treason indictments.   Instead of a description of the crime followed by a statement that it amounted to compassing the king's death, there arose the formula that A had imagined to destroy the king, or something
similar, and to attain that end had committed X, Y and Z,
which were clearly specified acts including, of course,
mere words. (75)

The act of 1534 also made it treason to call the king
in writing or by spoken word a heretic, a schismatic, a
tyrant, an infidel or an usurper of the crown.   This was
very much a specific response to a specific problem.
Such abusive descriptions were becoming daily more frequent all over the country.   No one was arraigned for
treason in the later medieval period for calling the king
a heretic, schismatic or infidel, but that there was no
new principle involved is demonstrated by the history of
the last of the derogatory terms.   As early as the beginning of the fifteenth century calling the king a usurper
was held to be wishing, and therefore imagining, his
death. (76)

Both of these different types of treason, causing bodily harm to the king, his queen or heir or seeking to de-

prive him of his title by spoken words or writing, and
calling him herétic, tyrant or the rest had to be uttered
maliciously if they were to be traitorous.   Quite a few
historians have held the word 'malicious' was only put
into the act to get it past the commons who were very
critical, but recently it has been argued that the word,
which appears in both surviving drafts, was there from the
beginning. (77)   By this thesis the 'sticking in the commons', to which Bishop Fisher referred, is explained as a
determination by the lower house not to insert 'malicious'
into the act but to keep it in. (78)   The word 'malicious' seems to have been in the minds of the king's lawyers for some time.   In 1530 a draft for a treason bill
included activity maliciously contrived to annoy the
king's ambassadors on the part of an English subject when
in another realm.   Closer both in time and sense was the
first succession act where it referred to those who maliciously did, or procured to be done, things to the king's
peril, or maliciously by writing, printing, deed or act
caused him to be disturbed of the crown, or caused things
to the prejudice or slander of the Boleyn marriage. (79)
Since offences were to be misprision if committed by words
spoken maliciously.   'Maliciously' had been used in reference to treason for some time before there was any dispute with Rome but in an indictment, not an act.   At the
trial of the duke of Buckingham in 1521 it was reported he
had said that if committed to the Tower of London he would
seek an interview with the king and when in his presence
stab him.   These words were recorded in the indictment as
having been said traitorously and maliciously. (80)   The
use of the adverb 'maliciously' was not common and it may
only have started in Henry VIII's reign.   The usual ad-
verbs in legal records alongside the descriptions of particular treasons are 'falsely' and 'traitorously'.   Historians' interest in the word 'maliciously' has usually
been provoked by the complaints about it by Sir Thomas
More and Bishop Fisher at their trials.   More argued apparently that but for the word 'maliciously' nothing in
the indictment disclosed an offence.   The judges, however, rejected the argument.   Fisher also questioned the
word and to him the judges replied that malicious was
superfluous. (81)   They were probably correct.   It is
quite possible that when 'maliciously' appeared for the
first time in a statute, the first succession act, the
drafters were lacking a derogatory adverb to precede the
misdeeds penalized.   It was usual to insert the word
'traitorously', yet since procuring deeds to the king's
peril or slandering the Boleyn marriage was only to be
misprision if committed by words, an adverb indicating

treason was out of place.   Hence 'maliciously' was substituted.   There was nothing sinister about the word.
It was included probably out of a desire to be doubly
sure nothing illegal was being done, a feature of most of
the Henrician treason legislation.

Another category of treason found in the act of 1534,
which had antecedents in earlier drafts, was witholding
from the king his castles, ships or ordnance for more than
six days after order to surrender them had been proclaimed. (82)   Those expected to commit this offence must
surely have been of gentle blood or holders of military
office.   The only treason cases known which have even a
distant relevance were those involving Rhys ap Griffyths
(1531) and William, Lord Dacre and Greystock (1534).
Griffyths was tried and found guilty of treason in the
king's bench for apparently plotting an alliance with King
James of Scotland for the purpose of conquering England, (83) and Dacre, who was warden of the west march,
was accused before the lord high steward of traitorous
agreements with various Scots to the injury of other English border magnates. (84)   Both Dacre and Griffyths must
have had castles and contingents of men under their authority and thus have been a military threat to the king,
but a clear connection with the 1534 act is very hard to
discover even if an uncle of Griffyths' had fortified himself in his castle against authority in 1530.   The intention of the crown in this matter cannot have been other
than to frustrate open rebellion, which although it did
not occur was certainly in men's minds.   Chapuys wrote
that men at this time were reminded of the upheavals of
1470 and the flight abroad of Edward IV. (85)   It is
worth noting that there are no known examples of these offences being brought into court in the Middle Ages.   If
they did occur they would most likely have been dealt with
by the king's council as was most usual when the king's
writ or proclamation was disobeyed.

One clause of the treason act of 1534 which has frequently been passed without comment but which was of prime
importance concerned forfeiture.   Again the idea, indeed
almost the precise form in which it appeared in the act,
was anticipated in the earlier drafts for a treason law.
The act stated that all convicted of treason were to forfeit all lands, tenements and hereditaments which they had
of any estate of inheritance in use or possession.   This
meant the loss of possessions held in fee tail or held by
others to the traitor's use as well as his fee simple.
Thus there was to be no need in the future for acts of
attainder in order to reach those special types of possessions which according to the common law did not belong to

him. (86)   Most important of all was the proviso that
such total forfeiture was henceforth to be standard for
everyone convicted of high treason, not only for those
found guilty under the act of 1534.

The new treason act did not make use of all the ideas
set down in earlier drafts.   Hostile behaviour against
the king and his representatives on the part of English
subjects who went overseas was either forgotten for the
moment or proved impossible to define as treason in a satisfactory legal formula;   it was, however, to loom large
at the end of the decade.   Of the general fairness of the
act of 1534 there can be little doubt, as long as by fairness we mean its observing of legislative and legal precedents and we do not set out to judge the severity of the
sixteenth century by the relative tolerance of the twen-
tieth.   Basically, the statute was intended to outflank
the judges' power of declaration in cases of suspected
treason where the overt act was spoken words only, and
this it did successfully.   The law was certainly made
more precise, though this precision benefited the king
rather than his subjects.   Henry VIII and his ministers
had reversed the tendency whereby greater definition
worked against the crown and this was achieved, although
they did not admit it, by driving their carriage through
the loophole in the act of 1352 which allowed for further
declaration of treason in the future. (87)   They did not
start from scratch once more, but developed the old to
meet new exigencies of state.   There was never any
thought of abolishing the statute of 1352;   it is doubtful if it even suffered a temporary eclipse.   Within a
very few years it was found to be still the most important
of all treason acts.   The act of 1534, although it filled
a number of notable gaps in the law, cannot by any standard be called comprehensive, for there was much legislation on treason yet to come in Henry's reign.   Nor can
its drafters be complimented on its coherence, at least as
far as provisions touching on definition were concerned.
Almost four years of consideration had removed inherent
contradictions, yet despite the labour the impression of
it being an instrument ad hoc still remains.

When Henry VIII married a third time, and wished to
protect the marriage and the new order for the succession
by an act, spoken words appeared as treason again.   The
second succession act (28 Hen. VIII c. 7) made it high
treason to claim the crown against the provisions now laid
down or seek to stop them operating;   also to disturb the
plans for the guardianship of the royal heirs after the
king's demise.   Where in the first succession act (25
Hen. VIII c. 22) which was now repealed it had only been

misprision of treason to give vent to words which were to
the peril of the king's person or the hurt of the recent
marriage, now they became actual treason, as deeds and
written words had done in the earlier act.   Similarly inflated was refusing to take the oath to the newly arranged
succession.   Quite new was making treason out of refusal
to take an oath to answer questions, or interrogatories as
they were commonly known, on any section of the act, or
refuse to answer, having taken the oath.   This emphasis
on pre-trial examination, which is what it amounted to,
was a symptom of the growing importance of legal procedure
in the law of treason and also very likely the result of
the behaviour of Sir Thomas More when questioned before
his arraignment. (88)   Forfeiture in the second succession act was set at the exact degree stated in its precursor.

Before the Reformation Parliament was dismissed there
were two other pieces of legislation which added to the
increasingly complex framework of provisions against treason.   One was the act which was described in the statute
rolls as extinguishing the authority of the bishop of
Rome (28 Hen. VIII c. 10). (89)   Those who defended papal
jurisdiction in England by writing or deed were to be punished as for contravening the *praemunire* act of Richard
II's reign (16 Ric. II c. 5).   This was mild treatment,
and suggests the king, or more probably his legal advisers, still wanted to keep the sanctions of the treason
law to deal with attempts on the royal person and not to
use them offensively, so to speak, in a situation where a
connection with previous cases and interpretations was
difficult to concoct.   The offence the act made treason
concerned the taking of the oath of supremacy.   This was
to be sworn by all holders of temporal or ecclesiastical
office, and refusing to do so was traitorous.   Like the
other statutes on treason enacted since 1534 it provided
its fellows with reinforcement and the crown with a weapon
very necessary to combat a particular set of circumstances.

Also passed in the last session of the parliament of
1529-36 was an act whereby was attainted of treason Lord
Thomas Howard, brother of the duke of Norfolk. (90)   His
offence was contracting a marriage with Lady Margaret
Douglas, natural daughter of the Queen of Scots, Henry
VIII's eldest sister.   The king must have felt the marriage was intended, if he died without heirs, to put
Howard in a good position to make a bid for the crown or
at least take support away from his wife's brother, the
King of Scots, another aspirant.   The behaviour of Howard
was held to be a manifest danger of interrupting the suc-

cession act recently proposed and which still awaited
royal assent.   The second part of Howard's attainder act
was concerned not with him but with generalizing the new
rule.   It was to be treason in the future to marry the
king's sister, niece or aunt without royal consent or
'defile or deflower' them, with physical punishment and
loss of possessions as was usual for that crime.   The
woman so offending was to suffer in the same manner.
There were no precedents for either part of the act.   No
medieval king had ever reckoned a subject's matrimonial
plans as treason.   The proposed marriage could perhaps
have been interpreted as being to the peril of the future
heirs of Henry and Jane Seymour and therefore treason
under the second succession act, but this was not yet law.
Either the king could not wait or he feared that if he did
the judges might not find the offence to fall within the
act.   Thus there was more legislation and, since there
was another example of this two-part type of act seven
years later, it must have been considered a success.   A
further point of interest is the statement in the attainder part of the act that Howard's behaviour, if it was not
an aspiration to the crown, was at least making a division
for the same.   The last reference to division where treason was concerned had been in the act which attainted
Elizabeth Barton, and it suggests the drafters may have
worked with that before them.   Previous to that it had
occurred in the indictment of Edmund Dudley in 1509.   It
never became a traitorous offence in a general treason act
and now disappeared for the rest of the century.

The legislation on treason passed in the years 1534-6
was regarded for the greater part of the remaining years
of the century as the zenith of severity.   In 1547 and
1553 there were to be returns from the Henrician code to
the treason law of 1352 as it was then understood, in 1553
expressly on the grounds the other laws were too extreme
and entrapped people.   Despite this wide provision there
was between 1536 and the end of Henry's reign recourse to
additional acts which again extended the scope of treason,
to some rather strained constructions on the part of the
judges and to acts of attainder which convicted for treason without demonstrating clearly there had been anything
committed which was traitorous under the law of the land.

Of the new acts which concerned treason in general
three were the result of the king's matrimonial ventures,
and of these two were perhaps to be expected once Henry
had started in the path of supporting his marriages with
the sanctions of treason.   The act which declared the
marriage with Anne of Cleves void (32 Hen. VIII c. 25)
made it high treason to take by word, writing or deed,

that union as good and lawful.    The statute protected
itself by also classifying as treason any attempt to seek
its repeal, a proviso which had earlier found its way into
the succession act of 1536 (28 Hen. VIII c. 7) and originated no doubt in Richard II's short-lived treason act of
1397 (21 Ric. II cc. 3, 4).    The succession act of 1543
(35 Hen. VIII c. 1) gave the crown on Henry's death to his
son Edward and then, failing other male heirs to himself
or to Edward, to Mary and her heirs and then Elizabeth and
hers. (91)    A new oath for office-holders and those
sueing livery, which repudiated the pope's authority or
that of any other foreign 'potestate', commanded allegiance to the succession as defined in the act and affirmed the royal supremacy;   it took the place of the oaths
in two other acts concerned with treason, that is in the
second succession act and the act extinguishing the pope's
authority.    It was refusal to take this oath which was to
be high treason, with penalties and forfeiture as in the
laws on that offence, meaning presumably the act of 1534.

The act making a new treason that is very difficult to
justify concerned women the king might take to wife and
their reputations and their immoral behaviour after marriage. (92)    It stated that if a woman the king should
intend to marry 'esteeming her pure and cleane maide' when
the truth was otherwise, willingly espoused him without
revealing her unchaste past, she was to be guilty on conviction of high treason and suffer such death and forfeiture as was usual for that offence.    Furthermore if the
queen or the wife of the prince of Wales were to 'move by
writing or message or token persons to have carnal knowledge of them or someone to procure the same' then the
queen, the wife of the prince or the procurer was to be
guilty of high treason.    Failure on the part of any subject to report to the council or the king and failure by
the councillors to report to the king any knowledge of
'lightness of bodie' of the queen was to be punished with
the same penalties as the actual offender. (93)    The act
quite ignored the principles which had guided virtually
all treason legislation hitherto.    Except perhaps in
saving him from ridicule it did not really further the
protection of the king or his government.    It did not
even try to construe the cuckolding of the king as in some
way endangering his health and thus his life, or as leading to bodily ailment as in the case of Anne Boleyn. (94)
We cannot be certain, but the tone of the act suggests
that it was the handiwork of the king himself.

There was one other piece of legislation which enacted
new treason in this period, namely the act of proclamations (31 Hen. VIII c. 8).    This in its sixth section

stated that any one committing an offence contrary to the
act, that is to say refusing to obey proclamations issued
by the king on his council's advice, and afterwards contemptuously quitting the realm so as to avoid having to
answer, was to be adjudged a traitor and incur the usual
penalties.   This echoed the idea to be found in the
drafts for a new treason act of 1530-1.   The provisions
ascribed to 1530 said it was to be treason for a subject
to depart contemptuously from the realm, and those of 1531
decreed it treason to flee the realm after proclamation
had been made in a suspect's neighbourhood ordering his
appearance before the king.   Since the legislation on
treason of 1534-6 had omitted these original proposals,
perhaps until the whole matter of proclamations and what
they were supposed to do had been dealt with separately,
the appearance of treason sanctions for failing to answer
the king was to be expected.   As we have seen, the original proposals on the subject in 1530-1 were based on
incontestable precedents to be found in the fifteenth century.   It appears that the act of 1539 was intended to
regulate and afforce penalties for non-appearance, but it
was non-appearance before council rather than any of the
common law courts or parliament.   The punishment for
failing to appear before council was, of course, usually
limited to fines, mutilation or imprisonment.   In the
proclamation act, penalty as for treason was the most
severe among several categories of punishment set down for
various types of non-appearance.   Considered generally
and not merely for its relevance to the law of treason the
act is perhaps best viewed as an attempt to make effective
the judicial procedures of the king's council, especially
by fortifying its summoning instruments, namely the sub-
poena and *certis de causis* writs, devices which parliament
had objected to and had limited in the mid-fifteenth century.   Since council did not operate under the common law
there could be no outlawry and subsequent forfeiture of
possessions for those who, when asked to appear, refused.
Before which court the offender, if captured later, was to
appear the act did not state.   It is unlikely he was to
be tried by council or the body set up to operate the act:
probably he was to be tried in a common law court.   Since
no actual cases have yet been discovered further comment
is profitless. (95)
   The important trials which occurred between 1535 and
the end of the reign, much though they have been commented
on adversely, reveal in the main little that was unfair in
the interpretation of the scope of treason.   The indictments often stated under which act the suspect was being
accused.   Usually misdeeds concerned opposition to a

royal marriage or planning to deprive the king of his
crown or titles.    Charges would normally be based on the
first two succession acts or the treason act of 1534
either singly or in concert, but sometimes the act of 1352
was found necessary. (96)    This was when open revolt had
broken out, and imagining the king's death and the levying
of war were obvious charges.    With such a battery of weapons at their command there was likely to be little need
for unfair construction of the laws on the part of the
king and his legal advisers.    Even the displaying of the
arms of Edward the Confessor, as was done by the earl of
Surrey in 1546, could be argued fairly satisfactorily as
falling within the second act of succession through being
likely to jeopardize King Henry's crown. (97)    Never the
less there was construction and of an excessive sort.

    The case was that of Anne Boleyn.    In a long indict-
ment she was stated to have traitorously procured several
of the king's servants, including her own brother, to
become her adulterers and concubines, and specific days
were mentioned when illicit intercourse was supposed to
have taken place.    This behaviour was called traitorous
several times when it was being described in detail, and
then in summary all concerned were said to have imagined
the king's death at Westminster on 31 October 1536 and at
several times before and since.    This may have been a
reference to the adultery already mentioned, but it could
also have been connected with another charge which followed:    that Anne had often promised to marry one or other
of her suitors when the king should die, and had said she
would never love the king in her heart.    When the king
learned of these misdeeds, so it was stated, he was so
upset that certain harms and dangers beset his body.
Finally the deeds of the queen and her friends were described as being to the danger of Henry's person and to the
danger and detriment of his and Anne's issue and heirs.
The indictment did not make it clear which act the queen
and her alleged concubines had offended against.    It
could have been the act of 1352, since there were words
imagining the king's death, or the treason act of 1534
(attempting bodily harm to the king) or the first succession act (deeds to the peril, slander or disherison of
Anne's own issue) or all of them.    The only contemporary
to comment on the legal classification of the indictment
was John Spelman in his law reports.    Unfortunately he is
of little help to us since he seems to confuse offences
mentioned in the first succession act with those in the
1534 treason act quoting without criticism Anne Boleyn as
saying that 'slander on the issue begotten between her and
the king' fell under the 'statute of the twenty-sixth'

year'. (98)   Whichever act the offences were held to have
fallen under, it was an excessive piece of construction.
There was nothing in the history of treason to suggest
that adultery on the part of the queen was traitorous.
The blame belongs not only to the king and his ministers
but to the judges who must have been consulted.   There is
no evidence they put up resistance as they had in the case
of Elizabeth Barton.

Although in 1536 the judges permitted Anne Boleyn's
adulterous behaviour to be found treason, there is some
evidence that they objected to a similar arrangement in
regard to Katherine Howard in 1542.   Henry VIII's fifth
queen had offended in much the same way as Anne Boleyn.
In one indictment she and a former lover, Francis Derham,
were stated to have planned to continue their former prom-
iscuous fornication even after she married the king.
Furthermore she had, when queen, fallen in love with
Thomas Culpeper, incited him to have criminal intercourse
with her and arranged to do so. (99)   In conclusion
Katherine, Culpeper and Derham were stated to have compassed not only the scandal of the royal marriage but also
the danger of the king's person and even his final destruction.   This was mainly a construction of the 1352
act, but the misdeeds might also have come within the
treason act of 1534 (bodily harm to the king) or the
second act of succession (deeds to the peril of the king
or his heirs).   As in the only case which was similar,
that of Anne Boleyn, the statutes were being used for a
purpose not intended.   This may have caused some opposition amongst the professional judges since the queen and
Lady Rochford, the procuress in the case, were, although
indicted, not brought to trial.   Instead they were attainted by an act, which took the form of giving approval
to the indictment, in the parliament which met on 16 January 1542. (100)   Katherine, Lady Rochford and Culpeper
were said in the bill of attainder to have perpetrated
many abominable treasons 'to the most fearefull perill
and daunger of the distruccion of your most royall person';   the bill like the indictment could have been based
on any or all of the three relevant acts mentioned above.
There is an indication that the attainder act drew opposition within parliament, for it was introduced on 28 January and not passed until 11 February, and there were two
second readings. (101)   Conceivably the delay was occasioned by procedural points like the confirming of an indictment by an act rather than going to trial, or the
king's giving his consent to the act by letters patent instead of in the usual form, but just as likely as a cause
of the hiatus was complaint about the actual construing of
the offences as treason at all.

An attainder act equally unsatisfactory, judged by what
it labelled as treason, was that which attainted Thomas
Cromwell in 1540. (102)   The crimes Cromwell was held to
have committed were reckoned to amount to both treason and
heresy.   The treasons were not at all clearly labelled,
being mixed with other non-religious offences, including
what would have been called in the fourteenth century accroaching or usurping the royal power and in the fifteenth
century misprision, which meant misusing the king's dele-
gated powers or simply seizing power for some illegal purpose.   Of this type of offence there were only two with
any proximity to treason.   One was Cromwell's setting
free on his own authority certain of those apprehended on
suspicion.   By the act of 1424 it was treason for one
suspected of that crime to break out of prison, and since
accessories to treason were held equally guilty with principals it may seem that Cromwell's deed could be construed
as traitorous.   Yet it was the first time this had been
done.   The other offence of a borderline nature was Cromwell's saying that if the king turned against the new doc-
trines (meaning Lutheranism) he would fight him in the
field in his own person with his sword in his hand.   For
making a statement to Henry IV of similar substance a
friar may have been convicted of high treason in
1402 (103) and Sir William Stanley, as we have seen, was
reported as having been accused in 1495 of treason because
he made a statement in the conditional tense about taking
sides in battle.   Neither of these reported conditional
statements had appeared in a formal legal accusation and
we may say that the act of attainder, if judged alongside
others of its class, was ill-founded as far as the treason
element was concerned.   It was also a thoroughly slovenly
piece of work, which suggests that its concoctors were
scraping the barrel or in such a hurry or aroused emotional condition that they were incapable of logical or legal
arrangement. (104)

One other attainder act of this period calls for comment.   Wriothesley's chronicle says that executed on
Tower Hill at the same time as Cromwell was Walter, Lord
Hungerford 'for treason of buggery'.   Stow says Hungerford suffered 'as it was said, for buggery'. (105)   The
act which said Hungerford had committed the offence with
his servants seems to have included another misdeed as
well, that is the procuring of a chaplain and two others
'to conjure and show how long the king should live'. (106)
This crime, as shown already, had been held as treason on
occasions in the past and may have been the reason for
Hungerford's conviction as a traitor, but the act is not
clear on this.   There had been recent legislation against

unnatural offences such as Hungerford's.   An act of 1534
(25 Hen. VIII c. 6), because as yet there was not a 'sufficient and condigne punishment appointed for buggery with
mankind or beast', decreed it was to be henceforth adjudged felony.   This act was, however, only to last until
the next parliament and does not seem to have been renewed.   The practice before 1534 may have been to classi-
fy unnatural sexual offences as treason.   We find mention
in a letter to Cromwell of a John Lawton indicted for
treason 'for carenadge' (unnatural carnal knowledge?).  (107)   This case may have been responsible for
the 1534 act.   In the reign of Edward IV there is said to
have been a case in which a man was charged with treason
'quod cognovit mulierem contra naturam'. (108)   It would
thus be unwise to assume that Henry VIII and his legal advisers were the inceptors of this form of treason.

Finally in this survey of innovation in the treason law
in Henry VIII's later years, notice must be taken of
charges relating to forgery.   In 1536, in the act 27 Hen.
VIII c. 2, the category in the statute of 1352 which made
it treason to forge the king's great or privy seal or
counterfeit his coin was extended to include forging the
king's signet or sign manual, thus reflecting new methods
in administration.   This addition to the law seems to
have been the result of the counterfeiting of the royal
sign manual on the part of a keeper of the king's palace. (109)   In contrast there may have been in 1546 that
rare occurrence, a narrowing of the scope of treason.   A
law report tells us that a chaplain who affixed an ancient
seal to a patent of non-residence made by himself was
reckoned by the justices only to have committed misprision
of treason since he had merely misused an old seal and not
counterfeited a new one. (110)   This decision seems to go
against one given in a similar case in 1400 where an old
seal had been put to a fraudulent commission for collecting taxes. (111)

If the changes in the definition of treason in the
years 1536-47 are judged not by modern standards but by
those of the sixteenth century, they still seem arbitrary,
severe, and above all too many in number to gain the respect of the population at large and thereby remain per-
manently on the statute rolls.   If the act about proclamation, the one declaring the Cleves marriage void, the
third act of succession and the new rule on forgery can
be defended, then the attainder act against Cromwell, the
one against Katherine Howard, the general act concerning
the moral conduct of royal brides which was joined to it,
and the construction of treason used in the trial of Anne
Boleyn, must be decried.   They were without respectable

precedent and based on no principle save that anything
which annoyed the king was to his peril and thereby traitorous.   The increased use of attainder acts suggests a
hardening of resistance on the part of the judges, who
must have been asked to construe as treason deeds and
words they thought were not really traitorous.

Who should take the blame for this unsatisfactory legislation?   The answer seems to be that the king himself
was largely responsible.   Henry was never loth to tell
his ministers what the law should be.   In February 1531
Chapuys reported to his master about the law of praemunire
that its interpretation lay solely in the king's head and
that he amplified it and declared it at his pleasure,
making it apply to any case he pleased.   In 1540 Marillac
reported to his master Francis I that a new act concerning
aliens had been drafted by the English king in
person. (112)   Recently it has been argued that it was
Henry who was responsible for the passing of the sodomy
act of 1534.   We also know that in February 1531 the king
went himself to the house of lords to further the bill
against poisoners and later that year was the proposer of
a new clause for the draft for a new treason law offering
pardon and reward to those who first detected any traitorous offence. (113)   Henry did not always get his own
way.   Despite Chapuys's asseveration that when the king
came to dispute about treason there was no one who would
dare to contradict him unless they wished to be reputed
stupid or disloyal, Henry on that occasion (the matter of
whether Elizabeth Barton's crimes amounted to treason) did
not prevail. (114)   From 1533 much of the drafting of
acts and drawing of indictments was probably in the hands
of Cromwell yet he does not appear to have ever been in
sole charge.   The king must have given him instructions,
especially when royal emotions were involved as with the
indictment of Anne Boleyn, and advice was undoubtedly
forthcoming from the royal lawyers to whom Cromwell recognizing his own deficiencies frequently turned.   One of
Cromwell's memoranda runs 'Item how the kynges lernyd
counsaylle shalbe with me all this daye for the full con-
clusyon of the Indytmentes.' (115)   In 1534, so it has
been suggested, the new treason act which had probably
been designed by Cromwell was 'tightened and cleaned up'
by Audley, the lord chancellor.   In the first act of succession Cromwell's intent to make it treason to attack the
Boleyn marriage by spoken words as well as by writings
seems to have been changed on the advice of lawyers. (116)
Cromwell must take some of the blame for the indictment
against Anne Boleyn but it is fair to say that the bad
acts on treason occurred when he was no longer there to
advise the king.

In conclusion some notice must be taken of an important
area where the treason law did not reach, the region of
words, which although they were likely to provoke disaffection and disturbance in the realm did not quite amount
to treason.   Cases involving such words were plentiful.
A recent investigation of the years 1532-40 suggests that
of 394 reported cases of words thought to touch on treason
at least 184 and perhaps over 250 were found subsequently
not to be treason at all, (117) yet they caused much concern and some of them may have created for the government
as much danger as deeds actually traitorous.   The form
such words might take were many but usually they amounted
to commenting adversely on the behaviour of royal advisers, criticizing the sexual life or procreative ability
of the monarch, misinterpreting government policies in a
dangerous manner, showing open hostility to the ruling
class or spreading rumours about general disaffection.
The suggestion has been made that this offence was not
covered by any law but this is incorrect. (118)   The
first statute of Westminster (3 Edw. I c. 34) made clear
provision for the handling of those who devised tales
whereby discord might arise between the king and his
people.   The act had been renewed, admittedly with the
emphasis now on the part referring to false news and horrible lies concerning the great men of the realm, in 1378
(2 Ric. II c. 5) and 1388 (12 Ric. II c. 11).   The statutes of 1275 and 1378 did not say where such cases
should be tried but affirmed simply that a miscreant
should be taken and imprisoned until he brought into court
the first author of any such tale.   Presumably this meant
either his friends sought out the deviser or the prisoner
himself admitted to authorship.   In 1388 a rider was
added to this provision.   If the prisoner could not produce the originator of the tale he was to be punished 'by
the advice of the council'. (119)
Whether this resulted in time in all such cases being
handled either directly or by delegation by council is not
clear but there is a strong possibility it was so.   By
the 1530s at least the practice had become one of allowing
magistrates to act summarily against the utterers of seditious words not amounting to treason often by use of the
whip, the pillory or prison, and there is every indication
that the jurisdiction was that of the council.   In 1542
there seems to have been a partial change in method.   The
act 33 Hen. VIII c. 14 made one form of seditious talk,
that involving prophecy based on animals to be found in
the badges or cognizances of the upper classes, into felony without benefit of clergy or sanctuary.   The perpetrators, on conviction under the common law before those

authorized to try felony, were to suffer death and forfeiture as was usual for that category of crime.    Thus one
form of words was made clearly justiciable under the
common law, and the crown benefited from an ability to
impose a more severe physical punishment combined with the
forfeiture of lands, goods and chattels.    In 1555 this
tendency was developed further.    By the act 1 & 2 Ph. &
M. c. 3 the laws of 1275, 1378 and 1388 were declared to
be still in full force and, whatever the procedure in the
past, cases brought under them in the future were entrusted to the justices of oyer and terminer, of gaol delivery, of assize, and of the peace, who were all now empowered to examine, hear and determine.    The penalty for
those found guilty of speaking seditious and slanderous
words to the reproach and dishonour of the king and queen
was, for the first offence, to be the loss of ears or a
fine of £100 coupled with a term of three months' imprisonment.    Those who wrote such slanders were, on conviction, to suffer the abscission of the right hand, those
who merely repeated the stories were to lose one ear or
pay 100 marks, while anyone who committed their offence
more than once was to be imprisoned for life.    Also
worthy of note was the giving to justices of the peace the
power to commit to ward, without opportunity for bail, any
person 'vehemently suspect' of those offences.    The
effects of this act seem to have been entirely to the government's satisfaction, being found in 1559 to have proved
'very good and necessary' in dealing with those who disturbed the tranquillity of the realm. (120)    Therefore by
the statute 1 Eliz. c. 6, as there was thought to be some
doubt about its continuation into the new reign, the provisions of the Marian act were extended to cover the new
queen and her issue, and cases appeared with some frequency in the courts of common law. (121)

# 2

<hr>

# The Scope of Treason: 2

<hr>

From the death of Henry VIII to the death of Elizabeth the
scope of treason underwent periodic contractions and ex-
pansions.    Contractions occurred largely at the begin-
nings of reigns when a new monarch, probably in search of
additional popularity and keen to reward those who had allowed his accession, removed the most disliked features of
the treason law which his predecessor had operated.    This
provides an interesting demonstration of how feared some
of the definitions of treason were.    It also shows how
each of the last three Tudor monarchs and their advisers
ingenuously believed at the outset of their reigns they
could do without such sanctions, only to have their beliefs shattered by experience and to be forced to return
to the provisions of the Henrician laws.    Yet, despite
their severity, these provisions failed to provide the
answer.    Henry's heirs found need for treason sanctions
to combat dangers which the father had never had to face.
This was particularly true of the later part of Elizabeth's reign, when the activities of Jesuits and seminary
priests seemed particularly threatening.    The usual Tudor
remedy was another statute, but other solutions were tried
occasionally.    In Mary's reign the judges delved into the
past to discover for the first time that century a new
source of law on the subject.    This was the so-called
common law treason which, so it was argued, had existed
before the statute of 1352 and because it was not mentioned by that act still survived.    Common law treason,
which was of several varieties, found favour with the prosecuting lawyers of the crown in the middle of Elizabeth's
reign.    Then the reason was procedural, as for example to
avoid the need to produce witnesses at indictment or trial
as was required by some later sixteenth-century statutes
on treason, or from a desire to put a suspect on trial
after a time limitation was expired, as demanded by

others.    Attainder acts in this period were still fairly
common, but in the charges levied they followed closely
the laws of treason which prevailed at the time.    There
was nothing like the act against Thomas Cromwell;   nor did
they have attached to them new and general laws of treason.    In the matter of forfeiture they also obeyed the
letter of the law of the time, oscillating between the
provisions, or rather the lack of them, in the 1352 act
and those in the Henrician law of 1534.

Judicial interpretation, so crucial in the initial
years of the break with Rome, was again important, but
there was a difference in the general effect.    Judges'
declarations as to what was and what was not treason seem
in this period to have gone almost entirely in favour of
the monarch.    Another significant development in this
field was that the most celebrated of legal interpreters
was not a judge, but Edward Coke who was attorney-general.
His success in getting various popular riots and assemblies classified as treason brought the Tudor era to a
close with the establishment of a markedly royal interpretation of the scope of treason.    There remains one other
general factor to notice.    Although there was considerable and frequent alteration in the scope of treason in
the period 1547-1603, with an increasing number of laws
under which prosecution could be made, the very frequency
of treason cases made the crown more dextrous in their
handling and provided it with recent case law of a pro-
fusion which had never existed before.    In addition, the
absence of a revolution, like the breaking with Rome in
the 1530s, and the very length of Elizabeth's reign, give
an impression of adherence to the principles of law in the
handling of treason which only close examination can confirm or deny.

The first general treason act of Edward VI's reign (1
Edw. VI c. 12), having observed philosophically that it
was better for the king to be too clement than too severe
and better a subject should obey out of love than through
fear, went on to describe the laws of the recently decea-
sed King Henry as 'verie streighte, sore, extreme and
terrible' although some justification was found in the
troubled nature of the times in which they were
passed. (1)    Now conditions had changed and the 'more
calm and quiet reign of another Prince' made their repeal
desirable.    The act claimed to be a return to the definition of treason as embodied in the act of 1352, with certain additions which were then stated.    To say the king
was not the supreme head of the church, or that someone
else should be king, or to compass by words to deprive the
king or his heirs of the royal estate or titles, were all

to be treason, but only when the offence was committed a
third time.   If the misdeed was perpetrated by written
word or by deed then it was treason at the first offence.
It was also to be treason for anyone to claim the crown
other than according to the third succession act (35 Hen.
VIII c. 1).   By these provisions not only was the 1543
succession act preserved in some part but also the treason
act act of 1534 where it touched the king's titles ecclesi-
iastical and temporal.   If the break with Rome and the
Tudor dynasty were to be perpetuated, both were probably
essential.   Also left unrepealed in the end, although
their removal may have been intended initially, were acts
against the counterfeiting of coins and that of 1536 (27
Hen. VIII c. 2) against forging the king's sign manual.
The rule that the wives of those convicted of treason
should have their dower, and the general diminution of the
offence of concealing treason from treason itself to misprision of treason 'as heretofore hath been used' were
quite novel.   The latter reference was presumably to the
general part of the act which attainted Katherine Howard,
wherein failure to report the lack of chastity in a woman
about to marry the king was declared misprision of treason.   Here the 1547 act went directly against medieval
precedent;   to conceal treason which was in the form of a
plot to kill the king had always been as bad as being an
actual perpetrator, even in Bracton. (2)   The laws touching treason that were repealed in 1547  included the act
against poisoners (poisoning became murder), parts of the
act of 1534 (26. Hen. VIII c. 13), the second succession
act, the law against unauthorized marriage to the king's
aunt, niece or sister, the general part of the attainder
act against Katherine Howard about fornication with the
queen or the wife of the prince of Wales and the premari-
tal chastity of one who aspired to be queen, the act extinguishing the authority of the pope (28. Hen. VIII c.
10), the act against taking the Cleves marriage as lawful
and the statute on proclamations.
     If it did not really signal a return to the act of
1352, the one of 1547 was none the less important.   It
showed that there was widespread dissatisfaction with the
Henrician laws even if there were some, like the western
rebels of 1549, who supported them.   Above all it was the
interpretation of words as treason which had aroused an-
tagonism, no doubt because a man's life could depend on
the testimony of a couple of witnesses who might well be
his enemies.   We may imagine that it was a case where the
instrument of repression attracted to itself much of the
hostility that the more general measures of the Henrician
revolution had engendered.   Certainly the first Edwardian

treason statute was a measure bound to increase the popularity of the new regime.   Quite possibly the act was
drafted by Protector Somerset himself.   Its moderation
seems to reflect the liberal attitudes which historians
have frequently attributed to him.   However, recent argument pointing to his great greed for wealth and his ruth-
lessness towards others suggests that if indeed he was the
author then his purpose may just as well have been merely
political.   Furthermore, it should be remembered that
several sections of the act which tended to soften the
treason law, like the rule that accusations of traitorous
words must be brought within thirty days of the offence,
the need for two witnesses at indictment and arraignment,
and the degree of forfeiture which was stipulated, were
probably not government inspired but accretions from the
bill's passage through parliament. (3)   The act is worthy
of a special place in the history of treason because it
was the first substantially to alleviate that law since
Henry IV repealed the act of 1397.

Such treason trials as there were in the immediate
aftermath of the Edwardian act bear out that the government stood by its word, for prosecutions were under either
the act itself or the statute of 1352. (4)   Usually it
was the latter;   indeed there was only one important court
case where the 1547 act was utilized.   Somerset himself
was tried for treason partly under it, on the grounds that
he had compassed to deprive the king of his royal dignity
by acts such as assembling men for the taking and imprisoning of the earl of Warwick and other privy councillors,
compassing to seize the Tower and gain possession of the
great seal and inciting the citizens of London to insurrection. (5)   The act of attainder against Somerset's
brother Sir Thomas Seymour, Lord Seymour of Sudeley, was
also fashioned to follow the new Edwardian treason act.
He was said to have aimed at gaining control over the
young king through creating a faction and causing tumult,
uproar and sedition in the realm, acquiring offices, retaining large numbers of men, preparing a 'great furniture' of weapons and 'practising to make the king take to
himself the rule of the kingdom'. (6)   He had promised
that Edward VI should marry an English nobleman's daughter
and had himself sought to marry Princess Elizabeth.   In
summation, the act declared these deeds could not be other
than to compass to deprive the king of his royal estate
and title and to imagine his death.   All this was a perfectly reasonable indictment under the 1547 act and the
reference to imagining the king's death showed a proper
return to the statute of 1352 as the drafters of Edward
VI's act had intended.   Worthy of attention is the close

parallel between Seymour's attainder and the indictment of
Empson and Dudley in 1509.   Each had sought to govern the
king, but whereas in 1509 to interpret this as seeking his
death and therefore treason under the 1352 act was impugn-
ing the law, in 1549 against Seymour the king and his advisers were following the provisions of the new treason
act perfectly correctly, albeit in a bill of attainder in
parliament.

   Beside the act of 1547 must be set the second general
treason statute of Edward's reign (5 & 6 Edw. VI c. 11),
which restored much of the Henrician treason act omitted
in 1547.   There now appeared as treason calling the king
(or his heirs) a heretic, tyrant, schismatic, infidel or
usurper.   As in the earlier act, this crime was treason
the first time committed if perpetrated by writing (overt
deed was inappropriate here) but only on the third occasion if by speech.   The intention of the act must have
been to provide additional sanctions for the changes in
religion heralded by the second act of uniformity, particularly to stop any altercations arising from slanders
against the king which might lead to riot or rebellion.
Also reintroduced from the same Henrician act was the
treason of detaining the king's ships, fortresses, ordnance or munitions, though whether this was included because it was alongside slandering the king in the act of
1534 and thought to be of possible future use, or whether
the government had knowledge of actual deeds of this type
is uncertain.   Those convicted of treason were to forfeit
to the king 'all suche landes, tenements and heredytaments
which anye suche Offender ... shall have of any estate of
inheritance in his own right in use or possession'.   This
was by now the standard formula.   It meant the loss of
fee simple, fee tail and lands held to the convicted man's
use by others and was the same as provided by the act of
1534 and later treason statutes.   Unlike the main Henrician treason act and in direct contrast with the one of
1547, wives of those found guilty were not to be allowed
to sue for their dower.   The 1552 treason act was apparently drafted by six prominent lawyers, John Gosnold, John
Caryll, William Stanford, Anthony Brown, William Cook and
the recorder of London, but who gave instructions to the
drafters is not clear. (7)   It may have been Northumberland, but before condemning him for what was to all appearances a most severe act it is well to note that an
earlier bill on the subject had had to be withdrawn, presumably because of opposition from the parliamentary
commons, and two mollifications in the manner of prosecuting suspected traitors introduced.   At least the act was
based almost entirely on precedent, whereas the one of

1534 was only in small part.    Furthermore, words were not
specifically defined as traitorous in a first offence even
if they might be so construed under the hallowed act of
1352.

The 1552 treason act, so it has been suggested, (8)
originated in the desire for a law to take the place of an
expiring statute of 1549, but this seems doubtful.    The
1549 act (3 & 4 Edw. VI c. 5) made it treason for twelve
or more persons who had assembled together to murder or
imprison a member of the privy council or to alter the
laws of the realm, to remain together more than one hour
after being commanded to go home;  similarly for persons
numbering forty or more, who stayed together for more than
two hours, attempting to break down enclosures, damage
parks and commit other rebellious acts.    Forfeiture by
those convicted of these offences was to be as for felony,
with the addition of fee tail, but for the one life only.
The 1549 statute, which since it was read six times in the
lords and another six in the commons must have aroused
much opposition and suffered considerable amendment, was
probably intended as support for the reversing of Somerset's agrarian policy which took place in the same session.    Also the recent disturbances over enclosures in
East Anglia, the south, Gloucestershire, Wiltshire, Oxfordshire, and Buckinghamshire must have caused alarm
amongst the landholding classes and a desire for severer
sanctions against the troublemakers, since riot as a crime
was nothing more than trespass.    This was certainly
better handling of popular insurrection than in 1517.
The provisions in the act about attempted imprisoning of
privy councillors or altering the laws of the realm suggest they were based on actual occurrences, or at least on
fears substantially founded, in the trial of strength between the protector and the rest of the king's council.
'Altering the laws' was found a useful concept by the
royal lawyers and was to appear again in Elizabeth's time
both in actual treason acts and in treason indictments.

Until this time (1549) prophecies foretelling the
future, whereby the king's death, deposition or incapacity
were predicted, had frequently been interpreted as treason
under the clause of the 1352 act about imagining or compassing the king's death.    Now there was some relenting.
The act 3 & 4 Edw. VI c. 15 said that those practising
'fantasticall and fond' prophecies concerning the king's
majesty and 'honorable gentlemen and commons' to the peril
of the king and the realm, by words or writings, in order
to make a rebellion and who were convicted of the offence
should suffer a year's imprisonment and a £10 fine on the
first occasion and life imprisonment with forfeiture of

goods and chattels for the second.   The penalties suggest
that the crime had been put into the misprision of treason
category.

Despite the re-expansion of the scope of treason in the
later years there is little impression in Edward's reign
of the treason laws being operated with great severity,
nor is there any suggestion of sharp or illegal practice
by the crown lawyers in the prosecution of traitors in
court.   There was a trial which was mishandled, but since
it resulted in acquittal of treason it should not count.
The only illegality touching treason appeared in a proclamation of 2 July 1549 which dealt with the setting of
prices of victuals in times of dearth.   Those who sought
revenge against profiteers by force, riot, menace or unlawful assembly were to suffer 'extreme punishment' as
'high traitors'.   Whether such sanctions were in fact put
into operation is unknown.   The only other piece of sharp
practice, which was not really contrary to the law since
it was an act, was the stripping from Somerset's son and
heir in 1552 the title of 'Viscount Beauchamp, earl of
Hertford and duke of Somerset'.   Since the father's offence had only been found felony, his heirs should not,
according to the usual rules, have suffered any such
loss. (9)   Overall, the reign of Edward VI displayed an
improved rationality in the laws defining treason which
even the rising severity did not destroy.

The period of Mary's reign bore, superficially at
least, a pattern similar in the matter of variation in the
scope of treason to that of her predecessor.   There was a
contraction in that scope early on and a renewal of wider
definitions as the years went by.   These changes, however, did not occur until those who had opposed Mary's accession by supporting Lady Jane Grey had been tried and
convicted of treason, partly under the Edwardian acts.
In August 1553 Northumberland, John Dudley, earl of Warwick, his eldest son, and William Parr, marquis of Northampton, were accused in the court of the lord high steward, and Sir Andrew Dudley, Sir John Gates, Sir Thomas
Palmer and several allies before other commissioners of
oyer and terminer, of machinating and compassing to depose
the queen from her crown and dignity by asserting the
title of Lady Jane Grey and by levying war against
her. (10)   These charges were laid under the first treason act of Edward VI and the statute of 1352.   'Levying
war', which was treason according to the latter, was here
being used as the deed necessary if the offences were to
be treason on their first perpetration under the act of
1547.   This had been the form in indictment drawing since
that act.   Archbishop Cranmer was indicted of similarly

compassing to depose Mary from her crown and dignity, his
acts being that he sent men to assist Northumberland when
he levied war and had declared Lady Jane to be queen, and
honoured, received and proclaimed her as such.   Guildford
Dudley, her husband, was indicted of doing the same. (11)
Jane's offences, unless the indictments of Cranmer and her
husband were held to apply to her as well because she had
made no objection to their honouring, receiving and proclaiming, were limited to her signing various writings as
'Jane the Queen'. (12)   The only one of Northumberland's
supporters who seems to have been indicted unsatisfacto-
rily was his fifth son, Robert Dudley.   He was accused in
January 1554 of having on 18 July 1553 taken forcible possession in the manner of war of the town of King's Lynn,
proclaimed Jane as queen and tried to make certain of the
Lynn townsfolk withdraw their allegiance from Mary and
join his father in levying war against her.   Unless the
proclamation could be interpreted as imagining Mary's
death, and the indictment does not suggest it was, none of
these crimes was in fact treason and it is noteworthy that
Dudley was not said himself to have levied war. (13)   The
legal advisers of the new queen seem to have been guilty
of the rather deceitful practice of giving an impression
that war had been levied through the use of phrases which
to the non-lawyer seemed to mean that. (14)   It is significant that the crime of levying war against the prince
and its definition should have been scrutinized closely by
the judges in the next year or so.

The first general treason act of Mary's reign (1 M. st.
1 c. 1), like that of Edward VI's, started with a preamble
which announced that laws without extreme sanctions were
obeyed better than those with them and especially where
the offence was one of words and not deeds.   In addition,
the queen had been moved by the fate of those nobles who
for such offences had recently suffered shameful and un-
customary death.   In the future, therefore, treason and
the penalties for it were to exist only as in the statute
of 1352;   there were no exceptions or new provisos.   Thus
the Marian act was really quite different from the Edwardian act of 1547 which, although declaring a return to the
act of 1352, had added provisions making it treason under
certain circumstances to imagine to deprive the prince of
his crown, titles and dignity.   By sanctifying the act 35
Hen. VIII c. 1 about the succession, Edward's statute had
made it treason to claim the throne against that act and
set forfeiture for treason at the level originally laid
down by the Henrician act of 1534 (26 Hen. VIII c. 13).
In 1553 the queen was ready to renounce her right to the
possessions traitors held in fee tail and those which

others held to their use.   The reference in the Marian
act to men being entrapped by the laws 'many times, for
woordes onelye without other facte or dede doone or perpetrated' suggests that even the moderate Edwardian device
of making seditious speech treason only on the third occasion was much resented.   How well grounded in fact the
complaints were and how many men had been convicted of
traitorous words between 1547 and 1553 is as yet unknown.
It is possible that the preamble to the 1553 act was referring to convictions since 1534, not since 1547.   This
would certainly better explain the mention of noblemen
suffering an unusual and shameful death, since those of
Northumberland's faction who were convicted of treason
shortly before the Marian act were, as we have seen, found
guilty of compassing to deprive the queen of her title by
act, not words.   Because of this the act is perhaps best
viewed as a way of slighting the most notable piece of re-
pressive legislation which stemmed from the breach with
Rome, that is to say the statute 26 Hen. VIII c. 13.

Although in her first treason act Mary made major concessions towards leniency, a change of royal policy occurred before any benefit could be taken by offenders.
Early in 1554 the trial took place of Sir Nicholas Throckmorton, a sympathizer of Sir Thomas Wyatt's, which was the
occasion of important interpretations by the judges concerning the scope of the prevailing treason law.   According to the indictment, Throckmorton, with ten other
gentlemen and in the company of certain traitors, had compassed to deprive the queen of her crown and dignity and
destroy her, and to take the Tower of London and levy war
against her.   They were also said to have actually levied
war against her in Kent and London. (15)   Adhering to
those who were the queen's enemies and levying war were
perfectly reasonable charges (although Throckmorton does
not seem to have been guilty of them), since they were
based on the statute of 1352, but the other charges were
of very doubtful legality.   Compassing to deprive the
prince of his crown had been made treason in 1534 (26 Hen.
VIII c. 13) and again in 1547 (1 Edw. VI c. 12) but this
had been repealed in the first treason act of Mary's
reign.   To destroy the queen, which was appended to this
charge, was no doubt treason by the act of 1352 and therefore quite proper, but compassing to levy war was not
treason by any law. (16)

What seems to have happened was that those who drew the
indictment did so without having the recent amendments to
the treason laws in mind.   Compassing to deprive the
prince of his crown had appeared illicitly in the charges
against Wyatt and his adherents a few weeks previous-

ly. (17)    Quite possibly in all these cases the crown's
lawyers worked from the indictments of Northumberland and
his followers, who had been arraigned before the first
Marian treason act was passed.   Throckmorton, if we can
believe the account of the trial which appears in Holinshed, made some very telling criticisms of court procedure
and, what is relevant here, of the indictment.   'I ought
not', he told the jury at one point, 'to be attainted of
the treason comprised within my indictment considering the
statute of repeal [in] the last parliament, of all treasons other than such as be declared in the 25th year of
King Edward 3rd.' (18)   He was answered by Serjeant Stanford, who must have been aware that the crown's position
was unsound, for he argued that there was another fount of
treason in addition to the act of 1352:   'there doth remain divers other treasons at this day at the common law,
which be not expressed by that statute, as the judges can
declare'. (19)   What Stanford was saying was that the
1352 act simply defined or clarified a number of existing
treasons;   it did not purport to include all.   There was
only a small amount of truth in this.   Every type of
treason of importance had in fact been included save one,
namely failure to reveal a knowledge of intended treason.
The myth of common law (as distinct from statute) treason
probably originated in the fifteenth century in acts like
that of 1424, but no lawyers had developed the idea properly at that time. (20)   In 1554 the queen's hard-pressed
legal advisers renovated it.   Chief Justice Bromley, we
are told, boldly asserted that several cases had been adjudged treason 'without the express words of the statute'
and the crown lawyers quoted cases, inaccurately as we
know now, from the reigns of Henry IV, Richard III and
Henry VII in proof.   Although from our point of vantage
we can see that the indictment against Throckmorton was
illegal because it was partly under the Edwardian treason
act 1 Edw. VI c. 12 and not totally under the act of 1352
as it should have been, Throckmorton really took exception
on other grounds.   He claimed there was need for an overt
deed of some sort to be proved against him.   The prosecution argued on the other hand that if three or four conspired together a traitorous act, and then afterwards one
of them committed it, all were guilty. (21)   We may say
that this was quite correct where the crime was imagining
or compassing the king's death, since all in the conspiracy had been conspiring, but incorrect where the crime was
levying war or adhering to the king's enemies and the
other treasons in the 1352 statute.   Thus Throckmorton
was quite right and the crime of compassing to levy war
which had been laid against him was, according to statute
law at least, not treason at all.

In the face of Throckmorton's trenchant criticisms the
judges were apparently obliged to clarify the law of treason then and there.  They excused the charge seeking to
deprive the king of his crown as being the equivalent of
compassing his death, detaining a fortress against the
king as being equivalent to levying war, and aiding the
king's enemies as adhering to them. (22)  The second and
third interpretations were not at all unreasonable for
there had been medieval cases which had taken them as
such, but depriving the king of his crown could not really
be fitted into the 1352 act.  Nor did the judges satisfactorily explain the new offence of compassing to levy
war against the king.  How in fact it had arisen seems to
have been that, in the late fifteenth and early sixteenth
centuries it became increasingly difficult to decide when
men were levying war.  Noble rioters and rebellious mobs
often did not carry banners like fourteenth-century barons
in insurrection; and banners had been the accepted symbol
of traitorous revolt.  Thus often indictments were drafted to accuse the rebels of compassing the king's death
instead.  There was added, however, with increasing fre-
quence a reference to an act of levying war, the overt act
which became common form in 'compassing the king's death'
indictments.  In time it must have become very tempting
for the lawyers to amalgamate the two sections of the indictment and use the charge 'compassing to levy war' particularly as the war could be said to be aimed at the
prince's death.
    The declaration by the judges was quite unacceptable to
Throckmorton, who said they so 'handled the constructions
of the statute of Edward 3rd' that 'we be ... in much
worse case now than we were when those cruel laws [of
Henry VIII and Edward VI] yoked us'.  The latter, so he
argued, did at least have the merit of being designed 'to
admonish us and discover our sins plainly unto us;  and
when a man is warned he is half armed'. (23)  In contrast, the laws as now interpreted under Mary 'be very
baits to catch us and only prepared for the same, and no
laws'.  There can be no doubt that in his arguments
Throckmorton was largely correct;  that he detected an illegal indictment and caught out the judges misinterpreting
the act of 1352 in the face of precedents and against the
history of the law of treason.  We can only marvel at the
sagacity and adroitness of a layman who was able to do so
much after severe imprisonment and without the help of
legal counsel.
    The reconciliation of England with Rome and the mar-
riage of Mary to Philip of Spain, which were the dominant
features of English policy in 1554, coupled very probably

with an awareness that for reasons of propaganda and per-
manence the pronouncements on the scope of treason by the
judges at Throckmorton's trial ought to be embodied in a
statute, necessitated three new treason acts in the third
parliament of the reign which met in November 1554.   The
first (1 & 2 Ph. & M. c. 9), which faced considerable opposition in parliament, was occasioned by prayers being
offered at conventicles in London that the queen should
either change her religious views or die.   Those who
should pray in like fashion in the future were, on being
found guilty, to suffer the penalties of treason.   There
was, so to speak,  an escape clause for those indicted of
this offence during the present session of parliament.
If on arraignment they pleaded guilty and submitted themselves to the queen's mercy, they were to be given corpo-
ral punishment other than death.   The act is of particular interest because it set down categorically as treason
wishing or intending the king's death by words expressed
in a conditional sense.   Empson, Dudley and Sir William
Stanley had been convicted for something similar under the
'imagining the king's death' clause of the statute of
1352, but in 1554 the crown felt obliged to legislate.
   The second treason act (1 & 2 Ph. & M. c. 10) was of
more substantial importance.   To compass by words to deprive the new king of enjoying jointly with Queen Mary
'the style, honour, and kingly name of the realms and
dominions' pertaining to her, to destroy or levy war
against the king the queen or their heirs, to depose the
queen or her heirs, to say the king ought not to be king
or the queen queen or her heirs succeed, to say someone
else should be king or queen or succeed them, these were
all to be treason but only when committed a second time.
This was in the first and second clauses of the act.   The
third clause added that it was to be treason on the first
offence to compass the king's death by deed or writing or
by the same means affirm the king ought not to enjoy his
title or the queen hers, or her heirs succeed, or affirm
that someone else should be queen. (24)
   The discrepancies between the first two and the third
clause of the act are hard to explain.   Most noticeably
compassing to deprive the queen of her title by words was
omitted from the first clause, unless it was thought to be
covered by the reference to deposing the queen.   Compassing to levy war was treason for a second offence if by
words, and was also a new statutory crime, but it was
omitted from the clause on writing and deeds.   Perhaps
these categories of offence were left out because they
were thought to have been clearly declared as treason by
the judges at the time of Throckmorton's trial.   Maybe

they were omitted unintentionally, for certainly the frequent changes in the law affecting treason at this time
and the comments of the lawyers and the judges in response
to Throckmorton's criticisms suggest an element of confusion in their minds.   The act was attempting to provide
for a co-monarch protection of the type afforded to the
prince by sections of the act of 1352, although the crime
of adhering to the king's enemies was missing.   The parts
of the 1534, 1547 and 1552 statutes about depriving the
prince of his title or calling him usurper were brought
back into use, though there was no need for much of their
provision since neither king nor queen was likely to be
called heretic or schismatic and Mary had renounced the
title of supreme head of the church. (25)   Nor was there
any need for a rubric like the one in the treason act of
1534 which made treason of any words wishing bodily harm
to the king or queen, since something similar had been embodied in another treason act in the same parliament (1 &
2 Ph. & M. c. 9). (26)

     One of the most important clauses in the second general
treason act of Mary's reign was concerned with forfeiture.
Traitors convicted under the act of 1553 were only to
suffer forfeiture as in the act of 1352, which meant, unless there was an act of attainder in addition, the loss
of fee simple only, tenancies in fee tail and land held
by others to the traitor's use being protected.   In Edward VI's reign the second major treason act had made the
forfeiture of traitors to include not only goods and chattels and land held in fee simple but tenancies in fee tail
and possessions held by someone else to the traitor's use.
In 1555, in contrast, the provisions of the 1352 statute
which had been re-established in the first Marian treason
act were apparently allowed to continue.   What the act (1
& 2 Ph. & M. c. 10) said was that forfeiture was to be 'as
in case of high treason by the laws of this realm at this
daye of right ought to be forfeited'.   Perhaps this phraseology was intended to allow the judges to make their own
interpretation.   It is just possible that the queen's
lawyers had become confused, for an opinion in Dyer's reports from Michaelmas term 1554 states that when a tenant
in tail commits treason and is attainted, by the statute
law the entailed lands are forfeited to the king. (27)
This was certainly not the law under the act of 1352 yet
there was at that moment no other law on treason.   That
an act of attainder against Northumberland, Lady Jane
Grey, Cranmer and others of that faction was found to be
necessary supports this viewpoint.   Speaking of the 1555
act in general terms, we may say that it made the scope of
treason more extensive than it had been in 1553 without

approaching the severity of the later years of Henry VIII,
for obviously there were no provisions supporting the
queen's ecclesiastical supremacy or striking at those who
upheld papal authority, nor were there any treasons connected with royal marriage or infidelity by the prince's
spouse or stemming from proclamations.    Important trials
for treason subsequent to the second Marian act suggest
that it was quickly put into use and that it was a thoroughly effective instrument.    Thus, compassing to deprive
the king and queen of their crown and dignity and conspiring to levy war against them were the main charges against
John Throckmorton in April 1556, Henry Peckham, John Dan-
yell and William Staunton in May and June of that year and
John Dethick, John Bedell and William Rossey in June. (28)
They were all convicted.    There is no evidence that they
were able to pick holes in the indictment as Sir Nicholas
Throckmorton had been able to do.

The third act touching treason which was passed in the
parliament of 1554-5 concerned the importing of counterfeit copies of foreign coins currently accepted for payment in England. (29)    Henceforth such importing was to
be high treason.    Counterfeiting of foreign coin as such
had been made treason in an act of the parliament of 1553
(1 M. st. 2 c. 6) as had the forging of the queen's sign
manual, her privy signet or privy seal. (30)    The two
latter offences had initially been made treason in 1536
(27 Hen. VIII c. 2) and that act was therefore being renewed.    Why counterfeiting the privy seal should also
appear is a mystery, since it was included in the act of
1352 which had been renewed *in toto* earlier in the same
parliament of 1553.    It is a further piece of evidence
of insufficient care being taken in the preparation of
legislation, lack of care in checking precedents and the
continual fluctuation in the scope of treason causing
confusion even among the lawyers.

The last important matter concerning the scope of treason in Mary's reign arose from the insurrection of Thomas
Stafford, grandson of the duke of Buckingham executed in
1521, who in April 1557 landed at Scarborough, seized the
castle and announced his claim to the throne. (31)    With
him on the venture had come a Frenchman, John Sherlles,
and the question to be faced was whether he could be tried
for treason.    It was decided that an alien, born in a
country at peace with England at the time of his offence,
who should levy war alongside English traitors had in fact
committed treason. (32)    This was new law but entirely
reasonable.

In the history of the scope of treason the reign of
Mary was a time not of great repression, although severe

the law undoubtedly was, but one of ill-advised indictments, interpretations of existing laws, and legislation.
Early in the reign some indictments were drawn in an unsatisfactory fashion, there were some distinctly odd interpretations of the treason law by judges and there was
legislation which was superfluous in one case and woefully
defective in another.   The mistakes in the passing of
laws were probably not occasioned by deliberate policy but
rather by negligence or confusion.   It is harder to excuse the interpretations of the judges at Throckmorton's
trial.   Their behaviour gives every indication of being
motivated by a desire to evade legitimate criticism.
Despite this decline in the quality of the law and judicial processes on treason the position even when Mary died
was by no means as severe as in 1546.

    In Elizabeth's reign treason was first dealt with leg-
islatively in a supremacy act.   This was intended to repeal the act 1 & 2 Ph. & M. c. 8, which annulled all statutes against the see of Rome since 30 Hen. VIII, and to
revive certain laws on ecclesiastical matters of Henry
VIII.   In its course through parliament the act may for a
time have contained a clause which made treason out of
twice refusing to take the supremacy oath, but in the
final form such a provision was lacking. (33)   The statute also contained a section on treason which had as its
modest purpose the making into a traitorous offence of the
defending by words, writings or deeds on the third occasion of the spiritual or ecclesiastical jurisdiction of
any foreign prince or prelate.   This was very similar to
a provision of the first Edwardian treason act (1 Edw. VI
c. 12) of 1547, but in Elizabeth's second parliament which
met in January 1563 it was found necessary to make the
same offence (though now it was regarding not any prince
or prelate but the pope alone) together with refusing to
take the oath of supremacy into treason if either was committed a second time after an interval of three months (5
Eliz. c. 1).   However, conviction in this case was not to
carry with it corruption of blood, disinheriting of heirs
or forfeiture of wives' dower.   The act arose from fears
engendered by the recent ill-health of Elizabeth, the
council of Trent and the activities of Catholic propagan-
dists, and from pressure exerted by the Protestant extre-
mists.   The list of those who must take the oath of
supremacy was extended to include lawyers, university
graduates, schoolmasters and those in holy orders.   It
was the commons who, after bitter debating, added the
clause making treason out of refusal to take the oath of
supremacy;   it can hardly have pleased Elizabeth and her
advisers.   The section of the act which made a more ser-

ious offence out of extolling the power of the bishop of
Rome seems to have proved much less contentious.

These acts, although important, were by no means at the
heart of the Elizabethan treason code.   That place was
reserved for the act of 1352 which, while not mentioned in
early Elizabethan legislation, continued in existence from
Mary's reign.   This is shown by the part of the indictment which was concerned with adhering to the king's enemies against Thomas, Lord Wentworth, Edward Grimston, Sir
Ralph Chamberlain and John Harleston, who had recently
lost Calais to the French, at their trials in April and
December 1559. (34)   Other basic provisions for dealing
with traitors were considered a necessity and were to be
found in a general treason act (1 Eliz. c. 5) which was
intended, so it said to take the place of the Marian act
1 & 2 Ph. & M. c. 10, because the latter only extended its
protection to Queen Mary and her issue.   It simply rehearsed the earlier act, substituting Elizabeth for Mary
and her husband and missing out a section on guardianship.
It became treason at the second offence to compass by
words to deprive the queen and her heirs of their titles
or to destroy them, depose them or levy war against them.
If the offence was committed by deed or writing it was to
be treason first time.   The act was put to some use as is
demonstrated by the trials of Arthur and Edmund Pole in
February 1563.   They were held to have conspired to
depose the queen, cause her death and total destruction
and place Mary, Queen of Scots, on the throne, various
deeds being alleged in the indictment in support of the
general charge. (35)

In the parliament of 1571 the crimes that were classified as traitorous when done a second time by the act of
. 1559, were made treason for a first offence no matter how
they had been committed, whether it was by words, writing
or deeds (13 Eliz. c. 1). (36)   The reason given for the
new law was that it was doubtful if the present law was
'sufficient enough for the surety and preservation of the
Queen's most royal person'.   Severity was increased not
simply  through  the modification of the law of 1559 but
because the scope of treason was extended generally.   Two
additions to the earlier law were the offences of compassing the bodily harm of the queen and of stirring foreigners to invade any of the queen's dominions, the inclusion
of the latter probably being prompted by Dr Storey's machinations in the Netherlands.   This extension was justified by the judges on the grounds that such invasions must
tend to the destruction or great peril of the prince's
person. (37)   The Marian treason of compassing the levying of war against the queen was included and had appended

to it the phrase 'within the realm or without', the government perhaps having Storey in mind again or even the
northern rebels who had fled to Scotland. (38)    Another
addition was words or writing which called Elizabeth a
heretic, schismatic, tyrant, infidel or usurper, and was
obviously taken, like the provision about compassing
Elizabeth's bodily harm, from the Henrician act of 1534
(26 Hen. VIII c. 13).    The third clause of the 1571 act
made it treason to claim a right of succession to the
crown unless it was according to a forthcoming proclamation;   this is suggestive of the second Henrician succession act of 1536 (28 Hen. VIII c. 9).    The fourth clause
made denying the power of the common law or any act for
limiting the descent of the crown treason during the
queen's life:   this seems to have been new to the laws of
treason and the differentiation between common law and
statute was significant.
     The statute of 1571 set forfeiture for treason as
vaguely as had the second general treason act of Mary's
reign.    It was to be simply 'as for high treason'.    This
should have meant it followed the act of 1352 whereby because that statute in fact said nothing about forfeiture
at all, only fee simple was wont to be lost.    However, we
have seen that in 1554 some judges believed that lands
held in tail should be forfeited to the king 'by the statute law'.    Then in a case in the king's bench at Easter
term 1570 came the erroneous opinion by five judges (four
were against it) that the king had had the forfeiture of
the lands traitors held in tail even before the statute of
1534 (26 Hen. VIII c. 13). (39)    Indeed the king had
often had them, but only by parliamentary act of attainder
or sometimes when the traitor had died on the battlefield.
Sir Matthew Hale, writing in the later seventeenth century, was puzzled by all this and came to the conclusion
that the 1534 act 'stands unrepealed as to the forfeiture
for treasons within the statute of 25 Edward III', which
in fact was correct in regard to what was being practised
by the judges and the crown, although incorrect according
to the statute book. (40)    Further proof that by 1571 the
crown held that possessions in fee tail as well as in fee
simple were forfeited for treason under the common law
lies in the attainder act against the earls of Northumberland and Westmorland  passed that year in parliament.
The act declared forfeit all lands, goods, chattels and
other possessions held to their use, but a provision intended to reach their possessions in fee tail was deliberately left out, apparently because there was felt to be no
need for it. (41)
     The 1571 general treason act has a particular impor-

tance in the history of Tudor treason legislation.    Because of the chance survival of a diary kept by an unknown
member, we are able to trace with some accuracy the parliamentary history of the bill which eventually evolved
into the 1571 act (42) and, more importantly, are able to
get a fairly accurate idea as to how far the original plan
of the government had to be amended by way of compromise
in the face of opposition.    As devised by the queen's
learned counsel and presented to the commons, the bill
contained only provisions making it treason to imagine the
death or the bodily harm of the queen, to compass to deprive her of the crown, to levy war against her, to stir
foreigners to invade, or to declare such intentions by
words or writing;   or to deny the queen's title or call
her a heretic, schismatic, infidel or usurper.    At the
first reading a bill supplementing that of the government
and concerned with the succession to the throne was proposed by the puritan, Thomas Norton.    It was to the
effect that anyone who had claimed or should claim the
crown during Elizabeth's life, or refuse to acknowledge
her as queen, was to lose any title to it and it was to be
treason to maintain such a person;   it was also to be
treason to hold that the queen with parliament could not
determine the succession.    The debate which followed was
concerned largely with whether Norton's bill should be
joined to the official one.    Eventually the house decided
in the affirmative but not before much bitter wrangling
the highlights of which were the arguments by Norton and
by Goodere, a sympathizer of Mary, Queen of Scots, and a
friend of the duke of Norfolk, for and against retroactive
legislation.

Eventually, on the queen's intervention, the retroactive clause was removed from Norton's bill, which then
simply disabled from the crown anyone who, during the remainder of the reign, claimed or usurped the throne or refused to accept Elizabeth as queen when she put the question to them. (43)    As before the amendment it still made
a traitor of anyone who maintained the right of such a
claimant providing he had first been denounced by royal
proclamation.    In this form the combined bill was passed.
These insights into parliamentary debates and procedures
show much excitement over the issue of succession but
little concern at the extension of the treason laws.    One
MP, Yelverton, suggested that part of the original government bill was covered by the act of 1352, while another,
one of the Snagge brothers, said the same about Norton's
addition;   no one said that the scope of treason was being
unwarrantably extended.    It was rather the reverse.    A
vehement opposer of the government bill, like Goodere,

said he entirely approved of it and this seems to have
been the general feeling in the commons despite the recognition that it was in large part reintroducing the provisions of the treason act of 1534. (44)

The protests of Goodere had caused the retroactive
clauses in Norton's addition to the 1571 treason bill to
be removed, yet there is some indication that the act when
passed was none the less used retroactively, although for
offences contained in the first section, not the Norton
supplement.   The case was that of the duke of Norfolk,
and the evidence lies in his indictment.   Though some
offences mentioned could have also been based on the act
of 1352, this has the appearance of being framed according
to the 1571 act (13 Eliz. c. 1), especially the section
which accused him of bringing in divers strangers and
aliens who were not lieges of the queen to invade the
kingdom. (45)   No earlier treason act contains this offence;  it was peculiar to the statute of 1571.   Yet the
dates of the committing of his traitorous offences given
in Norfolk's indictment ranged from 23 September 1569 to
16 July 1571, there being only one which post-dated the
act and therefore properly triable under it.   A description of Norfolk's trial supplies further evidence of dubious procedure.   When the duke, during his arraignment,
was told one of his supposed treasons was within the compass of the act of 1352 he asked if all the treasons contained in his indictment were based on that statute.
Nicholas Barham, the queen's serjeant, and Gilbert Gerard,
the attorney-general, answered categorically that indeed
the charges were grounded on that statute alone. (46)
This was quite untrue;  not only was there stirring foreigners to invade the realm, but compassing to levy war,
originally appearing in the act 1 Eliz. c. 5, though probably based on a judicial interpretation of Mary's reign,
was also included.   We must conclude that very possibly
the queen's lawyers intended at one stage to use the 1571
act against Norfolk, but later reverted to the act of 1352
without bothering to make sure the indictment conformed
with that decision.

Norfolk's indictment was not the only one at that time
which has the appearance of being unsoundly based.   In
May 1572 John Hall and Francis Rolston were arraigned for
plotting to free Mary, Queen of Scots, then in the custody
of the earl of Shrewsbury, and elevate her to the English
throne.   One of the crimes listed in the indictment was
their procuring an army to invade the realm which was, as
we have seen, treason under the act of 1571. (47)   That
statute was supposedly applicable only to crimes committed
after June 1571, yet Hall and Rolston's offences were all

stated to have occurred in August 1570.    Whether the
crown's lawyers reckoned that this indictment, too, was
under the act of 1352 is not known.

The attorney-general and his fellow prosecutors never
had to explain what they meant by 'under the statute of
1352'.    Had they been hard pressed it is possible they
would have argued that the basic crime of Norfolk, Hall
and Rolston was imagining the queen's death as found in
the fourteenth-century act and that all other offences
listed in the indictment were simply overt deeds demonstrating this intent.    We may say that this was a better
way of justifying Hall and Rolston's indictment than Norfolk's, where the initial summary of the crimes to be described further on contains the offence of stirring aliens
to invade the realm, which therefore does not appear
solely in the *exemplaria* following the 'for bringing to
pass his intentions' phrase.

The 1571 act, which clearly stated that it was only
concerned with future treasons, should not of course be
blamed for the way the lawyers mishandled it in the courts
in their efforts to secure convictions.    Regarded simply
as a new page in the statute book, the act's most serious
fault was not its severity or scope but that it continued
the process of piling treason statute on treason statute
in an unmethodical manner when what was needed was a
statement of what exactly the scope of treason now amounted to, a codification in fact.    This would of necessity
have engendered an examination and clarification of the
inconsistencies which had arisen since 1553 and which by
1571 were a disgrace to the English law.    That there was
no such simplification or consolidation can be explained
partly by recognition that it would have been something
new to the legal customs of England, partly by the fact
that the queen and her legal advisers were finding it increasingly difficult to persuade parliament to pass treason laws in the form in which they were originally drafted
and partly by the fact that the government was beginning
to find that the shadow of confusion cast by the diffuse
treason laws could be to their own, very definite, advantage.    For the crown, at a time when those arraigned were
beginning to argue to some purpose in their own defence,
it was preferable that the treason law should remain complex and be interpretable only by judges and serjeants.

Instead of seeking to consolidate the laws which already governed treason and its scope, Elizabeth and her
ministers in the parliamentary sessions of 1571 and 1572
secured the enactment of no fewer than four other important statutes touching that subject.    Deserving the
greatest attention is the act commonly designated as

'against bulls from Rome' (13 Eliz. c. 2).   This was directed against subjects who obtained bulls to absolve them
from obedience to the queen and thereby put themselves
under (so it was argued) the pope's feigned and usurped
authority.   Henceforward putting any such bull into use
or giving or receiving absolution thereby was to be treason for the first offence. (48)   This was an extension of
the act 5 Eliz. c. ì which, pleading the necessity of
sharp restraint because of licentious boldness by 'fau-
tors' of papal power, had made it treason to defend or
extol by speech, writing or deed a second time the jurisdiction of the bishop of Rome.   This in turn derived from
the act 28 Hen. VIII c. 10, whereby the pope's authority
was originally extinguished.   It was from the time of the
papal bull of 1570 that treason indictments contained increasingly the phrase 'sought to change the established
religion' which, though not a legal requisite like the
word 'traitorously' nor yet part of the wording of an act,
showed a new close association in the minds of the crown's
lawyers between treason and papal sympathies.   Bishop
Stephen Gardiner is said to have remarked early in Mary's
reign 'thes ij be alwayes lynked together, treson and
herysy', but legal phrases connecting religious beliefs
with traitorous inclinations only became common from
1570. (49)
   Rebelliously detaining ships, castles, or ordnance for
more than six days after being ordered to surrender them
was the subject of the act 14 Eliz. c. 1.   These misdeeds
became high treason, as did wilfully destroying the
queen's ships or barring any haven.   Detaining royal
castles, ships and ordnance for more than six days after
proclamation to surrender had first been made treason in
the act of 1534 (26 Hen. VIII c. 13) and the 1572 act was
restoring one of the few sections of that statute not included in the second general treason act of Elizabeth (13
Eliz. c. 1).   As with the fourth clause of the same statute, this piece of legislation was not supposed to endure
for ever, only for the queen's lifetime, which perhaps was
an indication of some displeasure in parliament at the
continuing provisions against traitorous acts, or else
caused by suspicion of proclamation.   Also to exist for
the queen's lifetime only was an act (14 Eliz. c. 2) which
made it treason to conspire to effect the escape of those
imprisoned following conviction for that crime.   Previously, stated the act quite correctly, it had only been
treason when a deed to that intent had been committed.
There can be little doubt this act was caused by machinations to release either Mary, Queen of Scots, or the duke
of Norfolk.   The latter alternative is much more prob-

able, since a treason bill introduced in the same session
against Mary, Queen of Scots, contained a clause making a
traitor of anyone who tried to rescue her or gave assistance in the enterprise.

These new statutes on treason were not considered by
the lords or commons to be the main business of the parliamentary session as they had often been in the past;
that privilege was reserved for the bill against Mary,
Queen of Scots, which has just been mentioned.   This
dealt almost entirely with future treason on her part, and
although it never found its way into the statute book,
being left in limbo by the prorogation of parliament in
June 1572, it offers interesting glimpses of how learned
counsel and members of parliament viewed traitorous behaviour at that time.   It stated that if Mary should thereafter pretend an interest or title in the English crown
or give her consent to the invasion of the realm by a foreign power or consent to or commit any action which would
be traitorous if done by a subject, or even if there was
war, insurrection or invasion made on her behalf, then she
should be held a traitor.   Furthermore, it was to be
treason to support her claimed title by words spoken or
written, to rescue her from incarceration during the current reign or give aid or comfort for the same purpose, or
to practise for her marriage without the queen's consent.
A clause which did not directly concern Mary made it treason knowingly to procure or assent to anything intended to
re-establish in England the authority of the bishop of
Rome. (50)

In these provisions the key phrase was probably the one
concerned with committing or consenting to any action
which would be traitorous if committed by any of Elizabeth's subjects.   To pretend an interest or title in the
crown, to consent to the invasion of the realm, would no
doubt have been found treason under the act 13 Eliz. c. 1
(i.e. denying the queen's title, stirring foreigners to
invade or claiming a right of succession contrary to a
proclamation) had the accused been an English subject.
However, Mary could hardly be called an English subject;
she was a Scottish queen held in England against her will,
even if it might be argued that she had entered the kingdom voluntarily, sought refuge, and now remained in prison
because of offences she had committed in her new home.
The majority of the remainder of the bill was intended,
once Mary had committed an offence labelled traitorous,
to make traitors out of her supporters.   Where the bill
really divorced itself from legal precedent and principle
was in making Mary a traitor once any war, rebellion or
invasion was made on her behalf.   No allowance was made

for the unlikely, although theoretically quite possible, occasion when someone took up arms on her behalf without her knowledge or approval.   In many ways, such as going outside the provisions of the prevailing treason law, the bill appears to have been intended to serve as a contingent act of attainder for the future, although the provision of some sort of trial shows it could never be exactly that.   No doubt the joint committee, which was responsible for the drafting of the bill, thought it was justified in going beyond normal bounds and virtually assuming the guilt of the party the act was intended to catch, because it had already consulted the judges about Mary's past misdeeds and they had answered that these constituted treason whether in her or anyone else.   Also important with the drafters must have been the fact that the bill was superseding an earlier one designed to become an actual act of attainder.

The bull of Pope Pius V, which in February 1570 excommunicated and deposed Elizabeth, commanded all her subjects to refuse her orders and subjected those who would not to a similar sentence of excommunication.   It must have greatly troubled many catholics who hitherto had acted according to a dual standard of obedience.   The treason act 'against bulls from Rome' (13 Eliz. c. 2), which judging by the proposed act against Mary, Queen of Scots, of 1572 was at that time intended to be supplemented by a new statute making it treason merely to procure or assent to anything which was aimed at re-establishing papal authority in England, was particularly designed to combat this danger, but it does not seem to have been put into use for some years.   Camden said that this was the government's policy despite the fact that 'some were apprehended who had faulted against it'. (51)   The first person to be convicted under the act he named as the seminary priest Cuthbert Mayne, who was executed at Launceston on 29 November 1577.   This information may well be correct; two charges against Mayne were apparently that he obtained from the Roman see 'a certain instrument printed containing a pretended matter of absolution of divers subjects of the realm' and later on published the document at Golden, Cornwall. (52)   Early in February 1578 John Nelson, a Jesuit, was put on trial for treason, but his indictment, like that of Thomas Sherwood, a catholic layman tried two days later, was probably based on the clause of the general act of 1571 which was concerned with saying the queen was a heretic or a schismatic. (53)

In the parliamentary session of January-March 1581 there was passed yet another act (23 Eliz. c. 1) concerning treason, the tenth of the reign.   Since 1574 mission-

ary priests from Douai had achieved considerable success
in their fight against conformity and in 1579 reinforcement appeared imminent when Dr Allen obtained the mission
of the Jesuits to England.   The statute referred to evil-
affected persons who practised contrary to the meaning of
the act 13 Eliz. c. 2 to withdraw great numbers of the
queen's subjects from their natural obedience so as to
obey the 'usurped authority of Rome' by means 'other than
bulls or instruments written or printed'.   The act, which
dealt with recusancy in general as well as treason, therefore set out, so it said, to declare the 'true meaning' of
its predecessor of 1571.   Practising to absolve, persuade
or withdraw subjects from obedience to their queen or with
that intent from the established religion so as to join
the Romish religion became treason, as did moving them to
promise obedience to any foreign potentate, including the
pope, or committing an overt act to that intent.   Withdrawal of obedience, which was the key offence in the act,
not conversion to catholicism, was of course right at the
heart of all treason, yet it had not appeared in any treason act hitherto.   This may have been because acts tended
to borrow something from previous acts and those of the
medieval period omitted the phrase lest it should remind
men of the *diffidatio* of earlier feudal times.   Now these
antecedents were forgotten.   The act of 1581 was aimed at
the seminary priests and the Jesuits, but those who willingly allowed themselves to be absolved and reconciled
with Rome or who promised obedience to a foreign prince,
were similarly to suffer as traitors, although aiders and
abettors in contrast with the usual provision for treason
accessaries were only to incur the penalties for misprision of treason.   Forfeiture for principals was again to
be 'as in cases of high treason', which meant by this time
the loss of possessions held in fee simple and fee tail on
conviction under the common law.

The act was first put to use in July of the year it was
promulgated.   On the 28th of that month a secular priest
named Everard Hanse was arraigned.   His indictment, if we
judge from a description in a contemporary pamphlet, was
based on both the act just passed and the general act of
1571 (13 Eliz. c. 1).   The charges were that he intended
to withdraw subjects from obedience to the queen and from
the established to the Romish religion and that he hoped
(and was thus an abettor within the meaning of the act)
the pope had not erred in declaring Elizabeth a heretic
and deprived of her crown. (54)   Following its use to
indict Everard Hanse, the act against reconciliation with
Rome seems to have suffered a sudden eclipse.   On 14 November 1581 in Westminster Hall Edmund Campion was arraign-

ed on an indictment which also accused William Allen,
Nicholas Moreton, Robert Persons, Thomas Forde and fourteen others, including Richard Sherwyn, Luke Kirby, James
Bosgrave, Thomas Cottam, Robert Johnson, Henry Orton and
Edward Rishton. (55)   The last seven alone appeared in
court.   The charges were that they had compassed to deprive the queen of her throne and title, to bring about
her destruction, to raise an insurrection, and to change
the government and religion of the country, and had stirred foreigners to invade.

These were offences only under the general treason act
of 1571 (13 Eliz. c. 1).   If the indictment can be partly
explained on the grounds that it was intended to display
to the English nation at large and to the world the traitorous nature of the seminarists' and the Jesuits' activities, and offences under the 1581 act like persuading subjects to withdraw from the established religion may not
have seemed important enough to include, the same cannot
be said about the indictments against John Mundyn, William
Tedder, John Nutter, Samuel Conyers and nine others of the
same persuasion in February 1584.   These men were accused
under the act of 1571 of the same crimes as Campion, Allen
and the first group, except there was no charge of stirring aliens to invade the realm. (56)   The lack of any
reference to the crime of reconciling English men and
women to Rome both in these two sets of indictments and in
general, suggests that the statute of 1581 was virtually
inoperable, if the suspects refused to co-operate by admitting, as had Hanse for example, such offences on examination. (57)   Witnesses and other evidence must have
been well-nigh impossible to obtain because of the clan-
destine nature of the need and because self-incrimination
under torture or threat of it might be denied at the arraignment.   William Allen, in his 'True, Sincere and
Modest Defence of English Catholiques' published in 1584,
claimed that

> not anie one priest of the Societie or Seminaries can
> be prooved to have absolved anie one man living from
> his allegiance or to have ever either in publique or
> private dissuaded anie one person in the Realme from
> his obedience.

Although, of course, what Allen meant by 'proved' was
hardly likely to be what the judges understood by it, the
statement does suggest that conviction under the act of
1581 was not easily obtained.   The calling of a conference of judges at Serjeants' Inn, apparently at the time
of Campion's trial, points in the same direction.   The
judges decided that for men merely to pretend to have
power to absolve or withdraw others from their allegiance

was traitorous even if they did not actually try to persuade them to that effect.   Furthermore, it was treason,
they opined, if anyone should actually try to change a
man's obedience even if the persuader did not have any
authority from Rome.   Here was a clear attempt to widen
the scope of the statute, yet of its efficacy in dealing
with the suspects the judges can have had no great opti-
mism since they also decided to declare that Allen's mission constituted conspiracy to levy war and that the
arrival of the Jesuits and seminarists in England was the
open fact of treason thought by contemporary lawyers to
be required for conviction. (58)

     It has been argued to some purpose that the act of 1581
was not the act the Elizabethan government wanted but a
compromise forced on it by opposition within parliament.
What the queen and her ministers may have hoped to see enacted was a statute which made those who received and
maintained Jesuits and seminary priests guilty of treason
rather than misprision of treason, and which compelled
parents and guardians to reveal the names of sons and
wards who had gone to study abroad and to summon them
home.   Failing to obtain the statute it desired, the government, on 1 April 1582, issued a proclamation, one
apparently unique in the history of sixteenth-century
law. (59)   This stated unequivocally that 'Jesuits, seminary men and priests' who entered the realm secretly were
traitors, that those who knowingly received and maintained
them in their homes should be deemed to be aiders of traitors and that English subjects who were then studying in
seminaries overseas and did not return within three months
should be held as traitors and their maintainers and comforters aiders of the same.   In essence these provisions
were creating new law. Making traitors out of Jesuits,
seminarists and priests who entered the kingdom secretly
must have been based on the decision taken by the judges
at their recent conference at Serjeants' Inn, and the proclamation was therefore founded on a construction of the
statute of 1581 (23 Eliz. c. 1).   Making traitors of
their maintainers and aiders, which would include those
who received them, was going beyond even the judges' construction.   Admittedly it had become the fashion for
treason statutes to inflict penalties on post facto accessaries, but except for those who were convicted under the
act of 1571 they were not made traitors.   Thus by the act
13 Eliz. c. 2 receivers were to suffer as offenders
against the praemunire statute of 1393, while according to
23 Eliz. c. 1, the parent act itself, they were to be held
culpable of misprision of treason.   The reputing as traitors of those who attended seminaries overseas must have

been based on the idea that since Allen's mission was conspiracy to levy war those training for the mission were
principal offenders now that there existed the overt fact
of the seminarists landing in England.

We could be less critical of the apparent illegality of
the proclamation of 1582 if it was clear that its intention was merely hortatory, being designed only as propaganda and never used as a basis for legal accusation, at
least not before a court of common law.  Even if as has
been argued, the proclamation was drafted in response to
the translating into English of Persons's 'De Persecutione
Anglicana', there is evidence that charges based upon it
actually came before the courts.  Only one accused, the
earl of Arundel, is known of at present, although it is
possible there were others.  On 17 May 1586 Arundel was
tried before the privy council in the star chamber.  The
offences laid to his charge were described generally as
'contemptes' and included receiving three Jesuits or seminary priests and making confession to them.  No reference
was made to the misdeeds being treason although the council noted that if perhaps the 'matter should fall out of a
higher nature then was to be delt with in this Court' the
elements which were not contempts might be dealt with
elsewhere.  There was nothing at all incorrect about
this;  offences announced by proclamations were frequently
tried under the jurisdiction of the privy council.  Novelty and illegality only occurred when Arundel was put on
trial a second time.  This was in April 1589 by commission of oyer and terminer before the lord high steward.
The earl's indictment stated quite clearly that anyone who
subsequent to the proclamation of April 1582 knowingly and
willingly received and comforted any Jesuit or seminary
priest was committing high treason and this Arundel had
done.  Admittedly this was only one count in the indictment and among the others were treason properly based on
statutes, yet that the proclamation and a charge based
upon it should appear at all was legally unjustified and,
in 1589 at least, of sinister implication.  However, the
tactic does not seem to have been repeated elsewhere,
probably because for such offences committed after March
1585 (Arundel's was in September 1584) there was the act
27 Eliz. c. 2 to rely on.

We may notice here that there was one other significant
case at this time where receiving was held as treason, but
it concerned secular conspirators, not Jesuits or seminary
priests.  On 15 September 1586 before commissioners of
oyer and terminer Robert Gage and Jerome Bellamy were
found guilty of high treason for merely comforting and receiving Anthony Babington, Robert Barnwell and Henry

Dunn, who were then in flight, knowing they had committed
treason.   This was new law.   Until this time all those
who were accessaries before the fact were as guilty of
treason as the principals, but no statute touched directly
on accessaries post facto, and, despite in 3 Hen. VII the
argument being offered in the Exchequer chamber in regard
to receivers of coin counterfeiters by Bryan C.J.C.P. that
felony is implied in any treason, they were not indict-
able.   In contrast with the case of the earl of Arundel,
the indictment was not even based on a proclamation, although there does exist a draft of one, dated 2 August
1586, which declared that those who concealed Babington
and his associates in flight should be held as abettors
and maintainers of traitors and be punished as 'appointed
by the laws of the realm'.   Coming so soon after Arundel's first trial, the Gage-Bellamy episode looks like a
deliberate attempt to extend the scope of treason at a
time when the passions aroused by a plan to assassinate
the queen had dimmed reason and lessened concern for
proper legal process. (60)

The unsatisfactory nature of the act of 1581 and the
need for temporary remedies by means of proclamation soon
convinced Elizabeth and her advisers there was again a
need for a new law and one which was more sweeping in its
compass.   It came in the parliamentary session of Februa-
ry-March 1585.   The statute (27 Eliz. c. 2) made it treason for Jesuits, seminary and other priests ordained by
Rome since 1 June 1559 not to have quit the realm within
forty days of the end of the session;  also for others of
that ilk born in England since the same date to enter or
remain in the realm after the same forty days.   Receivers of these traitors were to be held guilty of felony and
be excluded from benefit of clergy.   The act made an
attempt to reach priests in training at that time and in
the future.   Men being educated at a Jesuit college or a
seminary were to return within six months after proclamation made for that purpose in London and take the oath of
supremacy within a further two days.   Any of them who returned in other fashion were to be adjudged traitors.   In
many ways this was quite a reasonable act.   It gave Jesuits and seminary priests already active in England a
period of grace in which to leave and it did not categorically make traitors of their receivers as had originally
been proposed.   It struck at only those educated and ordained abroad and did nothing to hurt the old Marian
priests.   It only made traitors of those who were actually in the realm and would not leave or who in future entered it.   Against the act must be reckoned that certain
priests were made liable to the penalties for treason

simply by the fact of their priesthood, without compassing
any traitorous deed. Forfeiture, though perhaps only
coins were likely to be involved, was to be as was usual
for high treason, meaning all possessions held in fee
simple or fee tail.

The act proved of considerable value to the government
and there were a good number of commissions appointed to
operate it and indictments drawn under it against both
priests and their receivers in the years that followed (61) although more frequently the charges were combined
with others under other treason acts. This suggests that
the statute may not have turned out to be the universal
instrument originally anticipated. Obtaining evidence
that the accused were indeed priests proved in some cases
nearly as difficult as demonstrating intent of reconciling
men with Rome and the government had to give instructions
as to how suspects should be questioned so their clerical
status might be revealed. There was also a tendency for
the crown to argue that the act of 1585 was really nothing
more than a clarification of the statute of 1352, since it
was made, according to Thomas Bowyer, 'for the ease and
satisfaction of the country [i.e. jury] at tryall to prove
the overt fact'. (62) His argument was that the pope was
the queen's capital enemy since he had by sentence deprived her of her estate and absolved her subjects of their
allegiance. Therefore any subject adhering to the pope,
within which Bowyer included those taking priesthood under
his authority and returning to win the queen's subjects to
their faction, were 'even by the Commen Lawe to be adiud-
ged Traytors'. This explanation of the act of 1585 seems
to have found some favour among Elizabeth's judges and
legal officials. Very likely this was because it put religious proselytizing squarely under the provisions of a
venerated statute against disloyal political behaviour and
allowed the prosecuting lawyers to say the accused were
'deceyved to thinke they were in question for any matter
of religion', (63) and that the 1585 act merely described
what overt deed of treason under the 1352 act could amount
to. There may have been a second reason for the introduction of the fourteenth-century statute into the arguments of the lawyers and it concerned procedure. Most of
the treason acts of the later sixteenth century demanded
witnesses against the accused at indictment or trial or
both, although admittedly the act of 1585 did not. At
the arraignment the prosecution would therefore sometimes
say that all the treasons in the indictment, though based
on this or that act of Edward, Mary or Elizabeth, were
also treasons under the act of 1352. (64) This allowed
the witnesses to be dispensed with, which was often of

great assistance to the queen's case.   It usually meant
that the only evidence in support of the indictment was
the accused's confession (sometimes secured by physical
duress), which was often the source of the indictment as
well.

From 1580 for dealing with treason suspects who were
not Jesuits or priests the most serviceable act seems to
have been the general statute of 1571 (13 Eliz. c. 1).
Under this law John Somervyle was indicted in December
1583, William Parry in February 1585, William Shelley in
February 1586, Sir John Perrot  in 1592, Valentine Thomas
in July 1598 and Edward Squyer in November 1598. (65)
There were also laymen with definite political motives
behind their treason whose indictments were phrased in
such a way that they could have been based on the 1571
act, the 1352 act, or both.   In this category can be
placed the charges against Abington, Tilney, Jones, Travers, and Charnock in September 1588, Philip earl of Arundel in April 1589, Patrick O'Cullen in March 1594, Dr
Lopez in February 1594 and the earls of Essex and Southampton in February 1601. (66)   The clearest evidence that
the indictments were made to follow two different acts
comes from the trials of Edward Abington, Francis Throckmorton and the earl of Arundel.   According to one source,
when Abington was arraigned he was told by one of the justices, Sir Edmund Anderson C.J.C.P., that he stood indicted 'by the common law and the statute of 25 Edward 3' not
by the statutes 'of the 1st and 13th of this queen', this
despite the indictment copying closely the form of the act
of 1571. (67)   The reason behind this arrangement was, as
in the case of the Jesuits and priests mentioned above, to
avoid the need for two witnesses since, as the solicitor-
general remarked, 'traitors will never reveal their cogi-
tations unto honest men but unto such as themselves'.
Thus, if witnesses were essential, many treasons would
never come to light.   Another reason for the use of the
1352 act lay in the time clause in the 1571 general statute.   Under this an indictment had to be made within six
months of the misdeed, a proviso which had no parallel in
the fourteenth-century law.   Francis Throckmorton in May
1584 and the earl of Arundel in 1589 each tried to defeat
their indictment on this count, but were told they were
being prosecuted under the act of 1352. (68)   In criticism of this argument we may say that the indictment of
Arundel at least in its phraseology seemed to owe little
to the fourteenth century act but rather to follow the act
of 1571.

Thus far the provisions of the sixteenth-century treason statutes concerning witnesses or accusers, for men at

this time were not drawing a clear distinction between
them, have been omitted.   In essence what the acts said
was this.   The first Edwardian treason act (1 Edw. VI c.
12) stated that there should be no indictment, arraignment, or conviction for treason save on the accusation of
two lawful and sufficient witnesses or on the suspect's
own confession;   it did not say if the witnesses were
necessary in person at the arraignment.   The second Edwardian act (5 & 6 Edw. VI c. 11) demanded two accusers
(they were not called witnesses) but said more clearly
they should be brought face to face with the accused at
the arraignment and maintain the charge stated in their
bill of indictment.   The first Marian treason act (1 M.
st. 1 c. 1), while declaring only those deeds to be treason which were such in the statute of 1352, omitted any
mention of witnesses at all.   The act 1 & 2 Ph. & M. c.
10, omitting the word 'indictment', made it obligatory
once more for two accusers to appear before the party arraigned and repeat their accusations.   This rule was repeated in the first treason act of Elizabeth (1 Eliz. c.
5) and the second (13 Eliz. c. 1).   Unfortunately the
matter cannot be left there, for other complicating factors impinged.   In the act 1 & 2 Ph. & M. c. 10 there
seemed to be a contradiction, since clause eleven demanded witnesses-accusers when any one was accused under it,
yet clause six said treason trials were to be by the
'common law' which did not allow such accusers.   A meeting of judges and law officers of the crown on 25 October
1556 referred to in Brooks New Cases (50-2) decided,
apparently for the purpose of clarification and explanation, that in cases of treason under a statute, by which
they meant under a sixteenth-century statute since the
1352 statute in their eyes was only a declaration of
common law treason, two accusers or *testes* should always
be at the indictment.   If the offence was within the act
of 1352, this was unnecessary since the common law operated, they said, by jury and witness and not by accusers.
They noted that if the offence came under the recent act 1
& 2 Ph. & M. c. 10, then witnesses-accusers were required
at the arraignment as well as the indictment.

A clue as to what was behind these provisions and deci-
sions is to be found in the act 5 Eliz. c. 1, which made
it treason to extol a second time the authority of the
bishop of Rome.   It said nothing about witnesses-accusers
at the arraignment, but insisted that indictments should
only be allowed if the accusations were, in the grand
jury's estimation, founded on good and sufficient testimony and proof, which presumably was what the two accusers
were usually there to show.   All the treason statutes

mentioned above were concerned to a substantial degree
with words, written or spoken, as treason, and the
clauses about witnesses must have owed their insertion to
a desire on someone's part, members of parliament no more
than royal officials, that men should not be brought to
trial because of allegations that were quite unfounded and
promoted perhaps out of malice or a desire for profit.
In the fourteenth century the commons of parliament had
tried to insist that accusations should be properly founded in law and not based simply on popular clamour or
notoriety.   In the fifteenth century the kings had encouraged informing, whereby a man was not liable to any
severe consequences for making frivolous charges.   The
Tudors, concerned very much with seditious speech, wanted
all the information they could get, but they had to con-
cede that it should come from two witnesses rather than
one, who should then repeat their original allegations in
court so that the petty jury could see how the accused re-
acted.   Those making the charges are probably best regarded as accusers or informers rather than witnesses as we
know them.   Elizabeth and her ministers, where they
could, liked to indict suspects under the act of 1352 because, since it contained no rules about procedure, there
was nothing about manner of accusation and therefore the
chances of conviction were considerably increased.
     One aspect of treason prominent at the end of Eliza-
beth's reign which demands our attention was the interpretation put on the crime of compassing to levy war against
the prince, a traitorous offence at that time under the
general act of 1571.   On 29 June 1595 some London and
Southwark apprentices threw stones at the warders of the
Tower street ward, were arrested and, on judgment before
council in the star chamber, were whipped and pilloried.
Whereupon others in retaliation conspired to set their
colleagues free, kill the mayor and seize weapons from two
houses near the Tower.   They then persuaded a crowd of
300 to assemble at the Tower 'ou ils avoint Trumpet et un
que tient sur un pawle un cloke en lieu de un Flagge' and
in pressing on towards the mayor's house they offered violence to the sheriffs and others who were there to oppose
them.   What all this amounted to in law was debated by
the two chief justices, the master of the rolls and two
barons of the Exchequer. (69)   All decided that such misbehaviour was treason, and a draft of an indictment shows
that the apprentices were charged with compassing war, rebellion and insurrection against the queen and expediting
the same by words against the act of 1571 (13 Eliz. c.
1). (70)   On 11 June 1597 were arraigned Richard Bradshawe and Robert Burton, very likely under the same act,

for compassing by words to levy war, rebellion and insurrection against the queen.   The 1571 act referred in fact
only to compassing to levy war, not rebellion or insurrection, which had crept into indictments in 1572 alongside
other treason charges.   Now they appeared with levying
war alone which suggests a deliberate policy of extension.
What Bradshawe and Burton had done, although the indictment gave few details, was to seek to assemble the men of
Oxfordshire at Enslow hill. (71)   They were so incensed
by the high price of corn that they intended to destroy
enclosures, and they had planned to acquire arms and
horses from the houses of the local nobility and gentlemen to further their designs. (72)   Interpreting these
offences as treason was undoubtedly straining the law, although perhaps more in the second case than the first.
Coke, who from 1594 was attorney-general and may have been
rehearsing what the judges decided before the trial,
argues that the indictment for treason of the Oxfordshire
insurgents was justified because the offenders took on
themselves the reformation of not one but a whole class of
grievances, an argument which seems as weak in this context as it does in regard to the London riots of
1517. (73)   Clearer in logic and more revealing as to
what was going on in the minds of the crown's lawyers was
the point made by the chief justices and their three colleagues in the case of the London apprentices that in compassing to levy war, so long as the compassing was directed against something the queen 'per son ley ou Justice
doit ou poit faire en government come Reign', that is to
say against her authority or policy, it was immaterial
whether they intended harm to the queen herself. (74)
This interpretation was a new one but by no means unreasonable.   The medieval law had not known intent to levy
war and had not paid much attention to the ultimate aims
of the levyers;   the crime was 'to levy war ... against
the king' *tout court*.   The unsatisfactory feature of the
judges' construction in 1595 was rather in their viewing
riot or intended riot as intention to levy war.   There
was perhaps one justification for their decision.   The
sounding of the trumpet, the carrying of the makeshift
flag, were traditional proof of levying war itself even if
on this occasion the rioters were not in martial harness.
The best explanation of both charges of treason is that
the government was thoroughly frightened by an enemy
within (the appointment of a provost marshal in London in
July 1595 shows this), and was able to persuade the judges
to reach interpretations which were quite different from
those of earlier periods when both types of misbehaviour
would probably have been classed as nothing worse than
riot.

These two cases had an important bearing on charges
brought against the earls of Essex and Southampton and
their confederates after the failure of their bid to seize
power in 1600.    An account of their trials tells us that
Coke, the attorney-general, when he led for the crown
against the confederates, argued that if the law
> made such construction of the acts of mechanical men,
> what shall be thought of the acts of earls and other
> strong persons intending to surprize the Tower, to take
> the city, possess themselves of the court, to call a
> parliament, to change government, to tolerate religion?
These intents of force must needs tend to treason. (75)
Coke's line of reasoning, though plausible, is not convincing, for it was probably he who had persuaded the
judges to find the London and Oxfordshire riots as treason
in the first place, drawing, so it seems, on his defective
knowledge of the May Day riot of 1517.    The actual indictment accused Essex and his allies of imagining to
depose and slay the queen and Essex himself of endeavour-
ing to gain the throne and usurp the royal dignity. (76)
These were treasons under both the general treason act of
1571 and the statute of 1352, and as such unexceptionable.
What was open to criticism was the construing of the behaviour of the earls and their followers as these
offences.    Chief Justice Popham, one of the judges at the
trial of some of the lesser lights of the conspiracy, made
the revealing remark that 'by force to compel the prince
to any government is in itself treason'. (77)    At the
same trial Coke, in addition to his *a fortiori* argument
based on the riots of 1595 and 1597, reasoned that servants coming to their masters with armed petitions, which
was roughly what the earls did, 'tendeth to their destruction'. (78)    Francis Bacon, putting the crown's case
against Sir John Davis, argued that every rebellion implied the destruction of the prince, which was unsound
historically but doubtless very palatable to the queen and
her ministers. (79)    Serjeant Yelverton propounded that
'to alter the state, change the religion, inforce the
prince to settle power, and for subjects to sway things at
their list is *crimen laesae majestatis*.    Lese-majesty was
a term virtually never used by the common lawyers and suggests some desperation or new policy on the part of the
queen's legal advisers. (80)    To alter or subvert the established religion or government was a piece of political
phraseology which had become increasingly common in treason indictments from about 1570, but it was not part of
any particular act and was thus not essential for their
soundness in law. (81)    Forcing the prince to yield power
and attempts by subjects to control him or the equivalent

had not occurred in an indictment since the trial of Dr
Mackerell in 1537, and before that at those of Empson and
Dudley in 1509, when it could not be justified under the
existing treason laws.   It might have been possible to
argue that, since the earls and their followers had been
proclaimed traitors, swords had been crossed and a life
lost, that war had been levied against the queen, but for
some reason this approach was omitted from the strategy of
the royal lawyers. (82)

There was in fact a gap in the law when the matter was
one of armed factions seeking not the bodily harm but the
coercion of the prince, and it needed to be filled.   What
Elizabeth and her advisers were unwilling to do was to
accept that fact and legislate.   Maybe the queen did not
do this because it would have meant using the act retroactively.   An act of attainder would have been another
way of proceeding, but the device had not been used since
the 1570s, being made superfluous in most ways by the
large number of treason laws and a judicial interpretation
about forfeiture for that crime, which for the crown left
little to be desired.   Furthermore, an attainder act,
like any new treason act, had to be put through parliament, which was not an enterprise to be undertaken lightly
at a time when decisive action was essential.   Once the
trials had finished and the chief participants in the insurrection had been found guilty the crown was provided
with a precedent of exceptional value for, as Catlin
C.J.K.B. told Norfolk at his trial in 1571, 'usage is the
best expounder'.   Rebellion of all types was thenceforth
a traitorous act and that very word which in earlier times
had been associated with the withdrawal by peasants from
their legal obligations and with assemblies of a riotous
nature became synonymous with treason.

The history of what treason amounted to between 1485-
1603 is anything but a simple tale, nor is it an edifying
one.   Perhaps the greatest failing of the government and
its legal advisers in the framing of indictments was the
misinterpretation of the past, particularly of the act of
1352 and fourteenth- and fifteenth-century precedents.
This was demonstrated, for example, at the trials of
Empson and Dudley, the May Day rioters, Sir Nicholas
Throckmorton, the London apprentices in 1595 and the Oxfordshire rioters in 1596-7.   The policy, which was quite
apparent later in the sixteenth century, of framing indictments so that they might be said to be founded on several statutes was a deceitful subterfuge to gain procedural benefits, like avoiding the need to produce witnesses
or to indict within a certain time after the crime was
committed.   It is obvious that, when there was some doubt

about the scope of the law, the professional judges were
pressured to interpret in the manner most beneficial to
the prince, and usually their conferences ended with their
doing just that.   They may have misunderstood the history
of the treason law, or they may have misconstrued it
deliberately. (83)   It is, however, possible that the
supercession of statute by statute and the superimposition
of others created genuine confusion in some cases, particularly in the period from the accession of Mary to
1571.   Many of these weaknesses and difficulties might
have been resolved if the scope of the treason laws had
been open to criticism.   Unfortunately, the heightened
political and religious tensions tended to make men curb
their tongues for fear of being regarded as betrayers of
their prince, church and realm.   Very noticeably, there
was no opposition by the nobility as the fourteenth- and
early fifteenth-century kings had met with when they
sought to change the scope of the treason laws. (84)   The
magnates of those times had been great experts on illegal
accusations and precedents in general, but in the sixteenth all those with a good knowledge of the law seem to
have been in thrall to the crown.   With no accepted and
organized opposition for much of the period, there was not
the same need to observe the letter of the law so strictly.   Finally, there is the question of attitude.   The
way in which the Tudor kings and queens failed to follow
accurately some of the provisos of the acts defining the
scope of treason, acts which they could presumably have
altered eventually if they so wanted, tells us a great
deal about the fundamental nature of their government, and
the stress it was under.

# Apprehension, Examination, and Indictment

For the government, a case of treason began when a traitorous deed or spoken words were reported to a royal official.   The report might be made by a mere chance obser-
ver or overhearer, a renegade conspirator or a government
spy.   It was the duty of everyone to report suspected
treason.   Not to do so had itself been declared traitorous at least as early as the thirteenth century.   The
legal treatise writers of that period, Bracton, Britton
and Fleta each remarked that the king or his ministers
should immediately be informed about treason or intended
treason by the discoverer. (1)   Bracton said that a man
who acquired knowledge of treason should not delay in one
place for two nights or two days together nor attend to
his own business before telling the king.   By the fifteenth century to have known of intended treason but not
to have revealed it was always held as traitorous even if
the potential informant pleaded an intent to find out more
about the plot so as to reveal it in due course more completely. (2)   So it was if he argued a plan of joining
the conspiracy in order to frustrate it, unless of course
he was a government spy directed to do just that. (3)
The government, at a time when the country was restive,
could expect to receive from ordinary citizens a good
number of reports about activity of a supposedly traitorous nature.   It has been pointed out in regard to the
period of Thomas Cromwell's ascendancy that 'information
came and did not have to be sought for';   furthermore that
the conveyers were not professional informers or governmental spies but ordinary loyal Englishmen.   Occasionally
the first information about suspected treason came in the
form of a presentment by a jury.   In such a case the
crime would very likely be of lesser importance, like the
counterfeiting of coin and in answer to a general charge.
When the matter was dangerous to their safety the Tudor

monarchs expected to tell the grand juries about the treason rather than be told by them.

The recipients in the first instance of most pieces of information about suspected treason were the local justices of the peace.    It was their duty to pass this knowledge on to the king's council.    To save time and to show that the information was soundly based the justices, although they were not really empowered to examine suspects in treason cases, sometimes took sworn statements from the informers or witnesses which they passed on with comments of their own. (4)    Naturally enough, the large majority of the cases which were reported initially to the local magistrates concerned not incipient rebellion or plots to assassinate the prince but seditious words uttered and overheard in public places.    These, although important as indicators of public feeling, were not the most dangerous of cases.    The king was more concerned with conspiracies proper, because they threatened his hurt or overthrow more directly and the problem was how to induce defection amongst the plotters.    No law was ever passed which promised indemnity or reward to such turncoats but one was under active consideration at the end of 1531.    A surviving draft shows that anyone involved in the plotting of treason who was the first to give information to the king or any councillor upon which convictions of the others could be secured was to have a pardon and a quarter of the lands and goods forfeited by a traitor. (5)    How it was that the clause was omitted from the treason act of 1534 can only be conjectured.    Perhaps widespread objection was feared, for the measure was singularly at odds with the principles of the common law.    Perhaps by the time a new treason act was passed there was less need.    In Starkey's 'Dialogue between Reginald Pole and Thomas Lupset' Pole was made to say 'in the accusing of treason there is meseemeth over great liberty' meaning that accusers often brought charges which were very flimsy or unfounded.    Lupset argued in answer that as the crime was so great there must be no punishing of those who brought accusations of treason subsequently found to be without substance, since then everyone would wait until the deed was committed: 'wherefore, not without cause, upon suspicion only, every man may freely accuse other of treason'. (6)    If these statements accurately reflect contemporary trends, and a recent study of the years 1532-40 seems to bear them out, then there were plenty of reports of intended treason and many of them were without proper foundation often being prompted by malice, the desire to embarrass a personal enemy.    There is also the possibility that the intended provision of 1531 was actually put into operation, although not in a law but by means of a proclamation.   In May 1533 Chapuys, the imperial ambassador, wrote to Charles V that King Henry had proclaimed that informers against those who spoke against the Boleyn marriage should have 'a certain sum' of money. (7)   If this was true it was a proclamation with no basis in any statute.

There were occasions in the sixteenth century as in the fifteenth when the crown showed quite clearly that it approved of the principle of inducements to promote informing.   Set rules of procedure were established and size of reward decided on, but they were limited to particular offences and, except perhaps in two small categories, treason was excepted. (8)   Despite the lack of overt inducement there were never the less to be found professional treason discoverers, particularly in the later years of the reign of Elizabeth.   Robert Bernard wrote to Sir Francis Walsingham, probably in 1581, asking for pay which he had not received for three months.   He explained he was now in full credit with the papists and had access to all the prisons in London. (9)   In December 1582 another professional informer who operated in the gaols, Walter Williams, wrote to Walsingham that he could get nothing more out of 'the papist' and asked to be released 'having lain for a month on the bare floor without any bed'. (10) Some informers may have actually been placed in prisons for this purpose but more often the discoveries came from those who, already in prison, offered or were persuaded to inform for a period so as to achieve their freedom.   Thus in May 1594 a Mr Beard in the Fleet, who provided Lord Keeper Puckering with information about seminary priests at court, offered to point them out if given his liberty. In December 1581 John Hart, a seminary priest imprisoned in the Tower of London, offered in hope of a pardon to find out the designs of Dr Allen. (11)   There were also at this time Catholic priests who gave information not so much out of a desire for reward or pardon but simply because they had lost sympathy with their mission.   For example, in 1592 Thomas Bell, a seminary priest, changed his beliefs and loyalties and furnished the government with much information about recusants in Lancashire and the priests among them. (12)

When treason or intended treason had been reported, then arrests had to be made and the bodies of the suspects secured by imprisonment or sureties taken for future appearance before the legal authorities.   Usually this was accomplished without too much difficulty; certainly few of those accused of seditious words took to flight, yet there were times when extensive search was necessary.

In April 1486 Thomas Cokesey was commissioned by Henry VII
to find the Yorkist, Humphrey Stafford, who had recently
escaped from sanctuary at Colchester and was probably intending to seize Worcester.    Cokesey employed no fewer
than 400 men in his search of a wood near Bewdley to which
Stafford had been tracked. (13)    More typical perhaps was
the search early in 1538 for John Davey of St Sidwell's in
the suburbs of Exeter.    When accused of treason he fled
the county, and the inquiries of Sir Thomas Denys, Richard
and Sir Hugh Pollard were without success until they heard
that he was known to be in Westminster.    Then they sent a
messenger who knew Davey to tell Thomas Cromwell about the
matter, no doubt hoping for his assistance in making an
arrest. (14)    Searches on most occasions were conducted
by the justices of the peace or the sheriff and their servants and not left to the constable of the township or the
hue and cry by the local inhabitants.    In 1586 Anthony
Babington and his fellow conspirators, who fled when their
plot was revealed, were discovered in the woods near London by what one of those arrested called 'the careful and
vigilant watchmen of her majesties true subjects';    but
there was another side to the coin.    Burghley informed
Walsingham of the stupidity of the watchmen stationed on
the road to London to catch the same conspirators and complained of the negligence of the justices in appointing
such foolish men. (15)

It helped in securing a conviction in the courts and
for general purposes of propaganda if the searchers could
discover written evidence of traitorous intent.    Following the suppression of the Yorkshire rising of 1540,
houses and chambers in Wakefield of those suspected of
being involved were searched by the Yorkshire undersher-
iff.    In 1580 the house of William Balle at Hadley, Suffolk, and a river nearby were searched for stamps and instruments used for the counterfeiting, clipping and washing of coins. (16)    In 1584 there were intensive searches
of country houses, the quarry being not only seminary
priests in hiding but also popish relics and 'papistical
books'. (17)    The correspondence and memoranda of arrested traitors, because they were of great value in the formulation of interrogatories and subsequently of indictments, were looked for after arrest with great keenness.
Letters found in Bishop Fisher's study provided no fewer
than forty interrogatories for his examiners.    In June
1537 the duke of Norfolk reported to Cromwell that Sir
Ralph Ellerker and three of his servants had been sent to
Beverley to seize Thomas Strangwishe and to search his
house for writings 'that might teach the king'. (18)
Thomas Cromwell obviously set much store by the discovery

of writings by or to a suspect traitor and was thought by
one searcher to be worthy of commendation for his thor-
oughness in this respect. (19)
    Power to arrest those suspected of treason was in
reality confined, as with other breaches of the peace, to
constables, bailiffs, mayors and justices of the peace.
An ordinary citizen was obliged to make an arrest only if
he knew a felony (which would include treason), or a trespass which might lead to a felony, had been committed, or
if he was told to by one of the officials named
above. (20)   If he thought a felony had been committed
but was not certain, he could make an arrest but was not
obliged to do so.   If, of course, he possessed a royal
warrant or commission he could arrest with impunity.
Complaint about unjustifiable search and arrest was undoubtedly made, although only infrequently.   In one
example, from 1596, John Ardern wrote to Sir Robert Cecil
that the knight marshal had searched his house and chamber
on suspicion of treason and taken him to the marshalsea,
all without any warrant.   Nor was it unheard of for men
who had been arrested to retaliate. (21)   William Perry,
who at the time of Wyatt's rebellion attached one Mitchell
as a suspect in Camarthenshire, was sued by the latter in
an action of case.   The government was obviously perturbed by this reaction and ordered the Camarthen 'high justice' (presumably the senior justice of the Camarthen
great sessions) to ensure that Perry was not further molested 'so that no other so serving be hereafter troubled
for service'. (22)   The searching out and arrest of treason suspects was usually of only a small number at any one
time.   Naturally enough at a time of general insurrection
the net was widened and the methods became more ruthless.
Thus at the end of December 1569, when the rebellion in
the north was at its height, Sir William Cecil proposed a
plan for the arrest of the principal insurgents.   Their
names were to be ascertained by imprisoning under oppressive conditions other rebels who would thus be persuaded
to reveal their leaders.   When these 'head persons' were
known, they were 'at one night and one instant' to be
apprehended and their possessions seized.   This large
task could be undertaken because, since it was a time of
open rebellion, there were soldiers on hand to provide the
manpower.   They were to be led, not as we might expect by
justices of the peace, but simply by 'discreet persons',
which no doubt meant local loyalists. (23)   Whoever
actually effected any arrest on suspicion of treason, the
decision to apprehend was nearly always taken, even in
times of insurrection, by the members of the king's council, by the chief of his ministers or by the king himself,

such was the importance to the government of the right
handling of any seditious activity.   The fear of arrest
for treason was, as one French traveller recorded, (24)
very great at times and the attention men gave to the
arrest of others enabled them to recognize omens for the
prisoner's future in the very act of apprehension.   An
open arrest and the conducting of the captive along busy
thoroughfares was believed to herald a bleak future.   It
was said after the arrest of the duke of Norfolk and his
son, the earl of Surrey, in December 1546 that because
Norfolk had been deprived of his staff of office and
Surrey was led publicly through the streets to the Tower
their hope of freedom was small.(25) This proved to be so.

There were suspect traitors who fled not merely to the
next county or to London but escaped into Scotland,
France, the Low Countries or even Germany.   It was typical of the Tudor monarchs that they never ceased to work
for the extradition of these fugitives and that while this
was being negotiated they would try to acquire their possessions.   The suspect, when in a foreign land, could be
indicted in any county of the realm and subsequently outlawed. (26)   If the offences came under the treason act
of 1352 only the suspect's fee simple could be seized by
the king as forfeit;   if they came under the treason acts
of 1534 or 1552 or were committed after 1554 then the
king might take possessions held in fee tail and, until
1540, held by others to the suspect's use.   Outlawing
would take five months to accomplish at least, but if by
chance the suspect could be held to have levied war
against the king he might be proclaimed as a traitor and
his possessions seized immediately.   In Mary's reign the
judges decided that if a subject refused to return to the
realm when the king so ordered his lands and goods should
be seized to the king's use. (27)   This mode of procedure, which presumably reached as far as lands held in fee
tail, gave the king instant possession while awaiting outlawry or the passing of an act of attainder.

The extradition of traitors had hardly figured at all
in the history of English treason before the sixteenth
century, but in the reigns of Henry VIII and Elizabeth it
became an issue of importance.   The return of fugitive
traitors had been promised by Henry VII and James IV of
Scotland in the peace treaty of June 1502.   Neither was
to receive, succour or favour traitors or rebels (who in
this case were those as yet only suspected, not convicted
or outlawed) of the other, but was to deliver them back to
the prince offended. (28)   The provision seems to have
been put to little use immediately and it was not until
the time of the break with Rome and thereafter that the

English government had to face in earnest the problem of
the traitor who had fled outside the realm.  Henry VIII's
first request for extradition seems to have been in 1528
under the 'Intercursus Magnus' of 1505, while his second
was made under the treaty of Cambrai (1529) to the emper-
or, Charles V, and concerned William Tyndale.  Henry
claimed that Tyndale was spreading sedition, but the emperor expressed his doubts and argued that he must examine
the case and discover proof of the English king's asser-
tion before delivering the wanted man. (29)  This, he
said, was necessary according to the Cambrai treaty, other
conventions between the princes of England and Burgundy,
and the privileges granted to the English in the Low Countries.  What his investigation of the case revealed is unknown, but Tyndale was not handed over.  At the beginning
of 1540 Henry requested the delivery of Robert Brancetour,
an associate of Reginald Pole, and met with a refusal
which was quite definite.  Charles claimed he had consulted the treaties between the two princes and had found he
was not compelled to surrender Brancetour because he was
already convicted and there only remained his execution.
(30)  Therefore the emperor resolved to banish him, which
was the most he was obliged to do.  When the English ambassador requested the emperor should hand over Gerald
Fitzgerald and other rebels a few months later Charles
again refused, pleading the treaty, and promised banishment instead.  This reluctance was no doubt partly caused,
as Sir Thomas Wyatt hinted, by Henry's 'stirring up the
Almains' but an inability to understand the processes of
the common law probably also played a part. (31)  To gain
the co-operation of the emperor, Henry would have to have
given up the outlawry or attainting by act of fugitive
traitors, which at that time he was not prepared to do.
     When in February 1540 Henry asked James V of Scotland
to deliver to him Dr Hilliard, a chaplain of the bishop of
Durham, as a fugitive and rebel who had laboured to sow
sedition in the realm, he met with refusal based on another principle.  James said that in regard to Dr Hilliard
'and other kirkmen' he took 'no great regard' but left the
correction of their faults 'to the Halikirk'. (32)   In
March 1541 the issue arose again.  In answer to a request
by Henry for the handing over of several English rebels
and traitors the Scottish king said he would arrest and
surrender all who were laymen but that friars, priests
'and other kirkmen' should be left to the handling of
their ordinaries, archbishops and other prelates. (33)
James maintained that 'the treaty', which was presumably
that of 1502, made a distinction between ecclesiastics and
others and for this Henry took him to task, remarking with

some asperity that if he allowed churchmen to avoid trial by the temporal power, he was setting up a new kingdom in his realm. (34)

The answer of Henry VIII to the obstructive tactics of these and other monarchs like Francis I of France and Queen Mary of Hungary varied according to circumstance. One device was to approach the fugitives directly through agents or ambassadors and by blandishments and promises persuade them to return of their own free will.   In April 1540 the English king ordered that the suspect priest Gregory Botolf, then at Louvain, should be sent a letter giving him hope of a benefice if he would go to Calais. Botolf refused the bait of preferment, and therefore the English agents turned instead to accusing him of certain crimes so as to bring about his arrest by the mayor of Louvain. (35)   The ruse apparently put Botolf first in the mayor's custody and then in the gaol of the bishop of Liège at Diest until at least the end of August, without his being put on trial.   The English ambassador in the meantime pressed for either his extradition or his trial and judgment. (36)   This was not the first time such a plan had been adopted.   In February 1538 Wriothesley, the English ambassador to the regent of the Netherlands, Queen Mary of Hungary, asked her for the extradition of the fugitive traitor, Henry Philips, on the grounds that he had stolen a large sum of money from him.

Quite different tactics were used in an effort in 1540 to extradite the traitor 'Blancherose' whose real name seems to have been Richard Hosier.   Francis I, in whose territory he resided, at first made objection to the English requests on the grounds that Hosier had been born in Orleans and was thus subject to the law of France.   Henry VIII in reply instructed his ambassador to point out that 'Blancherose' never the less had an English father, meaning no doubt that he was therefore an English subject. The argument met with no success, so Henry changed his tack.   His instructions in 1541 to his emissary Lord William Howard were that he should not display any desire to have 'Blancherose' delivered but should show the French king certain writings and depositions revealing the wanted man to be a murderer and common thief. (37)   The shift in emphasis from a political crime to mere felony was obviously expected to meet with a more sypmathetic response, partly no doubt, on account of Francis's known willingness to return common criminals in flight.

A scheme which was more likely to secure extradition than most was one planned by Thomas Cromwell just before his fall.   He ordered Pate, the ambassador at the imperial court, to tell the emperor that two of his Flemish

rebels had recently arrived at Calais.   If he was asked
their names he was to say he would get them:   'if he
desire their delivery say you are sure the king will not
harbour traitors'.   It seems these men were to be used
as bargaining counters and that an exchange of fugitives
was to be made. (38)   The most direct attempt, and it was
a successful one, to secure a fugitive traitor occurred in
August 1570.   Dr John Storey, then in Antwerp, was persuaded in his official capacity as searcher to go aboard
an English ship, was imprisoned below and shanghaied to
Yarmouth.   His trial and execution for treason soon followed.   Although the capture does not seem to have been
sponsored officially by the government some minister may
well have had a hand in it.   English agents, with or
without the knowledge of their king, were willing it seems
to go to even greater lengths than kidnapping. (39)   A
surreptitious pursuit in 1543 of George Dudley, son of
John Sutton, Lord Dudley, who was en route to meet Reginald Pole, persuaded them they must either get him detained or kill him. (40)   The second alternative was only
ruled out because it would lose the king his confession.
     The Tudor monarchs were quite consistent in their at-
titude to suspect traitors who had fled overseas.   They
did their utmost to get them into English gaols.   The
policy stemmed from the reasonable fear that if left un-
harried such men would have the opportunity to 'work their
feats of treason'. (41)   So important was extradition to
Henry VIII that in June 1543 it figured as a reason for an
ultimatum of war to the French ambassador.   'Your
master', said the council, 'has maintained divers of our
sovereigns rebels as namely the son of a cobbler who
boasted that he was of the blood royal and called himself
la Blanche Rose'. (42)   The success of a demand for extradition depended not only on having a treaty with the
country concerned which included that issue but also, as
might be expected, on political conditions existing at the
time when the request was made.   When the French king or
the emperor had subjects in rebellion or who were at odds
with them, then action was much easier to obtain.   If
their territories were quiescent they were likely to find
many excuses for sliding out of their obligations.   The
Tudors were much more successful in getting extradition if
the fugitive had fled to Scotland, the reason being a
combination of explicit treaties, (43) a tradition of returning wanted men under marcher arrangements and the fact
that England was the more powerful country.
     Until 1534 suspect traitors could find a satisfactory
refuge, though of a restrictive sort, without ever leaving
the realm.   This was in any of a number of sanctuary

places where a felon in flight could find perpetual
refuge, in contrast to the forty days he was allowed in
ordinary churches.   Most of these sanctuaries were under
ecclesiastical jurisdiction as at Westminster, Beaulieu,
Colchester, Culham, and St Martin's-le-Grand in London.
They numbered more and covered a greater area north of
the Trent.   There was the whole of the county palatine of
Durham and its non-adjacent members, the liberties of the
archbishop of York of St Peter's Beverley, Ripon and Hex-
hamshire, the liberties of the prior of Tynemouth, and the
lay franchises of Tynedale and Redesdale. (44)   In none
of these areas did the king's writ run.   There were also
places in Lancashire, Cheshire and the Welsh marches which
had the same privileges and an equal popularity among
criminals in flight.   In the fifteenth century the kings
had shown increasing concern about these bolt-holes, not
just because they sheltered traitors but because they were
thought to support crime in general. (45)   Through their
judges kings began to insist that to protect a sanctuary
seeker the grant of sanctuary must mention his type of
crime in express words.   The case of Humphrey Stafford,
who sought sanctuary at Culham in 1486, displayed that to
operate a sanctuary the claimant of the privilege must be
able to show a royal grant with the crimes covered stated
specifically, an allowance in general eyre and incontestable examples of usage.   Stafford was removed into custody because treason was not expressly stated in the
charter. (46)   Henry VII, although probably grateful for
the protection which sanctuaries had afforded his own
supporters before Bosworth, (47) was particularly keen to
reach traitors in sanctuary, and, having obtained the
decision of the judges in the Stafford case, seems to have
made good use of it to take other traitors from other
sanctuaries in later years, even if he never introduced
legislation to settle the matter once and for all. (48)
     The next serious blow against traitors in sanctuary was
struck in February 1518 in the trial of John Cowley, whose
chief crime was that after arrest on suspicion of treason
he had broken out of the Marshalsea gaol, which was itself
a traitorous offence under the act of 1424.   In flight he
had made his way to St Martin's-le-Grand where he had been
seized on 11 February 1518 by Sir Thomas Lovell and others
and put in the Tower.   When asked in court how he wished
to acquit himself, Cowley simply asked to be put back in
sanctuary.   Asked if he wished to answer to the treason
(and heresies) of which he was indicted, he said no, he
only wanted privilege of sanctuary.   The attorney-general, Erneley, argued that this he should not have on
account of his heretical views, a rather implausible argu-

ment.   He then asked that Cowley be put to execution
forthwith.   The judges, however, remanded the accused
into the custody of the sheriff for a few days, either to
give him time to change his mind about not offering a plea
or to try to force him to do so by duress in gaol.   When
he appeared in court, Cowley stood by his original response and, the court 'having examined every matter', he
was adjudged by the justices to be executed as a traitor
immediately. (49)   This was a remarkable end to the case.
Usually those accused who would not plead guilty or not
guilty but made a response judged by the court as inadequate were sent to *peine fort et dure*, which was pressing
to death.   In the case of Cowley the judges simply gave
judgment and sentence.   There was no recourse to a petty
jury through the device, not unknown, of taking the
accused's refusal to plead as a plea of not guilty. (50)
There may well have been an intent on the part of the
justices to frighten other treason suspects who were already in sanctuary or might intend to flee there.   The
relation of sanctuary to high treason was finally settled
in 1534 by its abolition.   The act 26 Hen. VIII c. 13 removed 'the benefit or privilege of any manner of sanctuary' from both principals and accessaries.

   After being arrested, the suspect traitor was placed in
gaol, there to remain until either he was arraigned or he
was released on bail, on payment of a fine, or because of
lack of evidence.   This pre-trial period of captivity was
one of the most crucial stages in the whole legal process.
Furthermore, because of the duress frequently inflicted
it was the one which reflects most unfavourably Tudor governmental policy towards treason.   For the imprisonment
of a treason suspect before arraignment, any county, mun-
icipal or London gaol might be used, although the more
notorious of prisoners would usually be moved, if not sent
there initially, to the Tower of London.   This was the
most important treason gaol, followed by the King's Bench
at Southwark, the two London Counters (one in Bread and
Wood streets and the other in the Poultry), Newgate, the
Gatehouse, the Fleet, the Clink (in Southwark), the Bridewell and the palace of the archbishop of Canterbury at
Lambeth. (51)   To argue that a prisoner had something
like a choice of gaol is going too far, but there is some
evidence that his ability or that of his friends to pay
for the costs of his keep might enable him to stay in a
more preferable gaol for a time. (52)   The conditions
under which treason suspects lived in prison varied considerably but in general they were harsh even by the standards of the times.   The intention was quite clear to
both officials and captives:   to weaken the prisoner's

body and thus his resolution, so that incriminating evidence and information about fellow conspirators or overt rebels should be forthcoming.

The time which a prisoner suspect of treason had to remain in gaol before his arraignment varied enormously. It could be only a few days or it could be more than a decade.   Because of a desire on the part of the captors to elicit information and compare it with that supplied by other suspects, less than a month or two was unlikely unless it was a time of general insurrection.   If the prisoner was of social or political importance then the period was usually longer.   Sir Thomas More was committed in mid-April 1534 and only put on trial on 1 July 1535 although he was attainted for a lesser offence than treason in parliament at the end of 1534.   The duke of Norfolk, when tried on 16 January 1572, had been in captivity of one sort or another for twenty-six months since his original arrest on 2 October 1569.   The earl of Arundel, when he was arraigned on 18 April 1589, said he had been a prisoner four years 'and twenty-five weeks close prisoner'. (53)   These suspects were eventually found guilty of treason, and there was strong evidence against them, but against Thomas Mountayne, who was imprisoned 'in the Marshalsea' at the beginning of Mary's reign on suspicion of treason and heresy and kept there three years in irons before securing his liberty, there was 'never any man laid anything' to his charge. (54)   The longest periods in gaol before trial were suffered by catholic priests, for whom two or three years was in no way exceptional.   For example John Robinson, committed to the Clink in June 1585, had to wait three years for his trial.   John Finch, arrested probably in December 1580, was able to answer when examined before indictment that he had been in prison, partly in the earl of Derby's house, partly in the New Fleet at Salford and partly in the house of correction in the same town or a dungeon nearby, for three years and three months.   A considerably longer term was the misfortune of the priest Thomas Woodhouse, who was put in the Fleet prison in May 1561 and arraigned for treason only in April 1573. (55)   This seems to have been the longest period of pre-trial imprisonment for a treason suspect under the Tudors.   Edward, earl of Warwick, was put in the Tower in 1485 and eventually tried and executed for treason in 1499, but he was originally committed for fear of treason rather than on suspicion of it.   Mary, Queen of Scots, was in captivity of a sort even longer, but she likewise was not initially a treason suspect.

Despite the considerable number of such suspects who were in gaol at any one time, the government seems usually

to have known the whereabouts of each and even perhaps the
conditions of confinement.   In this way the Tudors were
better informed than their medieval predecessors, one of
whom, Edward III, had to admit in May 1350 that he did not
know why certain important prisoners were in the Tower and
therefore ordered them to be examined to find out how long
they had been there and on what grounds they had been
arrested. (56)   Concern about men detained in prison on
suspicion of treason unreasonably never really arose in
the sixteenth century.   There was an examination by the
judges of the law regarding commitments in 1596 but it
was concerned primarily with private actions and said
little about treason suspects.   What it did say helped
the suspect traitor not at all.   Any person committed by
command of the queen or by order of the council for high
treason was not to be set free without due trial and acquittal and the trial could be delayed or prevented if the
cause of committal was certified to the judges. (57)
There was thus virtually no restriction on the length of
pre-trial imprisonment at all since trial could be delayed
indefinitely except where the offence was reckoned to come
under a treason statute like 13 Eliz. c. 1, which required
the offences referred to in the indictment to have been
committed within a certain period. (58)
   Within the gaols suspect traitors were afforded special
treatment and whenever possible kept apart from the other
prisoners, although towards the end of the sixteenth century the London gaols at least had become so crowded that
efforts had to be made to reduce the number of existing
inmates when arrests of more than a few other traitors was
expected. (59)   If the prisoner was of great value the
government was quite ready to spend money to renovate old
prison premises to provide the right sort of confinement.
For Dr John Storey, who was put in the Lollards' Tower in
the Tower of London, the locks and bolts which had been
broken off when Queen Mary died were refitted.   On one
occasion so severe was the shortage of individual rooms in
the Tower of London that it was suggested the lodgings of
the king and queen should be taken over so as to provide
accommodation. (60)   The problem was made worse by the
desire to keep suspect traitors of high social position in
conditions suitable to their status.   The earl of Northumberland in Elizabeth's reign was thus allowed the liberty of five large chambers and two large entries, 'three
of which chambers and one of the entries lay upon two fair
gardens within the Tower wall'.   The windows, furthermore, were reported as 'letting in much air and
light'. (61)
    In many English gaols there was an area in which pris-

oners were put as a special form of punishment.   Most
must have been below ground and entered only by a trap-
door.   Names like 'the pit', 'little ease', and 'limbo',
suggest their unsavoury nature and the intent behind their
use.   The 'pit' was in the Tower of London and has been
described as 'a subterranean cave, twenty feet deep entirely without light';   it seems to have held not more
than three persons.   The Tower also possessed a dungeon
called 'little ease' where, according to the sister of one
prisoner, it was impossible to stand, lie or sit, and
another known as 'the grisely dungeon called Whalesbourne'
(perhaps in Coleharbour Tower or under the White Tower)
which was 'a very deep cavern, absolutely dark and shut in
on all sides', and also 'the dungeon amongst the rats'.
The last was a cell below the Thames's high water mark and
totally dark, 'where the flesh has been torn from the arms
and legs of prisoners during sleep'. (62)   There were
similar places of extreme rigour in other gaols.   There
was a 'little ease' in the London Bridewell and a 'limbo'
in Newgate, which was referred to by the Jesuit Robert
Southwell as 'the most darksome dungeon'. (63)   Nor was
there any shortage of dungeons outside London where the
prison buildings, many of which were parts of castles,
were usually of greater age than those in the capital and
had a worse reputation.   The length of a prisoner's stay
in a dungeon varied from a few days to many months.   The
Jesuit Alexander Briant it seems in 1581 was put in the
Tower 'pit' for eight days.   Thomas Felton, probably in
1588, was confined in 'little ease' in the Bridewell for a
mere three days but later on was in the 'limbo' of Newgate
for fifteen weeks.   Thomas Sherwood, a catholic layman,
was put naked into the Tower 'dungeon among the rats' for
three months from mid-November 1577.   The catholic priest
Stephen Rowsham was reputedly in the Tower's 'little ease'
for about eighteen months from 14 August 1582. (64)   When
a prisoner was moved to a dungeon in the Tower it was
usually a sign that he was soon to be examined under torture.   If this examination did not provide the information the government required then the prisoner was returned to the dungeon until he was tortured again or until he
was put on trial.
    Soon after his arrest, a suspect who was not of noble
rank might find himself shackled in irons.   There were at
least three reasons why this should occur.   There was the
fear the arrested person would escape, a fear which seems
to have afflicted gaolers chiefly in the early stages of
imprisonment. (65)   If the shackles had to be worn continuously for more than a week or so the intention was probably to weaken the prisoner's resolve to withold informa-

tion through the sheer discomfort.   Very often those put
in dungeons for special punishment were kept in shackles. (66)   Another reason seems to have been simply a
desire to force the prisoner or his friends to purchase
release from the irons.   Gaolers were allowed a certain
amount of discretion about keeping their charges en-
chained, although they were dangerously at risk if a suspect traitor whose shackling had been ordered by the king
escaped.   Type of irons and method of shackling varied
from gaol to gaol.   The priest John Nutter, put in gaol
at Dunwich, had fastened to his foot an enormous iron
chain with a heavy wooden block at the end. (67)   A well-
informed contemporary source tells us that Richard White,
a catholic layman, was forced when in Ruthin gaol to wear
heavy handbolts on each arm and heel which did not allow
him to lie on his side. (68)   In 1535, prior to their
trial, three Carthusian monks, Middlemore, Exmew and New-
digate, were chained upright by the neck, arms and legs to
posts in some part of the Tower for thirteen days. (69)
These types of shackling were no doubt considerably less
common than the simple chaining of legs together or the
fastening of one leg by chain to a wall, pillar or post.
That there were different degrees of shackling is quite
clear.   Dr Storey, on his capture, begged that there
should not be put more than one iron on his legs;   Richard
White had to suffer an increase to two pairs of irons on
his legs after making a pert answer at his trial. (70)
Although the length of time spent in irons was usually to
be measured in days rather than months there is reference
to John Body, a catholic layman, being shackled from 5
September 1581 to 28 April 1582, and Thomas Mountayne in
his autobiography affirms that he himself was in irons for
three years. (71)   A very long period in irons was uncommon not because of compassion on the part of the government or the gaoler but because they knew from experience that it might affect the circulation of the blood and
cause the flesh to putrefy.   Because of such a mishap
Nicholas Horner, a catholic tailor, had to have a leg am-
putated while in Newgate in 1587. (72)   There can be
little doubt that the prisoner's behaviour at his pre-
trial examination played a big part in deciding whether he
should continue to wear irons.   If he provided the information his examiners were seeking then the shackling would
probably cease.   If he proved truculent the irons would
be kept on until the next examination or until he was put
on trial.
     In most sixteenth-century English gaols there was
little segregation of prisoners, partly because of over-
crowding and partly because the prison buildings provided

few separate rooms.   Most prisoners could therefore com-
municate with each other without difficulty, but this was
not the case with those suspected of treason.   In the
London gaols at least, instructions were often given on
committal that such persons were to be held as close prisoners. (73)   When the duke of Norfolk was first placed in
the Tower on 2 October 1569 orders were issued to Sir
Henry Neville,who was given charge of him, that the prisoner should have no conference with any other person.
Eleven months later on the committal to the Lollards'
Tower of Dr Storey the same strict command was given. (74)
The phrase 'no conference' probably included communication
by writing as well as by speech;   also it prevented visits
by those in the outside world.   The policy of keeping
suspect traitors incommunicado must have been difficult to
enforce, for there were many ways of passing messages sur-
reptitiously to fellow prisoners.   The earl of Warwick
communicated with Perkin Warbeck by, so the indictment of
the former recounts, knocking on the vault of his chamber
and later making a hole which enabled them to speak together. (75)   The gaoler or his family or servants might be
prevailed upon to ignore their duties and give assistance.
In 1584 it was discovered that the daughter of the lieutenant of the Tower was passing letters between the prisoners in the Tower and those in the Marshalsea.   Earlier
in the century Sir Thomas More and Bishop Fisher seem to
have had no difficulty in communicating with each other in
the Tower, despite the suspicions of the authorities, and
reporting their respective answers before the council.
In this case the courier was frequently George, a servant
of the lieutenant of the Tower. (76)   It was even possible to smuggle books to prisoners in gaol.   At his trial
in 1572 the duke of Norfolk was told by the attorney-general that although he had complained of his close keeping,
which prevented him having law books to help in the preparation of his defence, never the less it seemed very
likely that in fact he had acquired them. (77)

Visitors to imprisoned treason suspects were supposedly
forbidden during the pre-trial period, but although relatives and friends might be kept away not everyone was.
In Elizabeth's reign catholic priests were persistent and
occasionally successful in their efforts to visit co-
religionists.   George Haydock, a catholic priest, although languishing in an obscure cell in the Tower in
1582-3, was visited, according to one account, by another
priest who gained access to him by a stratagem.   In some
gaols officials seem to have turned a blind eye to the
visits of catholic priests or to have allowed them subject
to search on entry and departure. (78)   Visits by rela-

tives and friends, either with the gaoler present at the meeting or not, occurred only after trial or the admission of guilt.   Quite correctly they were taken by the public at large as a sign, like the awarding of such privileges as the 'liberty of the Tower' or 'liberty of the leads' (i.e. the roof), that the prisoner would soon be leaving either for his home or the scaffold. (79)

The closeness of their imprisonment seems to have had a disturbing effect on the spirits and mental faculties of quite a few suspect traitors, so several of them avowed at the time of their trials.   Sir Thomas More said his health had been impaired by his imprisonment and that he was fearful his memory would now fail him.   Sir Nicholas Throckmorton at his trial in 1554 told the court that his memory was 'much decayed since my grievous imprisonment with want of sleep and other disquietness'.   In January 1572 the duke of Norfolk told his judges that 'closeness in prison, evil rest, have much decayed my memory'. (80) Lesser men living under worse conditions may have suffered proportionately more, although not necessarily so since they were more accustomed to enduring discomfort.   There is a dearth of information on this subject but we may surmise that the lack of sleep and the occurrence of bodily ailments were the result of most places of confinement being without heat.

Quite often the lot of the suspect traitor in prison was made worse by his being deprived, either wholly or in part, of his food.   The intention was usually deliberate and the aim was to create a form of duress which would persuade him to divulge information.   At the end of December 1569 Sir William Cecil, in his instructions for the doing of justice on the northern rebels, ordered that the principal offenders should be put in gaol, put in fear, and pinched with lack of food and pains of imprisonment, so they should reveal those who had given them aid. (81) The Jesuit Alexander Briant, who was arrested and committed to the Counter at the end of April 1581, was believed by the government to know the whereabouts of Robert Persons and therefore instructions were given to the gaolers that he should be allowed to see no one and that he should be kept without food or drink.   Burghley, who mentioned the incident in a tract, admitted that Briant turned to eating 'clay out of the walls' and had 'gathered water out of the droppings of houses', but argued he had only his own wilful obstinacy to blame.   Briant was apparently deprived of sustenance for a mere two days and two nights, but a prisoner in the Tower where he was taken on 5 May stated that in the Counter Briant had in fact almost died of thirst. (82)   Ralph Sherwin, a seminary priest, after

being twice racked in the Tower in December 1580 was said
to have been kept without food for five days and nights,
presumably to gain information which the racking had
failed to elicit. (83)   These were not the only examples
of the use of starvation as a form of duress   but there
was no great number of such cases, the reason probably
being that it was impossible to prevent sustenance reach-
ing the prisoner from fellow captives or the gaoler's servants for more than a very short period.   The only suspect traitors who may have been killed by starvation were
nine intransigent Carthusian monks who were chained to
posts in Newgate on 29 May 1537.   A woman called Margaret
Clement seems to have brought them food for a time with
the prison keeper's connivance but was then stopped. (84)
Seven of the nine died in June, one in August and the
other in September.   What in this case the king intended
is not entirely clear, but since there is no evidence that
the deaths were hastened by disease he must bear full res-
ponsibility.

As with prisoners accused of other offences, the treason suspect was usually expected to pay the keeper of the
gaol for fires (when allowed), light, food, drink and bed-
ding, everything in fact beyond space in which to lie on
the gaol floor.   If he had any money in his possession on
arrest and if it was not immediately taken from him by his
captors then the gaoler soon found ways to mulct him of
it.   There might be a fee merely to enter the gaol or to
be allowed to live in a pleasanter area than custom dic-
tated, or even a better prison.   For example, we are told
that John Finch, a catholic layman, was kept in the Salford New Fleet until his money ran out in the autumn of
1583 and was then moved to the local house of correction. (85)   Payment was commonly made by prisoners for
being allowed freedom from irons, the keeper arguing that
he would be at risk if the suspect escaped, and we even
hear of monetary gifts when a prisoner was put into irons.
Perhaps the payment in this case was so that they should
be affixed in a manner which would not cause excessive
discomfort.   Generally speaking, unless authority had
decreed a special type of imprisonment, the suspect traitor could escape the worst of prison conditions by dis-
bursements of his own or his friends.   In the earlier
part of the sixteenth century there was little reference
to payments by friends, so presumably no one dared to risk
association with the prisoner in that way, but in Elizabeth's reign catholic laymen were sometimes willing to
come forward and pay to alleviate the rigours of prison
for their suspect co-religionists.   In 1581 they brought
alms to James Fenn, then a prisoner in the Marshalsea but

not known to the government as the seminary priest he was,
so that he might pass them on to fellow treason suspects
there. (86)   If such support was not forthcoming and the
prisoner had no money nor any possessions which the king
could draw money from, there was never the less little
chance he would be allowed to perish from starvation as
might someone else suspected of mere felony.   This was
because it was royal policy to make public examples of all
traitors and a death in gaol offered little in the way of
propaganda.   The suspect traitor would not of course be
allowed, as felons sometimes were to supplicate for alms
beyond the confines of the gaol.   Thus the crown had to
pay for the diet of such indigent prisoners as well as for
the special watch it kept over all suspected traitors.
Rates, whether paid by the prisoner or the king, seem to
have varied considerably according to rank and the place
of imprisonment.   Thus for the maintenance of Richard
Leigh, a seminary priest, the lieutenant of the Tower requested payment at Michaelmas 1588 at a rate of 13s. 4d.
a week plus the fees of a keeper at 5s. a week and with a
further 4s. a week for fuel. (87)   A list of recent prisoners in the Tower perhaps dating from 1537 shows clearly
the difference in rates of maintenance:   for Lord Darcy
and Bishop Fisher the payment authorized was 20s. a week,
for Sir Thomas More and Rhys ap Griffyths 10s. a week, for
various priors the same and for Carthusian monks 40d.
only.   The same document adds further that as for the
Lady Anne (Boleyn), Lady Rocheford, Sir Francis Weston,
Mark Smeaton and two others 'these persons had lands and
goods sufficient of their own', meaning the king did not
therefore have to pay from the royal coffers. (88)

Pre-trial imprisonment was used not only to force treason suspects to reveal their own illicit activities and
the names of confederates but occasionally towards the end
of the sixteenth century, through the assistance of ministers of the church of England, to try to change their
traitorous intentions by altering their religious opinions.   There were several examples of catholic priests
being taken forcibly to listen to the words of preachers.
According to the 'Diary of the Tower', in 1581, on 15 January, 26 January, 5 February and then every Sunday until
Pentecost following, all catholic prisoners there were
dragged to hear 'heretical sermons' in the church of St
Peter ad Vincula. (89)   How this treatment was in vogue
at that time is demonstrated by an example from Wrexham in
May of the same year.   A catholic layman, Richard White,
was carried to church in chains by six of the sheriff's
men and laid down under the pulpit.   White retaliated, it
is said, by so rattling his shackles that the preacher

could not be heard. (90)    There were also occasions when catholic prisoners were taken before a number of protestant clergy who intended by disputation to achieve, if not a change of belief, then the exposure in public of the treason behind the facade of religion.    Edmund Campion, in 1581, with Sherwin, Pound, Bosgrave and others was taken to the council chamber in the Tower and the Tower chapel on four different occasions to argue with the deans of St Paul's and Windsor and other ecclesiastical notables. (91)    In 1582 or 1583 George Haydock was visited in the Tower by a protestant minister who was keen to dispute with him and they became involved in a fierce argument over Queen Elizabeth's title as head of the English church. (92)    Other pressures of a non-physical kind there must have been, even if clear evidence of them is rather scanty.    One of the few cases which provides a reasonable amount of detail concerned the catholic layman John Finch.    He was arrested by the earl of Derby in December 1580 and threatened, so it was said, with torments and with reminders of the great misery his wife and family would suffer if he failed to reveal his misdeeds. When this had no effect his captors attempted to bribe him by promising preferment and material rewards. (93)    This must have been a common experience among suspect traitors of his sort.

    In view of the duress which gaol conditions imposed on treason suspects, the knowledge that they might be tortured and the unlikelihood of being acquitted when they came before a court, attempts to escape, and even to commit suicide, were surprisingly few.    Like other escape plans the scheme of the earl of Warwick and Perkin Warbeck in August 1499 to set fire to the gunpowder in the Tower, escape in the confusion, and sail overseas with the king's jewels and treasure, was probably known to the king soon after its conception. (94)    Three of the very few successful escapes were by Jesuits and seminary priests.    In October 1597 John Gerard, a Jesuit, and John Arden, a catholic gentleman, broke out of the Tower by swinging across a rope tied to the Tower wharf.    Edward Kenyon, a seminary priest, fled from the garden of Winchester gaol in 1599, but it was easily done since he was free of any irons and the under-keeper in whose charge he was placed had gone drinking in the town with two other prisoners. Kenyon was apparently the third person to break out of the gaol that day.    This lax surveillance was quite exceptional and there was a thorough investigation into it. The escape in August 1588 of the seminary priest William Watson from the London Bridewell was the work of Margaret Ward, who carried a piece of rope concealed under the

loaves and pies she was allowed to take into the prison
from time to time. (95)   The London gaols, with their
frequent searches which amounted to a count of the prisoners and an inspection of their irons, were able to retain virtually all suspect traitors committed to them.
Doubtless the penalties which a gaol keeper would suffer
if any escaped were well known and ensured constant vigi-
lance.   The development of circumstances within the gaol
which might assist prisoners to break out was viewed with
the greatest concern and the matter reported to higher
authority.   In the Tower, according to one Elizabethan
report, every prisoner had his own keeper.   From another
source we learn that in 1551 the 'warders' numbered no
fewer than sixty, which indicates how highly the government rated the close keeping of important treason suspects. (96)   Cases of prisoners attempting to kill themselves while in gaol awaiting trial were very few.   In
February 1554 William Thomas, sometime clerk of the council and a protestant confederate of Sir Thomas Wyatt, who
had plotted the assassination of Queen Mary, stabbed himself in the chest without inflicting a mortal wound;   on
21 June 1585, in the Tower, the earl of Northumberland
shot himself through the heart. (97)   These were the only
clear-cut cases of attempts at suicide.   John Finch, who
has been mentioned above, was reported as having in November 1583, while under guard, leapt into a river at Man-
chester crying 'Yesterday I damned my soul and today I
will destroy my body', but may only have done so as a
penance. (98)
     As rare for treason suspects as the successful escape
was the granting of bail.   Treason had been listed as an
irrepleviable charge in the statute of Westminster of 1275
(3 Edw. I c. 15), and since it was unmentioned in the acts
on bail 3 Hen. VII c. 3 and 1 & 2 Ph. & M. c. 13, remained
as such.   There were, never the less, at least three
occasions when bail was permitted to men thought to have
acted traitorously, although in two of the cases it may
not have been given with the king's approval.   In May
1534 Sir Edward Guildford wrote to Thomas Cromwell to tell
him that he had allowed bail to Robert Oldham, parish
priest of Pluckley, Kent, lately accused of seditious
speech, because he had named the pope inadvisedly in his
beads.   What Cromwell decided is not known, but, if there
was any supporting evidence, arrest was sure to have been
commanded.   In another case, which occurred in April
1559, the sheriff of Essex was told that the council
'found it strange' that John Harleston, late captain of
the castle of Ruysbank near Calais, who had been indicted
of treason for surrendering it to the French, was allowed

to go at liberty. (99)   He was to arrest him and bring him
to the Tower.   The third case involved two priests, Thomas
Abel and Dr Edward Powell.   There is some evidence that in
1540 they were allowed out of Newgate, or the Marshalsea
of the king's bench, on bail without Cromwell's permission
so as to solicit alms.   The keeper who had permitted this
was himself imprisoned for his generosity. (100)

Once the suspected traitor had been arrested and placed
in custody, there followed the examination or questioning.
This was a procedure which had developed in the later
Middle Ages but its origins are unknown.   It may have
started from the practices of the king's council, of the
ecclesiastical courts, of the labour legislation of 1349-
51, or even of the coroner's inquest.   There was questioning of principals in criminal cases by justices in the
early fourteenth century which was quite separate from the
arraignment. (101)   In the fifteenth century examination,
despite protest by the parliamentary commons, became increasingly popular through being specifically sanctioned
in a number of acts, the majority of which were connected
with deceitful commercial practices.   Here the examination was to be conducted by justices of the peace and the
results used for the most part in place of a presentment
by a grand jury.   By the sixteenth century a prisoner
arrested for felony and anyone who could give information
were examined by two or more justices of the peace who, as
long as the offence was not irrepleviable, then released
the suspect on bail and certified as much as was necessary
to prove the felony to the justices, the information
apparently to be used as evidence at the trial. (102)   In
treason cases procedure was different, since justices of
the peace normally had no authority over the crime and
there could be no bail.   The justice of the peace who
made the arrest would question the prisoner and quickly
investigate the circumstances as best he could;   then he
would report his catch to an important minister, the king
himself, or the council.   Articles, or interrogatories as
they were sometimes called, which were leading questions
the suspect must answer, were composed by king, minister
or council or all three for the purpose of the second and
more serious examination.   For example in 1533 Elizabeth
Barton was examined on interrogatories concocted by Cromwell, in 1587 Des Trappes, the French ambassador's secretary, on those of Burghley, and in January 1537 John
Hallam the Yorkshire rebel on those of the king and his
council. (103)   Unless one minister was exceptionally
powerful, or the prince particularly interested in the
case, the council was the usual drafter of treason interrogatories.   Although there were medieval precedents for

examination, there was no statute until 1555 which sanctioned its general use in cases involving serious criminal
offences, thus it is of considerable interest that in the
Tudor period prior to that date there was only one occasion reported when the process was subjected to serious
criticism.   This was in 1549 when Lord Seymour of Sudeley, who was suspected of a number of treasons, refused to
answer any interrogatories before he was actually arraigned.   The privy council therefore decided not to reveal
the interrogatories to him, intending no doubt he should
not know with what he was charged and therefore not be
able to prepare a defence before he was put on trial.(104)
In 1590 the essential legality of all examinations whether
for common law or conciliar purposes was challenged by
John Udall, suspected not of treason but felony, who argued convincingly that since the act 42 Edw. III c. 5 said
no man should be put to answer without presentment before
justices or things of record, or by due process, or writ
original, he need not answer. (105)   The point caused
some discomfort among the examiners, who were unable (even
the solicitor-general) to prove him wrong.

Those who were entrusted with the formal examination of
treason suspects were drawn from all ranks of royal servants, from chief minister to local gentry.   The prince
alone seems never to have taken part, although Henry IV
did so at the beginning of the fifteenth century.   The
choice of examiners depended largely on the degree of importance of the treason, the rank of the suspect, and
where he was being held.   When at Oxford early in 1538
two priests accused each other of traitorous words, the
mayor was appointed by Cromwell to take their examination. (106)   John Hallam and his confederates in custody
at Hull were examined on 24 January 1537 by a special commission comprising the mayor and five members of the local
gentry.   Sir Thomas More, on the other hand, was examined
on 7 May 1535 by the attorney-general, the solicitor-general, two civilians and Cromwell himself.   The choice of
examiner also reflected the nature of the suspected treason.   In August 1533 Elizabeth Barton was examined by
Archbishop Cranmer, although the examination was based on
interrogatories designed by Cromwell. (107)   Sir Francis
Walsingham, secretary of state, or an underling like Topcliffe or Young, among whose chief duties was the pursuit
of seminary priests and Jesuits, was usually present when
a suspect of that type was being interrogated.   There was
a short period in 1536-7, at the time of the rebellions in
Lincolnshire and the north, when the king looked to civil
lawyers to conduct examinations.   On 19 February 1536
Gerald Rede, a servant of Sir Thomas Percy, was examined

in the Tower before John Tregunwell, Richard Layton and
Thomas Legh, doctors of law, in the presence of John ap
Rice, notary.    In April of the subsequent year the rebel
leader Robert Aske was examined by Legh, Dr Petre and the
lieutenant of the Tower, also with ap Rice present.    Perhaps the civil lawyers were thought necessary because, as
we find stated in a case of February 1537 which concerned
William Morland, a monk of Louth Park, they were able to
examine 'more exactly'. (108)    This may have meant they
had more dexterity in sifting evidence and the depositions of witnesses.    It may also sometimes signify the
use of physical duress.    Certainly the presence of the
lieutenant of the Tower at the interrogation of Robert
Aske seems very sinister in the light of his inquisitorial
role later in the century.    From this time the examination of treason suspects seems to have become increasingly
the task of the privy council.    The act 33 Hen. VIII c.
23 specified that trial for treason could be where the
king wished it to be, as long as three members of the
council, before whom the prisoner was examined, vehemently
suspected his guilt.    By this reference and another in
the same act, which was to men 'virtually proven traitorous by exam and witness before the council', that body was
referred to in a treason statute for the first time;    yet
it showed that examination of treason suspects by it was
commonplace. (109)

To elicit information of any value from a suspected
traitor the examiners needed other information on which
to base their questions.    The less they knew about his
deeds, his intents and his associates beforehand, the
longer and harder it was to discover his guilt and any
future danger to the realm or the prince.    The questions
examiners put were therefore usually based on answers
given by previous examinees, or on any incriminating evidence found on the suspect's person or in his house.
Thus, in January 1587 Burghley apparently concocted the
interrogatories for the examination of Des Trappes out of
the confession of Michael Modye.    An order in January
1579 for the examination of Robert Blades specifically
asked for interrogatories to be made for him from his
papers. (110)    Depending on how much the government knew
already, and also on the size of the traitorous design,
the scope of any examination could be very wide or very
narrow.    The widest types of interrogatories seem to have
been offered to those who had taken part in open revolt.
The questions designed in 1537 to be put to Kendall, vicar
of Louth, are a good example. (111)    They asked where and
when he had received knowledge of the Lincolnshire insurrection and 'with whome, what facion, menys and days de-

vysed you to sett the sayde insurrection forward and by
whoys hayde, comforth or consell?'   The vicar was to be
asked what he had done day by day and why, who persuaded
the people to follow him, how they were mobilized, how
they were armed and fed, who aided and counselled them,
how they were kept under arms, how it was they dispersed
after the royal proclamation and who opposed their going
home.   When such general interrogatories were used, the
main aim of the government must have been simply to provide itself with information about the extent of the disaffection, the numbers of the rebels and the names of
their leaders.   Getting the vicar to incriminate himself,
though desirable, was probably of secondary importance.

A good example of an examination intended largely to
reveal the guilt of the suspect himself was that undergone
by John Finch at Lancaster in April 1584. (112)   He was
asked if he had ever been in any of the pope's seminaries
for Englishmen, where he had travelled, and by whom he had
been relieved, in the last six years, what priests he knew
and where they were, whether he had ever been conversant
with seminary priests or Jesuits, whether he was himself
reconciled, and whether he had reconciled others to the
Roman church, whether he had heard mass and how often if
he had, whether he thought Pius V's excommunication of
Elizabeth was lawful, whether he took Elizabeth to be the
lawful queen of the realm, whether the earls of Northumberland or Westmorland and their followers had risen in
insurrection lawfully or not, whether he took Elizabeth to
be head of the church, whether he had persuaded anyone to
forsake their allegiance to the queen, and whose part he
would take if the pope, or someone else by his authority,
should make war on the queen for the reforming of religion.   The more precise nature of these interrogatories
stemmed from a desire to get Finch to admit he had broken
a treason statute, for many of the questions were based on
specific acts.   Since these narrower questions were not
apparently derived from information provided by other suspects we may take it that techniques of examination had
advanced considerably since the earlier part of the century.

The reason for this development was twofold.   There
was first, the skill of the seminary priests and Jesuits
in offering evasive answers.   For example, the priest
John Mundyn, who was questioned by Sir Francis Walsingham
himself in February 1583, when asked what he thought of
Nicholas Sanders's landing in Ireland, said he knew nothing about it and that Sanders should answer to it, not
he.   When it was demanded of him if he accepted Elizabeth
as the true queen both de facto and de jure, he replied he

did not know what the terms meant. (113)   Most evasive of
all were the answers given to the 'bloody question', which
the government had devised as the simplest method of dis-
tinguishing traitors.   This question which had, as we
have seen, been anticipated as a test as early as the
reign of Henry IV, was usually expressed 'whose side would
you take if the bishop of Rome or other prince by his
authority should invade the realm with an army intending
to deprive the queen of her position'.   Even to this
question evasive answers were given.   Mundyn claimed he
was not theologian enough to give an answer.   John
Nutter, another seminary priest, gave as his reply that he
would act as became an honest and catholic priest.   Another priest, Edward Campion, at his third examination on
15 August 1588, when asked whether he would assist the
pope's forces or the queen's should they come into con-
flict, said he hoped the catholic Romish forces would prevail but refused to say which side he would join. (114)
The second reason why examinations became narrower in
their scope was that the answers were to be used not
merely as the basis for an indictment as had probably been
the practice in the fifteenth century, but offered also at
the trial as evidence.   Thomas Bowyer tells us how at the
arraignment of the priests Ralph Crockett, Edward James,
John Oven and Francis Edwardes in September 1588 their examinations were read out in court 'which proved sufficiently the matters conteyned in their several inditement-
ments', and Serjeant Yelverton at the trial in 1600 of Sir
Christopher Blunt, Sir John Davis and other confederates
of the earls of Essex and Southampton, told the court that
for 'particular proofs and plain convincing' there needed
only to be offered the things admitted in the examinations
of the accused. (115)
   Many a suspect traitor must have been given not one but
several examinations.   Sir Geoffrey Pole, tried for treason on 4 December 1538,was examined on the preceding 26
October and 2, 3, 5, 7, 9, 11, 12 November, there being
seven separate sets of questions in all.   One George
Barkworth, committed to Newgate on suspicion of being a
seminary priest at the end of the century, claimed he had
been examined on no fewer than nine occasions. (116)
Obviously one set of answers provided material for a second set of questions and so on.   Sometimes the later sets
must have been based on information newly received from
other sources, and there may also have been some intent of
wearing down the examinee's resistance.   Answers to interrogatories were not always given orally.   There is
considerable evidence that the suspect, if he could read
and write, was given the questions in writing and allowed

considerable time to think out and set down his answers.
A set of articles was left with the duke of Norfolk on 7
September 1571 so he could write down answers since he did
not want to give them orally.   John Finch was said to
have asked for, and been given, the articles in written
form, and been allowed pen and paper for his answers.
Robert Aske wrote at least some of the answers to his 107
interrogatories himself.   A variation of this method was
used with Lord Lawarr in December 1538. (117)   He was
examined by the council, which failed to find sufficient
grounds for putting him in the Tower of London.   Therefore he was commanded to write down everything he had already confessed or could call to mind.   Presumably the
intention was to test Lawarr's answers for consistency.
Whenever possible it was the practice to exact an oath to
tell the truth from the examinee before the examination
began.   On completion the answers would be read out by
the questioners who appended their signatures and the man
asked to sign it 'withought constraint or promise' as a
true record.   In this form the answers would make strong
evidence in court, particularly if one or more of the examiners was present in person to affirm on oath that the
replies had been given in the words set down. (118)

As the sixteenth century progressed it became more frequent, when interrogation failed to provide the information
required, to put the suspect traitor to some form of torture.   This might take the form of simply keeping the
person without food until details of confederates and
machinations were forthcoming, but usually it meant recourse to the rack or some other mechanical device for
causing great and immediate pain.   Deliberate torture on
the orders of the king was virtually unknown in medieval
England, being against the tenor of the common law, as
Fortescue in his 'De Laudibus Legum Anglie' emphatically
pointed out. (119)   There were three cases reported, it
is true, but they all occurred in the second half of the
fifteenth century and suggest that torture was employed
only under the king's prerogative.   Sir Edward Coke believed that torture had been introduced into England by
John Holland, first duke of Exeter and constable of the
Tower of London, in 1445-6 as part of a scheme concocted
in conjunction with William duke of Suffolk for bringing
the imperial civil law to England. (120)   There had, in
fact, been torture used before this but only once.   In
1310 Edward II approved its use against the Templars and,
since at that time there was no one competent in England
to inflict it properly, expert torturers had to be imported from abroad. (121)   This was really under the ecclesiastical law.   The cases in the later fifteenth century

occurred in the Yorkist period.    In 1468 a servant of Sir
Robert Whittingham called Cornelius 'Sutor', who was captured while carrying letters from Queen Margaret to Lan-
castrian sympathizers in England, was put in the Tower and
then persuaded to divulge certain secrets by being burned
in the feet.    One of those he incriminated, John Hawkins,
a servant of Lord Wenlock, was then also committed to the
Tower where, according to Stow, 'he was brought to the
brake called the duke of Exeter's daughter'. (122)    The
only other torture case recorded concerned Sir Henry Wyatt
who, according to his son, writing in the reign of Henry
VIII, was racked on the orders and in the presence of
Richard III. (123)

Henry VII may not have resorted to torture at all, but
if this was so he was unique among the Tudor monarchs.
The asseveration of Sir Thomas Smith, like Fortescue a
century before, that torture was not used in England must
be taken as meaning that it was not a general method of
investigating offences before trial, not that it was unknown.    Smith argued that torture was unacceptable because if a man was subsequently acquitted 'what amends can
be made him'.    He said that torture was futile, since any
man on arraignment could deny depositions made under it.
He also suggested that the information obtained by such
duress was valueless, as men would say anything to be released from the pain, and that a jury, out of pity, would
acquit anyone who had been so handled.    Thinking of
Roman law and the practices of continental Europe Smith
emphasized that under English law no confession was necessary for conviction.    The length of this writer's remarks
about torture suggests a genuine concern about the possibility of its more general use in England in the future,
as well as a personal knowledge of recent application. (124)

The evidence that torture was being administered at the
time when Smith wrote, and that furthermore it had been in
regular if not frequent use since the reign of Henry VIII,
is irrefutable.    Although there was no specific sanction
for torture in the common law, it secured mention in one
statute at least.    The act 27 Hen. VIII c. 4 against pirates, which dealt with the difficulty of providing witnesses to their misdeeds, made reference to torture in a
way which suggested that the government was well acquainted with its value.    The clearest evidence of its use,
however, is to be found in references among the minutes of
council proceedings, of which, according to Jardine, there
are forty-eight between November 1551 and April
1603, (125) and in the domestic state papers of Henry
VIII, particularly the papers of Thomas Cromwell.    From

these latter documents it is clear that torture was in
persistent use in England in the 1530s.   In July 1533
Cromwell suggested to Henry VIII that two grey friars
of Greenwich might be profitably 'examined by pains'.   In
the August Stephen Vaughan argued in a letter to Cromwell
that certain friars who had been arrested in London should
be put to the 'brake'. (126)   Although there followed no
great wave of torturings they seem to have occurred thereafter at fairly regular intervals, and for a variety of
suspected crimes, until Henry VIII's death.   Thomas Cromwell was a favourer, even perhaps the instigator, of examination under torture, but there can be little doubt
that the king entirely approved. (127)   The minutes of
the privy council do not, of course, tell the whole story,
for there were cases of torture being inflicted in provincial gaols and under other authority, but they suggest
that the periods when the government turned to torture
most frequently were in Mary's reign and from 1577 on-
wards.   Although these were times of strong religious
dissension the heightened emotionalism created cannot be
used as the only explanation for the employment of torture
in treason cases, since in Mary's reign many of the offences concerned were not treason but everyday felonies.
For the later period also the records of the privy council, while they demonstrate that torture was used mainly
on suspect traitors, clearly reveal that it was applied,
in addition, to those thought to have been guilty of lar-
ceny, robbery, murder, witchcraft and even riot. (128)
It was only in treason cases that torture was employed in
the fifteenth century, but as early as 1534 and perhaps
even a decade before that was extended to deal with other
crimes.   In March of that year it was reported that John
Bawde, a servant of the lieutenant of the Tower responsible for the escape therefrom of the wife of John Wolfe,
was to be racked, then hanged, for his felony. (129)
There were several other similar cases before the reign
ended.   No doubt the handling of treason started a trend
in regard to other crimes as well and it is important evidence that the study of sedition should not be divorced
from the study of the history of English criminal law as a
whole.
     To the question 'What was the means of applying torture
to suspect traitors?' there is a plentiful supply of information.   The most primitive method has already been
referred to above.   It was to 'pinch' with lack of food
and pains of imprisonment, the latter usually meaning incarceration in a particularly foul dungeon. (130)   In
1583, according to one catholic source, John Finch was put
into 'a deep, dark, cold and stinking dungeon' in the

middle of a bridge at Salford where 'they pinched him with extreme hunger, feeding him on fishdays with sodden beans only and upon other days with small pieces of beasts liver and they would be sure to give him little enough of both'. Alexander Briant, the Jesuit, developed such an extreme thirst in confinement that he 'assaied to take with his hatte the dropps of raine from the house eeves, but could not reach them'. (131)   This method of torture was not particularly popular with the government, no doubt because it took so long to produce results and might kill.   The rack, on the other hand, which was the most frequently used method of torture, had neither of these disadvantages.   There was only one rack in England and it was in the rack-house of the Tower of London, although exactly where this was is not known for sure. (132)   The intended victims were lodged in close confinement very near to the scene of the torturing.   Sometimes it was believed that the mere sight of the rack would be sufficient to elicit the wanted answers from the suspect.

In June 1570 the privy council commanded that John Felton should be delivered to the lieutenant of the Tower 'wherebye he may be brought to the place of torture and so put in feare thereof'.   Only if Felton continued in his refusal to confess was he to be actually laid on the rack and 'feele such smarte'.   Similarly, in November 1574 it was ordered that Humphrey Needham should be brought to the rack 'without stretching his bodye to th'intent he might discover the trothe'. (133)   According to a pamphlet incorporated in Holinshed, possibly the work of Thomas Norton in 1581, the rack was operated with great care, never in haste but slowly, with constant urging to the prisoner to tell the truth. (134)   There is no contemporary verbal description of how exactly the rack was constructed although there are what purport to be drawings of it.   Nor do we know precisely how the victim was laid upon it despite there being plenty of descriptions of how vigorous some rackings might be.   Thomas Norton, the rackmaster, was reckoned in 1581 to have pulled Alexander Briant 'one good foote longer than ever God made him'. According to Thomas Mountayne, Thomas Storynge in 1553 was laid on the rack and 'so pulde that he began to crak under the armepytes and yn other partes of his bodye'. (135)

Another method of torture was by means of an instrument usually referred to as 'the brake' but sometimes as the 'Scavenger's daughter' or 'Skevington's irons'.   It was devised according to an early seventeenth century report a century before by Sir William Skevington, nicknamed 'the gunner' when lieutenant of the Tower but more likely by his son Leonard when he held the same office later on.

This contraption apparently took the form of a broad hoop
of iron made in two parts joined together by a hinge.
The prisoner was made to kneel or to bend forward and the
hoop put under his legs, then fastened over his
back. (136)   Thomas Mountayne states that 'the body
standeth double the head being drawen towards the feete'.
Pain was thus inflicted by compression rather than stretching.   The torture was applied usually for periods of no
more than an hour and a half.   It tended to cause bleed-
ing from the nose and the mouth;  even, so some reports
had it, from the fingers and the feet.   It was in the
'Scavenger's daughter' that the unfortunate Thomas Storynge was put after a period on the rack, there to stay for
an entire night. (137)   Though less popular with the
authorities, there is no substantial evidence that the
brake was a form of torture merely supplementary to the
rack.   According to Matthias Tanner, the former inflicted
considerably more pain than the latter. (138)   Similarly
there was only one example of the brake and it was to be
found, according to a committee of the parliamentary commons which made an enquiry in 1604, in the dungeon in the
Tower called 'little ease'.   The committee members found
the place 'very loathsome and unclean' and not used for a
long time as a prison or other 'cleanly purpose'.   There
is in fact no reference to use of the brake subsequent to
the torturing of the seminary priest Luke Kirby and the
Jesuit Thomas Cottam in December 1581 and December 1582
respectively. (139)
From about 1590 a new form of torture was used with increasing frequency against suspect traitors.   This was
the 'manacles' or 'gauntlets'.   Apparently the victims
were hung up by the hands or wrists against a wall, their
feet being unable to touch the ground.   One description
of this mode of torture says that iron gauntlets were used
which could be contracted by means of a screw.   'They
served to compress the wrists and to suspend the prisoner
in the air from two distant points of a beam.   He was
placed on three pieces of wood, piled one on the other,
which when his hands had been made fast were successively
withdrawn from under his feet'. (140)   Richard Topcliffe,
the priest hunter, who was often commissioned to conduct
examinations using this form of torture, said sadistically
when anticipating the predicament of the Jesuit Robert
Southwell 'It will be as though he were dancing a trick or
a figure at trenchmore'.   John Gerard, a Jesuit who experienced the torture of the manacles said that at the
time he thought that 'all the blood in my body rushed up
into my hands ... and I was under the impression that the
blood actually burst forth from my fingers, my arms and

at the back of my hands.' This was a mistake however; the sensation was caused by the swelling of the flesh over the iron which bound it. (141)   The use of the manacles seems to have been reported for the first time in November 1583.   Richard White, a catholic, with four other prisoners was 'laid in the manacles' at Bewdley or Bridgenorth, the form of the duress being referred to as 'a kind of torture at the Council, not much inferior to the rack at the Tower of London'. (142)   'The Council' was the council of the marches and the manacles must have been its own invention.   How the manacles became the most common form of torture was explained in a letter by Richard Verstegan to Robert Persons in August 1592.   He claimed that because of popular complaint Topcliffe the previous year had been given authority to torment priests in his own house and that his choice of instrument was the manacles. (143)   The usual place for the operation of this mode of torture was not, however, the house of any examiner but the London Bridewell, and there was throughout the 1590s a steady stream of council injunctions for the removal thither of treason suspects and those suspected of other notorious crimes and their putting to torture. (144) Eventually, by 1597, the manacles made their appearance in the Tower of London as well.   The length of time which a prisoner, supposing he refused to give information, was left in the manacles was usually two or three hours at most.   John Gerard however was tortured for at least five hours one day and probably as long the next being told initially at least that he must be put to torture day after day as long as his life lasted until he gave the information demanded.   Robert Southwell was left hanging by his hands while Topcliffe, who had been examining him, went off about his other business.   In time Southwell became unconscious and Topcliffe had to be called back by a servant.   The most suffering was endured by the Jesuit Christopher Bayles who was allowed to hang for a whole 24 hours.   Southwell, who was tortured in this way on seemingly ten different occasions, said at his trial he would much have preferred to endure ten executions. (145)

The rack, the brake and the manacles were the standard methods of torture but other, more ad hoc, methods were used as well if only infrequently.   Thomas Bell, a protestant minister who was converted to catholicism but became an informer against his new co-religionists, was hung upside-down for three days. (146)   In July 1543 the duke of Suffolk and the bishop of Durham wrote to the council to report that to loosen the tongues of William Brewer and William Shepherdson, servants of Roland Walle, they had fitted them with new shoes full of grease and set them in stocks close to a hot fire. (147)   Margaret Ward, who in August 1588 smuggled a rope into a London prison so as to effect the escape of the seminary priest William Watson, was said to have been 'flogged and hung up by the wrists, the tips of her toes only touching the ground, for so long a time that she was crippled and paralysed'.   The intent was apparently to ascertain who had assisted her in her plan. (148)   Tortures such as these were never commanded by the prince or his council in the specific form which they actually took.   Their instructions usually referred to examination by means of the rack, brake or manacles, but sometimes because the proper apparatus was unavailable it was left to the discretion of the examiners.

Those who were commissioned to examine suspect traitors with the power, in case of stubborness, to resort to torture were a select band.   There was no supposition by the government that any person who had handled the more formal aspects of interrogation should be entrusted with the more serious work of torture, and we may assume that both willingness and the requisite knowledge were at a premium. In the later years of Elizabeth the same few men were called on repeatedly.   A large percentage of the torturing took place in the Tower and therefore it was natural that the constable of the Tower in the person of his lieutenant should always be present on those occasions. (149) This had also been very much the case in Henry VIII's time.   In few cases did the lieutenant alone supervise the application of torture. (150)   Appointed to assist him were men who in their careers seem to have acquired a special knowledge of examining by or by threat of torture. They were civilians like Dr John Hammond or diplomats with some legal training like Robert Beale, Thomas Randolph and Thomas Bodley, who may have acquired knowledge about torturing in their missions abroad.   Towards the end of the sixteenth century the queen's legal servants, in the persons of the attorney-general and solicitor-general, were frequently in attendance, as was the clerk of the privy council and the recorder of London, although to find judges of the two benches there was uncommon. (151)   Two men who fell into none of these categories yet who were primarily responsible for torturing suspect seminary priests and Jesuits were Thomas Norton and Richard Topcliffe.   If the others undertook the task as an onerous burden these two took a certain delight in their work. Norton, a common lawyer of puritan leanings and a frequent member of the house of commons, whom Camden described as 'of surpassing wisedome, remarkable industry and dexterity, singular piety and approved fidelity to his Prince and Country', was official censor of Elizabeth's catholic subjects and known in some quarters as 'Mr. Norton the rackmaster'.   In a letter to Walsingham he took exception to a statement by the author of 'a seditious book' that Alexander Briant at his racking had been preserved from feeling pain, claiming that of all those racked  no one had made 'so grevous complaining and showed so open signes of peine as he'. (152)   However, he disclaimed the major part of the credit, pointing out that he was not in fact the rackmaster but the meanest of those in the commission, being like a clerk under the directions of the lieutenant of the Tower.   The enthusiasm for the work of examining and torturing suspect priests on the part of Richard Top-cliffe was well known and his eager anticipation of the forthcoming sufferings of Robert Southwell has already been not ced.   Verstegan, in his letter of 3 August 1592 to Robert Persons, wrote of Topcliffe that his 'inhuman cruelty is so great as he will not spare to extend any torture whatsoever'.   Southwell, referring in a letter to the putting of suspects in the manacles wrote that 'Unum istud purgatorium timemus omnes, in quo illi Catholicorum carnifices Topcliffus et Youngus omnem habent cruciandi libertatem'. (153)   Topcliffe's zeal was so excessive that complaints about it to the privy council caused Burghley to imprison him in gaol for a period on the grounds that he had exceeded the powers given him by war-rant.   In the 1590s Topcliffe's pre-eminence in examining by torture was challenged by Richard Young  about whom there was no comparable outcry.

   The effect of the torture in its various forms is an issue of considerable importance.   There can be little doubt that at the moment of application the pain was very great, the testimony of those tortured shows that, and the manacles seem to have created more than the rack or the brake.   Other evidence shows the rack and the manacles were able to cause serious injury and even death.   Thomas Pormort, a seminary priest, was racked in 1591 so severely that 'his body was all disjointed and his belly broken'. According to the Jesuit Henry Walpole, James Atkinson in 1595 was kept so long in the manacles that 'he was at last taken away for dead after many hours suffering and, in effect, died within two hours'. (154)   Anne Askew, tor-tured in 1546 as a heresy suspect, had to be carried to her execution at Smithfield in a chair as she had been crippled by the rack. (155)   Yet such torturing seems to have been unusual in its severity.   The official explana-tion about torture in the pamphlet 'A Declaration of the Favourable Dealing of Hir Maiesties Commissioners appoin-ted for the Examination of Certeine Traitors' apparently compiled to rebut certain slanders then current, claimed

that the 'formes of torture in their severitie or rigour
of execution, have not beene such and in such maner performed as the slanderers have maliciously published'.   It
stated that Edmund Campion

> before the conference had with him by learned men in
> the Tower wherein he was charitably used was never so
> racked but that he was presentlie able to walke, and
> to write and did presentlie write and subscribe all his
> confessions.

Francis Throckmorton's racking was explained in similar
terms.   He was put on the rack, so it was said,

> and somewhat pinched although not much:  for at the end
> of three daies following he had recovered himselfe and
> was in as good plight as before the time of his rack-
> ing:  which if it had then or anie other time been
> ministred unto him with that violence that he and his
> favourers have indevoured slanderouslie to give out,
> the signes thereof would have appeared upon his lims
> for many yeares. (156)

The effect of the rack seems in some cases to have been a
temporary paralysis of the arms and legs.   Thomas Sherwood, a catholic layman, tortured in December 1577 was
said to have lost the use of his limbs.   Of Edmund Campion at his trial Dr Allen wrote that his arms were so be-
numbed from his rackings that he could not hold up his
hands on arraignment 'as custome is in such cases'.
Allen also tells us that Alexander Briant, the day after a
racking, had 'his senses dead and his blood congealed (for
this is the effect of the racking)'. (157)   How the body
of the tortured person was affected over a longer period
of time is difficult to determine, since it was a maxim of
the crown that only those known, although not yet proven,
to be guilty should be tortured.   Almost all were subsequently executed and usually within days rather than weeks
of their last torturing.

How successful was torture in obtaining the desired information?   Certainly it did not persuade every examinee
to reveal his secrets.   Some were confident they would
never confess anything.   The soldier Captain Edmund Yorke
was said to have boasted that he wondered at any man's
wronging of his friends for a little torture and that he
was armed to face such pain.   Edmund Campion wrote that
he would never disclose any secrets of the catholic gentlemen in whose houses he had been entertained 'come rack
or rope'. (158)   This bravado was not common.   More frequent was the attitude of Richard Williams who in August
1594 said he would die rather than betray his friends but
if he did reveal anything while on the rack he would deny
it all later.   The position taken by Dr Roger Lopez was

also fairly typical.   At his trial in 1594 he admitted
to confessing certain incriminating facts at his examination but said he had invented them in order to escape
being racked. (159)   In fact, few of those actually tortured managed to withold the information their examiners
sought.   If they refused to give it during one session on
the rack or in the manacles then there would be others.
By their own reckoning Robert Southwell was tortured ten
times and Henry Walpole, another Jesuit, fourteen. (160)
It is very difficult to be certain that a victim of torture successfully witheld the information which was demanded of him, particularly as from 1583 the crown was keen
to announce in court that the accused had never been tortured, but a number of Jesuits, seminary priests, and
catholic laity like Alexander Briant, Southwell, John
Gerard and Thomas Sherwood, may have been able to do so.
Some, like Edmund Campion, who gave the names of those who
had sheltered him but not their secrets confessed to him,
probably divulged a number of details without revealing
everything that the examiners wished to learn.   Of Francis Throckmorton, Holinshed states 'the second time he was
put to the racke, before he was strained up to any purpose
he yeelded to confesse any thing he knew ...'. (161)
Total revelation of this type must have been by far the
commonest outcome of any torture session.

   To defend or excuse the torture practices outlined
above is well-nigh impossible, yet there were certain features which must be borne in mind.   First, as Thomas
Norton put it,

> none was put to the rack that was not first by manifest
> mater knowen to the Counsel to be gylty of treasons, so
> that it was well assured aforehand that there was no
> innocent tormented.   Also none was' tormented to know
> whether he were gylty or no but for the Queen's safe-
> tie to disclose the maner of the treason and the com-
> plices. (162)

Here there was something of the medieval idea that a misdeed, by being notoriously known, allowed the normal
judicial procedures to be altered, a notion which seems to
have found some reinforcement in the act 33 Hen. VIII c.
23, which allowed those vehemently suspected by three members of the council of treason or murder to be tried where
the king wished.   Norton also pointed out that no man was
tortured for religious matters, that is to say over points
of doctrine or faith, but only concerning plots against
the queen or attempts to alter by force those laws of the
realm which dealt with religion.   In addition, according
to a tract included by Holinshed, no one was tortured unless first he had said he would not tell the truth al-

though the queen commanded him to. (163)    If anyone being
examined said he did not know, or could not remember, and
would 'so affirme in such maner as christians among christians are beleeved' this was accepted so long as there was
no evidence suggesting the contrary.

That these were in fact the conditions which governed
the use of torture seems very likely.    In the later sixteenth century at least there was no torture without careful consideration of each particular case by the prince
and his immediate advisers.    As Norton said, no one was
put to the rack 'but by warrant of six of the most honorable of Counsel' and this of course was why the common
lawyers could accept the practice.    It was not an inte-
gral part of their law but a special procedure operated
under the prerogative of the prince and on his orders or
those of his ministers. (164)    What usually persuaded
the government to resort to torture was its realization
that the case was one particularly dangerous to the commonwealth.    Naturally enough most traitorous plots fell
into this category but so also might a very dangerous riot
or a most heinous murder or theft.    The other element
common to cases where torture was authorized was governmental recognition that as well as the suspects already
taken there were other persons involved whose names and
locations were not known but which must be discovered with
the utmost celerity.

There were certain types of treason suspects who were
always safe from being put to torture.    These were the
various classes of the nobility.    As William Shelley, a
servant of the earl of Northumberland, told his master by
letter,

> the earl in respect of his nobility was not in danger
> to be dealt withal in such sort as he the said Shelley
> was like to be, being put a private gentleman and
> therefore to be used with all extremity to be made to
> confess the truth. (165)

Despite the general obnoxiousness of torture and the unfair way one class was protected from it there was little
opposition to it among the population as a whole, except
on two occasions.    The rackings with which Norton was associated gave rise to complaints early in 1582, and he was
commanded to keep to his own house for a time.    As we
have already seen, at some point before August 1592 Topcliffe was given authority to torture suspect priests in
his own house because 'the often exercise of the rack in
the Tower was so odious and so much spoken of of the
people'. (166)    According to Camden, Queen Elizabeth in
1584 gave orders for a cessation of the execution of seminary priests and Jesuits, the exiling of seventy of them

instead, and commanded there should be no more torture by
examiners. (167)   Such periods when torture was outlawed
were of short duration, as the crown soon discovered how
much more difficult it was to elicit information without
it.   When Elizabeth died torture was as firmly established as it ever had been.

In the second half of the sixteenth century the use of
torture was frequent not only in investigating suspected
treason but also in gaining information about other serious forms of crime, like murder.   There can be little
doubt that the use of the rack, at least, spread to the
handling of these from its use in the field of treason.
Later it seems to have gained something in sophistication
and obnoxiousness from its new use.   Thus in April 1573
instructions were given that George Brown, a suspected
murderer, should be examined and tortured on the rack, if
necessary with the brethren and friends of the murdered
man present and assisting in putting the interrogatories. (168)   During Mary's reign permission was given for
the use of torture against suspect witches, robbers, horse
thieves and even mere rioters.   This utilization in
crimes less than treason was still apparent at the end of
the century and the crown was suspected almost automatically of using it in almost any criminal case of importance.   This was reflected in the way at trials the
king's lawyers, whenever possible, emphasized that those
arraigned had confessed voluntarily, without use of violence.

As a subject, torture has suffered from almost total
neglect in recent study of the Tudor period.   Usually
mention of it has been avoided altogether or references
have been of the matter-of-fact variety implying that it
was an institution inherited from the past and merely continued.   As we have seen, the latter view is largely
erroneous for, although there were one or two medieval
precedents and even the odd example in the early years of
Henry VIII, there was no established system of torture as
we find existing after the beginning of the English Reformation.   Thomas Cromwell, seemingly the first major user,
may have acquired his belief in the value of torture from
his travels abroad in his earlier years or his service
under Wolsey.   Very likely examination of suspects became
such a vital weapon in Cromwell's battle against traitorous activities because it was far more successful than of
yore;   this success was made possible by the use or the
threat of torture.   Once the government acquired the reputation for being willing to use the rack, brake or manacles on those who refused to provide information, suspects
probably hastened to unburden themselves of secrets that

mere imprisonment, even of an oppressive kind, had never persuaded them to divulge before.   Torture did not always succeed;  there were some notable refusals to yield, nearly all by persons who considered that the tenets of their religious faith were at stake.   But its general success meant that the crown, through the extended use of examination, had acquired a dominance over the process of prosecution which it had never possessed before.   There can be little doubt that the old processes of the common law were thereby dealt a considerable blow, although the crown was usually careful to disguise the fact by ensuring that those examinations actually alleged in court as evidence were not the ones gained by torture, although they were often preceded by others which had.

The king's council, which had such an important role to play in the definition of treason, was often entrusted in addition with the crucial task of directing and co-ordinating the investigation of suspect traitors.   Its power in this field was at times virtually unlimited.   When a traitorous deed was reported to a justice of the peace it was common for him, because of the limited nature of his commission, to tell the council or, what was virtually the same thing, tell one of the prince's chief ministers. Sometimes the informant went not to a justice of the peace, but directly to the council.   If the matter reported seemed important, and treason by its nature usually did so, the council would summon the informer or accuser to appear before it, or command the justice or other officials to investigate further, very possibly supplying the interrogatories for the examination. (169)   If there was to be torture, then the council would warrant it. When a report arrived which revealed the suspect treason as a widespread or well-organized plot or involving men of high station, the council might depute some of its own members to undertake such a task.   On 23 February 1549 all the privy council, except the archbishop of Canterbury and the speaker of the house of commons, went to the Tower to examine Lord Seymour of Sudley.   The next year there was an example of the council going a step further and acting as if it were a grand jury.   The accused was the duke of Somerset. (170)   Instead of simply being examined by council, he was charged by the councillors, so we are told, with a number of misdemeanours and high treasons set down in twenty-nine articles.   This was a time when, because the king was not yet of mature years, the power of the council, or of some of its members at least, was very great.   The incident should remind us of the difficulty of defining the role of council in regard to treason in exact terms, for it was a body whose competence and authority varied in this period virtually year by year.

One most important task of the council was to decide
who should try each treason suspect.   Justices of the
peace had no power of trial, but they could enquire into
certain traitorous misdeeds and receive the relevant indictments.   According to William Lambarde, these powers
extended to 'the treasons of defending by word, writing or
deed for a third time the jurisdiction of a foreign prince
(1 Eliz. c. 1), putting into use papal bulls or giving or
receiving absolution thereunder (13 Eliz. c. 2) and attempting to absolve or withdraw English subjects from
their natural obedience (23 Eliz. c. 1).'   The justices
of the peace also had the task, says Lambarde, of keeping
the statute 3 Hen. V cc. 6 and 7, which made treason out
of the clipping, washing and filing of coins. (171)   In
fact they were given power only to make enquiries and
begin judicial process, since trial for the counterfeiting
of coins was usually handled by the justices of assize or
gaol delivery.

High treason was generally tried before a commission of
oyer and terminer.   This commission had been the principal judicial instrument to deal with treason in the fourteenth and fifteenth centuries.   In minor cases justices
of the peace might be appointed to serve on such a commission but usually the places were taken by magnates and men
high in the royal service.   On occasion an oyer and terminer commission might appear to be nothing less than the
council acting in a judicial capacity.   The number of
those appointed to any one commission could be as many as
thirty to forty.   Frequently the commissioners numbered
between a dozen and a score but there might be as few as
three. (172)   Sometimes four or five were named in the
commission as being members of the quorum, that is to say
of an inner group whose presence was essential when sessions were held.   The reason for this device was to ensure there should be available in court proper legal expertise and sufficient knowledge about the background to
the case, the members of the quorum being often judges of
the two benches, notable royal lawyers, and even prominent
ministers.   Thus for the trial of Sir Thomas More there
were named in addition to six judges the lord chancellor
(Sir Thomas Audley) and Thomas Cromwell. (173)

It was common for professional judges and serjeants at
law to be in a minority on any oyer and terminer commission appointed to deal with treason.   They might form a
majority of any quorum which was named, but such shorter
lists appeared less and less as the sixteenth century progressed, when the formula at the end of the commission was
simply to the effect that the trial could be held by any
four or five of the commissioners.   There is the possi-

bility that the role of the judges was lessened, because their legal expertise made them critical of the crown's tactics in investigation and prosecution and much less amenable to the mixture of legal argument and political propaganda propounded by the attorney-general and the solicitor-general than were the magnates and the holders of non-legal offices who sat with them.   The only treason trials where professional judges or law officers of the crown were in a majority among the commissioners were those involving peers of the realm and held before the lord high steward.   On such occasions their influence and opinion was, perhaps, considered to be counterbalanced by the jury of twenty-four peers.   At the arraignment of William Davison, secretary of state, on 28 March 1587, Chief Justice Wray, describing the work of himself and his fellows of the queen's bench, said 'in the Term we hear matters of Treason by reason of our office;  and out of the term by Commission of Oyer and Terminer associate with others'. (174)   From this we should expect to find that all the important state trials were held out of the legal term and before oyer and terminer commissions.   In fact some were held during the term although before special commissions and not in the king's bench.   The prince was obviously determined to have both the most favourable court and a time which suited himself.

The choosing of the members of any oyer and terminer commission which was to deal with important treason must have been done, as long as he was interested in the case, by the king himself.   When he was not interested then a chief minister, or failing that the council, would decide. We may fairly surmise that, despite the unpleasantness of the task because the lives and possessions of friends and enemies were often at stake, there must have been much political jockeying among men of substance to secure appointment.   Unequivocal information about the mode of selecting special commissioners in treason cases comes unfortunately in only a single instance.   To choose the fourteen commissioners who were to examine and give judgment on Mary, Queen of Scots, a complicated electoral process was followed.   Two lesser members of the privy council were to name three lords of privy council, two of the privy council lords to name three other lords, 'two of the elder barons to name the three earls, two of the Privy earls to name the three barons'. (175)   How far this copied the selection of commissioners for other state trials is difficult to determine but since the commission's powers were unique, it is quite likely that the appointment procedure was hardly based on precedent at all.   No person arraigned for treason in this period

seems to have challenged any of the judges appointed to
try him, and this despite several known examples of notorious enemies of the accused serving as commissioners.
The relative authority of the various members of any oyer
and terminer commission is another problem yet to be
solved.   There must always have been a chief commissioner
who acted as chairman of the sessions.   To him no doubt
went the king's instructions about the necessity of securing a conviction and how the case should be handled,
and it was his task to apprise the other judges of the
same. (176)   What powers he had over his fellows we do
not know, but that he might possess some is suggested by
the terms of the exceptional commission set up to examine
and sentence Mary, Queen of Scots.   This stated, as if in
distinction from the usual practice, that 'all men's
voices are free and of equal power'. (177)

Although the king, as we noticed at the outset of this
chapter, would probably hear first of traitorous conspiracy from the mouths of informers, the only ways in which
accusations of treason could be made before a court were
by appeal or indictment.   Appeal, that is to say the formal accusation originally by spoken word, but always in
great detail, by one man or woman of one or several
others, had been in decline for a long while, although
there were sufficient examples in the fifteenth century to
show it had not been forgotten.   It involved the taking
of sureties from the appellor, when he first made the
charge, to prosecute his appeal at a later date;   on his
part there was an offer to prove the veracity of the accusation by armed combat.   There was an instance of such
trial by battle in Ireland as late as 1583.   In the later
Middle Ages appeals were most commonly made by approvers,
men already indicted of treason who had decided while in
gaol to confess the offence and accuse their accomplices.
Theoretically the reward for an approver for an appeal
which was successful (whether the trial was by jury or
battle) was either prison for life or having to leave the
realm. (178)   In practice the successful appellor might
receive a pardon.   There are no examples in the sixteenth
century of imprisoned treason suspects approving (or
'appeaching' as it was often called) their fellow conspirators as traitors in the old manner, although there were
cases where suspect felons accused their confederates of
felony.   Thus in 1583, as Holinshed tells us, one Ditch,
a notable horse stealer, was 'nineteen times indicted
whereof he confessed 18' between the time of his apprehension and his trial, and 'appeached manie for stealing of
horses'. (179)   Ten were convicted and hanged and Ditch,
no doubt on this account, escaped the gallows.

There were, of course, many occasions when suspect
traitors held in prison, or being examined, accused others
of the very crimes imputed to themselves.   What happened
then was that the accusation was used as interrogatories
in the examination of the new suspects or, if the original
suspect had not yet been indicted at the time of his revelations, produced in court as evidence.   If the accuser
already stood indicted then those arraigned would perhaps
object to such a deposition, yet usually they gained
little profit from the move.   The accuser, or informer as
we should call him, if there was found to be nothing true
in his charges, might be tried like any medieval approver
would have been for the offence he tried to blame on
others. (180)   From the later fourteenth century informing
about certain categories of offences though not treason
was positively encouraged by the government, for example
in the matter of illegal retaining and granting of live-
ries, riot, and the contravention of economic regulations.
Those who informed about the latter were called 'promo-
ters', and were allowed a proportion of any convicted person's possessions, and laws were passed setting out the
method of procedure they must adopt and the penalties for
its contravention.   There was also provision for the use
of informers in the act of the six articles (31 Hen. VIII
c. 14), which gave power to bishops and their officers to
deal with offences mentioned in the act by taking informations and accusations by oaths and depositions of two able
and lawful persons as well as enquiring by the oaths of
twelve men, that is to say by means of a grand jury.
This act formalized the way in which information was to be
offered under it, by decreeing that the informer must include the name, surname and dwelling place of the offender, as well as the day, year, place and county where the
crime was committed.   Although there were no similar
statutory provisions to deal with treason, and indeed the
final form of the act of 1534 omitted a draft clause which
was to sanction and reward informing, the manner in which
the relevant indictments were compiled in the sixteenth
century showed an increased reliance on informers drawn
from the general public, together with the development of
standardized procedures for their acquainting grand juries
with their knowledge. (181)
    Nearly all treason trials were preceded by the drawing
of an indictment.   This had been approved by a grand jury
which passed it on to the justices for the purposes of the
trial.   It was not, however, solely the handiwork of the
jury, although the jurors might well have had a say in its
composition.   Usually what happened was that the king or
his council heard that treason had been committed, or was

likely to be, and that particular persons and districts
were involved.   This information they turned into interrogatories which were used in the further examination of
those suspected.   If, when these were returned, it seemed
that the suspects were so incriminated that they might be
tried with profit, then one or several grand juries were
appointed to provide the indictments.   Of course, in many
cases the report was not thought to justify indictment or
trial and it has been argued in regard to the years 1532-
40 that the total of treason reports which were probably
dropped amounted to 223 out of 883.   Names of suspects
and details of misbehaviour were acquired by grand jurors
in a variety of ways.   Sometimes the king's 'learned
counsel', that is to say the royal legal advisers, sent
to the grand juries bills they had compiled themselves
which described the offences, the culprits and the particular laws broken.   This was done in a way which was so
comprehensive and already so close to the form of an
actual indictment that the jurors needed only to approve
and send them on to the justices. (182)   Sometimes the
bill of accusation was put forward also on the crown's behalf but by someone of less eminence and less skilled in
legal form.   These types of indictment can be easily dis-
tinguished in the legal records since they usually com-
mence with the words 'inquiratur pro rege'.   There was
nothing particularly novel in this practice of prompting
on the part of the king, for examples are plentiful in
fifteenth-century records. (183)   Quite obviously with
certain crimes, such as the committing of treason abroad,
it was the only way in which a jury could obtain the necessary information.   Where the members of the grand jury
had played a more substantial role in its composition the
final form of the indictment usually began with the words
'juratores presentant pro domino rege'. (184)   In this
case the jurors were responding to a general charge by the
court that they should announce the names of those they
suspected of a general category of crime, in this instance
treason.   However, we should be ingenuous if we believed
that until that moment the jurors had no knowledge of what
they were likely to be asked in the courtroom.   The accusations embodied in this type of indictment may have
come largely from the jurors' own knowledge about the
crime and its perpetrators or from the knowledge of the
justices there to hold the trial.   (185)   More commonly,
however, the members of grand juries set themselves to receive accusations from the people of the locality.

What the jurors preferred increasingly to hear was not
mere common report, 'noise in the country', or notoriety
as it was sometimes called, but charges by those who had

definite knowledge of events through their proximity to
the traitorous persons or plot - we should call them witnesses.   According to Sir Thomas Smith, writing early in
Elizabeth's reign, any man who had a charge to make had to
put in a bill which went first to the justices 'to see if
it be conceived in forme of law'.   If it was thought to
be drafted in an acceptable manner, the complainant then
delivered it to the grand jury 'and after being sworn ...
declareth to them what he can for the profe of it'. (186)
To make an indictment without having such accuser-witnesses, who would affirm their charges with an oath, had
become, even by 1537, a practice which could lead to
official investigation. (187)   The statutes on treason
soon made similar demands.   By the first Edwardian treason act (1 Edw. VI c. 12) there was to be no indictment
for treason except on the accusation of two lawful and
sufficient witnesses or on the suspect's own confession.
This was confirmed and clarified at a meeting of judges
and royal lawyers at Serjeants' Inn in October 1556. (188)
In cases of treason which came within a sixteenth century
statute, although not within the act of 1352, two accusers
or  *estes* were to be at the indictment.   When the charges
came from the king and his council they would often be
accompanied by a copy of the suspect's examination, or his
formal confession if there was one, or the examinations or
confessions of accomplices.   These seem to have been
accepted by the grand juries as the equivalent of the testimony of two witnesses, although no doubt they had to
come from at least two persons. (189)   By the end of the
sixteenth century the drawing of treason indictments was
subject to another rule as well.   It concerned the time
which had elapsed since the misdeed was committed.   The
act 1 Eliz. c. 5, which made it a traitorous offence to
compass for a second time to deprive the queen and her
heirs of her titles and dominions or destroy or depose
her, contained a provision that, if the deed had been perpetrated by words, prosecution, and therefore, no doubt,
the compilation of the indictment, must occur within six
months of the offence.   The treason act of 1571 (13 Eliz.
c. 1), which made immediate treason out of the misdeeds
quoted in the act 1 Eliz. c. 5 as traitorous only on being
committed a second time, said more clearly that those who
offended against it must be indicted within six months of
the committing of the misdeed if it occurred within the
realm, or within a year if it was perpetrated abroad.
    Indicting juries usually contained twelve jurors, al-
though there could on occasion be twice as many.   They
were all supposed to be men of substance and, in practice,
a fair proportion had held offices in local government.

There was no bar on their being related to the accused and some definitely were. (190)   There was no property qualification, but clergy, women and aliens were excluded. Throughout the Middle Ages the position had been elective, jurors being chosen by two men nominated in each hundred or borough by the bailiffs.   In the sixteenth century, when the government felt it to be necessary, it did not hesitate to appoint the jurors itself. (191)   It might even go further.   The duke of Norfolk in May 1537 informed Henry VIII that he had just appointed two grand juries at York, one of twenty gentlemen and the other of twenty-one, and had then declared his mind to them.   This probably meant telling them that since he and the king believed in the veracity of the informations or bills of indictment before them, they should also.   In general, when the issue was treason there was little reluctance to find the accusations *billa vera* and thus to indict, even if during Cromwell's ascendancy there were a number of occasions when the government met with a refusal to indict in cases of seditious words and popular insurrection. (192) An important question, and one to which we have no good answer, is whether the accused was supposed to appear before the grand jury when the indictment was being compiled and, if he did, whether he was allowed to say anything.   There was one case where *billa vera* was found and a note made that the accused was absent. (193)   However, there were also cases where men complained at their trials that they had been unable to prepare a defence since they had no prior knowledge of what the charges against them were;   this presumably means they had never gone before a grand jury.

Treason indictments were always compiled with care, nearly always being preceded by careful investigation of the crime reported;   often, as we have seen, they originated with the legal advisers of the king. (194)   Sometimes even the opinion of the professional judges was solicited. With very few exceptions the treasons named were treason according to the statutes and common law as then interpreted.   Sometimes there was a reference in the indictment to the statute on which the charge was based, (195) but where there was not there was no claiming as treason offences which were not so.   There was nothing similar to the classifying as treason of mere felonious and riotous behaviour, as happened after the revolt of 1381. (196) The insertion of the charge of compassing to levy war and to deprive the prince of his crown in the indictment of Sir Nicholas Throckmorton seems to have come about through genuine confusion caused by recent changes in the law. (197)   A major reason for this studied legality was

that the process of accusation, although not entirely in
the king's hands since there was at this time no public
prosecutor, was none the less controlled precisely.

Concerning Tudor treason trials it has been suggested
on several occasions that the crown fabricated much of the
evidence against the accused.   In fact the essential
accuracy of the vast majority of descriptions of traitorous crimes contained in the indictments cannot be denied.
That is not to say there were not occasions when the dates
of the misdeeds quoted were given erroneously.   For example, the dates supplied for the departure of certain
English priests from the seminary of Rheims in 1582 were
quite inaccurate.   John Mundyn, William Tedder, John
Nutter and Samuel Conyers were said to have departed on
1 October of that year, but the Douai diaries show that
Mundyn left on 6 August, Tedder on 13 November and the two
last on 24 November.   For at least nine other priests who
were similarly arraigned for treason like discrepancies
can be shown. (198)   However, there is no validity in the
argument that as the dates in the indictment were wrong
therefore the actions accounted traitorous were never committed.   Doubtless the dates were erroneous because the
events occurred not in England but in France and information on such details was hard to come by.   All indictments had to give the date and place of the offence even
if, when the same sort of crime was committed by the same
party more than once, the indictment could contain the
formula 'and in other places and on other days before and
after'.

In the courtroom, as we shall see, considerable emphasis was placed on declaring the traitor's offences to the
world for purposes of political propaganda, but even if
the crown and the jurors used every piece of accusatory
material available in order to impress the petty jury and
secure conviction there is nothing to suggest that propaganda purposes affected the basic design of indictments.
In April 1535 in the cases of Augustine Webster, prior of
Axholme, and Richard Reynolds, monk of Syon, Archbishop
Cranmer pointed out to Thomas Cromwell that if no offence
was alleged against them other than offending against the
act which extinguished the authority of the pope (28 Hen.
VIII cc. 10, 11) 'It wilbe muche more for the conversion
of all the fawters'. (199)   The suggestion was not received with any favour and the suspects were in fact tried
under the act of supremacy (26 Hen. VIII c. 1) and the
treason act of 1534 (26 Hen. VIII c. 13). (200)   There
is, it must be admitted, one piece of evidence from late
in the century which at first sight seems more suggestive
of political interference.   In November 1598 Edward Coke,

then attorney-general, having attended to the drafting of
an indictment of Edward Squyer, asked Cecil for his opinion as a politician about what should be put in and what
excluded. (201)   Coke was obviously thinking about how
the indictment should sound to the crowd in the courtroom
and the degree to which Squyer ought to figure as a prime
mover of the traitorous conspiracy he was involved in.
There was thus nothing sinister or illegal occurring;
there was merely a decision to be taken about whether
those conspirators not yet captured should figure in parts
of the indictment or not.   Nor is there any other evidence which suggests that the crown was at any time other
than thorough and generally accurate in the drafting of
treason indictments.   It was not an area where chances
could be taken because a verdict of guilty, although the
usual outcome of any such trial, was by no means automatic.

The quasi-judicial procedures met by suspect traitors
between their arrest and their trial were of great importance both to the Tudor government and the development of
the law of treason.   This was an area where rules were
few and precedents ill-defined, and the crown had room to
operate in a high-handed, even ruthless, manner.   The
crucial tool in many successful prosecutions was the examination of the suspect and his accomplices.   The well-
handled examination produced the facts on which to base
the indictment, as well as the evidence to prove them.
Incrimination and, better still, confession, were sought
after with the greatest diligence by the government's servants, and for this purpose the use of torture was deliberately adopted.   When, seemingly because of opposition
in parliament, the evidence of witnesses became essential
at indictments and trial, the importance of examination
and confession remained undiminished, since the government
soon discovered that the prisoner's answers to interrogatories could be made to serve as evidence so long as testimony was forthcoming by some person present at the examination that these were indeed the prisoner's responses.
The Tudor monarchs and their ministers, had they been subjected to criticism on the issue of a type which they
could not ignore, would have defended the way they handled
examinations by saying that it was often essential in
treason cases to acquire information from the prisoner
soon after capture so as to preserve the prince and the
realm from destruction.   This answer, of course, has a
certain validity, but since they soon introduced the practice of torture into other sorts of criminal cases the
pretended reluctance of the Tudors to use such brutality
may be questioned.

Since the arrest-to-trial part of the legal process was
governed by few rubrics of the common law, common lawyers
may have considered they had an excuse for not raising
their voices in protest.   The beneficiary was undoubtedly
the council, under whose supervision most of the examinations of suspect traitors took place, and whose authority
over torture was well-nigh total.   Because of its ability
to get suspect traitors to confess and incriminate other
men before trial, and even before indictment, the role of
both grand and petty juries was considerably diminished,
particularly that of the former.   So, therefore, was the
popular, as distinct from the royal, element in criminal
judicial process.   The ability of the state to convict
those who acted or conspired against it was therefore much
greater than ever before.

# 4

# Trial

The majority of treason trials under the Tudors were held
before commissioners of oyer and terminer; some, especially later in the sixteenth century and concerning traitorous activities thought less dangerous were held before
justices of assize and gaol delivery. (1)   The local
councils like those of the north or of the marches of
Wales had power to try treason only if specially commissioned.   The court of king's bench dealt in the first
instance only with treason offences committed in Middlesex, though it received a number of cases moved up after
arraignment from the lesser courts by writ of *certiorari*
or of error.   This procedure was allowed, so it seems,
because the accused had made his peace with the king and
was soon to present a pardon, or because the crown had
been embarrassed by legal novelties or abnormalities
arising in the judicial process and was willing to admit
as much.   Both eventualities meant that the accused would
soon go free.   The relatively few trials which involved
persons of noble rank were held by special commission in
the court of the lord high steward.   This court of peers,
which had originated in the early fifteenth century, was
wont from the mid-sixteenth to meet in Westminster Hall
under the authority of whoever was appointed high steward
of England for the purpose of that particular trial.
Assize courts might be held in virtually any town of size,
at times in the most makeshift of buildings.   Suspect
traitors of any importance were usually arraigned before
justices of oyer and terminer and often in London.   Where
the king's bench usually sat, part of Westminster Hall,
was a common venue for such trials, but there are also
references to the use of the justice hall in Southwark,
the London Guildhall, and, in Elizabeth's reign, the 'justice hall in the olde Baylie'. (2)   Of these the London
Guildhall was by far the most popular, frequently taking

treason cases where the offence was held to have been committed in the city.   For that reason the lord mayor was
usually on the commission.

Until 1542 there had been difficulties in the way of
arranging for the trial of suspect traitors in London
since they had had to be indicted in the shire where their
offence had been committed and the petty jurors had had to
be drawn from the same locality.   If the case was moved
into the king's bench for trial, or tried before an oyer
and terminer commission in another county, the cost to the
jurors was heavy and absenteeism and delay a probable outcome.   The act 33 Hen. VIII c. 23 allowed, (3) if the
suspect confessed his crime or if three of the king's
council thought the prisoner 'vehemently suspect', for an
oyer and terminer commission to hold sessions wherever the
king decided and the qualification for the grand and petty
jurors to be not local residence but appointment by the
sheriff of the county where the offence had been committed. (4)   This change made for more trials out of the
county for a time but the act was revoked by the treason
statute 1 & 2 Ph. & M. c. 10.   At Hilary term 1570, at
the time of the northern rebellion, the judges decided
that suspect traitors should be indicted in the county
where the offence was committed and then the indictments
removed, if required, into the queen's bench or before
justices of oyer and terminer in Middlesex. (5)   This
sending up to London for trial seems thereafter to have
become accepted practice in important cases as long as the
crown did not consider it more valuable politically to
have the trial and any subsequent execution in the home
locality. (6)

With the possible exception of the process of indictment, and the withdrawal from the courtroom of the petty
jury in order to consider its verdict, all parts of a
criminal trial under the English common law were held in
public.   As Sir Thomas Smith, who was making a contrast
with the continental civil law, pointed out, all was done

openlie in the presence of the Judges, the Justices,
the enquest, the prisoner, and so manie as will or can
come so neare as to heare it, and all depositions and
witnesses given aloude that all men may heare from the
mouth of the depositors and witnesses what is
saide. (7)

The natural interest aroused by the drama of treason trials, the ease of access to the court, the relative simplicity of the judicial process and, in the case of certain
catholic priests, the sympathy of co-religionists, encouraged many of the public to attend.   Chapuys told his imperial master that there were more than two thousand per-

sons present at the trial in the Tower of Anne Boleyn and
her brother. (8)   A report of the trial before the lord
high steward of the duke of Norfolk in January 1572 states
that there were 'a great number' of people present, and
that order within the hall was maintained by the knight
marshal and the warden of the Fleet prison and their servants with tipstaves.   An eye witness of the trial in
1595 of the catholic priest William Freeman remarked that
the throng was so great that he was too far away from the
prisoner to hear certain of his retorts. (9)   A treason
trial away from London could also draw the crowds, and on
occasion the crush might be so great that it threatened
the efficiency of the sessions.   When the catholic priest
William Lacey was arraigned at York on 11 August 1582 the
crowd was so numerous 'that the court was in great dis-
order and the justices of assize forced to make room for
themselves like ushers'. (10)

With such behaviour not unknown it might be thought
that the government would have attempted to dissuade
would-be spectators of treason trials, but rather the reverse was the case.   Christopher Hales wrote to Thomas
Cromwell in April 1538 telling him with evident satisfaction that for the arraignment of the suspect Knell 'there
was very good and great appearance of the country'. (11)
Thomas Bowyer's account of the trial of the seminary
priests James, Crockett, Oven and Edwardes shows that the
day of the trial had been chosen as a Tuesday 'to the
intent that greater resort from the further parts of the
shire might be present at it'. (12)   The only time when
there was obvious fear of disturbance being made by spectators which might lead to the accused's escape or injury
was in the case of Mary, Queen of Scots.   In October 1586
Queen Elizabeth wrote to Burghley and Walsingham that it
should be 'well considered whether it shall be expedient
to have the said proceeding against her so public that
every man may hear or that such only as be our commissioners and other our servants appointed to attend upon them
be admitted thereunto'. (13)

The social, occupational and religious composition of
the crowds which attended treason trials is unknown, although certain general features are obvious.   Friends and
relatives of those being tried, or those likely to be incriminated by the testimony were always present.   Also in
court were witnesses to the crimes imputed, although they
were only likely to be called to offer evidence if they
could assist the prosecution.   Sometimes confederates of
those on trial seem to have been drawn, fascinated, to the
courtroom, although without their presence being known to
the authorities; and there must have been in the crowd

accusers, informers, and enemies of the prisoners as well
as those who wrote reports of the trials, both official
and unofficial.   If the accused was a catholic priest or
layman accused under the Elizabethan treason laws then a
large attendance of co-religionists was commonplace.
Henry Cheke wrote to Lord Huntingdon concerning the trial
of William Lacey in August 1582 that the assembly at the
arraignment was 'very great, especially of Papists'. (14)
If the trial was one whose outcome was likely to have an
important effect on the king's policies abroad and therefore of interest to foreign governments, the king might
suggest that their representatives be present.   The clerk
of the privy council, on 30 November 1541, informing the
imperial and French ambassadors, the Venetian secretary,
and the representative of Cleves that Culpeper and Deram
were to be tried for treason the next day, advised they
should each send a secretary to witness the event. (15)
The only sixteenth-century writer to mention with any
clarity the social composition of the crowd at a treason
trial was William Allen, who claimed, perhaps for purposes
of propaganda, that at the arraignment of Edmund Campion
and his fellows

> there was such a presence of people and that of the
> more honorable, wise, lerned and best sort, as was
> never seen nor heard of in that court in our or our
> fathers' memories before us, or at any arraignement of
> the greatest dukes or peers of this land, excepting
> the number of lordes which are there in that case of
> necessitie. (16)

We should also remember that relatives and friends of the
accused or their confederates might be present as justices commissioned for the occasion.   Anne Boleyn's father
sat in judgment on his own daughter while the duke of Norfolk was on the bench at the arraignment of Deram and Culpeper, who were indicted of illicit intercourse of a traitorous nature with the queen, Norfolk's grand-
daughter. (17)

The vast majority of spectators attending a treason
trial were there, we may safely surmise, not so much out
of idle curiosity but because they believed the prisoner
was an enemy of the king and the realm and hoped to see
him found guilty of his heinous crime and thereby the
canker rooted out of the body politic;   or contrariwise
because they were sure the prisoner was unfairly accused
and hoped to see him acquitted.   There was emotional involvement in almost every case.   Some of those arraigned
were 'detested' by the spectators for their crimes, we are
told. (18)   In the case of others the announcement of
their acquittal was the signal for great rejoicing among

the crowd in court.    The verdict 'not guilty' on William,
Lord Dacre of the North, in July 1535 in the court of the
lord high steward caused the commons present to 'utter the
greatest shoute and crye of ioy that the like no man
livyng may remembre that ever he heard'. (19)    In 1553,
when the people present in Westminster Hall supposed the
duke of Somerset had been acquitted, they made 'such a
shryke and castinge up of caps that it was hard into the
large Acre beyonde Charinge Crosse'. (20)    According to
William Allen, there was a more rational interest prevailing in the minds of a section of the audience which attended the sentencing of Edmund Campion and his associates.
Whereas others of the crowd were there merely to see the
tragedy played out, some were present, said Allen,

   to behold whether the old honor of law and iustice
   wherein our nation hath of all the world had the
   praise, could or durst stand, notwithstanding any violent impression of power and authoritie to the contrary: whether there were any *Markhams* left in the
   land that would yield up coiffe, office and life rather
   then geve sentence against such as they knew in conscience to be innocent and in truth not touched by any
   evidence whatsoever. (21)

While it is entirely possible that a number of educated
catholics did, in fact, adopt this attitude, there is no
evidence that it was shared by others in the crowd.
    Despite the satisfaction shown by spectators at the
conviction of some prisoners and the rejoicing at the acquittal of others, so suggestive of a highly charged at-
mosphere, there was no actual interruption of the proper
course of any treason trial.    In outward appearances the
crowds, once the trial was under way, were well behaved
and quite inhibited, although if the accused answered the
justices or the king's learned counsel in a really arro-
gant manner with words directed against the king then mur-
muring might begin.    In 1584 Dr William Parry, on being
sentenced, said 'I here summon Queen Elizabeth to answer
for my blood before God.'    Incensed, the people present
cried out as he was led from the court 'Away with the
traitor'. (22)    If the prisoner attempted to defend the
reputation of a traitor already convicted, or hinted that
the treason lay in other quarters, then there might arise
a certain amount of noise from the audience.    This was
what happened in 1600 when Captain Thomas Lee at his trial
suggested that the earl of Essex was less a traitor than
his rivals were.    These incidents were trivial yet there
were none greater, which testifies not just to the good
stage management of treason trials, although there must
have been some of this, but also to the fact that treason

trials were conducted in the main like other criminal trials and these the public was long accustomed to view and,
as jurors, to participate in.

There can be little doubt that the government encouraged people to attend treason trials for the purpose of
publicizing the offences and the names of the miscreants.
It was hoped they would tell all their neighbours on return home.   As Sir Thomas Smith noted, it was customary
in all criminal cases at gaol deliveries for the justices
to announce in court the cause of their coming and to give
'a good lesson to the people', (24) and we may add that in
treason trials they and the king's learned counsel were
careful to provide in addition information about why the
law on treason took the form it did as well as the background and the political implications of the case for the
benefit of the courtroom audience.   Even in handling the
evidence, it seems, the prosecuting lawyers were wont to
address remarks as much to the spectators as the jurors.
There is only one clear reference to a prisoner at the bar
addressing the crowd directly.   In 1571 Dr John Storey,
becoming aggrieved at one point in his trial because his
plea that he was a subject of the king of Spain was rejected by the judges, 'turned him about to the people and
said "Good people I trust ye see how violently I am used;
and how unjustly and contrary to all justice and equity
they use me".' (25)   Never the less, like the prosecuting
lawyers, those who were accused frequently made remarks
which seem to have been addressed to a wider audience than
the judges and jurors.   This was particularly noticeable
when they tried to gain a pardon or save their necks by
openly admitting their guilt.   Their words took the form
of homilies about now realizing the need for loyalty to
the prince if the commonwealth was to subsist, interming-
led with pleas that no one else should copy their vicious
offences.

A treason trial began its course when the justices'
commission was read out and officers to whom any writs had
been directed brought them in and certified them;   then
the accused was brought to the bar.   Sometimes he had
only been informed that his trial was at hand a few hours
previously.   Storey complained to his judges that he had
had 'Scarborough's warning to come to this Arraignment;
for I knew nothing thereof until seven of the clock in the
morning'. (26)   The prisoner was sometimes led in with
arms bound, and if there were several accused to be tried
at once they might be led in bound or chained together.
Usually their bonds were loosed while they offered a plea
and made their replies, but this was not invariably the
case.   The catholic priest Cuthbert Mayne and his assoc-

iates, arraigned in September 1577, were reported as
appearing stripped of their upper garments, but whether
this was to hinder their escape, to embarrass them, or
mere chance, is uncertain. (27)   In contrast, in the
court of the lord high steward in 1571, the duke of Norfolk made his entry in a dignified manner with the lieutenant of the Tower holding his right hand and Sir Peter
Carewe his left. (28)

In theory the next step in the trial was for the grand
jury or juries to deliver the indictments to the judges.
Then the clerk of the court, after telling the prisoners
informally they were accused of treason and should 'have
their trial', would call them separately to the bar and
instruct them to hold up their hands. (29)   It was not
unknown for the justices at this stage to offer a pardon
if the accused would confess and recant.   This happened,
for example, in the case of Sir Thomas More. (30)   An indictment was then read out thus:   'Thou, A.B. that stand-
est there art here accused by name of A.B. of X., gentleman (or whatever), for that on ... thou didst ...' and so
on.   To this charge A.B. was asked to plead guilty or not
and then, if there were others on trial for the same offence, the charge was re-read to another prisoner, his
name being substituted.   He also made a plea.   When
there was more than one indictment the prisoners had to be
called separately each time, to hold up their hands while
each was˜read, and then plead to each. (31)   There was no
rule which prevented several accused being tried simultaneously and in fact this occasionally happened.   At this
point some prisoners tried to discuss the charges informally, as it were, with the justices before pleading, but
it was not allowed.   Others said that to some indictments
or parts of an indictment they wished to offer a plea of
not guilty, yet to other charges they were willing to confess their guilt.   They were answered that if they held
they were not guilty to any part of the indictment they
must plead not guilty to all 'and for such matters and
parts of the indictment as you can clear yourself the Jury
may find you Not Guilty and find you Guilty of the
rest'. (32)   Certain accused, like Sir Thomas Wyatt in
1554 and Robert Hickford, the duke of Norfolk's secretary,
in 1571, were quite willing to plead guilty as long as
they were allowed to speak afterwards and rebut infamous
charges bandied around but not contained in any indictment.   When this was conceded to Wyatt there followed
after his plea a series of questions from the queen's
learned counsel about his behaviour, which he answered at
some length. (33)   In 1571, in the court of the lord high
steward, the duke of Norfolk, before he entered his plea,

asked if the indictment was 'perfect and sufficient in
law, and whether in whole or in the part and in which
parts'.   He was told that it was perfect throughout and
that all points were treasons.   Thereupon the duke
pleaded not guilty. (34)

Sir Thomas Smith, writing in the earlier part of Elizabeth's reign, tells us that according to his observations
most robbers, thieves and murderers were wont to plead not
guilty, even if they had confessed the fact at their examination. (35)   Of those accused of treason in Tudor England the number who pleaded guilty seems to have been
quite large.   The proportion was perhaps as high as one
in four, which must have been greater than among those
accused of other types of crime.   It was also by no means
uncommon for indicted traitors to change their original
plea of not guilty to the reverse after the trial had been
in progress for some time.   At their arraignment in April
1535 the Carthusian monks Robert Feron and John Hale pleaded not guilty when brought to the bar initially, but when
the adjourned trial was renewed next day they altered this
to guilty. (36)   Sometimes the change of plea occurred
during the dinner recess or, as happened at the trial of
Sir Thomas Grey in March 1554, after the evidence had been
given but before the jury had retired.   At other times,
as for example when Sir Thomas Percy, Sir John Bulmer,
Margaret Cheyne and Stephen Hamerton were on trial at York
on 16 May 1537 for their implication in the risings in the
north, there were changes of plea while the jury was in
retirement considering its verdict. (37)   Very likely
most of these changes were induced by promises of merci-
ful treatment by the king.

Several of those indicted of treason, when asked to
plead, did not say 'guilty' or 'not guilty' but would
either not answer directly or refuse to make any answer at
all.   Had the offence been anything but treason they
would have thereupon been adjudged to *peine forte et dure*,
the Tudor form of which Thomas Smith described as being
'layd upon a table and an other uppon him, and so much
weight of stones or lead laide uppon that table while as
his bodie be crushed and his life by that violence taken
from him'. (38)   Since by dying in this manner the prisoner's possessions were not forfeited and since to the
king forfeitures for treason were doubly attractive because they did not have to be shared with any lesser lord,
it is readily apparent that the crown had the greatest
interest in not allowing *peine forte et dure* to be inflicted on suspect traitors.   When the offence was treason
the trial simply proceeded as if the accused had not stood
mute or refused direct answer but had made a plea of

'guilty'.    Judgment and sentence were therefore given
immediately.    This rule was stated officially for the
first time in the act 33 Hen. VIII c. 12, but the practice
had probably begun several years earlier.    We notice, for
example, that when no satisfactory answer was received
from John Cowley at his trial in 1517 judgment and sentence followed nevertheless, but not before he had been
remanded to the custody of the sheriff at Southwark to
help him change his mind.    This case may be indicative of
a transitional period between *peine forte et dure* and immediate judgment and sentence. (39)

When the indicted traitor had been asked how he would
plead and had given the answer 'not guilty', it was further demanded of him how he would be tried.    To this the
proper and only response was 'by God and the country',
'country' meaning a petty jury, or, if the accused was of
noble blood, 'by God and my peers'.    Periodically other
responses were made.    Richard White, a catholic schoolmaster, at his arraignment at Wrexham on 9 October 1584
is said to have answered, apparently, in all sincerity,
that he wished to be tried by the justices themselves not
a jury 'for you are wise and learned and better able to
discern the equity of our cause than the simple men of our
own country altogether unacquainted with such matters'. (40)    A similar argument, to the effect that many
important matters such as what authority was due to the
bishop of Rome were not resolved in schools and therefore
unlikely to be determined by lay jurors, seems to have
been propounded at his trial in 1581 by Edmund Campion.
Likewise at his trial in 1588 the seminary priest John
Hewett said he would not be tried by jury since he did not
wish ignorant men, who did not understand the case, to be
burdened with his blood.    None of these requests was
granted;  they were simply ignored and juries empanelled. (41)

When all those indicted had entered a plea, and as long
as one had pleaded 'not guilty', a petty jury was produced.    In theory, except in the years 1542-7 when the
practice was stopped, (42) the prisoner was told he might
object to each juror coming to take the oath if he had
proper reason to do so.    According to Sir John Fortescue
writing about 1470, the accused was permitted to challenge
in this way as many as thirty-five jurors, although there
is no evidence from the fifteenth and sixteenth centuries
that this ever happened.    In Tudor treason trials the
objection to ten by Sir Nicholas Throckmorton in 1554
seems to have been the maximum. (43)    If the prisoner
asked how many jurors he might challenge he was not told;
nor did he receive a proper answer if he enquired what was

a proper reason for objecting.   The justices would simply
answer that they were not there to provide him with legal
counsel, which in any case was not allowed to those accused of treason, and that as for a reason the prisoner
would surely 'know a cause in (his) conscience'. (44)   If
the trial was that of a nobleman taking place in the court
of the high steward there was little chance of removing
one or more of the peer-jurors.   The unchallengeable
position of these seems to have been first propounded at
the trial of Lord Darcy in 1537, and it was stated quite
categorically at the trial of the duke of Somerset in 1551
that a peer of the realm might not be challenged at all.
At the arraignment of the duke of Northumberland in 1553
this had been slightly modified to allow challenge 'only
at the prince's pleasure' and that was where the matter
rested for the remainder of the Tudor era. (45)   In treason trials outside the court of the high steward the
crown, as well as the accused, could make objection to
particular jurors but, in fact, it was a rarity.   The
only clearly reported occasion was the trial of Sir Nicholas Throckmorton on 17 April 1554.   The attorney-general
showed the sheriff's return of jurors to Sir Roger Cholm-
ley, one of the justices, 'who being acquainted with the
citizens, knowing the corruptions and dexterities of them
in such cases noted certain to be challenged for the
queen'.   Thereupon two jurors were challenged by Serjeant
Dyer. (46)   When Throckmorton asked for the reason he was
told that it need not be given.
     When any challenging of jurors was finished the clerk
of the court usually recited the indictments to the jury,
telling them the accused had pleaded not guilty and in-
structing them that they must enquire whether in fact this
was so. (47)   When a suspect traitor was being tried with
a number of ordinary felons, as for example at a sessions
of gaol delivery and not by commission of oyer and terminer, it was not unknown, if there was insufficient evidence to suggest the prosecution would be successful, for
a proclamation to be made at this point by the court crier
calling on anyone who could lay any charge against the
accused to come forward.   In the case of Thomas Mountayne
in 1554 this call was made three times.   No one appeared
to offer any charges so he was set free on sureties to
appear again at the next sessions. (48)   In the case of
Sir John Perrot in 1592, once the indictment had been read
to the jury, an 'oyez' was made 'to know if any man were
there to give evidence against the Prisoner at the bar in
behalf of her majesty'.   This seems more like an appeal
for supplementary evidence which could be used as the
trial wore on. (49)

If the offence was treason or a felony the arraigned
person was not normally allowed the advice or assistance
of legal counsel in the courtroom.   This was not new;   it
had been the practice throughout the Middle Ages. (50)
It caused more criticism than nearly every other feature
of the English criminal trial.   Perhaps this was because
men were aware of the value of legal counsel from their
experiences in personal actions, where it was allowed.
In 1541 the elder Sir Thomas Wyatt, recently the English
ambassador to Charles V, while in custody expecting to be
arraigned for treason, drafted an address to the justices
which he intended to deliver in court.   Significantly the
first point he thought it worthwhile to make was that his
response must lack polish and cogency since he might not,
as in France or under the civil law, retain counsel for
his defence.   Robert Persons, the Jesuit, in a general
criticism of the English common law laid considerable emphasis on the predicament of the man arraigned.   He
wrote:

> How is it possible ... that such a Man especially if he
> be bashful and unlearned, in so short a time as there
> is alotted him for answering for his Life without the
> help of a Lawyer, Proctor or other Man that may direct
> counsel, or assist him in such an agony;   how can he
> see all the parts or points that may be alleged for his
> defence being never so Innocent. (51)

The unlikelihood of being permitted to have legal counsel
did not stop some of those on trial for treason from asking for it.   Edmund Campion seems to have requested it.
To the similar entreaty of the duke of Norfolk in 1571 the
lord chief justice is said to have answered 'Your Grace is
to answer to your own fact only, which yourself best know
and may without counsel sufficiently answer.'   When in
1590 John Udall, who was accused of seditious libel, asked
for counsel to answer for him, Clarke, a justice, is reported to have said brusquely 'You cannot have it and
therefore answer to your indictment.'   Later in the trial
a justice told the prisoner, quite inconsistently, 'Mr
Udall your counsel hath deceived you', to which Udal bitterly replied that he had not been allowed counsel at any
time. (52)
If Udall had asked for legal counsel while in gaol and
it had been denied him then he may have been unfortunate,
for although the accused were not permitted to have someone to answer for them in court there are several examples
of lawyers giving them advice when they were awaiting
trial.   Thus Francis Throckmorton, after being arrested
on suspicion of treason in 1583, managed 'to talk with a
solicitor of his law causes who brought him certeine books

drawne or other like papers written, which he made show to
peruse'.   Throckmorton at that time was at the house of
the gentleman sent to apprehend him, and the solicitor's
visit may not have had official sanction, yet example can
be shown of learned counsel being permitted to enter the
Tower to give advice to a prisoner, although only in the
presence of some third person thoroughly trusted.   It is
of course possible that this advice was concerned not with
the prisoner's current predicament but with civil actions
then pending.   The evidence is not entirely clear. (53)
    Although a legal counsellor could not 'allege any
matter' or give evidence for a prisoner in court he could
nevertheless play a part in a treason trial in the right
circumstances.   These were that the prisoner should first
himself have alleged an error in procedure 'for it is to
be observed that in no case the party arraigned of treason
or felony can pray councell learned generally but must
show some cause'.   Such possible errors Coke listed as an
omission of the mention of an overt act when the indictment concerned compassing the king's death, an inaccuracy
in the indictment in respect of time or place or the
prisoner's name and rank, a lack of two witnesses at the
indictment or the trial, a jury drawn from the wrong
place, the statute under which the charge was brought not
being relevant to the case, or there being a general
pardon in operation which excused the crime in question.
There may have been other causes for allowing legal advice
as well.   In June 1486 the Yorkist Humphrey Stafford
seems to have been afforded the privilege.   When asked to
plead he would answer only that he wished to be put back
in sanctuary, having been forcibly taken from Culham in
May.   He was then assigned counsel. (54)
    Once an error had been claimed which seemed to the jus-
tices to justify the appointment of legal counsel, this
was done.   He had as his task not so much to argue the
point on behalf of the accused as to act as an independent
tribunal for its investigation.   If he found any error in
the legal process, then the court was informed and judgment stayed.   Coke added further that not only the accused but any person there present was allowed to point out
a procedural error 'lest the court should erre and the
prisoner unjustly for his life proceeded with'.   Perhaps
when Coke was writing his 'Third Institute' there was already some criticism of the way the accused, through lack
of advice, was often unable to challenge doubtful procedure unless fortuitously knowledgeable about criminal law.
At any rate he was prompted to offer a justification.
First, he said, when a man's life was at stake 'the evidence to convince (convict) him should be so manifest as

it could not be contradicted.' This meant that it was
best that any doubts about the guilt of the accused should
not be accentuated by the arguments of defence counsel;
unanimity in the court was desirable since it gave
strength to any judgment and sentence. Sir William Stanford, dealing with the same issue in the mid-sixteenth
century, argued that if counsel was provided for the accused the pair might be 'si covert in lour parlance' that it
would take too long to boult out the truth. On the other
hand, if the accused pleaded his own case, 'son gesture ou
countenance' would give some indication as to whether he
was speaking the truth. A second argument offered by
Coke against permitting counsel was that 'the court ought
to see that the indictment, triall and other proceedings
be good and sufficient in law; otherwise they should by
their erroneous judgement attaint the prisoner unjustly.' (55) The suggestion here was that to allow the
accused counsel jeopardized in the same way the legality
of the arraignment. This may have been because it was
suspected that a good defence would throw the crown's lawyers out of their stride, as Sir Nicholas Throckmorton did
of his own accord. It may also have stemmed from a realization that since no such legal advice had been allowed
in the past, its introduction might impugn the validity of
the judgments given, and upset legal convention.

Few of those arraigned for treason had accurate knowledge of what charges were comprised in the indictment
before it was read out to them in court. The sensible
prisoner, like the elder Sir Thomas Wyatt, tried to anticipate what the various counts might be and prepare a
rational defence. (56) Even when the trial had got under
way the accused was not allowed time or opportunity to
view the indictment so as to marshal his arguments or make
sure he had tried to answer every point laid against him.
He must think on his feet and woe betide him if his memory
was not good. Realization of this accounts in part for
the numerous lamentations made by prisoners at the start
of their trials about the way their wits were dulled and
their memory impaired through the arduous imprisonment
they had suffered. They often tried to make the best of
circumstances by asking for *aides memoires*, the chance to
take notes, or simply to have reasonable comfort in the
courtroom. Thus Sir Thomas More obtained permission to
sit down on a chair. Edward Abington, who was tried on
15 September 1586, is said to have requested after making
his plea that he might have a pair of writing tables 'to
set down what is alledged against me that I may yield a
sufficient Answer thereunto'. There came the answer 'It
was never the course here', and Sir Christopher Hatton,

one of the justices, added 'When you hear anything you are
desirous to answer, you shall speak an Answer at full
which is better than a pair of tables.' (57)   The favour
allowed to Sir John Perrot in 1592, which was to let him
bring with him into court his 'Writings and Letters', was
undoubtedly of considerable value.   This was a new step;
the lord chamberlain said that 'never was any man that
come to that place dealt withal so favourably as he was.'
Information about matters such as the prisoner having
notes or being given a few seconds to collect his thoughts
was probably regarded at the time as too trivial to be
worth recording.   The accounts we possess do not suggest
there was any great improvement on later medieval practice.   In the fourteenth century suspect traitors arraigned in parliament were wont to ask for the charges in
writing and for time to consider their answers.   On the
other hand to suggest that in the Tudor period such privileges were getting fewer would be quite wrong. (58)

Before any important treason trial commenced the king's
ministers and the learned counsel who were to prosecute
his case in court devoted time to planning crown strategy.
Kings did not attend treason trials in person, although
Henry VIII was present at the arraignment for heresy of
William Nicholson in 1538, putting questions and arguing
with the prisoner.   Instead they were accustomed to press
for 'more sore justice' and 'fearful warnings' from a distance, even if Elizabeth in the case of Mary, Queen of
Scots, showed a marked reluctance to allow proceedings to
go as far as the sentencing. (59)   Henry VII's failure to
get the judges to declare how they intended to deal with
Humphrey Stafford's plea of sanctuary before the case came
into court may have served to limit royal interference in
one direction for the future. (60)   The king's ministers,
however, had few inhibitions when it came to arranging
treason trials, as the activities of Thomas Cromwell pa-
tently reveal.   All reports of suspect traitors went to
Cromwell:  these he cross-checked, then drafted the interrogatories to be given, received back the examinations and
composed the indictment in collaboration with the king's
learned counsel.   Thus it was quite natural he should go
one step further and suggest how their guilt might most
easily be demonstrated in court by sorting out all the
evidence to be offered.   He was frequently to be found
advising the attorney-general and the solicitor-general
who in theory were responsible for the handling of the
prosecution both in and out of the courtroom. (61)   Other
ministers later in the century may have behaved as Cromwell had done but there is less material for the historian
to draw on.   Cecil was certainly capable of giving in-

structions about the conduct of a treason trial.   He
wrote to Attorney-General Coke on 19 February 1601, when
Essex and Southampton were on trial, to instruct him not
to let certain words in Sir Christopher Blunt's examination be read out, since they might suggest he had an
ability to prophecy the future. (62)   This relatively
trivial piece of interference is important because it
shows that the professional work of the royal prosecutors
was not thought to be sacrosanct or incapable of improvement.   Perhaps the clearest and most impressive example
of a minister of state giving directions for a treason
trial is to be found in the scheme drafted by Burghley in
1586 for handling the evidence and the introduction of
witnesses against Mary, Queen of Scots.   It was most precise.   First, Ballard's dealings with Mendoza and Paget
in France were to be shown, then Ballard's dealings with
Babington, then Mary's decision to contact Babington,
these to be followed by the reading of Babington's letter
to Mary and hers to him.   'This being opened and the
matter thus far proved,' says the plan at this point,
'then to see what answer she will make hereunto ... and
... then to reply.'   The intended rejoinders by the crown
were set out in a similarly precise fashion and were based
on other letters written or received by Mary.   Provision
was made for attestation of the latter by her secretaries,
who were also to provide a description of their mistress's
system of correspondence. (63)
     It is also worthy of note that, as well as planning the
handling of evidence, royal ministers were to be found
sitting as justices at the trials of suspect traitors
whose prosecution they themselves had helped to dev-
vise. (64)   In turn the king's learned counsel, as well
as receiving advice from men close to the king, frequently
sought the opinions of the professional judges (though not
those presiding) and other law officers before and during
the trials.   They might also in particular cases obtain
the services of those with a specialist knowledge if it
was thought necessary to introduce matter of an unusual
sort.   For example, for the trial of Edmund Campion and
his associates Dr John Hammond, a civilian, was asked to
prepare points from the writings of Sanders and Bris-
towe. (65)
     It was usual for the king's learned counsel at any im-
portant treason trial to number three, the attorney-general, the solicitor-general and a king's serjeant, or the
attorney-general and two serjeants.   Thus against Sir
Nicholas Throckmorton in 1554 counsel comprised Attorney-
General Griffin, Serjeant Dyer and Serjeant Stanford;   at
Campion's trial it was Attorney-General Popham, Solicitor-

General Egerton and Serjeant Anderson;   against Sir John
Perrot in 1592 it was again Popham and Egerton but with
Serjeant Puckering.   For trials in the court of the high
steward learned counsel seems to have numbered not three
but four.   At the arraignment of the duke of Norfolk in
1571, sitting directly before the bar and prosecuting for
the queen, were Gilbert Gerard the attorney-general,
Thomas Bromley, solicitor-general, Nicholas Barham,
queen's serjeant, and Thomas Wilbraham, queen's attorney
of the court of wards.   At the trial of the earl of Arundel on 18 April 1589 the queen's learned counsel consisted
of the attorney-general and solicitor-general and serjeants Puckering and Shettleworth.   It was usual apparently for the various members of counsel to divide the
different parts of the case between them, as for example
by each alleging a different confession or exam, or a related group of the same, to the prisoner. (66)

The main part of a treason trial, which was the offering of the evidence, frequently began with a speech by the
king's counsel, often in the person of the king's serjeant.   This summarized the charges recently read out in
the indictment.   'Then Serjeant Puckering', so an account
of Perrot's trial tells us, 'rehearsed to the Jury the
principal points contained in the Indictment aforesaid.'
On other occasions, which were not so common, although by
no means infrequent, the serjeant reviewed instead the
political background to the offence.   At the trial of
Edmund Campion and others Serjeant Anderson gave an address which reminded those in the court of recent rebellions and traitorous conspiracies, and pointed out how the
pope, through Jesuits and their associates, had been
largely responsible.   It was now papal policy, said
Anderson, to recruit Englishmen 'to dissuade the people
from their Allegiance to their prince, to reconcile them
to the pope, to plant the Romish Religion'.   This speech,
says one account, was 'very vehemently pronounced with a
grave and austere countenance' and dismayed all the accused for 'it sounded very criminously to their Trial'. (67)
Both of these varieties of opening remarks might lead to
criticism from those arraigned on the grounds no effort
was being made to deal with the evidence.   From descriptions of Perrot's trial in 1592 and that of four seminary
priests, James, Crockett, Oven and Edwardes, at Chichester
on 30 September 1588, it seems as if there was also a
third method of opening.   In these cases the prosecuting
lawyers clearly stated the statutes on which the indictments were based, explained the scope of the treason laws
and outlined what the crown ought to show to prove its
case.   All these initial remarks were intended primarily
for the jury. (68)

Many of the accused asked of the court, either at this
point or just after they had pleaded, that they might not
have to wait to answer until all the evidence against them
had been alleged but might make a response to each matter
as it was broached.   The earl of Essex in 1600 is said to
have asked 'Will your Lordships give us our turn to speak?
for Mr. Attorney playeth the orator'.   'We beseech your
Lordships,' he added, 'that it may please you to allow us
first to answer generally to that wherewith we have been
generally charged, and afterwards to every particular
piece of evidence as it is delivered for otherwise we
shall soon confound our own memories and give liberty and
advantage to our enemies for lack of precise answer to
each particular objection.'   What Essex was saying was
what many prisoners said, namely that their memories were
not good enough to recall at the end all the points
brought against them.   Nearly always learned counsel was
willing to accept such suggestions;   said Serjeant Puckering to Sir John Perrot 'You shall be remembered of every
matter piecemeal'. (69)

Amongst the weapons which the prosecution used in order
to prove its case, pride of place went to the introduction
of examinations and confessions.   These might derive from
the accused himself, for it was by no means unheard of for
a man to confess to the offences or part of them beforehand, yet plead not guilty in court.   Usually, however,
they were examinations of the accused, and confessions and
examinations of confederates.   It was the fashion to read
them out and then interpret them, so to speak, to the
jury.   For example, in regard to the fourth indictment
against the seminary priest Cuthbert Mayne, Mayne's own
exam, in which he confessed to bringing into the realm
twelve or thirteen *Agnus Dei*, was alleged and then the argument was offered that, since he had only eight or nine
in his possession on capture, he must have delivered the
rest, which was reckoned an offence under the act 13 Eliz.
c. 2.   From the crown's point of view it was best if the
associates in crime, whose depositions were used, were as
yet unconvicted.   Sir Nicholas Throckmorton made great
play of the fact that Cuthbert Vaughan, whose confession
was alleged against him, was a condemned man 'whose testimony is nothing worth by any law'. (70)   As we shall see
below, it also assisted the crown's case if the person who
had devised the examinations or confessions and also the
examiner who had interrogated, made an appearance in court
to vouch for their veracity in front of the accused.   So
important had examinations and confessions become in the
process of trial by the mid-sixteenth century, that Chief
Justice Bromley, when arguing with Throckmorton about the

treason act of 1352, was prompted to say that the phrase
'attaint by people of like condition' meant not, as
Throckmorton rightly held it did, petty jurors of similar
estate to the accused, but the confessions of confederates, in his case, Sir Thomas Wyatt and followers. (71)

In the same category as examinations and confessions
were incriminating documents like letters or memoranda
which had been discovered in the possessions of the accused or his confederates.   Against the duke of Buckingham
in 1521, his own writings were produced;   against Dr
Bocking, a sponsor of the Nun of Kent, a book. (72)   At
the trial of the duke of Norfolk in 1571, a letter from
the earl of Murray, and another from the bishop of Ross,
to Mary, Queen of Scots, were used to show that the duke
was bent on marrying Mary at the time of the conference at
York.   At the trial of Cuthbert Mayne in 1577 the queen's
counsel produced as evidence a letter between Mayne and
'his master' concerning some points of religion, a 'paper
wherein were contained divers questions concerning also
matters of religion with resolutions to the same', and a
letter from Gregory Martin, whom counsel called an 'arch-
priest from Douai'. (73)

Each statement by counsel alleging confession, examination, documents, witnesses' evidence, or point of law,
tended to take an interrogative form and the accused was
expected at natural junctures to deny or explain away the
allegations.   There might even be questions specifically
directed at the prisoner.   At Sir Nicholas Throckmorton's
trial Serjeant Stanford began for the prosecution by saying he intended to show that the accused was rightly indicted and arraigned, and his second sentence apparently
was 'How say you Throckmorton, did not you send Winter to
Wyatt in Kent and devise that the Tower of London should
be taken?'   Serjeant Barham, alleging the duke of Norfolk's intention of marrying Mary, Queen of Scots, is reckoned to have said, 'First ... we pray your Grace [speak-
ing to the lord high steward] that my Lord of Norfolk may
directly answer whether he knew that the Scottish Queen so
claimed;   if he deny it, we will prove it.'   When the
duke, being so instructed, prevaricated, Barham said to
him, 'Say plainly.   Did you know it or no? for if you say
nay we can prove it.'   Thereupon Norfolk claimed he was
being handled severely and said he would 'answer directly
to the whole matter of my dealing with her'.   This was
unacceptable to Barham, who rejoined 'You must answer to
the parts as they fall out.'   Some prosecuting counsel,
it would seem, were quite willing to try to lead the accused directly into admitting treason if they could.   At
the trial of Richard White, John Hughes and Robert Morris

at Wrexham on 9 October 1584, Simon Thelwall asked the
'bloody question', namely 'whose part would you take if
the pope came with power to invade the realm and fight
against the queen?', and other counsel asked the prisoners
whether the queen ought to be supreme head of the
church. (75)   If evidence was given by witnesses the
prisoner was expected, if he could, to take exception to
it;   sometimes the justices actually demanded what he had
to say in his own defence, expecting him to try to show
that the witnesses' evidence was not credible.   There
was, therefore, some resemblance between the way a prisoner was handled at the actual trial and at the foregoing
examination, save that the former took the form, as Sir
Thomas Smith said, of an 'altercation' between the accused, the justices and the king's counsel.

What answers could the prisoner at the bar offer to
repel the attacks of the king's counsel and thus impress
the jurors?   If he was reasonably sharp-witted, knew some
history, and had at some time attended a treason trial as
a spectator, he might have learned that the prosecution,
although impressive against the less mentally agile, could
be flurried and even embarrassed by the right responses.
The first move was perhaps for the accused to interrupt
the prime serjeant or the attorney-general as he made the
usual opening statement, or address him the moment he
ended, asking that specific offences only be charged.   At
this point in his trial Henry Cuffe, secretary of the earl
of Essex, arraigned 1 March 1600 is reported to have said
'I will beseech Mr. Attorney that we may insist on some
point certain and not as in a stream have all things at
once brought upon me with violence.'   As the king's counsel began the case against Sir John Perrot, the prisoner,
we are told, 'prayed serjeant Puckering to lay aside words
and to proceed to the matter of the Indictment.'   Edmund
Campion, in response to the crown's opening speech 'demanded of Mr. Anderson whether he came as an orator to accuse
them, or as a pleader to give in evidence.'   He asked if
indeed the laws of England allowed 'the trial of any man
for life and death by shifts of probabilities and conjec-
tural surmises without proof of the crime by sufficient
evidence and substantial witnesses'.   The shaft went
home, for the lord chief justice said defensively 'You
must have patience with him and the rest likewise;   for
they being of the Queen's Council they speak of no other
intent than of duty to her majesty.' (76)

Nicholas Throckmorton's trial did not begin in this
manner.   Serjeant Stanford, the report tells us, made a
definite accusation and asked Throckmorton to deny or
affirm it.   Throckmorton denied it and demanded Stanford

should prove his charge.    Stanford's answer was to read a
confession by one Winter.    Throckmorton's counter shows
another gambit open to the prisoner: he gave his own
account of the facts related in Winter's confession.    It
was Throckmorton also who protested about learned counsel's practice of reading out confessions only in part.
Having pointed out that Serjeant Stanford had 'gathered
the place as you think, that maketh most against me' he
asked that Stanford should read further so that 'hereafter
whatsoever become of me, my words be not perverted and
abused to the hurt of some others'. (77)    Another tacti-
cal rule can also be gleaned from the report of this
trial.    Throckmorton must have owed much of his success
in gaining acquittal to the fact that he knew what had
been happening since his arrest in the bringing to justice
of the Wyatt conspirators.    Thus he was able to reduce
the value of the testimony of the witness Cuthbert
Vaughan, when he was produced in court to swear to his
confession, by saying 'He that hath said and lied will not
being in this case [that is, under sentence of death]
stick to swear and lie.'    He explained further that
Vaughan must either 'speak of some man or suffer death'.
Edward Abington, at his trial in 1586, went so far as to
argue that all the witnesses produced against him were
confessed or condemned traitors.    Another sally by
Throckmorton, which demonstrated the value of keeping well
informed although languishing in prison, came in answer to
Chief Justice Bromley's rather odd admonition to the
king's counsel to read out Sir Thomas Wyatt's accusation
of the accused.    The latter replied that whatever Wyatt
had said about him 'in hope of his life, he unsaid it at
his death.'    Another justice, Hare, said that nevertheless Wyatt had stated at his execution that all he had
written and confessed to the council was true.    Answered
Throckmorton, 'Nay sir by your patience Master Wyat said
not so, that was master doctor's addition', meaning Dr
Weston, the priest on the scaffold.    Sir Richard Southwell, one of the justices, remarked ruefully 'It appeareth
you have added good intelligence.' (78)
     The most telling response the accused could offer, al-
though the most difficult for a man with little legal
knowledge to fabricate or substantiate, was a challenge to
learned counsel on a point of law.    In 1521 the duke of
Buckingham seems to have argued at one stage in his trial
that no overt act of treason was charged against him.    Dr
Richard Benger, when on trial for words at Kent assizes at
about the time of Cromwell's fall, objected strongly to
the alleging of examinations and depositions not sworn to
by those who had administered or deposed them.    In 1589

the earl of Arundel challenged his indictment on the
grounds that it was inaccurate or inadequate in regard to
details of time and place.   However none of these accused
won his point.   Buckingham's objection caused Chief Justice Fineux to say that 'icy cest entente fuit prove par
... paroles', that is to say the duke's words were the
overt act.   The cool response given to Arundel was that
details about the time and place of the offence in the indictment mattered very little as long as the matter of
fact were proved. (79)   Throckmorton at his trial, when
the attorney-general had asked the presiding justice to
sum up, objected that his case could not properly be
brought under the treason act of 1352 since no overt deed
of compassing the queen's death or adhering to her enemies
had been alleged.   This piece of reasoning threw the
queen's counsel and the justices also into a great flurry
and their limp explanations were easily demolished by
Throckmorton, whose knowledge of legal history was much
the superior. (80)   What particularly assisted Throckmorton here was the fact that the scope of treason at that
time (1554) was not clearly delineated, there being, as we
have seen, several illogicalities in the law.
     Very important for any successful defence were proper
objections to the testimony of prosecution witnesses, for
it was they and their examinations and confessions which
dominated the Tudor treason trials and secured so many of
the convictions.   The history of the scope of treason reveals quite clearly how their importance increased
throughout the Tudor period.   Witnesses had appeared in
some medieval criminal trials but since there are few descriptions of the proceedings we cannot be absolutely sure
of their role and the rules governing their appearance at
that time.   Chief Justice Fortescue pointed out that witnesses were not vital to the process of trial under the
English common law even if they might be in other courts
in England.   The jury of twelve men, he added, was the
best and most effectual method for the trial of the truth,
and no cause was ever decided by witnesses alone. (81)
Only in the 1530s, during the drive to suppress treasonable words which were being expressed against the king's
marriage and religious policies, did witnesses become an
important issue.   How the law stood at that time was demonstrated at the trial of Sir Thomas More, who was convicted on the testimony of the solicitor-general, Sir Richard
Rich, alone, and more clearly perhaps by the arraignment
of Bishop Fisher.   Fisher is reported to have asked
'whether a single testimony of one man may be admitted as
sufficient to prove me guilty of Treason for speaking
these words or no? and whether my answer, negatively, may

not be accepted against his affirmative to my availe and benefit or no?'  The reply he drew from 'the judges and lawyers' was quite clear:  being the king's case 'it rested much in the conscience and discretion of the jury', and they would find judgment on the evidence given before them. (82)  This shows that, although it may have helped the king's case to have several witnesses attesting to the guilt of the accused, he had by no means lost if he had only one, or none at all for that matter.  There was nothing at that time in any treason law which demanded two witnesses.  The first succession act 25 Hen. VIII c. 22 referred to offenders 'lawfully convict ... by present-ment, verdict, confession, or process according to the laws and customs of the realm', a clumsy formula which was soon truncated.  The general treason act 26 Hen. VIII c. 13 merely asked for the accused to be 'lawefully convicted accordinge to the Lawes and Customes of this realm'.  The act against papal authority 28 Hen. VIII c. 10 referred to offenders being convicted 'according to the laws of the realm'.

However, from about 1537 or 1538, the government, and especially Thomas Cromwell, showed an increasing interest in witnesses.  This may have been brought about by the number of cases, some dating from as early as 1533, where treasonable words were reported but where, because they were uttered in private conversation, there was only the accuser as witness.  In September 1537 Lord Audley, the chancellor, reported to Cromwell that Thomas Nevill, the brother of Lord Latimer, had been accused of traitorous words, but there was only one witness, a woman.  Audley, a lawyer, was obviously doubtful if Nevill should be brought to trial.  In Cromwell's own memoranda of about November 1539 there is a note concerning Giles Heron, a treason suspect, which reads 'what shall be done with him for as much as there is but one witness?'. (83)  Govern-mental concern over witnesses may also have been prompted by happenings in the courtroom.  In May 1537 two northern rebels, Levenyng and Lutton, indicted for treason, were acquitted.  On the subject of Lutton's acquittal the duke of Norfolk wrote a letter to the king saying that Sir Ralph Ellerker 'alone gave evidence against him and that but slender'.  Quite possibly only Ellerker testified against Levenyng as well; certainly the enquiry into the verdict mentions him alone as witness.  The jury, which was divided for a long while, found a verdict of not guil-ty because a majority felt that Ellerker spoke out of malice, since he had already been granted part of Leven-yng's lands by the king. (84)  The king's legal advisers could not have failed to notice that another witness might

have won the case.   They may even have given some thought
as to whether, if two witnesses were made obligatory at
arraignment, the mere production of that number might not
stop the petty jurors giving too much attention to the
actual weight of the evidence.

However, the Henrician government passed no law about
witnesses at treason trials.   What it did do was to introduce provision for witnesses into legislation promoting
religious obedience.   In the statute 34 & 35 Hen. VIII
c. 1 for the advancement of religion, suspects being tried
before joint commissions of bishops' officers and justices
of the peace or king's councillors for teaching contrary
to the act were permitted 'trial by witness' and allowed
to try to purge their innocency by offering as many or
more witnesses than had deposed against them.   The act 35
Hen. VIII c. 5 provided in one of its clauses that preachers offending against the act of 'six articles' should
be accused within forty days of the offence, unless sufficient cause why this could not have been done was shown
by two sufficient witnesses.   This, and the provision in
the same act that suspects under the six articles statute
were only to be accused by indictment, show that the government was having to legislate for the first time about
witnesses and evidence, although as yet cases of treason
were not involved. (85)   Very likely the close contact
with canon law, which the drafting and operating of religious laws engendered, was influential.

How legislation affected the role of witnesses in legal
process in general has already been touched on above, but
since the matter is of great importance the historical
development of the law touching witnesses at arraignment
may be briefly rehearsed here.   Reaction against Henry
VIII's treason laws seems to have been one of the reasons
for the statute 5 & 6 Edw. VI c. 11, stipulating that
there should be two accuser-witnesses (*testes*) at arraignment who should be brought in person before the party
accused and 'avow and maintain that that they have to
say'.   Thereby it went beyond the treason act of 1547
(1 Edw. VI c. 12), which did not make it at all clear if
the witnesses were essential at both indictment and arraignment.   The first Marian treason act said nothing
about witnesses at all, but the second (1 & 2 Ph. & M.
c. 10) made it essential for two witness-accusers to
appear before the party arraigned.   At the conference at
Serjeants' Inn on 25 October 1556, between the judges and
the law officers of the crown, the 1554 act was interpreted as meaning that two witness-accusers were necessary if
the indictment was based on a sixteenth-century act but
not if it was drawn under the act of 1352, since the

latter was a declaration of common law. (86)   Two accuser-witnesses were also required to appear against the accused by the Elizabethan treason acts 1 Eliz. c. 5, 5 Eliz. c. 1, 13 Eliz. c. 1 and 23 Eliz. c. 2.   Why these statutes should contain rules about witnesses when other laws on treason, like 1 M. st. 2 c. 6, 1 & 2 Ph. & M. cc. 9, 11, 1 Eliz. c. 1, 14 Eliz. cc. 1, 2, 23 Eliz. c. 1 and 27 Eliz. c. 2, did not, is to be found in the offences they were designed to combat.   Rules about witnesses appeared when one of the misdeeds with which an act dealt was speaking traitorous words. (87)   The statutes dealing with simple deeds like counterfeiting coins, detaining the king's ships, castles and ordnance, and practising to withdraw the queen's subjects to the Roman faith, did not need to introduce provisions for witnesses, since those types of offence were more overt than a few words of private conversation, and thus there was usually more evidence available.   Parliament obviously did not fear there might be unfair prosecutions for crimes of that sort.

The gaining of this guarantee against unfounded accusations must have owed as much to demands made by those on trial as to concern in parliament and the crown's own sense of fair play.   Lord Seymour, in February 1549, told the privy council, which had come to the Tower of London to examine him, that he expected an open trial and his accusers brought face to face with him.   The duke of Somerset at his arraignment on 1 December 1551 objected 'many things against the Witnesses and desired they might be brought face to face', but the request was fruitless and he was proceeded against upon their depositions, which were read out in court.   This, William Rastell is quoted as saying, led to the act 5 & 6 Edw. VI c. 11. (88)   The response of the Elizabethan government, when it found it had no liking for the appearance of witnesses as demanded by some of the new treason laws, was really one of subterfuge.   When the duke of Norfolk in 1571 asked for Banister, Leddington and the earl of Murray to be brought face to face with him, he was told by Serjeant Barham that that particular provision of the law 'hath been found too hard and dangerous for the prince and it hath been repealed.' (89)   Barham seems in this instance to have meant that by the Serjeants' Inn decision of 1556 those indicted, as was Norfolk, under the statute of 1352 were not automatically entitled to the privilege of meeting the witnesses against them.   This was hard on Norfolk for, as we have seen above, although he was told he was indicted solely under the fourteenth-century act, the charges included categories of treason first legislated on in the reigns of Mary and Elizabeth.   Thus it seems as if the

queen's legal advisers set out to indict Norfolk under the
act 13 Eliz. c. 1 and then reverted to using the act of
1352, but without ensuring that the indictment totally
conformed.    One reason for the change of mind must have
been a desire to avoid having to produce certain witnesses in court.

Some of the argument at the trial of Edward Abington on
15 September 1586 was most revealing on this point.
Abington objected to the confession of Anthony Babington
being read out against him and asked for two lawful witnesses face to face, not witnesses who had confessed their
guilt or were already convicted.    As in Norfolk's case,
the indictment appears to have been based on the act 13
Eliz. c. 1, which required two witnesses at the arraignment.    None the less, Chief Justice Anderson in reply
said Abington was being tried under the statute of 1352,
which did not require witnesses.    The solicitor-general
then showed very clearly how the crown was interpreting
the laws of treason at that time.    No treason would ever
be sufficiently proven, he said with some exaggeration, if
two lawful witnesses had to be produced every time.    The
statute of 1 Eliz. required them to prove overt act 'but
the statute of 25 Edward 3 is, Who shall imagine'.    'How
then', he argued, 'can that be proved by honest men being
a secret cogitation which lieth in the minds of traitors.'
These would only reveal their intentions 'unto such as
themselves'.    He was, in fact, putting the cart before
the horse.    The crown had itself chosen to say the indictment was under the 1352 statute when some of the deeds
referred to were only offences under the act 13 Eliz. c.
1.    Lest we should be tempted to consider the aim in
cases like this was invariably the sinister one of doing
without witnesses, or of preserving witnesses of dubious
veracity from facing the prisoner, it is well to remember
that the earl of Arundel, at his trial on 18 April 1589,
was also told he was indicted under the act of 1352, yet
at least nine witnesses were called into court to affirm
what learned counsel had just specified. (90)

From Arundel's trial until that of Sir Walter Raleigh
in 1603 the issue of witnesses being brought face to face
with the accused does not seem to have reoccurred in treason trials, although John Udall, who was indicted of
felony, touched momentarily on the subject at his arraignment in 1590.    As was the case earlier in Elizabeth's
reign, when the crown was willing to admit that charges of
treason were brought under an act which required witnesses at the arraignment then witnesses appeared, even if on
one occasion at least the evidence was of the hearsay
variety.    There is no evidence that the crown ever tried

to argue that all treason arraignments were governed by
the common law and that therefore no witnesses were necessary.   It has been argued in regard to the trial of Sir
Walter Raleigh at the beginning of James I's reign that
'the procedural question of the witnesses was unanswered',
but this seems incorrect. (91)   Raleigh, quoting statutes
of Edward VI and Philip and Mary and also the Old Testa-
ment claimed he was entitled to be confronted by two witnesses.   In answer, Chief Justice Popham pointed to the
summary of treason legislation and the decisive declaration about witnesses contained in the statute 1 & 2 Ph. &
M. c. 10.   This statute, so he argued, demanded witnesses only for offences mentioned by itself;   otherwise
trial for treason was to be as it was at common law, in
which he included the act of 1352. (92)   This indeed had
been the policy of the Elizabethan government all along,
although the new treason statutes which demanded trial
witnesses were an addition to the requirements of the act
of 1554.   Where Elizabeth and her ministers were guilty
of sharp practice was in construing certain offences, and
thus certain indictments, as coming within the act of 1352
and thereby depriving the accused of any right to face
witnesses against him.

There is no evidence that when witnesses against the
accused were actually available the Tudor government ever
showed reluctance to use them.   Rather it was wont to
order the appearance in court of as many as was thought
would help the king's case.   One report of the trial of
the earl of Arundel in 1589 gives the names of nine and
says there were also 'divers others' who were brought into
court to affirm 'viva voce upon their several oaths' evidence given against the accused.   When Sir John Perrot
was called to judgment on 26 June 1592 the lord chamberlain drew attention to the fact that as many as thirty
different witnesses had been produced against him at the
arraignment.   This seems to have been the grounds for
the lord chamberlain's next statement, which was that 'he
never saw any Traitor have such indifferent Trial and such
sufficient proofs produced against him', an interesting
admission that witnesses in court made for a fairer trial.
Lord Buckhurst supported this opinion, stating that he had
seen 'divers Traitors condemned of Treason upon a tenth
part of the evidence that was against him yet justly condemned'. (93)

Although the practice was infrequent, it was apparently
quite in order for the crown to introduce hearsay evidence.   At the trial of Sir Nicholas Throckmorton a deposition by the duke of Suffolk was read out in which he
stated that his brother, Lord Thomas Grey, had told him

that the accused was 'privy to the whole devices against
the Spaniards'.   Throckmorton rightly asked why was not
Lord Grey's deposition brought against him instead.   As
if by way of reply, the judges at the trial of William
Thomas two weeks later went as far as to declare that one
witness of his own knowledge and another by hearsay from
him, although at third or fourth hand, were two sufficient witnesses in cases of high treason.   The conference
of judges and law officers of the crown at Serjeants' Inn
in October 1556 did not make any pronouncement on this
matter at all, and thus whether the rule of 1554 survived
is not clear. (94)   Coke went so far as to argue that
'the strange conceit in 2 Mar William Thomas's case that
one may be an accuser by hearsay was utterly denied by the
justices in the Lo. Lumleys case' in Hilary term 14 Eliz.
Certainly it is very noticeable that the crown avoided
bringing hearsay witnesses into court or even their examinations.   Only in a report of the trial of the earl of
Arundel in 1589 do we find something which may refer to
such practices continuing.   'There were then brought in
court', we are told, 'viva voce upon their several oaths
Anthony Hall and Richard Young, a justice of the peace,
who aimed something by hearsay to the proof of the former
matter.'   In the trial of Sir Walter Raleigh at the beginning of the next reign there was, however, a clear demonstration of the use of hearsay evidence and of bitter
objection to it by the accused.   Chief Justice Popham,
refusing to allow Lord Cobham to testify, argued that
'Where no circumstances do concur to make a matter probable then an accuser may be heard; but so many circumstances agreeing and confirming the accusation in this
case, the accuser is not to be produced', which amounted
to saying that a hearsay statement was sufficient if
otherwise corroborated.   At another point in the proceedings Raleigh, when the examinations of three witnesses had
been read out, remarked that he was only being accused by
hearsay evidence. (95)   The justices answered that this
was perfectly all right, and quoted the case of William
Thomas and Sir Nicholas Arnold.   Said Raleigh bitterly,
'If this may be, you will have any man's life in a week.'
   Such were the court rules which governed the use of
witnesses in the Tudor period.   Like Raleigh, those accused were wont at times to challenge both the witnesses and
their testimony, although the grounds they gave for so
doing were different.   One defendant tried in an assize
court probably in 1541 drew attention to the fact that
those who deposed against him were not sworn.   Frequently
the accused would argue that the witness was a confessed
traitor or felon, and thus his testimony was unacceptable.

The duke of Norfolk at his trial claimed that all the witnesses against him were incapacitated, one because he had
confessed to treason and the others because they were outlawed or attainted of treason.   To this Chief Justice
Catlin answered that none were outlawed or attainted of
treason, or yet indicted.   Apparently it did not matter
if they had confessed to treason;  they were still proper
witnesses so long as they had not been indicted or attainted at common law.   Another possible challenge and one
that always caused great denials by the crown, was to suggest a witness had been compelled to make the answers he
did by duress or fear.   The thought that this challenge
might be made seems to have stopped the crown offering
testimony from those it had tortured, and even prompted it
to produce secondary witnesses who would testify that the
primary witnesses had not been put to the rack or the
manacles. (96)   A third objection, but one with perhaps
even less chance of success than the others, was to say
that the witness came as an accuser.   These were unacceptable as witnesses because by definition they offered
themselves to accuse and did not, as witnesses were supposed to do, await their turn to be called.   In the later
Middle Ages for a person to appear in court without invi-
tation and say he knew something about the matter in hand
was considered maintenance, that is to say the illegal
assistance of a man in his suit when it did not concern
one personally.   However, one result in the common law of
the first twenty years of the Reformation was the growing
acceptance of accuser-witnesses, and by the reign of Elizabeth it became customary for the crown to proclaim in
court at a certain time that if there was any person who
wished to make accusations against the prisoner he should
now do so.
     One cause of the old suspicion of the eager witness was
a belief that an eagerness to accuse came from malice,
which was likely to corrupt the testimony and turn the
testifier into a false witness.   This was a line of argument frequently resorted to by those on trial and sometimes it met with success.   As we have noticed already,
the jury which tried William Levenyng eventually decided
to acquit him because they thought the evidence given by
Sir Ralph Ellerker was maliciously prompted by his desire
to have the prisoner's lands when forfeit. (97)   Sir John
Perrot at his trial objected several times to the witnesses brought against him on the grounds that they were his
mortal enemies and lewd and wicked men.   When brought
into court later for the pronouncing of judgment he complained of 'the hard and false dealings of the witnesses
towards him in these causes ... who falsely, maliciously

and perjuriously accused him'.   He claimed, furthermore,
that all the witnesses who 'proved treason against him'
were Irishmen who had 'no respect of an oath' and that
'for a small value a man might procure a number to swear
anything'. (98)   This defaming of witnesses' characters
was also employed by the earl of Arundel, who said of the
witness Walton that he was 'a naughty lewd fellow who had
sold that little land he had to three several men'.   He
called other witnesses 'bad men and prisoners', whose
words 'were worth little credit'.   Thomas Gerrard, another witness and an important one, the earl tried to shake
in his testimony by demanding he look him in the face and
tell nothing but the truth 'as he would answer before God
in whose presence he spoke'.   Gerrard was terrified, but
it did not save the earl. (99)   A challenge which must
have particularly perturbed the judges and the queen's
learned counsel was that made at their trial at Wrexham on
9 October 1584 by Richard White, John Hughes and Robert
Morris.   The accused took exception to the crown's three
witnesses on the grounds that one had been in the pillory
for perjury and the others had been bribed to bear false
evidence.   They named a gentleman of the parish as having
told him about the bribery.   He was called to the bar and
informed of the prisoners' statement:   'the which he re-
iterating before all the hall justified to be true'.
'Whereat', says the report of the trial, 'the assembly
were greatly astonied, and the judges themselves not a
little daunted.'   The 'deputy justice', however, immediately denied any man would give money to obtain false
witnesses since no one would profit from the prisoners'
deaths.   Later on, while summing up, he made a point of
'extolling the witnesses' and 'dispraising the prisoners',
which must have contributed to their eventual conviction. (100)

Although they might challenge the witnesses which the
crown brought into court to support its case, the accused
were rarely permitted to cross-examine them.   This we
might expect, remembering the reluctance of the government
to allow witnesses to meet the prisoner face to face.
When cross-examination did occur it seems to have been
occasioned by the witness putting a question to the accused.   Cuthbert Vaughan is reported to have said to Sir
Nicholas Throckmorton 'How say you Mr Throckmorton, was
there any displeasure between you and me to say aught
against you?'   This allowed Throckmorton to rejoin 'how
say you Vaughan, what acquaintance was there between you
and me....?' and to this he received a proper
answer. (101)   This was the only time in the trial a witness was questioned by the prisoner and the descriptions

of other sixteenth-century treason trials suggest it was
no commoner elsewhere.   It was a chance occurrence and
rare, perhaps, because it was likely to be futile, since
the witness was not obliged to give any answer.

If this was a handicap to the accused, much more so was
his inability to offer witnesses of his own.   Several
times in the sixteenth century prisoners tried to obtain
leave from the court to do so.   John Udall offered several witnesses to testify on a single matter at one point
in his trial, but he and they were answered that 'because
their Witness was against the queen's majesty they could
not be heard'.   The duke of Norfolk at his trial, after
the bishop of Ross's depositions had been read out, complained 'nor have [I] been suffered to bring forth witnesses proofs, arguments, as might have been made for my
purgation'.   When John Fitzwilliams presented himself at
the bar ready to speak on behalf of Sir Nicholas Throckmorton, the attorney-general asked the justices not 'to
suffer him to be sworn, neither to speak'.   Despite
Throckmorton's sarcastic comment 'why be ye not so well
contented to hear truth for me as untruth against me?'
Fitzwilliams had to leave the court without saying anything.   Later on in the trial Throckmorton managed to
raise once more the matter of witnesses on behalf of the
accused, pointing out to Chief Justice Bromley that he
knew Queen Mary had enjoined that

> notwithstanding the old error amongst you which did not
> admit any witness to speak or any other matter to be
> heard in the favour of the adversary, her majesty being
> party, her highness's pleasure was that whatsoever
> could be brought in· favour of the subject should be
> admitted to be heard.

Bromley's answer was that the words were addressed, not to
him, but to Morgan the chief justice of common pleas, and
that Throckmorton himself had no reason for complaint
since he had been allowed to say as much as he wanted. (102)   The implication was that it was for the
judges to decide if witnesses for the accused should be
permitted and that in Throckmorton's case the opportunities allowed him to answer back and question the bench
were generosity enough.   It is possible, although the
evidence is not strong, that the prisoner was allowed to
have some say as to who was examined before the trial, and
that the examination of someone whom he selected might be
offered in court.   The duke of Norfolk at his trial in
1572 is reported as saying he had 'divers times prayed
that if anything which I said were denied to be true, I
might be driven to the proof of it.'   Lord Burghley in
reply said that he had not 'heard it reported to her

Majesty that you made any such request or desired to have
any particular witnesses examined or proofs heard, on your
part'.    What the duke responded to this is not reported. (103)    The dialogue certainly suggests that testimony on behalf of the accused might be allowed in certain
circumstances but that these did not obtain in Norfolk's
case nor apparently in any other reported treason trial in
the sixteenth century.

So far we have been largely concerned with treason trials where there was but one accused at the bar.    This was
the normal practice, but there were occasions when several
accused were on trial at once.    One of the most instruc-
tive of these was the arraignment of Edmund Campion and
seven associates in November 1581.    Campion, we are told,
protested to the justices that he and the other accused
should have been 'severally indicted and that our Accusations carrying so great importance and tending so nearly
unto us as our lives, each one might have had one day for
his trial'.    He pointed out that 'all the Evidence being
given or rather handled at once must needs breed a confusion in the Jury', which might take the evidence against
one as being against all.    That each ought to have been
tried on a separate day Chief Justice Wray readily admitted, but he added that it was impractical as the time did
not permit.    The procedure that far and to come he none
the less firmly defended, pointing out that 'evidence
shall be particularly given against every one and to the
matters objected everyone shall have his particular answer
so that the jury shall have things orderly'.    By being
tried together the prisoners, in this instance, benefited
from the fact that Campion was able to speak not merely in
his own defence but on behalf of any other of the accused,
as in turn evidence was alleged against each of them.
When Bosgrave was nonplussed by one accusation Campion
spoke to excuse him.    When a little later Cottam was
taxed with having a seditious book in his baggage and
seemed unable to account for it, Campion came to his
rescue, arguing that the volume in question was a purely
spiritual work.    As the trial drew to a close it was
Campion again, who had acted throughout rather as counsel
for the defence, who summed up the case for the accused. (104)    There were other treason trials when several
persons were arraigned at once, for example that of Babington and his fellow conspirators on 13-15 September
1586, but there is no evidence that any of the accused was
permitted to answer on behalf of his confederates.    We
may suspect that the device of a common trial was favoured
by the crown not merely to save time, but when the prosecuting lawyers were forced to rely heavily on the pre-

trial examinations and answers of the accused and there
was little supporting evidence.   Once one of the suspects
had been arraigned and convicted then his examinations and
replies in court were no longer available as evidence in
subsequent trials, since he was an attainted traitor.   If
all received judgment at the same time this obstruction
was avoided. (105)

So far we have assumed that the accused pleaded not
guilty.   If, however, he pleaded guilty trial procedure
obviously differed.   We might expect to find that judgment was pronounced straight away and the convicted man
quickly taken from the court.   This was certainly the
pattern of events in felony trials, but frequently, when
the matter was treason, the arraignment continued for a
considerable time after the admission of guilt.   When
John Savage, one of Babington's fellow conspirators, had
pleaded guilty, the queen's learned counsel addressed the
court to the effect that there was really nothing further
to be done in the case except to proceed to judgment on
Savage's confession yet, because the crown wanted the
spectators in court to be satisfied and 'all the world to
know how justly he was to be condemned', they asked permission to give such evidence as would fully prove the indictment.   This was granted, and the clerk of the crown
read out Savage's confession.   At the arraignment of Dr
William Parry two-and-a-half years earlier, the government's determination to ensure that a plea of guilty did
not remove the propaganda value of the trial was even more
clearly revealed.   Parry admitted he was guilty of everything contained in the indictment and said he wished to
die.   This was far too succinct a response for the prosecution and the clerk of the crown told Parry he must confess his guilt in the manner in which it was contained in
the indictment.   Parry said he did so and his confession
was 'recorded', presumably on the plea roll, but the crown
had not yet finished.   One of the justices, Sir Christopher Hatton, stated that the matters contained in the indictment were of great importance as they touched the
queen's majesty and 'the very state and well being of the
whole Commonwealth'.   'Wherefore I pray you', said Hatton
to the other justices, 'for the satisfaction of this great
multitude let the whole truth appear that every one may
see that the matter of itself is as bad as the Indictment
purporteth, and as the Prisoner hath confessed.'   He argued that the crimes were only summarized in the indictment, and more was necessary to satisfy the world at large
even if all the requirements of English law had been met.
Next the accused was asked to declare that all his confessions were made freely and willingly and not extorted by

threats, which he did.    Parry's confession was at that
point read out by the clerk and then offered to its author, who viewed every page, as well as two incriminating
letters, and vouched for their authenticity.    Unfortunately for the crown, much of the propaganda effect of
these proceedings was quickly obliterated as Parry, with a
remarkable volte-face, just as the justices were about to
pronounce judgment, interjected to claim that what he had
said previously was not true and that his confession had
been extorted by threat of the rack. (106)

It is quite possible that, before trial began, the
crown came to an agreement with certain prisoners that if
they would plead guilty they should be allowed to give an
extended account of their crimes.    The existence of such
arrangements cannot be proven, but the way the court which
tried Sir Thomas Wyatt on 14 March 1554 agreed instantly
to his request that if he pleaded guilty he should have
leave to say what he wanted, certainly points in that direction.    Wyatt plunged into a homily on the just desserts
for treason and its 'beastly brutishness', saying how much
he repented of his offences.    Then the queen's learned
counsel interrupted to point out that he had drawn the
duke of Suffolk into the plot and tried to involve Princess Elizabeth, and asked Wyatt one or two questions about
his behaviour during the insurrection which were seemingly
intended to confirm what he had written in his confession.
At one point a letter Wyatt had written to the duke of
Suffolk was shown to him. (107)    All this was obviously
an exercise in propaganda.    The crown already knew almost
everything there was to know about the rebels and their
intentions, and there is little likelihood that the episode was a further examination at the last moment before
sentence, even if learned counsel always hoped for some
implication of Elizabeth.

When the justices thought the evidence had been heard
and the prisoner had been given sufficient time to make
his replies, the case was summed up for the benefit of the
jury.    This task was usually undertaken by one of the
senior justices, and how he performed it would play a
large part in deciding the prisoner's fate.    The elder
Sir Thomas Wyatt, in the speech he intended to give in his
defence when put on trial, said he knew 'the force of a
small word of their Lordships' to the jurors.    When John
Udall was being tried for felony, one justice said bluntly
to the jurors just before they retired 'You being ignorant
of the law and we being sworn as well as you are you are
to hear us and take our exposition of the law.'    We are
told that at the arraignment of Bishop Fisher, before the
jury retired, 'the case was so aggravated to them by my

lord chancellour, making it so hainous and dangerous a
treason, that they easily perceived what verdict they must
returne.'   Some of the other justices charged Fisher, at
this point, with 'obstinacy and singularity', saying how
presumptuous he was to stand against what parliament had
agreed on, and all the other bishops given their consent
to. (108)   The summing up at the trial of Sir Nicholas
Throckmorton came when the accused himself suggested that
the court was tired of his interjections and therefore the
lord chief justice should repeat the evidence against him
together with his own objections 'if there be no other
matter to lay against me'.   Upon this Chief Justice
Bromley 'remembered particularly all the Depositions and
Evidences given against the prisoner' but 'either for want
of good memory or good will the prisoners Answers were in
part not recited.'   These omissions, however, were remedied by Throckmorton, who 'did help the Judge's old memory
with his own recital'.   This seems to mean that the accused was allowed, if he wished, to make a last address to
the jurors after the prosecution ahd finished.   At the
trial of Sir John Perrot, so we are told,

> the queen's learned Counsel prayed the Jury to consider
> well of that which had been said and willed them to go
> together.   Then Sir John Perrot willed them to consi-
> der their Charge and have a conscience in the matter;
> and to remember that his blood would be required at
> their hands if they dealt further than their conscience
> did warrant them. (109)

Short addresses of this sort seem to have been the custom
on both sides, although the actual words and arguments
used are frequently omitted in reports.

One of the few detailed descriptions of a more than
cursory summing up by an accused is to be found in the
report of the trial of Edmund Campion and his associates.
Campion began by reminding the jurors of the account they
must render on Judgment Day, and begged that their deliberations should be 'substantial'.   He drew attention to
what he called the 'presumptions and probabilities' offered by the queen's learned counsel, remarking that 'the
constitutions of the realm exact a necessity and will that
no man should totter upon the hazard of likelihoods'.
As to the 'points of doctrine and religion' which had been
discussed, like excommunications, books and pamphlets, the
authority of the bishop of Rome, and 'how mens consciences
must be instructed' these, said Campion, were not matters
of fact triable by jurors, nor indeed part of the indictment.   The only valid part of the evidence, he observed,
was the testimony of the witnesses, yet this was not
truthful.   'Call I you to your remembrance', he is said

to have begged the jurors, 'how faintly some have deposed,
how coldly others, how untruly the rest', describing one
of the witnesses as a confessed murderer and another as a
well-known atheist who had destroyed two men already.
Finally, he suggested the jurors themselves should examine
the two other witnesses. (110)    Just how typical Campion's summing up was we cannot be sure.    It was the
sophisticated address of an academic, and therefore probably exceptional.    From the point of view of practical
effect it had one definite strength, namely the castiga-
tion of the witnesses, and one great weakness.    This was
its failure to descend to arguing facts, controverting
details, or alleging errors of law, as Sir Nicholas
Throckmorton seems to have done. (111)    One feature of
general historical interest was that Campion seems to have
been the first man reported as having suggested that the
guilt of the accused ought to be proven beyond reasonable
doubt before a verdict of guilty was justified.

Petty jurors were supposed to be men of substance who
lived in the hundred where the crime had been committed.
By an act of 1414 the minimum size of this substance had
been set at the holding of lands worth forty shillings a
year 'above all reprizes'.    If jurors were discovered to
possess less they were replaced;    in fact as many as seven
were replaced at the trial of Edmund Dudley in July
1509. (112)    The intention behind setting a qualification
of wealth was to ensure that the jurors were less likely
to be corrupted by bribes.    In the sixteenth century the
crown was rarely satisfied with jurors who only just met
the minimum requirement, and sought rather to empanel
those whose rank and wealth was equivalent to that of the
accused.    Thus, for the trial of the May Day rioters in
1517 the justices decided that the petty jurors must have
lands and goods to the value of a hundred marks. (113)
When the earl of Surrey was tried at the London Guildhall
in 1546, the jurors, because his title came 'by nativity
not creation' as the eldest son of the duke of Norfolk,
were knights and squires of Norfolk.    Rather remarkably
there seems to have been no law which forbade the sitting
on juries of those who held office under the crown.    On
one occasion at Gloucester in 1538 Bishop Roland Lee,
president of the council of the marches of Wales, put several justices of the peace, 'the best of the bench', on a
petty jury, although one of them protested. (114)

Peers, that is to say lords of parliament, who were indicted of treason were tried in the court of the lord high
steward.    The jurors, who were always of noble station,
numbered usually between fifteen and thirty.    They were
drawn from all ranks of the nobility, not just that of the

accused.   At the arraignment of the duke of Buckingham in
1521 there were present on the jury one other duke, one
marquis, seven earls, eight lesser noblemen, and the prior
of St John of Jerusalem.   At the trial of the duke of
Somerset in 1551 the jury comprised one marquis, eight
earls, one viscount, and seventeen lesser lords. (115)
Queen Anne Boleyn faced a jury which had on it a duke, a
marquis, eight earls, and sixteen noblemen of inferior
station.   For lesser nobility, like Lords Darcy and
Hussey, tried for treason on 15 May 1537, there were as
jurors a marquis, six earls, a viscount, and thirteen
lesser lords. (116)   A bishop who was indicted of treason
was not entitled to trial before his peers and his life
was as much at risk as any layman.   This had been demonstrated by the trials of Thomas Merkes, bishop of Carlisle, in 1400, and of Richard Scrope, archbishop of York,
in 1405.   For John Fisher, bishop of Rochester, in 1535
the jurors were freeholders of Middlesex and comprised two
knights and ten esquires. (117)

The selection of the members of the petty jury was very
much in the hands of the crown since, although in theory
they were appointed by local electors, in practice it was
by the sheriff.   At his trial Sir Nicholas Throckmorton,
hoping to have a jury which was unbiased, reminded the
court of a case where one justice said to another, 'I like
not this jury for our purpose, they seem to be too piti-
able and charitable to condemn the prisoner', but the
second replied there was no cause for apprehension:   the
prisoner would 'drink the same cup his fellows have done'
since the jurors were 'picked fellows for the
nonce'. (118)   Usually the government was justified in
its confidence in the jurors but this did not mean that
packing was unrestricted or that rules about choice of
jurors did not exist.   An act of 1352 excluded as petty
jurors members of the grand juries which had brought the
indictment, but only if challenged by the accused.   Thus
it was very likely that some men sat on both, which may
have been a help in gaining a conviction.   There was a
medieval rule that no petty juror should be directly related to those on trial, but that in the sixteenth century
it was sometimes ignored cannot be doubted.   Ensuring
that the jurors were of the right mind to find the accused
guilty was not left merely to the process of selection.
When empanelled they might be given instruction outside
the courtroom by some 'learned man', who would explain the
nature of the offence and also, no doubt, the likelihood,
as the crown saw it, of the prisoner's being guilty. (119)
A variation of this device was to summon the jurors, before the date fixed for the trial, into the star chamber

and 'deliver' the evidence to them.   On occasion members
of the jury might be removed and others, known to dislike
the accused and wish his death, be substituted. (120)   As
far as we can tell, few jurors failed to appear when once
selected for service, although some might have to be changed because they were found to be insufficiently wealthy.
One of the few exceptions seems to have been at the trial
of Campion and his fellow catholics in November 1581.
William Allen states that 'three of the first of that im-
panel being Squiers belike fearing God and doubting that
iustice should have no free course that day' failed to
appear. (121)

When the jurors retired, Sir Thomas Smith tells us,
'they have in writing nothing given them but the endite-
ment, the clarke [of the court] repeating to them the
effect of it and shewing more, that if they finde him
guiltie they shall enquire what goods, lands and tenements' the accused possessed when the offence was committed.   Smith, at this point in his book, was referring to
trials for felony but there is little evidence that when
the offence was treason there was any difference.   The
place where the jurors debated their verdict was usually
apart from the courtroom.   It might be elsewhere in the
same building, but it could be a house or church nearby.
There in theory the members of the jury were carefully
confined with a bailiff or other official keeping guard so
as to ensure that no one tried to speak with them.   In
the earlier sixteenth century, if they seemed to the justices to be taking too long to make up their minds, they
were not permitted to have meat, drink, candle, fire, or
in some cases even furniture to sit upon, the intention
being to persuade them to arrive at a verdict more speed-
ily.   By the time Smith wrote his 'De Republica' the
jurors were prevented from having these luxuries from the
moment they retired. (122)   If they wanted to hear any
witness again, or at greater length, they could summon him
for questioning.   What opportunity the petty jurors had
to play detective, and discover for themselves the facts
of treasonable conspiracies, in the time between being empanelled and the arraignment, we do not know.   They may
well have had less freedom here than their medieval for-
bears, but neither had the chances which jurors who were
to try lesser offences had.   Meeting restriction in one
area, the jurors may have tried new initiatives in another.   Towards the end of the sixteenth century, and at
the beginning of the seventeenth, there were one or two
instances of jurors interrupting the giving of the evidence to ask a question on a particular point, which was a
new method of gaining information.   At the trial of the

earl of Arundel in the court of the lord high steward in
1589 Lord Grey and Lord Norris, when a witness named Mark
Bennett denied writing a particular letter, interrupted to
ask him 'if he knew of the letter, yea or no?'   At the
arraignment of Sir Walter Raleigh in November 1603 Sir
Thomas Fowler, one of the jury, asked 'Did sir Walter
Raleigh write a Letter to my lord [i.e. Lord Cobham]
before he was examined concerning him or not?', to which
the attorney-general replied in the affirmative. (123)

While in retirement the jurors were by no means cut off
from the world outside.   They may even have had the
right, as Campion's summing up speech suggests, of summoning in and examining for themselves the witnesses in the
case.   Occasionally, and no doubt with the approval of
the justices, they sent a message to the accused urging
him, before they returned a verdict, to submit, that is to
say to admit guilt by changing his plea and putting himself on the king's mercy.   Several times in the sixteenth
century treason juries sought the advice of the justices
on points of law.   At the trial of the earl of Arundel
the peers of the jury debated their verdict for an hour
'and in points of law they consulted the opinion of the
judges and serjeants'.   At the arraignment of the earls
of Essex and Southampton in 1600 the lords sent for the
two chief justices and the chief baron of the exchequer
and drew from them the important opinion that to compel
the prince to govern in a way he did not choose was manifest rebellion, and that every rebellion intended the
prince's death and was therefore treason. (124)   We also
have evidence that the jurors might be visited by the
sheriff and that he might speak to them 'very vehemently'.
If this is not conclusive proof of interference there is
stronger.   At the trial of Richard White, John Hughes and
Robert Morris the jury retired to a church where it remained all night with its keeper, 'saving that two of
them, about an hour after their coming were sent for to
confer with the judges to know of them whom they should
acquit and whom they should find guilty'. (125)

About the deliberations of the jurors we know little,
since we must rely almost entirely on chance remarks and
passing references.   Something, however, may be gleaned
from the length of time they were out of the courtroom.
The jury which tried Robert Southwell the Jesuit needed
but fifteen minutes to confer, and the one which tried Sir
John Davis and Sir Gellis Merrick, supporters of the earl
of Essex, returned in half an hour.   Sir John Perrot's
jury was out for three-quarters of an hour, while the
fellow peers of the earl of Arundel decided on his guilt
in an hour, a time which was about average. (126)   In

cases like these there was probably little difference of
opinion, although we cannot be categorical about this
since in the trial of Bishop Fisher the jury returned
shortly, but it was 'no doubt full sore against their conscience as some of them would after report to their dying
daies, onely for safety of their goods and lives which
they were well assured to lose in case they acquitted
him'.   The jury which acquitted Sir Nicholas Throckmorton
was out at least three hours, possibly five, and the one
which acquitted Levenyng and Lutton in 1537 debated the
issue from nine o'clock Friday morning until Saturday
night, despite efforts by the duke of Norfolk to cut short
the discussions.   The jury was divided over Levenyng
seven to five in favour of acquittal until late on Saturday night, when 'they fell all to prayer ... and rose upe
... and agreed to the acquitting ...'.   Apparently the
majority had thought that the chief witness, Sir Ralph
Ellerker, spoke out of malice and that Levyning had joined
Sir Francis Bigod's uprising under duress.   The minority
held out, it seems, largely because of the presence
amongst them of a strong loyalist, Thomas Delaryver, who
said, so he claimed later, much about the penalties they
would incur if they brought in an acquittal. (127)

When the jurors had reached their decision, which according to one contemporary was signalled by their shouting out the words 'a verdict', they told the justices.
They were then ordered to return to court and the prisoner
was brought once more to the bar.   The justices asked if
the jury was agreed on its verdict and its members usually
answered with one voice 'Yea'.   'Who shall speak for
you?' was the next question, suggesting that either it was
not always the foreman or that, if it was, the election to
that office occurred while the jury was in retirement.
The accused was ordered to hold up his hand and the jury
to look upon him and say if they found him guilty, yes or
no. (128)   In the court of the high steward procedure was
somewhat different.   The twenty-four noblemen of the jury
returned from their place of retirement, such as the court
of chancery nearby, without giving notice they intended to
return.   While they were out the lord steward remained in
his seat.   When they had been 'again placed by Garter
King at arms' and the prisoner conducted out of hearing
the lord steward or the clerk of the crown asked every
juror, beginning with the youngest baron and progressing
to 'the highest', whether the prisoner was guilty or not.
Invariably they all gave the same verdict, which, if it
was 'guilty', was announced with each 'laying their hands
on their hearts' and protesting 'in their consciences'
that it was so.   In lesser courts, at least, if the ver-

dict was 'not guilty' the jurors were supposed to enquire
if the accused had fled to escape arrest.   If he had then
his goods and chattels were forfeit, as Stanford says
'pour le vehement presumption que adsurde vers luy auxi
bien per son fues ou retrait come per lenditement'.   If
he was found guilty the jurors were expected to enquire
what lands, tenements, goods and chattels he had in his
possession at the time the treason was committed or at
any time since. (129)   Usually the reply to this question
was that they did not know, and the crown expected it.
     Referring to criminal trials in general, Sir Thomas
Smith said that jurors might decide to acquit the accused
if the justice who summed up the evidence gave them a hint
that he thought it unsatisfactory.   Whether this ever
occurred in a treason trial we do not know.   Certainly
contemporary reports do not mention it.   Smith also held
that if they saw that the prisoner during the trial was
being pursued maliciously by a justice 'or some other
man', or they suspected the subornation of witnesses, the
jurors might bring in an acquittal.   Conceivably Smith
was thinking here of the trial of Sir Nicholas Throckmorton.   Conviction of the accused was thus by no means
automatic.   As the elder Sir Thomas Wyatt wrote in the
address intended for his judges 'yt is an naughtie fere
yf any man ... so thinke a queste dare not acquyte a man
of treason ... for it were a fowle slaunder to the kynges
majesty, god be thanked he is no tyrant ... he will but
his lawes.' (130)   The crown put its best endeavours into
the prosecution of suspect traitors, of that we can be
sure, yet there were quite a number of acquittals.   As
well as Sir Nicholas Throckmorton, Levenyng and Lutton,
who have already been mentioned, there were acquitted
amongst the more notable of suspects Ralph and Edward
Chamberlain (involved in Sir Robert Chamberlain's treasons in 1491), two of John Cowley's associates (Henry
Spencer and Edward Young)  in 1519, Lord Dacre of the
North in 1534, Sir Ralph Vane, Sir Thomas Arundel, Sir
Miles Partridge and the duke of Somerset in 1552, and
Thomas, Lord Wentworth, in 1559.   A recent study of treason cases in the years 1532-40, admittedly a period involving several insurrections and a very large number of
treason trials, has found no fewer than 32 acquittals out
of 600 arraignments.   The king could never be certain a
suspect traitor would be convicted until the verdict had
been returned, even if there was always a strong likelihood of conviction.
     When a jury acquitted the accused, unless the trial had
been held in the court of the high steward, there was
likely to be a governmental investigation.   If a peer had

been acquitted then the king put on a brave face;   at
least, contemporaries do not seem to have detected any
royal malice against the noble jurors.   In 1541 Sir
Thomas Wyatt the elder wrote 'What dyspleasure bare he
Henry VIII to the lordes for the acquytinge the Lord
Dacres, never none ...'.   In contrast, when men of lesser
rank were on trial and were eventually acquitted despite
the strength of the evidence, then, said Smith, who was
referring to criminal cases in general, not only would the
jurors be rebuked by the justices but they would also be
threatened with punishment and 'many times commaunded to
appeare in the starrechamber or before the privie ccun-
sell for the matter'. (132)   Smith was quite right.
There are a number of examples of juries which had acquitted being summoned to appear before the council in the
star chamber to answer for their 'unjust' verdicts. (133)
Quite the clearest example of what might happen was the
fate of the jury which acquitted Sir Nicholas Throckmorton.   When the jurors persisted in their verdict of not
guilty, regardless of suggestions that they might have
omitted considering some of the evidence and despite
threatening words from Chief Justice Bromley, the attorney-general asked the court on the queen's behalf that
each juror should be bound in a recognizance of £500 to
answer, whenever called, what might be charged against him
on the queen's behalf.   The foreman of the jury, Whetston, begged they should not be molested 'for discharging
our consciences truly'.   Thinking, no doubt, of the
jurors' business commitments, he asked that they should
be given a date to appear, by which he meant be excused
committal to gaol.   The plea was ignored and eight of
the jurors, including Whetston, who refused to submit
themselves and say they had offended,·were kept in prison
for more than six months.   On 26 October 1554 they were
called before the council in the star chamber and, despite their plea that they had 'done all things in that
matter according to their knowledge and with good consciences', and their offer to submit themselves to the king
and queen 'saving and reserving their truth, consciences
and honesties', five of them were sentenced each to pay
1,000 marks and three £2,000.   In fact these enormous
fines were later mitigated to more realistic amounts of
£220 in some cases and a modest £60 in others.   The last
three jurors were not set free until 21 December
1554. (134)
   It must have been Throckmorton's jury to which Sir
Thomas Smith was referring when he wrote that he had seen
in a previous reign 'an enquest for pronouncing one not
guiltie of treason contrarie to such evidence as was

brought in ... not onely imprisoned for a space but an
houge fine set upon their heads which they were faine to
pay'.     It is important to notice that Smith regarded the
episode as exceptional, holding that usually enquiries
into acquittals were little more than empty gestures.
'This threatening', he said, 'chaunceth oftener than the
execution thereof, and the xii answere with most gentle
wordes, they did it according to their consciences, and
pray the Judges to be good unto them, they did as they
thought right and as they accorded all, and so it passeth
away for the most part.' (135)    Certainly there are lacking from later in the century references to juries who had
acquitted suspect traitors being punished for their leniency, even if the threat that they would have to appear
before the council if they acquitted may have been made
before or during the trial.
    As reprehensible in modern eyes as punishing the jury
which acquitted was the practice, infrequent it is true,
of putting the accused on trial a second time on the same
charges.    In 1551 Sir Robert Stafford, after the execution of one Appleyard of Northamptonshire for stirring up
rebellion, suggested that malice was responsible for his
death.    He said the dead man had been taken to Northampton, where the indicting jurors had failed to find a true
bill, then to Uppingham, where he was acquitted, and then
'reprieved' to the Leicester assizes, where he was convicted. (136)    Another example occurred in 1586.    A catholic, Robert Bickerdike, was arraigned first in the Common
Hall at York for aiding a priest and was acquitted.
Later he was put on trial at the Lammas assizes at York
for treasonable words.    This jury, says a catholic
account, seeing the malicious attitude of the justices and
those who had accused him, also found him not guilty.
'At which thing they [the justices] all stormed and said
he should not escape them so', and the queen's attorney
said he would frame a new indictment.    Bickerdike was
then arraigned a third time, but in fact the indictment
was the same as at the Lammas assizes.    Rhodes, one of
the justices, is reported as saying to the jury 'This
traitor had too favourable and too scrupulous a jury in
the town but I trust you will look otherwise to him, being
the Queen's enemy and a notorious traitor.'    The jurors,
after 'earnest pursuit' by the justices, complied. (137)
    The delivery of judgment on the convicted prisoner, and
any speech by the latter in the arrest of this delivery,
might follow immediately on the return of a verdict by the
jury.    On the other hand, when the jury had pronounced
the accused guilty, the court might then be adjourned for
several days, or even weeks if the crown wanted it so.

Sir John Perrot was arraigned on 27 April 1592 but did not
appear before the justices for judgment until 26 June.   A
delay like this was, however, uncommon enough to encourage
Perrot to try to persuade the court that deferral of judgment had been caused by the queen's concern at the 'hard
proceeding against him at his Arraignment'.   When judgment followed an adjournment the prisoner was usually kept
waiting at the bar for some time before the justices entered the court.   Then the king's learned counsel, saying
that the prisoner had earlier pleaded not guilty, put himself on a jury and been convicted, prayed on his majesty's
behalf that judgment might be given accordingly.   The
clerk of the crown thereupon asked the prisoner 'What hast
thou now to say for thyself, why thou shouldst not have
Judgment to die?'   To this, says Holinshed, there were
two types of response the prisoner might make.   He could
plead for mercy, or he could attempt to show that the indictment was insufficient. (138)

Most prisoners decided to plead for mercy.   In their
requests to have their lives spared many asked for the
justices, or if the case was in the court of the high steward then the nobles of the jury, to intercede with the
king on their behalf.   This those who were beseeched normally promised to do, although few lives were saved thereby.   Such mediation was probably more successful in regard to other, lesser, requests which prisoners made in
their pleas for mercy.   These were largely to do with
their families, possessions, servants, and debts.   The
duke of Norfolk asked the lords of his jury to be suitors
to the queen for his 'poor orphan children', and to 'take
order for the payment of my debts and have some consideration of my poor servants'.   The earl of Arundel at his
trial asked the lord high steward and·the nobles present
to be mediators for him with the queen, so that he might
have 'order taken for his debts and ... conference with
his officers and ... talk with his wife and ... see his
infant, born after his imprisonment, whom he had never
seen'.   He also begged that the queen would take the
child into her favour and patronage. (139)   Edward Abington, one of those involved in Anthony Babington's conspiracy, asked that his sister 'whose preferment hath also
miscarried', might be provided for 'in some sort' from the
revenues of his lands.   His fellow prisoner, Edward
Jones, requested that his debts be paid from what was
owing to him, adding that if his entailed lands were forfeited 'some consideration may be had of my posterity'.
The duke of Northumberland at his trial in 1553 requested
that the queen should be gracious to his children, but in
addition asked farsightedly for 'some learned man for the

instruction and quieting of his conscience', as well as
for the manner of execution 'which noble men had in times
passed', requests which were usually made when in gaol
awaiting death. (140)   Very few of those found guilty
were stubborn or courageous enough not to ask for some
alleviation of the expected penalties.   One who did refuse was the earl of Essex in 1600.   When the lord high
steward asked him to submit himself to her majesty's
mercy, acknowledge his offences, and lay open all matters,
the earl prevaricated, saying he was not so proud he would
not crave her mercy, yet without admitting any particular
offence.   He closed the episode by saying he would rather
die than live in misery, by which we may take it he meant
he preferred death to prolonged imprisonment. (141)
    Of the few prisoners who sought to arrest judgment by
showing the indictment was insufficient the most famous by
far was Sir Thomas More.   More, who by the chancellor's
error was nearly deprived of his chance to speak, advanced
as his main argument the thesis that the indictment was
invalid because the act on which it was founded was invalid, being contrary to God's laws and those of the church,
'the supreme government of which no temporal person may
take upon him'.   He said that the realm of England,
being but a small part of the church, should not make a
law which was at odds with the general law ecclesiastical.
In addition, he argued that the act of supremacy was contrary to Magna Carta and to the king's coronation oath.
When the chancellor expressed amazement, since all the
most learned men in the kingdom except More accepted the
act, the prisoner rejoined by stating that he was supported by the opinions of the majority of learned bishops and
virtuous men now dead;   that is to say he believed he had
the 'general council of Christendom' on his side.   Lord
Chancellor Audley, who according to one report of the
trial was 'loth to have the burthen of that Iudgmente
wholye to depend uppon himself', asked the chief justice
of the king's bench whether the indictment was sufficient
or not.   The reply came that it was sufficient as long as
the act of parliament was not unlawful.   Thus satisfied
Audley then gave judgment. (142)
    Although More's argument against the indictment was re-
jected, the justices had been willing to listen to it.
Later on that century they were not so amenable.   When
Sir John Perrot in 1592 asked if he might be permitted 'to
take any Exception against the Indictment' Chief Justice
Anderson replied bluntly that he might not.   It is possible that the attitude of the judiciary had hardened as a
result of a strong case to gain a stay of judgment made by
John Udall at his prolonged and remarkable trial for

felony in 1590-1.    Udall's arguments did not all concern
the indictment although the main one, which was that for
various reasons, including a lack of malicious intent,
there was doubt about his offence being felony, certainly
touched it.    The others concerned procedure:  the jury,
so Udall thought, had been misled by the justices in their
summing up;  the 'proof by witness' was insufficient since
the evidence was not 'pregnant' and the witnesses had not
been produced face to face with him;  he had also been interrupted in his pleadings.    Udall's speech caused delay
through the resulting argument, but it did not stop judgment being pronounced.    Some of the justices' answers to
Udall's objections appear distinctly flimsy, but since
there was no opportunity for him to appeal to a higher
court it did not matter. (143)

Not all the remarks of prisoners, when asked what they
could say in arrest of judgment, were directed towards the
seeking of mercy or finding error in the indictment or the
judicial process.    Many were simply excuses for their
misconduct.    They might say, for example, that they never
intended harm to the king, or never intended to commit the
crime of treason.    Seminary priests and Jesuits in Elizabeth's reign were very eager to say that they were true
subjects.    Edmund Campion, just before judgment was
given, is reputed to have stated that all he and his fellow    accused had to say was that if 'our Religion do make
us Traitors we are worthy to be condemned;  but otherwise
are and have been as true subjects as ever the Queen
had ...'.    Bishop Fisher, when asked what he had to say,
took his cue from Christ and asked God's forgiveness on
those who had condemned him, 'for I think they know not
what they have done'. (144)

Some criticism of the English judicial process in general has already been mentioned;  here we must consider
what contemporaries thought of the trial itself.    If we
judge by the paucity of deeply critical comment engendered, they were of the opinion that English treason trials
were fair enough.    It is true there was indignation at a
number of convictions in 1540, but there were no actual
trials in these cases, simply the passing of acts of attainder in parliament. (145)    This method of conviction
had been developed in the fifteenth century for use
against insurgents in the field or in flight.    It was
used in the sixteenth only in 1533, 1539-40, 1542 and
1549.    Thereafter, the Tudor monarchs were willing to
offer in every case trial in court, with a chance for the
accused to reply to the charges.    Those who might have
been expected to make the most bitter and telling criticisms of the English treason trial, the catholic priests

and laity forced to live overseas in Elizabeth's reign,
failed to do so.  The reason seems to have been their
lack of a sufficient knowledge about the common law.
What critical comment there was often took the form of
mistaken comparisons between English trial procedure and
continental criminal law.   Robert Persons alone offered
arguments of any validity. (146)   He drew attention to
the accused's lack of counsel, 'which is the greatest in-
justice that can be devised', causing innocent blood to be
shed;  also to the exaggerations and amplifications of
the crown's lawyers in their presentation of the evidence.
He pointed out how at times the latter by their ferocity
could provoke great fear and confusion in the accused.
In the place of the existing system Persons advocated
that before arraignment and while the prisoner was in gaol
some men 'of conscience and learning' should investigate
the case thoroughly, finding out what the accusers and
witnesses had to say, giving a copy of it to the prisoner,
and allotting a lawyer or proctor to help him.   If the
prisoner was impoverished and could not pay the fees then
he was to be allowed to call on 'a publick Attorney'
appointed by the crown whose services were to be free of
charge.   The suggestion about giving a copy of the charges and the evidence against them to the accused was a
reasonable one, and the allotting of legal counsel would
have had the merit not only of allowing him a proper defence but also of making the justices and the king's
learned counsel improve their knowledge of the law of
treason and show more consistency in its interpretation.

     Most contemporary criticism of treason trials was con-
cerned with the petty jury.   Edmund Campion and Richard
White asked to be tried by someone with more learning.
Robert Persons wrote of the accused's life depending on
'the verdict, malice, ignorance or little Conscience or
care of twelve silly little men', who had to decide 'without time or means to inform themselves further, than that
which they have heard there at the Bar'.   An account of
the trial of William Freeman in 1595, which is sympathe-
tic to the accused, depicts the jury in a very unbecoming
way.   It says that when one of the jurors, probably the
foreman, was asked how they had found Freeman guilty, he
answered that it was because he denied the queen was the
supreme head of the church.   The questioner denied this,
saying that Freeman simply refused to answer;  furthermore
there had been only one witness and he was 'insufficient'.
The juror replied that 'Harye the jailor heard hym speak
yt also, that he was priest'.   This was denied, the questioner pointing out that 'Hary did but depose he heard
Gregory [the witness] say so and I might have deposed the

same, for I heard hym say as much in the Hall'.    'Well,
well', said the juror, 'yt were no matter yf all such as
he were hanged.'    'Such', says the writer of this account
in disgust, 'was the honesty and conscience of this good
jury.' (147)    Yet the author spoils his case by observing in the next line that in the course of the trial one
of the jurors stood up and asked a justice whether he
might with safe conscience 'cast a man awaie for speakinge
a word in jest'.    This was an action which needed a fair
amount of courage;   the justices, as they were wont when
questioned in this manner, displayed frowning countenances
and vented sour remarks.

     Here was a weakness of the treason trial which contem-
poraries hardly touched on.    The justices behaved at
times in a way which was cavalier, almost flippant.    This
attitude was probably caused by having to deal with a
great many criminal cases each year, sometimes as many as
twenty or thirty a day, and by having had for so long
their own way without challenge over points of criminal
law.    Sir Nicholas Throckmorton alone argued with them
effectively about the latter, but he owed his acquittal in
part to the warning he addressed to the bench even before
he entered a plea.    'My lords I pray you', he is reported
to have said, 'make not too much haste with me neither
think not long for your dinner, for my case requireth
leisure and you have well dined when you have done justice
truely.' (148)    The judges' ire was aroused momentarily,
but the point was well made and the pace of the trial
slackened even as it began.    When a prisoner made a
proper criticism of witnesses, evidence, or procedure it
called forth a great deal of bluster from the bench.    The
temper of the justices rose noticeably and they would
often attempt to ridicule or overbear the accused by
quoting legal maxims of all sorts, some not at all suited
to the case.    They were unwilling to accept that any
prisoner could make a point of law against the legal expertise of the king's learned counsel or themselves.
This might have been excusable if their knowledge of the
relevant part of the criminal laws was really great.
They knew the statutes relating to traitors which had been
passed in the last thirty years or so, and something about
the act of 1352, but in operating the complex system which
was the sixteenth-century law of treason this was sometimes not enough.

     Despite these varied weaknesses the process of trial in
treason cases had much to recommend it.    If we examine
the evidence against each of the accused and read the circumstances of their trials, it becomes obvious that few
were found guilty when, under the laws as they then stood,

they should have been acquitted.    The nearest thing to a
total miscarriage of justice of which record has survived
seems to have been in the case of Thomas Mountayne, who
around 1553 had been arrested on Bishop Gardiner's orders
on suspicion of treason and heresy.    Although examined,
Mountayne had not been arraigned, yet one morning at
5 a.m. he was awakened by his gaoler to be told 'Your tyme
is neare at hand and that ys to be hangyd and drawne as a
trayetor and burnde as an herytyke;  and thys muste be
done even this forenoone.'   Mountayne asked if the gaoler
had a writ of execution or had received a command from the
council.   The gaoler said impatiently that Mountayne
asked these questions for 'no cause eles to prolonge the
tyme'.   Mountayne asked if he had ever seen a man put to
death who had not been condemned to die, as he had not.
The gaoler admitted that Mountayne had made a good point,
saying 'I have been greatly myseynformyd I crye yow
marsy.' (149)   We do not know who gave the gaoler his
instructions, but as it stands the story does only harm to
the reputation of Gardiner, even if the gaoler's ready
acknowledgment that a man must be properly convicted is
reassuring.   It is perhaps worthy of comment that cases
like those of Appleyard and Bickerdike, where there is a
suspicion that the niceties of judicial process were not
properly observed, occurred not in London but in the pro-
vinces, and they were not 'state trials' in the usual
sense.
　　There are several statements on record by prisoners
vouching for the fairness of their trials.   Sir Nicholas
Throckmorton said that 'the ... Lord be praised for you
the magistrates, before whom I have had my trial this day
indifferently by the law', although his generosity here
must have been inflated by relief at his acquittal.   Yet
others with less cause to be pleased were also generous.
In his speech in arrest of judgment Sir John Perrot said
he found no fault with the process of his trial, admitting
he had had 'good and orderly proceedings therein'.   When
one of the justices had summed up the evidence against
Edmund Campion and his associates, Chief Justice Wray
offered the prisoners another opportunity to speak 'if
ought rest behind that is untold', since 'we would be loth
you should have any occasion to complain on the court'.
To this the accused replied that 'they had found of the
Court both indifference and justice'. (150)
　　Any attempt at reconstructing the Tudor treason trial
has severe limitations;  there is no *embarras de richesse*,
but the reports of sixteenth-century witnesses, variable
of course in their reliability, provide sufficient information to enable us to be reasonably sure about how jus-

tice was actually dispensed.    There is thus a contrast to
be made with the treason trials of the later Middle Ages,
of which descriptions as distinct from the legal records
thereto pertaining are virtually non-existent unless they
happened to be conducted in parliament.    We have been
able to establish something of the actual scene in the
Tudor courtroom, the pleading to the indictment, the roles
and techniques of the various prosecutors together with
the interference of their masters, the responses of the
accused, all of which may be surmised in regard to later
medieval practice but rarely demonstrated.    Furthermore,
the nature of the evidence alleged is quite apparent,
showing the rise in importance at the arraignment of examinations taken after the prisoner's arrests and an increased frequency in the production of witnesses.    It is
evident also that there was a new and growing concern with
the role of the witness which produced a number of clauses
in treason statutes regulating their appearance;   these in
turn had an effect on general procedure in the courtroom.
As in the Middle Ages, prisoners asked for counsel and had
it denied them, if we mean by counsel someone who would
plead their case on their behalf.    On the other hand,
should the prisoner detect a procedural error, legal counsel was then made available for putting the matter to the
court in legal terms.    Whether the Tudor method of 'remembering' the prisoner of every charge 'piecemeal' so he
could answer each point in turn was the medieval practice
as well cannot be ascertained but since anything else
would tend to confusion and mystify the jury it seems
quite possible.    The way in which, when some prisoners
pleaded guilty, the king's learned counsel was allowed
regardless to rehearse the case for the crown and the
whole circumstances of the offence to.the assembled crowd
seems to have been a Tudor novelty, though not an unexpected one.    The part played by the justices in the course
of the trial by their explanation of the treason law in
general, and the indictment in particular, together with
their summing up, although these must have occurred in
some form in the Middle Ages, is exemplified for the first
time in Tudor trial reports.    Again, in the matter of the
jury and its deliberations we can draw on both the valuable handbook of Sir Thomas Smith and revealing contemporary comments on the trials of William Levenyng, Richard
White and Rorbert Southwell.    There are also good examples of speeches in arrest of judgment like those of Sir
Thomas More, Sir Nicholas Throckmorton, and if we include
seditious words, of John Udall.    In the Levenyng case we
also have a clear demonstration of the arguments offered
in the jury-room.

As to the fairness of Tudor treason trials, if there can be any value in seeking to judge such a quality four centuries after, we can only say that the procedure was weighted against the accused, but not to such a degree that Tudor trial methods seemed much more onerous to contemporaries than had later medieval treason trials to the men of those centuries.   The greater frequency than previously in examining witnesses for the crown and in alleging examinations taken before trial, the seeming greater attention given by the crown's lawyers to planning their court strategy and the greater consideration given to the evidence against the accused beforehand are all quite noticeable, yet it would be foolish to argue from the greater precision in prosecution that a prisoner's guilt was decided beforehand and trial was a mere formality. With juries like those which acquitted Levenyng, Throckmorton and Dr Richard Benger it could not be so.   These and the sizeable number of other acquittals testify to the fact that jurors, even if chosen with care by the crown, had minds of their own, minds which were likely to be conditioned as much by local sympathies and personal loyalties as by the pressures brought to bear on them by the justices and the king.   We must also allow for a toughness of mind which made jurymen ready to face the prospect of a large fine and imprisonment with steadfastness if not equanimity.

# 5

◇◇◇◇◇◇◇◇◇◇◇◇◇◇◇◇◇◇◇◇◇◇◇◇◇◇◇◇◇◇◇◇◇◇◇◇◇◇◇◇◇◇◇◇◇◇◇◇◇◇◇◇◇◇◇◇

# To the Gallows and after

◇◇◇◇◇◇◇◇◇◇◇◇◇◇◇◇◇◇◇◇◇◇◇◇◇◇◇◇◇◇◇◇◇◇◇◇◇◇◇◇◇◇◇◇◇◇◇◇◇◇◇◇◇◇◇◇

Few persons in Tudor England who had been convicted of
treason spent any length of time in gaol after their
trial.   There were, it is true, one or two notable exceptions, like the seminary priest John Pybush, who was tried
and found guilty on 1 July 1595 but executed only on 18
February 1601, and the earl of Arundel, who was tried in
April 1589 and died a natural death in the Tower of London
on 9 October 1595, but in general governmental policy was
either to execute convicted traitors forthwith, or release
them fairly soon after arraignment. (1)   This had also
been the practice in the fourteenth and fifteenth centuries.   Only when, through seditious words or failure to
report traitorous conspiracy, the accused had been found
guilty of misprision was the punishment of perpetual imprisonment inflicted. (2)

Those found guilty, whom the government was determined
to execute, were returned to a regime in gaol that was
often more strict than the one they had endured before
being tried.   The priest Thomas Woodhouse in 1573 was
sent back not to the Fleet, where he had been incarcerated
hitherto, but to the harsher climate of Newgate, where he
was placed in a most dismal part of that gaol.   The
priest James Fenn, after being convicted in the queen's
bench of treason in February 1584, was not returned to the
Marshalsea, but taken to the Tower, fettered, and put in
'the pit', where he remained for six days until execution. (3)   Except when the convicted person was of relatively high social rank, he was likely to be kept in irons
until the time of execution, as were, for example, Edmund
Campion, Luke Kirby, and Alexander Briant.   It was in
reference to Briant that William Allen wrote that 'when he
was condemned, yrons were commaunded upon him and the
rest, as sone as they came home to the Tower, and they
were never taken off, till they were fetched furth to be

martyred.'   Richard White, the catholic schoolmaster,
from the day his trial began until the day he was put to
death was 'coupled fast and chained with an huge iron
chain and horse-lock, and warded diligently day and night
with a band of men'. (4)

The reasons for this treatment were several.   Obviously the king did not wish to lose the person who was to be
the principal performer at the forthcoming execution
through escape or successful attempt at suicide.   In
fact, as in the later Middle Ages, there were few escapes
and apparently only a single post-trial suicide.   On 19
December 1583, while in Newgate awaiting execution, John
Somervyle, who had planned to shoot the queen and been
convicted of it at the London Guildhall three days previously, managed to strangle himself. (5)   Another cause
of the severe nature of renewed imprisonment was a hope
that the condemned man might be persuaded to give additional information about fellow conspirators who were
still at large, or even about other plots concerning which
they received information while in confinement.   There
was a belief that comfort during his last days on earth
was likely to make a prisoner more obdurate, less amenable
to suggestion at the time of his execution, and thus a
less satisfactory vehicle for propaganda both when apos-
tasy was the desideratum and when the end was plain admission of guilt. (6)

The crown did not rely simply on the discomfort of
gaol life to elicit new information.   It was quite ready
to use the weapon of terror, and not even the formal torture of the rack was categorically excluded.   When, in
April 1556, John Throckmorton asked if he could be racked
after judgment had been given he was answered in the affirmative. (7)   However, actual examples of post-convic-
tion torture are impossible to discover, and it seems as
if information was usually extracted from those condemned
by playing on their fears about the manner of their forthcoming execution.   Thus orders for the examination of the
earl of Northumberland in June 1572 about his fellow conspirators stated he should be terrified by the threat of
extreme punishment if he concealed anything.   In February
1601 the earl of Essex was allowed a private execution in
the Tower in return for supplying new facts about his
traitorous conspiracy. (8)   It seems likely that similar
deals with noblemen were made on other occasions, the
usual arrangement being for the king to allow the co-oper-
ative prisoner an execution by means of beheading in place
of the normal hanging and disembowelling.

There were a good number of occasions in the sixteenth
century when physical punishments of a much lighter nature

than the death penalty were awarded for misdeeds touching on treason.  These were when the offence was seditious words of a less serious nature, seditious words whose intent was to cause scandal and disaffection rather than the king's death.  During Cromwell's ascendancy and until 1555 justices of the peace were wont to use in summary fashion the punishment of the pillory, prison or the whip on those they thought were guilty of uttering such words. Perhaps the punishment awarded most frequently was a period of several hours on the pillory where it was not uncommon for the victim's ears to be nailed or cut off. Gilbert Pott, who was set on the Cheapside pillory on 11 July 1553, had 'both his eares nayled to the pillory and cleane cut of for seditious and trayterous wordes' while at the same time a trumpeter blew his trumpet and a herald read out a description of the offence.  Ears were not always cut off.  A month later John Daye, parson of St Ethelberga's in Bishopgate Street, and a surgeon, each had an ear nailed while also in the Cheapside pillory, but after languishing there for three hours 'the nayles were pulled out with a payre of pinsers and they were had to prison again'.  Two days later Day had his other ear nailed in like manner.  From 1555, as we have noticed above, jurisdiction over this category of crime was extended to the justices of oyer and terminer, gaol delivery and assize in addition, and the penalty was specifically set at the loss of ears or a fine of £100 for the first offence.  If an offender who had been punished in the pillory and suffered the loss of his ears continued in his seditious utterances he might be imprisoned for life:  so said the act;  or he might have part of his tongue cut off:  such was the opinion of Roger Manwood, then a justice of common pleas, in 1577. (9)  If he had written down rather than spoken the offending words the miscreant was to have his right hand cut off.  Use of the pillory was not introduced by the Tudors.  It had seen a fair amount of use in the later Middle Ages as a punishment awarded by town courts.  The new departure in the sixteenth century was the increased frequency with which this form of punishment was sanctioned and its use outside the boroughs. (10)

Another form of physical punishment was whipping. This, unlike the loss of ears, was not to be found in any act on treason or seditious and scandalous words, but must have been sanctioned by the king's council as in fact the act 12 Ric. II c. 11 allowed.  On 30 June 1553 in London a young fellow who had been attached to a post by a chain and a collar of iron was whipped by two men 'for pretended visions and sedicious words'.  On 22 May 1555 a youth

named William Featherstone, who claimed he was King
Edward, was taken from the Marshalsea in Southwark
'rydinge in a carre in a folles cote with papers written
on his head and brest' to the courts in Westminster Hall.
There he was stripped naked, bound to a cart, and whipped
through Westminster and London as far as Smithfield, where
he was given back his clothes and banished 'into the north
countrie'. (11)   Sometimes the pillory and whipping com-
plemented each other.   In June 1552 the privy council
ordered the London sheriffs to put John Lawton on the pillory next market day with a paper on his head inscribed
'a sceditious vagabounde';   then he was to be whipped out
of the city.   In December 1537 a fuller named Edward
Lyttelworke, who was reckoned to have spread a rumour of
the king's death, was ordered to be set on the pillory for
an hour at midday on a market day, his ears cut off, and
'to be tyed to a cartys ayrse and to be strypped naked to
the wast of his body and so to be whypped round aboute the
towne'.   Then he was to be imprisoned at the king's
pleasure. (12)   Whipping was no penal novelty either.
Medieval ecclesiastical courts had awarded it frequently
for moral offences.   What was new in the Tudor era was
its infliction under the authority of the lay power.

Whipping for seditious words was apparently reserved
for men, while the pillory might be used for offenders of
either sex.   Women alone were liable to a third form of
physical punishment, namely the cucking stool.   On 23 May
1554 the privy council gave orders for two wives of Stepney to be set on the 'cooking stoole' for creating false
and seditious rumours.   In August 1553 Lord Mordaunt and
Sir John St John were instructed to examine for seditious
words a woman prisoner in Bedford gaol, and if necessary
to punish her 'by the cuckingstoole', or some other suitable way. (13)   This was another punishment with medieval
antecedents, but as with the pillory it had in earlier
centuries been awarded only by borough courts which had
been able to plead ancient custom.   Another mild form of
punishment for treason, one which seems to have been tried
on only a few occasions, was banishment.   On 15 January
1585 commissions were issued to the lord chancellor and
others authorizing them to banish two Jesuits, eighteen
seminary priests and one layman whose names were given.
Some, like James Bosgrave, Edward Rushton, and Henry
Orton, were already convicted of treason and others, like
William Tedder, Samuel Conyers, and Arthur Pitts, stood
merely indicted.   In addition, the commissioners were to
apprehend and then banish all other Jesuits, seminary
priests, and other 'wandering and massing priests'. (14)
According to Holinshed, on 21 January 1585 subsequent to

this order, twenty-one of these who had been in prison in
the Tower, the Marshalsea, and the King's Bench, were put
aboard ship at the Tower wharf for a free passage to Nor-
mandy.   Before sailing each prisoner signed a document
which certified he had been 'verie friendlie and honestlie
intreated', and conveyed 'with carefull diligence'. (15)
It seems as if all had been given a pardon with proviso
that they left England within twenty-one days.   For such
banishment, as distinct from the legal antiquity known as
abjuration of the realm, there were few medieval precedents, and all save the exiling of Hereford and Norfolk in
1398 had been prompted by magnates in opposition to the
king.   The novelty of the device of 1585 was reflected in
a clause of the commission which, in order to tie it in
with normal legal process, instructed that certificates of
the proceedings of the commissioners were to be returned
from time to time to the king's bench and there enrolled.
Holinshed made much of this example of royal clemency but
it was not unique.   In addition to this group numerous
other priests were exiled in 1585-6, the Douai diaries referring to as many as seventy-two in the former year.
Nor was this the last that was heard of the banishment of
priests.   In November 1602 there was a proclamation which
ordered all Jesuits and seminary priests then in England
either to take an oath of allegiance or quit the realm.
If they did neither the law was to be operated against
them. (16)

One of the least severe punishments on traitors, although it was not necessarily the whole of the penalty
inflicted, was to compel them to demonstrate their guilt
in a public place.   The most celebrated example was perhaps that of Elizabeth Barton and her supporters.   When
accused in the star chamber, they all-confessed to the
fraudulence of the nun's visions, and 'their feined hipo-
crisy and dissimulated sanctitee and treiterous purposes
and intentes'.   For this the council adjudged them to
stand at St Paul's Cross.   Each had to give to a preacher
a bill explaining his misdeeds, which no doubt was read
out, and then the subsequent Sunday, while standing on a
special stage, they each rehearsed their offences in person.   According to Chapuys it was intended that the miscreants should later be taken 'through all towns' to repeat their declarations. (17)   There was a similar public
admission of guilt and error in 1544.   John Heywood, at
St Paul's Cross one Sunday in July, denounced his own
blindness in believing that the bishop of Rome was the
supreme head of the universal church, and admitted to concealing and favouring this and other erroneous and traitorous opinions like an untrue subject. (18)   Very likely

Heywood's crimes, like those of Elizabeth Barton and her associates, had been investigated before the council and confession of guilt obtained.   Those who were found guilty of, or pleaded guilty to, accusations of treason at common law would have the opportunity, if they wished, of speaking at their execution but they were never exhibited like Heywood or Elizabeth Barton.

Although in the early Middle Ages convicted traitors may have been dragged to execution actually tied to the tail of a horse, it was the practice in the later medieval period to tie them to a hurdle.   The reason for this was very likely, as Maitland pointed out, to provide the executioner with a living body. (19)   On the day of the execution in the Tudor period the sheriff's officers tied the condemned man's hands behind his back and fastened him to a wicker hurdle.   This was done at the door of the gaol, and it was then that relatives and friends sometimes had a last opportunity to bid him farewell.   We hear of occasions when, before being bound, the prisoner distributed money given him for the purpose to the poor who were gathered round. (20)   From the gaol victim and hurdle were dragged through the town to the place appointed for the execution. (21)   Sometimes the prisoner was able to speak to those who lined the route.   Edmund Campion was even reported to have had the dirt wiped from his face by one bystander.   There were a few prisoners who suffered considerably while on the hurdle.   Accounts tell us the priest Thomas Prichard, when being drawn to execution at Dorchester on 21 March 1587, was so battered that he was almost dead when he reached the gallows.   Cuthbert Mayne, in November 1577, was, according to a contemporary description, 'uneasily laid on a hurdle and so spitefully drawn, receiving some knocks on his face and his fingers with a girdle'. (22)   Occasionally, as at the drawing of Thomas Ford, John Shert, and Robert Johnson on 28 May 1582, the prisoners were admonished as they went by 'zealous and godly men', in this case including the sheriff 'who in mylde and loving speeches made knowen unto them how justly God repayeth the reprobate'. (23)   Thomas and Christopher Norton, as they were drawn from the Tower to Tyburn on 27 May 1570, were accompanied by, among others, a preacher, who rode beside them asking they should acknowledge their misdeeds, discharge their consciences, and be truly repentant.   This became the fashion, and especially when the victims were Jesuits or seminary priests. We read also, again in regard to catholic prisoners, that in Elizabeth's reign a shouting mob might accompany them to the gallows 'uttering all manner of harsh and savage abuse'. (24)   Only in Mary's reign is there reference to cries of goodwill on the part of the bystanders.

How the actual execution of traitors was handled and
how the victims behaved at the gallows was of prime importance to a government greatly concerned with the propaganda value of the event.   Rather surprisingly, with the
exception of the beheading of Mary, Queen of Scots, there
is a shortage of record material relating to the technical
arrangements made by the crown for these executions.   Although occasionally the judges who gave judgment specified
that the execution should take place within a certain
length of time, the actual date seems to have been decided
on by the monarch or the privy council.   In every case
there had to be a warrant or writ of execution.   It was
clearly stated in 1587 that when a prisoner had been convicted in court and delivered to the lieutenant of the
Tower, or other gaoler, 'it shall not be lawfull for hym
to execute that condemned person withoute any more a-doe,
but the Queen's expresse direction there is to be expected'. (25)   The warrant, if the prisoner was of some
note, was drawn up by the solicitor-general, sealed, and
sent to the gaoler in whose charge the prisoner lay.   The
gaoler had the task of telling the man that the time of
his execution was at hand, although it seems he could
often decide for himself at what hour he should do so.
His freedom of choice in this regard was not entirely unlimited.   When, as was often the case, the execution was
planned for eight or nine o'clock in the morning, the
warrant usually reached the prison the evening before.
Thus Sir Edmund Walsingham, lieutenant of the Tower, told
Bishop Fisher the time set for his execution, which was
9 a.m., only four hours previously.   Sir Thomas More was
treated in the same way. (26)   In some cases the reason
for the delay may have been a desire to protect the prisoner from the fear of death until the last possible moment in others the intent was to gain a response to a
final question.   Largely, however, it must have been engendered by a fear of escape, or suicide, or of weakened
prisoners killing themselves through excessive devotions.
If the government feared none of these eventualities then
two or three days' warning might be given, perhaps through
the visit of an ecclesiastic, who was supposed to teach
the prisoner quiet and patient suffering and show him how
to prepare for death. (27)
     Despatching the writ of execution was accompanied or
preceded by a number of other administrative orders on the
part of the crown.   A reasonable number of 'officers and
other appointed men' had to be instructed to be present so
as to restrain any disturbance provoked by elements of the
crowd and apprehend overt sympathizers.   There is evidence that when the execution was for heresy, householders

in the vicinity might be compelled to keep their apprentices and servants within doors, but there was apparently
no comparable rule when the crime was treason.   The records of the town of Plymouth show that there the sheriff
was provided with a horse to draw the hurdle and 'a dozen
faggots and a quarter of reed' for the fire which was to
burn the victim's entrails. (28)   Then there was the
choosing of the site of the execution.   Unless the condemned persons were of great political importance, and
therefore reserved for execution in London, it was common
for them to be executed near where their offence had been
perpetrated, or where sympathy for their conspiracy had
been demonstrated.   For example, in 1537 Robert Aske was
sent to York for execution, in 1543 Adam Damplip was sent
to Calais, in 1557 the followers of Thomas Stafford were
executed at Scarborough, Hull, Beverley, and twelve other
places in Yorkshire, and in 1597 Richard Bradshawe and
Robert Burton, leaders of the Oxfordshire insurrection,
were put to death at Oxford. (29)   To serve as a warning
locally must similarly have been the reason why the seminary priests William Marsden and Robert Anderton were executed in 1586 in the Isle of Wight at the places where
they had made their landing.   For traitors who were to be
executed in the capital Tyburn was the place normally designated by the justices who pronounced sentence, although
sometimes when those convicted were of noble rank the king
allowed execution to take place in the Tower or its vicinity. (30)   In addition to these arrangements the king and
his advisers had to find suitable executioners and their
assistants, a task that was not always easy.   On at least
one occasion such men had to be imported from abroad,
while at other times amateurs had to be employed, like a
local butcher or a cook.   There were also gallows, scaf-
folds, sand and straw, to see to.   Often the two former
had to be newly constructed for the event.   Thus for the
execution in London of a number of seminary priests and
Jesuits in August 1588 six gibbets were specially erected.
In February 1554 between twenty and thirty gallows were
set up to deal with insurgents who had taken the part of
Sir Thomas Wyatt;   in 1571 Dr John Storey was hanged on a
pair of gallows recently constructed in a novel triangular
manner. (31)   For the beheading of the duke of Norfolk a
new scaffold had to be made as it was the first execution
on Tower Hill for fourteen years;   for the execution of
Mary, Queen of Scots, there was built a special scaffold
in the great hall of Fotheringay castle. (32)
   The detailed instructions given about the height and
position of this scaffold should remind us that the intention was that all those present should be able to see the

execution;  this was standard practice. (33)   That attending the putting to death of traitors was a popular
pastime there can be little doubt, though the numbers of
those present are hard to calculate.   On Tower Hill for
the death of Bishop Fisher there were assembled citizens
in 'no small number'.   To see the intended execution of
the duke of Northumberland at 8 a.m. on 21 August 1553
came, so it is said, about 10,000 men and women with all
the men of the Tower, the warders, the guard and the
sheriff's officers standing 'in order with ther hol-
bardes'.   At the executions of a number of seminary
priests and catholic laity in August 1588 there was reported as being 'an extraordinary concourse of citizens and a
crowd surging on all sides'.   Anne Boleyn was executed
within the Tower, but even then the crowd allowed inside
the walls was estimated at between one and two thousand
and there were in addition others watching through the
open gates. (34)

Among the spectators all classes were represented.
Chapuys, writing early in May 1535, noted that among those
who had recently watched from close by the deaths of a
number of Carthusian monks were the dukes of Richmond and
Norfolk, the earl of Wiltshire and his son, and other
lords and courtiers. (35)   This he thought was quite
novel.   In 1535 it may have been, but it was to be a common practice for the rest of the century.   At some executions nobility and gentry were in a majority.   This was
when a magnate was executed in private, that is to say
within the walls of a fortress, and only a limited number
of watchers were allowed entry.   Stow states that at the
execution of Mary, Queen of Scots, at Fotheringay there
were about 300 persons of gentle blood present, which must
have been virtually the whole crowd.   At the beheading of
the earl of Essex in the Tower in 1601 there sat on forms
three yards from the scaffold the earls of Cumberland and
Hertford, Viscount Bindon, Lords Thomas Howard, Morley,
Darcy, Compton and Grey, and about a hundred knights, gentlemen, and aldermen, who must have comprised the majority
of the watchers. (36)   In any execution crowd there were
likely to be those who sympathized with the condemned person, either because they were fellow conspirators not detected, or, when priests and Jesuits suffered, because
they were co-religionists;  or even, as the autobiography
of Thomas Mountayne demonstrates, simply because they were
neighbours and friends.   In each case they might have
come from many miles away.   There was never any overt
attempt to rescue the prisoner as had happened on occasion
with felons in the Middle Ages.   The most suspicious incident was at the execution of Babington and his assoc-

iates in September 1586 where a Captain Gray was arrested
with a 'dagge' under his coat. (37)
   When the condemned man reached the gallows it was customary for the king's commission to be read out.   Sometimes this was accompanied by a proclamation that those
present should move back twenty feet if they had not been
appointed to do execution. (38)   The only persons allowed
to stay close by the prisoner were the executioner, with
perhaps an assistant, a chaplain, and the sheriff.   From
the hurdle the convicted traitor was led under the gallows
and placed either in a cart or on a ladder.   Then the
rope was put round his neck.   If he had been allowed the
privilege of decollation the prisoner was usually led on
foot, sometimes by a minister or fellow magnate, the short
distance from the prison to the scaffold.   At this point
it was expected of the victim that he would make a speech.
Henry Dunn, a fellow conspirator of Anthony Babington,
'demaunded whether the people did expecte anie thinge'.
He was told they did, and thereupon he addressed the
crowd.   Almost every prisoner said a few words, some a
fair number, and what they had to say was listened to
carefully by the sheriff and the chaplain, who quickly in-
tervened to silence the speaker should he say something
deemed inappropriate.   In 1594 a catholic priest named
William Dean had his mouth gagged with a cloth and was
nearly suffocated because his words were thought harm-
ful. (39)   What was to be permitted in this respect at
the execution of Essex in February 1601 was clearly laid
down in a letter from Cecil and others to the constable
and lieutenant of the Tower.   The prisoner was to confine
himself to confessing his treasons and 'his sins towards
God', and to his 'hearty repentance and earnest and inces-
sant prayers to God for pardon'.   If, however, he entered
into 'any particular declaration of his treasons or accusation of any of his adherents therein' the constable and
the lieutenant were to 'forthwith break him from that
course' as the time was 'not fit'.   The reason given was
that all this had been published at full length at the
arraignment.   Similarly, if Essex should try to justify
himself by saying that his intent was not malicious but
merely directed against private enemies, he must be diver-
ted, since it would contradict what he had said to the
lords of the privy council.   These instructions in some
form were doubtless passed on to the condemned man.   Whether such detailed rulings had been the practice earlier
in the Tudor period is difficult to say.   Probably prisoners were simply admonished, as was Sir Thomas More, not
to use too many words, and it was left to the officials on
the scaffold to decide if they were saying the wrong
things. (40)

Leading speeches by royal officials or notables, although an obvious way of explaining the condemned person's
crimes and of justifying the sentence of death were uncommon, the crown preferring to supplement the speech of the
condemned man, if it was thought deficient in any way, by
getting the officials present to put to him questions designed to elicit responses which demonstrated more clearly
his evil designs, his guilt, and in some cases his religious beliefs and his contriteness.   Taking the lead in
this examination were usually the sheriff and the minister
of religion appointed by the crown to give spiritual comfort to the prisoner.   The ministers were not welcome on
the scaffold in the eyes of many of the condemned.   The
Jesuits and seminary priests objected particularly, but
the most notable protest occurred in 1554.   The duke of
Suffolk told Dr Hugh Weston, the dean of Westminster who
was chaplain for the occasion, not to accompany him up the
steps of the scaffold.   When the request was disregarded
the duke tried by physical force to prevent Weston from
so doing and a scrimmage resulted.   Most execution chap-
lains addressed the prisoner in a standard manner.   At
the execution of the catholic conspirators Ballard, Babington, Savage, Barnwell, Titchburne, Tilney, and Abington in 1586, Dr White, the minister, asked each, just before his turn came to die, to acknowledge his offences,,
confess his sins, make a confession of faith, and ask for
the queen's forgiveness. (41)   Into what detail about religious belief a minister was willing to go even at this
late hour is demonstrated by the conversation between the
seminary priest William Freeman and Andrew Boardman, the
Tower chaplain, in 1595 at the former's execution.   The
pair argued at length over mediation and intercession of
saints 'and such lyke'. (42)   Then Boardman, as ministers
usually did when the condemned man was a catholic, suggested they should pray together or that Freeman should pray
with the crowd, only to be told by the other, as was also
quite customary, that this was unacceptable and he would
pray in Latin by himself.   Where there was variation in
this course of events it was caused by the prisoner asking
his friends in the crowd to pray for him.   Ballard is reported as saying 'Praie for me I beseeche you;  and I
desire all those that came with me to saie the creede for
me, for that is a speciall meanes to strengthen our be-
liefe.'   Babington asked all his friends to pray for him
both at that moment and after his death.   Mary, Queen of
Scots, refused to hear a 'godlye admonition' by the dean
of Peterborough and said that protestant prayers would
avail her little.   She asked instead that her servants
should pray for her.   Robert Southwell the Jesuit,

'desired all Catholiques to ioyne with him in prayer to allmighty God'. (43)

The minister or priest appointed by the king to be present at the execution was not the only man of religion to address the prisoner, but he was the only one who did so from on the scaffold or under the gallows.   Sometimes, especially if those who were to die professed a faith different from the one prevailing at the time, there were other clergy present in an official capacity.   Placed near the condemned man, yet amidst the crowd, might be found 'pulpit men', whose job it was to preach to the prisoners in an effort to gain a last-minute change of faith.   Hugh Latimer, bishop of Worcester, wrote to Thomas Cromwell in May 1538 to say that, if the government wished him 'to play the fool in his customable manner' when Friar Forest was to suffer, he would like his 'stage' to be near enough the prisoner for him to hear and perhaps be converted.   We are told that John Hewett, a seminary priest who was executed on 5 October 1588 at Mile End Green, actually 'disputed openly with the preachers' at the gallows. (44)   There were also a few occasions when the preachers talked not about religious faith but about political matters.   At the execution of Luke Kirby on 30 May 1582 'Field the preacher' read out for all to hear the condemned man's answers to 'six articles' originally put to him by the privy council.   These amounted to asking whether the pope might lawfully depose the queen, and Kirby's response had been that if any prince fell into 'turcisme atheisme or paganisme' the pope might indeed act in that way.   Kirby was then asked by Field if he thought Queen Elizabeth had so fallen, to which Kirby replied only that he 'knew his conscience'.   Similar answers to the 'six articles' as administered at their examination were read out at the execution of the seminary priests William Filby and Lawrence Richardson the same day. (45)

It was the usual practice to allow questions concerning allegiance, politics, and the finer details of the treason, to be put by the sheriff or some other lay official whose duty it was to be in attendance.   When Robert Barnwell was on the gallows' ladder, Radcliffe, the sheriff, asked him why he concealed Babington's traitorous conspiracy for so long, and then whether he 'were at the courte at Richmonde walkinge in the greene', where the queen noticed him.   At the execution of Edmund Jennings, a seminary priest, on 10 December 1591 was present the notorious examiner of priests and Jesuits, Richard Topcliffe.   He asked Jennings to lay open his treason and ask the queen's pardon. (46)   If the offer was to be made at all it was usually left to the lay officials to suggest that a plea for monarch's forgiveness accompanied by a change of opinion might even at that late stage be successful.

Another class of person who might be in close attendance on instructions from the king was the witness who had been the cause of the condemned man's indictment and conviction.   When Thomas Ford was put up into the cart under the gallows he announced he was guiltless of any treason.   Sheriff Martin answered that his guilt had been made manifest, saying according to one report 'here be thine owne answers to shew, affirmed under thine owne hand (i.e. his examination) and other witnesses to repove thee'.   Thereupon the witness John Munday, a government spy, was called forward, 'who iustified the causes to his face, that at his arreignement was laid to his charge'. When Luke Kirby was awaiting execution that same day he claimed there was no one who could prove him to be a traitor.   The sheriff said there was, and Munday again came forward.   This time there was an altercation between witness and condemned man as to whether Munday, on a visit to the Tower, had acknowledged he could not truly charge Kirby with anything although he had done so at the trial. Munday denied he had made such a statement, and the sheriff said the prisoner's guilt was obvious.   There was a similar scene when a third seminary priest, Robert Johnson, was placed in the cart a short time later.   Munday was summoned to speak once more, and told the prisoner that he himself had been privy to the horrible treasons of which the other had been properly convicted. (47)

Persons attending the execution of traitors on governmental instructions did not have a monopoly of the questioning.   Members of the crowd asked serious questions and were often given a reply.   Henry Cuffe, secretary to the earl of Essex, when about to die, disclaimed any disloyal thought claiming he was not a party 'privy or consenting to that tumultuous assembly' at Essex house. Whereupon he was interrupted, says a report of the execution, by one who asked had he not in court, after judgment had been given, confessed that he was justly condemned? After Cuffe had continued his speech a little further he suffered another interruption.   'How dare you', said a voice, 'decline from the good example of the penitent death your lord made that now go about to justify yourself?   You must confess your sin and make satisfaction to the world that you are justly condemned ....'   These sound very much like the words of a nobleman.   The speaker was followed by Lord Grey, who added that it was no time for logic on Cuffe's part: 'I am sorry that those good parts which God hath bestowed upon you and by your own industry have attained unto, should be thus abused in

justifying yourself.'   A third member of the audience
then said that Cuffe, if not a party to the fact, was
certainly privy to the intent, 'and therefore your words
are but fig leaves to cover your shame'.   Then, so we are
told, speakers accused the prisoner of seducing Sir Henry
Neville 'and requested him to speak the truth of that
matter and also of his [Neville's] slandering the city in
giving out that of the 24 aldermen 21 were assured to the
Earl.' (48)   From the tone of their statements we may
surmise that all the speakers were probably men of importance.

On other occasions when there is reference to questions
being put this was certainly the case.   Just before he
was hanged Dr Storey was asked by the earl of Bedford the
most important question 'Are you not the queen's subject?'
In 1601 Sir Walter Raleigh asked the prisoner Sir Christopher Blunt, who had adhered to Essex, to tell the truth
concerning the earl's plan to bring an Irish army to England.   Men of social standing like these did not even
hesitate to tell the sheriff his duty.   When at one stage
the latter interrupted Blunt's speech to announce 'the
hour was past', Raleigh and Lord Grey told him to allow
the prisoner to finish his prayers and confessions.
Curiosity was one major cause why magnates attended the
executions of traitors but there were others as well.
Raleigh was said to have been at Essex's death 'to feed
his eyes with the sight of the earl's sufferings and to
satiate his hatred with his blood', but many were there
to make an instant response if, perchance, they should be
accused or incriminated by the prisoner's gallows
speech. (49)

The content of the speeches made by condemned traitors
was not constant, but certain common elements are quite
apparent.   Most speeches can be classified as being basically an admission of guilt or a denial, but few prisoners denied all, or admitted all, of the offences with
which they were charged.   More admitted some degree of
guilt than made a form of denial, but relatively few were
willing to confess they had committed treason actually
using that word.   Those like John Savage in 1586 who is
reported to have said unequivocally 'I must confesse that
I was guiltie of this treason', or even like John Ballard
who said 'For the matter for which I am condemned I am
guiltie', were quite uncommon.   They might, however,
admit they had consented to the committing of treason, or
had failed to report a knowledge of intended treason to
the authorities.   Edward Jones described some aspect of
Babington's conspiracy and then said 'I confesse I concealed these treasons'. (50)   Lady Jane Grey announced on

the scaffold that she had consented to a deed against the
queen but had not procured it.    Chidiock Titchburne admitted that he had kept silent about the Babington conspiracy and therefore could be held to have consented to
it, but like so many others he denied he had intended the
queen's death. (51)    Prisoners seem to have refused to
recognize that under the law such behaviour was as much
treason as directly attempting the monarch's assassination.

Sometimes the prisoner admitted he had offended against
the law or against the king.    We are told that Sir Thomas
Palmer in 1553 said 'I am come hether to dye for I have
lyved heare under a lawe and have offended the same and
for my so doinge the same lawe fyndethe me guilty.'    In
1554 the duke of Suffolk is reputed to have said 'I have
offended the queen and her laws and thereby am justly
condemned to die and am willing to die.' (52)    In 1521
the duke of Buckingham admitted to offending the king
through negligence, and Thomas Salisbury in 1586 said he
had grievously offended her majesty. (53)    Such statements show that the condemned man had no complaints to
make about his trial but felt that his offence was somehow
less than treason proper.    There were many others who
thought their plight was directly attributable to God.
Thomas Cromwell, for example, gave thanks 'to my lorde God
that hath appoynted me this death for myne offence'.
Anthony Babington, who, we are told, vaguely described his
offence as such 'that nothing can satisfie but the shed-
dinge of my hartes bloode', thought 'it hathe pleased God
to bringe me to this.'    John Storey, without referring to
the treason for which he had been condemned, said the kidnapping which led to his trial and forthcoming death was
wrought by God. (54)

In contrast with those who admitted some degree of
guilt were others who, when on the gallows, firmly denied
any treason or traitorous intent.    The yeoman Appleyard
in 1551 denied he had stirred up rebellion.    The aged
countess of Salisbury, executed in 1539, is said to have
refused to lay her head on the block saying 'So should
traitors do and I am none'. (55)    On 26 February 1552
were executed four of the duke of Somerset's henchmen who
protested they were entirely guiltless of any plot against
the king or the lords of council.    In 1584 William Parry,
who had been charged with conspiracy to dethrone and slay
the queen denied he was ever guilty of any intention of
harming her. (56)    This was an attitude which was quite
common among the seminary priests and Jesuits executed in
the reign of Elizabeth.    Edmund Campion said he was only
a traitor 'if you esteem my religion'.    Thomas Ford, when

asked by the sheriff to beg the queen's forgiveness and
'change his former traitorous mind', said 'in no other
treson have I offended than my religion which is the
catholicke faith wherein I will live and die'.   William
Freeman is reckoned to have said 'I protest I am guilty of
no externall acte of treason', by which he meant the real
cause of his conviction was his religion. (57)   Some convicted traitors, while not going as far as to deny their
guilt, showed themselves completely unrepentant, even
truculent.   William Hacket, a mentally unbalanced puritan
who saw himself as king of Europe, cried out that he was
Jehovah and apparently said to the hangman 'Thou bastard,
wilt thou hang Hacket thy king?'   The Irishman Brian
O'Rorke, says Stow, at Tyburn on 3 November 1591 refused
to ask either the queen's or the world's forgiveness, or
to forgive them.   When Edward Abington in 1586 was asked
before dying to request royal forgiveness he announced in
a prophetic manner that there would soon be great blood-
shed in England, saying the country was hated for its in-
iquities, even by God. (58)   Men who behaved as these did
were very much a minority.

It was a common practice, whether prompted by the chaplain in attendance or not, to ask for the monarch's forgiveness and to wish or pray openly for his health and the
prosperity of the realm.   Anthony Babington asked for the
forgiveness of God and Queen Elizabeth, as did Sir Charles
Danvers in 1601.   In 1586 Charles Tilney asked to be for-
given by the queen and by all those others he had offended, while John Felton in 1570 asked the forgiveness of
the queen and 'all the people'. (59)   As for asking God's
blessing on the prince there was Henry Dunn (1586) who is
reported as saying 'I beseeche God from the bottom of my
hart to blesse' Queen Elizabeth, and Bishop Fisher who
asked God to save the king and the realm.   According to
one eye-witness, William Freeman, more dramatically, said
'As for the Queen her finger should not ake yf my hart
could helpe it.   God blesse the Queene, God blesse hon-
ourable Councell, God blesse the wholl realme.' (60)   All
pronouncements and requests like these were received with
great favour by the crowds.   There were also one or two
occasions when those about to die requested forgiveness
from enemies or acquaintances who were actually present.
Sir Christopher Blunt enquired from the scaffold 'Is Sir
Walter Raleigh there?'   When told he was, he asked his
forgiveness 'both for wrong done you and for my particular
ill intent towards you'.   Raleigh answered that he forgave him most willingly 'and besought God to forgive him'
also.   William Freeman and Boardman, the Tower chaplain,
who disputed on religious matters until almost the moment

of execution, mutually asked and received forgiveness of
any offence they had given each other. (61)

It was required of the prisoner that when he spoke he
should not describe his misdeeds with the intent of justifying them.   If he did then he was stopped.   When the
duke of Norfolk in 1571 spoke about 'the state of my offences as in my own conscience I judge them' and claimed
he had seen Ridolfi but once and had never dealt with him
Sheriff Bramch told him he had come to be executed not to
purge himself and charge his peers.   He was allowed to
continue, but when he denied consenting to rebellion or
invasion he was 'vehemently interrupted' and told such
matters were not to be dealt with.   Ralph Crockett, a
seminary priest executed at Chichester on 1 October 1588,
'spake somewhat in excuse of himself' saying he died 'for
religion and coming to execute his function of priesthood'.   He was immediately stopped by two justices who
were present, who said that he was condemned for treason,
not for religion.   There could be other forms of interference with a condemned man's last speech. (62)   Robert
Widmerpool, a catholic layman, when he tried to address
the crowd, was howled down;   the catholic priests who were
convicted at the sessions at the Old Bailey in August 1588
were not permitted by the authorities to make any speech
at all.   Just occasionally the officials present showed
what amounted to either great tolerance or laxity.
Richard White was allowed to tell his hearers that they
should reconcile themselves to the catholic church three
times over before the sheriff interfered. (63)

Descriptions of sixteenth-century executions for treason show that it was not uncommon for the victims in their
last words to make requests concerning their debts, money
that was owed to them and provision for their wives and
children.   Henry Dunn forgave 'all that was owing to him
and craved forgiveness of what he owed'.   His fellow conspirator Titchburne is reported as saying with equal brevity 'I lefte a note of my debtes with my wife;   I beseeche you that it maie be paide'. (64)   Edward Jones, a
third member of the same conspiracy, was much more precise.   We are told he requested that Sir Francis Knowles,
who was then present, should be 'a mean to her majesty
that there be some care had of my creditors and debtors'.
He had written down the amount of his debts:   they total-
led £980.   Sums that were owed to him, he said, reached
£1,600.   He warned that anyone who examined his accounts
would find evidence of sums owing him in the amounts of
£100, £200 and £300, but in fact these had almost entirely
been discharged.   He did not want the accounts to be misinterpreted and cause any man's undoing.   As to depen-

dants, Sir Thomas Wyatt asked Secretary Bourne to inter-
vene with the queen on behalf of his wife and children,
but received no reply. (65)   Anthony Babington, referring
to his wife and child, said he did not know 'howe they are
lefte, but her frends be riche ynoughe.   I would humblie
desire that favoure might be showed them'.   To whom this
request was directed, the queen, royal officials, or members of the public there present, is not clear.   Dr
Storey made a request clearly intended for sympathizers.
He asked that anything they might have intended bestowing
on him 'I beseech you, for charity sake, bestow it yearly
on my wife who hath four small children ...', adding, says
the report, that 'now my daughter Weston and her three
children are gone over to her and I know not how they
shall do for food'. (66)

Execution speeches of the various types outlined above
have sometimes been referred to as 'confessions', and it
has been implied that they were wrung from those condemned
either by fear or distant hope. (67)   Even if we consider
only those which made some degree of admission, this seems
to be too severe a judgment.   Certainly harsh conditions
of confinement in prison may have weakened any will to
maintain a defiant attitude at execution, but those who
were most defiant were the Jesuits and seminary priests
and they had frequently had the worst of imprisonment,
whereas the least defiant were the nobility and gentry
and they seem to have had the best.   Fear of how the executioner had been told to perform his gruesome task, a
quick death or a slow one, may have had more influence,
and a man of relatively high station who had been granted
permission by the king to suffer by beheading may have
been terrified at the thought of being hanged and disembowelled instead.   Another explanation of the victims'
apparent reconciliation to their fate is that most rea-
lized they had committed a crime which, even if they were
not very willing to admit as amounting to treason, was
none the less very serious and carried the death penalty
under the law.   For this self-deception that they were
not traitors the complex state of the treason law must be
held partially responsible, although the ability of the
human mind to delude itself in such situations has been
the same throughout the ages.   Another reasonable explanation of good behaviour on the scaffold was the obvious
desire among prisoners who were possessed of some wealth
for their heirs not to be disinherited:   they hoped that
although they themselves were convicted of treason the
penalties in regard to possessions would be as for felony
and the inheritance would not be lost to the family for
ever.   A suitably contrite and loyal attitude at execu-

tion might persuade the king not to visit his wrath on the condemned man's children;  it might even within a few years persuade him to favour them.    Thomas Cromwell made a speech to which neither king nor rivals could take objection, and his son Gregory was made a peer the same year. (68)

Words by condemned traitors to the effect that they had been convicted under the law are best interpreted not as an indication that they accepted the verdict because it was a decision of the law which itself was an expression of the king's will, but simply as a neutral statement explaining how they came to be in the predicament they were, and as a way of avoiding comment on their trials.    There can be little doubt that the majority of the victims believed God himself was responsible for their discovery, accusation, conviction and forthcoming execution, and that He had been influenced by their sinful way of life in general as much as by any seditious conspiracy or uprising.    Their requests for forgiveness, their forgiving of enemies, and blessings on the monarch and the realm, even if prompted by the chaplain in attendance, were the natural output of minds and consciences being put into exemplary condition for the journey to the next world.    Their owners were eager to make a good christian end.    If, bearing in mind all these factors, the contriteness displayed at the gallows still seems partially unexplained, we should remember that the vast majority of those executed for treason were very likely guilty of committing that crime.    There is also the possibility that good behaviour on the scaffold was induced by hope of reprieve at the last moment.    There were strong rumours to this effect circulating about the duke of Northumberland in 1553. The hopes of the condemned may have been kept alive by knowledge of actual offers of pardon made to others on condition that they would comply with the king's wishes. (69)    Such an offer was made to John Fisher in 1535.    It was reported that Thomas Plumtree, who had participated in the northern rebellion of 1569-70, at his execution on 4 January 1572 was offered his life if he would give up his catholic faith and become a protestant. At the end of May 1582, when there were several executions of catholic priests at Tyburn, at least four of them, John Shert, Robert Johnson, Luke Kirby, and William Filby, were told by the sheriff that if they admitted their fault, were sorry for their treasons, asked forgiveness of God and the queen so that 'we shall perceive in thee any such motion that thou wilt ... become a good and faithfull subject' 'we will carrie thee backe againe.'    This seems to have been regarded as a novelty.    Those in the crowd, so

we are told, said amongst themselves 'O exceeding mercie
and favour.   What a gracious princess we have.'   Each of
the four prisoners refused to allow that he had committed
any treason and the offer was spurned. (70)   It does not
seem as if other men convicted of treason were ever given
a similar choice.   However, that pardons were actually
given to traitors at the gallows cannot be doubted.   John
Ferne, a priest, secured one on Tower Hill on 4 May 1535,
and in 1546 Johan Edling, wife of the purveyor of the
king's oxen, who was guilty of clipping gold coins, received hers when actually bound to the stake at Smithfield. (71)

On arrival at the scene of execution the person condemned might first be compelled to watch the deaths of one
or more confederates.   This occurred, for example, at the
execution of Anthony Babington and his associates, and it
was a fairly common practice when Jesuits and seminary
priests were being put to death.   Thus James Bell, a
seminary priest, when taken from the hurdle, was made 'to
looke upon his companion (John Finch) that was a-quarter-
inge'.   At Chichester on 1 October 1588 the priests
Edward James and Francis Edwardes had to observe the
death of their fellow Ralph Crockett.   The purpose in
this case was quite clear.   It was thought that their
resolution was less than Crockett's, and that they might
be persuaded to conform and acknowledge the queen's ecclesiastical supremacy if frightened sufficiently.   James
died without changing his opinions, but Edwardes yielded
and was spared. (72)

That Tudor England was not well provided with profi-
cient executioners cannot be doubted.   There were sufficient who were able to perform the office of hangman,
but the more demanding arts of decollation and disembowelling, which were peculiar to the crime of treason, were
rarely practised with great competence.   For the beheading of Anne Boleyn the government decided to import an
executioner from Calais or St Omer;   for that of the earl
of Essex it took care to send two executioners 'because if
one faints the other may perform it to him'. (73)   In
1536, when Anne was executed, there was plying his trade
one Gratwell, who was recognized as 'the hangman of
London', and who had 'done execution in London since the
Holy Mayde of Kent was hanged'.   He was described by
Wriothesley as being 'a conninge butcher', yet he must
have been thought unsuitable for the beheading of the
queen.   Perhaps he was not reckoned good enough with the
axe, there being few opportunities to use it in a land
where hanging was the common mode of execution.   Outside
London executioners were frequently of doubtful compe-

tence.   The catholic priest Thomas Prichard, put to death
at Dorchester in 1587, was described as being 'most cruel-
ly mangled' 'the executioner beinge a cooke and unskilfull
or careles'.   In September 1593 since no one could be
found to put to death at Beaumaris Richard Daye, another
priest, his execution was delayed for three or four weeks
until a butcher of Chester offered to perform the task for
a fee of 40 shillings. (74)

The condemned man did not usually see the executioner
until he arrived at the gallows, although the priest John
Mundyn was actually placed on the hurdle at the Tower gate
by the man who was to put him to death.   This executioner
was exceptional in another way as well.   He openly rel-
ished Mundyn's forthcoming death, saying to his charge he
would treat him as he deserved, and accusing him of corrupting certain youths whom he had taught.   Usually we
find the executioner, on bended knee if his victim was of
noble rank, explaining he must fulfil his function, and
asking the prisoner's forgiveness;   sometimes he requested
it more than once. (75)   None of the victims, as far as
we can tell, ever refused the request.   The duke of Norfolk in 1572 even gave his executioner encouragement,
telling him not to fear 'as he would lie quietly and hand-
somely for him'.   Quite a number of victims went as far
as to pay the executioner a sum of money as a form of
reward. (76)   There was even one occasion when the prisoner tried to convert the executioner to catholicism.
The Jesuit Thomas Cottam reminded Bull, the London hangman, who was about to put him to death, of how the executioner of St Paul had had his soul saved by the martyr's
blood which had fallen on his garments.   There was also
the occasional jest.   Richard White advised his hangman
to change his occupation since it was 'but simple'. (77)

Unless the victim had been granted by the king the
nobleman's death of being beheaded, the grisly process of
execution began with hanging.   The prisoner, who was
often stripped down to his shirt and had his arms bound in
front of him, was placed on a cart or a ladder.   The executioner, who throughout took his orders from the sheriff,
put the noose round the victim's neck, setting the knot to
the ear;   he might also cover his face with a piece of
cloth. (78)   When the sheriff made the signal either the
cart was drawn away, leaving the condemned man swinging in
space, or the ladder was turned over with the same result.
How long the victim was allowed to hang varied greatly.
If he was left he might die by strangulation in a few minutes, although there were examples in the later Middle
Ages of men and women being taken down many hours later
and surviving.   It was the task of the sheriff to decide

when the 'topman', who sat aloft on the gibbet, or an officer with a halberd, should cut the victim down. (79) If he, or the government, wished the latter to be fully dead or totally insensible when he was disembowelled, then not only would he be permitted to hang for some time but the sheriff's men, or even members of the crowd, might pull on his legs and hit his chest in order to hasten death.   At the execution of John Payne, a seminary priest, at Chelmsford on 2 April 1582 'they very courtesly caused men to hange on his feete'.   When Richard White was being executed the hangman 'leaned upon his shackles of purpose to despatch him out of his pains the sooner'. (80)   However, the sheriff was usually very concerned that the victim should not be dead, or seemingly dead, when cut down, since in accordance with the sentence given by the justices, he was supposed to be disembowelled alive.   This was likely to cause some outcry from the crowd if the hanged man was popular in the locality, or had said the right things in his last speech like asking for the king's forgiveness and calling on God to bless him and the realm.   When the sheriff gave the order for White to be cut down 'the people desired him to take compassion upon the poor prisoner and to let him die, the same also two or three gentlemen which were present requested, by whose earnest entreaty he was stayed yet a little longer.' There were also occasions when the crowd demanded the victim be cut down immediately, or before there was any chance of total insensibility.   This happened in the cases of the seminary priest Cuthbert Mayne in 1577, and the much hated William Hacket in 1591. (81)   Sometimes when the victim was cut down very quickly contemporary opinion attributed it to malice and caused by some deed the government found particularly obnoxious.   Thus in around February 1592 Patterson, a catholic priest who was treated in this way was thought to have been made to suffer the more because he had converted six felons to catholicism while he was imprisoned in Newgate. (82)

It was when the victims came to be disembowelled that the experience of the executioner, or the lack of it, was plainly revealed.   The biographer of Richard White obser- ved shrewdly about the man who put to death his hero, that 'although thieves and murderers were well acquainted with the hangman's office, yet he wanted skill to do this execution answerable to the bloody wills of the magis- trates ...'.   On being cut down from the gibbet prisoners sometimes managed to stagger to their feet.   If they did they were tripped up by the hangman, or his assistant, and carried or dragged, as were those who lay insensate, to the fire which had been prepared nearby. (83)   Occasion-

ally they seem to have been transported on the hurdle on
which they had been drawn from the gaol.   In one instance
in 1540 two priests were reported as being laid on a board
and kept there 'fast bounde' for the rest of the execution.   There followed next the abscission of the victim's
'members' (genitals), in order, Coke tells us, to show his
issue was disinherited with corruption of blood;   then
there came the slitting of the stomach, the putting out of
his entrails and the cutting out of the heart.   Finally
heart and entrails were burned.   This reason for this
butchery lay in the medieval belief that it was in the
body of the traitor that his treasonable thoughts had
their birth, and that his entrails therefore must be pur-
ged by fire.   At the execution of Sir Thomas Blount in
1400, so we are told, the executioner 'luy fendy le ventre
dessoubz la boudine et luy tyra les boiauz hors du corpz,
puis coppa le boiel dessoubz lestomacq lequel il lya dune
laniere bien fort adfin que le vent nentrast ou corps, et
ce fait gecta touz yceulz boiaulz ardoir dedens le
feu'. (84)   In contrast with such expertise we hear in
the sixteenth century of the gruesome task of disembowelling being badly botched.   The executioner of Richard
White 'having made a little hole in his belly ... pulled
out of the same his bowels by piecemeal;   the which device
taking no good success, he mangled his breast with a butcher's axe to the very chine most pitifully'.   At Dorchester in 1587, at the putting to death of Thomas Prichard, the executioner 'being ... unskilfull or careles
first cut him over thwart the belly' and 'all over the
hand'.   In this case the victim gave assistance to the
inexpert executioner.   A contemporary description tells
us that 'the Priest reised himself and putting owt his
hands cast forward his owne bowells crynge out "Misere
mei"'. (85)   A report of the execution of Bridgettine
and Carthusian monks in 1539 speaks of the executioner not
being allowed to remove their hair shirts as he did other
garments so that 'propter duritiem cilicii quod gladio
resistebat saepius ferire antequam penetrare acies posset
cogeretur, jam non secam corpora sed laceram videren-
tur'. (86)

If a victim on being cut down quickly recovered from
the hanging and suggested by his attitude he might be
ready to put up some resistance, assistance was sought
from the sheriff's officers standing by.   In the case of
Peeke, a catholic layman, executed at Dorchester in July
1591, they 'stretched out his hands and with their Hal-
berts thrust them thorowe and fastned them to the ground'.
After John Storey had been cut down 'and when the executioner had cut of his privy members he rushing up upon a

sudden gave him a blow upon the eare to the great wonder
of all that stood by' but then he was held down by three
or four men so that the rest of the disembowelling could
proceed. (87)   When a prisoner's entrails had been removed the executioner cut out the heart.   Until this
point many of the victims were still conscious.   The
priest Edmund Jennings, we are told, cried out for his
patron St Gregory to assist him and 'the hangman, aston-
ished, said with a loud voice "God's wounds! His heart
is in my hand and yet [St] Gregory is in his mouth"'.
The heart, which was frequently described as 'leaping and
panting' in the executioner's grasp, was then put in the
fire, or on a boiling pan, and precaution taken that it
did not jump out again.   Finally the executioner took an
axe, cut off the victim's head, and held it on high,
which was greeted by the plaudits of the multitude. (88)
   Beheading was a much easier form of death both for the
victim and the executioner.   As with hanging the executioner asked for and received the condemned man's pardon,
and was often given some money by him in addition.   The
duke of Norfolk gave as much as 'four sovereigns of gold
and eighteen shillings and six pence of silver'. (89)
The executioner was entitled to the clothes in which the
victim came to the scaffold and, although these were worth
but little in the case of most hangings, they must have
brought him a sizeable sum when death was by the axe.
The victims seem frequently to have been dressed in some
of their best clothes, albeit black or very dark in col-
our.   The earl of Essex, we are told, 'was apparelled in
a gown of wrought velvet, a satin suit and felt hat, all
black'.   Norfolk in 1572 wore a velvet gown, black satin
doublet, white fustian waistcoat and velvet nightcap.
Mary, Queen of Scots, who was described as being dressed
'as gorgeously as she was wont to do upon festival days',
was attired in a gown of black satin 'embroidered with a
French kind of embroidery of black velvet, her hair seemly
trussed up with a veil of white lawn'. (90)   Only in
Mary's case does the executioner appear to have been refused the victim's clothing.
   When the condemned person had finished both his speech
to the crowd and his private prayers, he took off, or had
taken from him, any part of his clothing that might hinder
the executioner performing his office.   Essex, 'asking
what was fit for him to do for disposing himself to the
block', had his doublet taken off.   Anne Boleyn took off
her mantle and her hood, put a linen cap over her hair,
and fastened her clothes about her feet. (91)   Lady Jane
Grey's gown was removed by two women in waiting.   Mary,
Queen of Scots, 'was by two of hir weomen and the two

executioners disrobed into her petticote'. (92)   At his
execution the duke of Norfolk took off his gown and doublet then, when he put his head on the block, it was found
that 'his shirt truss being very straight' would obstruct
the stroke, so he had to get up again and have it cut
open.   The victim then had the choice of having his eyes
bandaged or not.   Anne Boleyn, Lady Jane Grey and Mary,
Queen of Scots, had each a hankerchief as a blindfold, but
men usually refused. (93)   To receive the executioner's
blow the victim had to lie, not merely kneel, in the straw
on the scaffold, and place neck and head over a small
block.   Then the executioner would probably check to see
'his neck (was) sure upon the block', and the condemned
man would revert to prayer.   The duke of Norfolk asked to
see the axe, but the dean of St Paul's, who was in attendance, begged him to refrain 'from adding more terrors
than the occasion needed'. (94)

Usually the executioner decided to bring down the axe
while the victim was praying, although the earl of Essex,
according to one report, gave the signal to strike himself.   Quite often the head was severed at a single
stroke.   Even if it was not, it seems, as in the case of
Essex, that 'the first was deadly and depriving all sense
and motion'. (95)   To ensure that death was instantan-
eous special precautions might be taken.   Thus the dean
of St Paul's reminded the duke of Norfolk 'to stretch out
his neck and to bend his chin downward'.   Bull, the
common hangman of London, who executed Mary, Queen of
Scots, seems to have arranged for his 'bloody and unseemly
varlet attending upon him' to hold down her hands. (96)
Despite the fact that the executioner cannot have been
very skilled in the use of the axe, at least not upon
human victims, few executions were botched.   The worst
errors seem to have concerned women.   The first blow on
the neck of Mary, Queen of Scots hit the knot of her
blindfold 'and scant pierced her sacred skin', and she
could still speak.   The only real disaster was the execution of the aged Countess of Salisbury in 1541.   Chapuys
said that, because the usual executioner was absent, 'a
blundering *garconneau*' was chosen, who hacked her head and
shoulders to pieces. (97)   We must set this report
against the statement made more than a hundred years later
to the effect that the cause of the trouble was the countess's refusal to hold her head still.   Finally the executioner held up the victim's severed head, a move that
was greeted with sighs and groans by the assembled popu-
lace, and either he, or the sheriff, or the chaplain, said
something which amounted to 'so let all the king's enemies
perish'.

Rope and axe were not the only methods of executing for
treason but they account for 99 per cent of such deaths.
In theory the proper death for a female traitor was to be
drawn to the place for execution and burned.   The sen-
tences passed on Anne Boleyn and Lady Jane Grey were that
they should be burned, or beheaded, according to the
prince's pleasure, although eventually it was the latter
which was decided on.   There may not, in fact, in the
period under review have been a single instance when a
woman was burned for high treason. (98)   It is true that
Stow records two cases, one in September 1592, the other
in April 1594, where burning did occur, but on both occasions the victim had been found guilty of poisoning her
husband. (99)   The offence therefore was very likely
petty rather than high treason, the act of 1530 which made
poisoning high treason having been revoked in the legislation of Edward's reign.   Another quite distinct method of
execution was inflicted on traitors who had been convicted
of heresy as well as treason.   On 22 May 1538 the friar
John Forest was 'hanged about the middle in chains of iron
on a paire of gallowes alive, a great fire made under him
and about him and so was burned for his said heresie and
treason'.   This was a method of execution hallowed by
time, being modelled apparently on that used on Sir John
Oldcastle in 1417.   In Forest's case death was caused by
the flames, but there were a few cases where men died for
treason by means of being hanged in chains.   On 2 December 1549 Robert Ket, the Norfolk rebel leader, and William
Ket, his brother, were both hanged in chains, the former
on top of Norwich castle and the latter on the steeple of
the church at Wymondham, their home village.   Another
example is mentioned in a letter from the duke of Norfolk
to Thomas Cromwell in 1537.   The writer states that Sir
Robert Constable, a leader in the northern insurrection,
'dothe hang above the highest gate of the towne [i.e.
Hull] so trymmed in cheynes ... that I thinke his boones
woll hang there this hundrethe yere'.   The purpose of
these exceptional executions was clearly to display the
corpse for as long as possible, so that it should remind
the people of that region of the penalties for insurrection. (100)
Whilst those executed for murder were usually buried
alongside the gallows, the disembowelled bodies of dead
traitors were often accorded a more special treatment.
Most of the decollated corpses were cut into quarters and
these, with the head, were then put into a basket and carried off in a cart to be parboiled.   If the execution had
occurred in London the boiling was probably done in Newgate gaol. (101)   The body of the victim who had secured

the privilege of being beheaded was usually put into a
coffin of some sort, although, if the traitor was a man,
the head might be retained so that it could be displayed
on a pole somewhere near at hand.   If the victim was
female and noble the removal of the body was probably
left to the women of her household. (102)   One exception,
however, was the body of Mary, Queen of Scots: 'her ser-
vauntes were incontynentlye removed and order taken that
none should approache unto her corps, butt that yt should
be embalmed by the surgeon appoynted'.   In the later
years of Elizabeth, with the execution of many catholic
priests, there arose a desire among co-religionists to
have some memento of the victims, a feature of execution
not noticeable previously, although bystanders were reputed to have dipped their hankerchiefs in Sir Thomas
Wyatt's blood.   At the execution of William Hart at York
in March 1583, so it is said, members of the crowd 'pressing round the gallows' took his shirt, clothes and shoes
'et sanguis et ossa colligebantur, et vi quodamodo e
carnificis manibus auferebantur'. (103)   Following the
execution of the seminary priest Richard Thirkeld, also at
York, the following May, in order to prevent catholics
collecting blood-stained souvenirs a large fire of straw
was made at the gallows.   A letter of August 1588, apparently by the Jesuit Robert Southwell, stated that it had
by that time become the practice of the authorities, who
recognized that certain catholics were willing to risk
their lives to secure some relic, to put a guard round the
gallows after execution. (104)   The quarters of the victim's corpse and the head, when parboiled, were sent to
locations where the treason had been conspired, or where
the traitor had found support.   There, when displayed on
town gates, walls, or gibbet, either affixed to poles or
to chains, they were supposed to act as a reminder of the
penalties for disloyalty towards the prince.   Relatives
who wished to preserve these bodily parts, or give them a
decent burial, had to wait until they were officially
'thrown down' so as to make room for the remains of later
traitors.

   That executions for treason were considered by the pop-
ulace to be a moving spectacle is obvious.   Whether it
considered them cruel and gruesome seems doubtful.   Tudor
opinions as to what amounted to cruelty may seem to us in-
consistent.   Holinshed was disgusted at the patronizing
of beargardens.   When there was the collapse of a scaffold at the Paris garden in January 1583, killing eight of
the audience, he felt moved to write it was 'a freendlie
warning to all such as more delight themselves in the
crueltie of beasts to see them rent each other'.   Yet he

seems to have fully approved of disembowelling and quartering.   Wriothesley, when referring to the execution of
two priests at Calais for treason, who had 'their bowells
brent afore them and spake alwaies til their harts were
pulled out of their bodies', felt moved to add that it was
'a piteous death'. (105)   Yet usually he displays, like
Holinshed, no emotion or sympathy when describing traitors' deaths.   Despite this evidence it would be wrong to
conclude that the spectators or commentators never extended their sympathy to any person executed.   Holinshed
himself describes with obvious emotion the hanging in
Fleet Street on 2 June 1582 of Philip Prise, whose 'great
repentance', 'pathetic speeches', 'plentiful tears' and
'vehement sighs and greevous grones' much affected those
present.   He continues 'most yea in maner all (where of
some were such as a man would have thought had never a
teare to shed at such a sight, having viewed diverse the
like and more lamentable spectacles) with wet eies beheld
him.'   But Prise's crime was murder, not treason;   when
the offence was the latter the attitude of the spectators
was much more stern and their compassion disappeared.
Such hard-heartedness, we may suspect, was increased
rather than diminished by the relative composure of the
victims.   Although there were no others capable of making
sardonic quips at their execution and ending their life
'with a mocke' as did Sir Thomas More, the bravery which
most of them displayed was outstanding. (106)   In
accounts of executions of those whose social rank was
above the labouring class, we find only a single case
where the condemned person was so distraught that the time
appointed had to be set back to allow some recovery.   In
descriptions of the behaviour of victims of all classes,
and both laity and clergy, on their way to and actually at
the place of execution there is virtually no reference to
any displaying fear. (107)
     Drawing to execution on a hurdle, hanging, disembowel-
ling, and quartering, had been the medieval method of
putting traitors to death, and the Tudor monarchs cannot
be said to have introduced any part of the ritual;   nor do
they appear to have increased its severity although there
is clear evidence that certain members of the house of
commons called for such a measure when William Parry's
treason came to light.   What the historian may have expected to meet was some lessening of the barbarities involved.   Certainly a good number of those condemned who
were of higher social standing were granted the privilege
of decollation, but again this was traditional.   The only
evidence of mitigation is to be found in the reign of
Elizabeth and concerns in part the queen herself.   Appar-

ently , when told of 'the severity' used in executing
Babington and some of his associates on 20 September 1586,
'and detesting such cruelty', she gave instructions that
the other conspirators, Abington, Tilney, Jones, Travers,
Charnock, Bellamy, and Gage, should the next day be 'used
more favourably'.    Therefore they were allowed to hang
until fully dead before being cut down and disembowelled.
In 1588 the government appears to have gone a step further.    At the sessions of oyer and terminer held 26-29
August in the Old Bailey the catholic laymen and seminary
priests condemned for treason were apparently spared that
part of the sentence which decreed being disembowelled and
quartered.    Unfortunately, this did not herlad a universal or long-lasting policy.    Later on that year other
traitors were disembowelled, though outside London, and
the practice of cutting the victim down alive was restored. (108)

Conviction led not only to execution but also to what
was dreaded quite as much by the victims' dependents, the
forfeiture of his possessions.    Forfeiture for treason
has a complex history, and changes were most frequent of
all in the Tudor period.    The act 1 Ric. III c. 3 had
declared that neither sheriff, escheator, bailiff, nor
other person, should seize the goods of a person arrested
on suspicion of felony before he was conficted.    In regard to treason practice seems to have been different.
Goods and chattels of the suspect were seized and inven-
toried on indictment and were as good as forfeited, since
the crown felt no obligation to return them if their
owner was later acquitted.    The law as it related to
possessions other than goods and chattels, that is to
lands, was, prior to 1534, enshrined in the statute of
1352 whereby conviction of treason in a court of common
law meant the automatic loss of possessions held in fee
simple although not of fees tail or property held to the
traitor's use.    To reach these the king had to rely on a
parliamentary act of attainder declaring forfeiture in
each case.    In 1534, and on occasions thereafter the
rules of forfeiture under the common law were the subject
of amendment in new laws on treason.    These several
changes have been noticed above. (109)    Here we may point
out that the general tendency was for fees tail and lands
held to the traitor's use ('all lands in possession or
seised to or held to their use' was the common formula) to
be made the standard forfeiture penalty in each act which
altered the scope of treason.    By the last years of the
reign of Henry VIII this had become simply 'forfeiture as
in cases of high treason'.    Such a formula and such a
degree of forfeiture remained standard throughout the rest

of the Tudor period save for brief returns to the act of
1352 in 1547 and 1553.   It is worthy of note, however,
that in 1554 the judges of the two benches opined that
lands held in tail were forfeit 'by statute law', and this
at a time when the 1352 act was held to prevail.   Again
in 1570 they argued that the king had had the forfeiture
of entails without a parliamentary act of attainder even
before 1534.   Both statements were quite erroneous historically. (110)

    When the law governing treason was held to be that of
1352 the king, if he wished to have as forfeit the lands
held in tail by a traitor and those which other men held
to his use, was forced to obtain a parliamentary act of
attainder.   Such acts were frequent in Henry VII's reign.
Edward, earl of Warwick, John, earl of Lincoln, Perkin
Warbeck, Edmund de la Pole, earl of Suffolk, John, lord
Audley, were all so attainted (each save Suffolk posthumously) in the parliament of 1504.   Sir William Stanley
and his fellow conspirators were similarly dealt with in
1495.   There were no attainder acts passed in the first
fourteen years of Henry VIII's reign but the duke of Buckingham was attainted in the parliament of 1523, Rhys ap
Griffyths in the session of 1532, and Elizabeth Barton and
her backers in that of 1534.   From 1534-42 attainder acts
were quite frequent;   thirteen were enacted which dealt
with treason, although not necessarily exclusively, and
three with misprision of treason. (111)   That they were
drafted and passed at all shows that the king's intent was
not merely to obtain entails and possessions held to the
victim's use, since the act 26 Hen. VIII c. 13 provided
him with these.

    A small number of attainder acts were the outcome of
the king's desire to convict a person of treason without
trial before a court of common law.   Why the crown did
not want such a trial was usually because the evidence
against the accused was felt by the king's legal advisers
to be of doubtful sufficiency, or of such a type that it
could not be made public, or because the offence did not
seem to fall within the existing treason laws.   Thus the
attainders of Thomas Cromwell and Queen Katherine Howard
fall within the first category, that of Elizabeth Barton
within the second.   Although this method of conviction
cannot but be decried it is wise to remember that the
charges proposed for, or contained in, the bill of attainder might be examined and argued over in both or either of
the two houses of parliament at some length, with evidence
being considered and witnesses heard.   Bishop Burnet
thought that in Henry VIII's reign the passing of attainder acts was preceded by the reading of depositions in

both houses of parliament.   Certainly the next reign revealed quite a sophisticated juridicial procedure in
operation there.   On 25 February 1549 the bill of attainder against Admiral Seymour was put into parliament
and passed by the lords 'uppon mature deliberacion, hearing thexaminacions, deposicions and wytnesses'.   On 3
March it was decided by the house of commons that the
evidence against Seymour 'shall be heard orderly as it
was before the lords; and also to require that the Lords
which affirm the evidence may come hither and declare it
viva voce.'   There followed another prolonged debate,
the bill only being passed when 'no man was able to say
the contrary, being divers tymes provoked thereunto by
the Speaker'.   Katherine Howard was even offered the
opportunity to defend herself before parliament, but
turned it down. (112)   Sometimes the purpose of an attainder act was to confirm the conviction of men whose
guilt had been established by outlawry, or by verdict of
jury.   For example the earls of Westmorland and Northumberland, the countess of Northumberland, Leonard and
Edward Dacre, Sir John Nevill, and five other northern
gentlemen, of whom it was said that some had been indicted, had fled and stood outlawed, some had been merely indicted, and some had been convicted by law, were the victims of an act of attainder in 1570 which approved and
confirmed the conviction of those found guilty in court,
or who had been outlawed. (113)   It is worthy of note
that attainder acts which decreed the forfeiture of the
lands of a man who was not convicted in court, or outlawed, but merely stood indicted were very few in number,
as were those which attainted persons who, since they had
never been formally accused, had not come under the common
law at all.
     Another group of sixteenth-century attainder acts,
while they stated they were designed to confirm conviction
which had occurred in a court of common law, had as their
main purpose to give the prince immediate possession of
the traitor's landed property without the delay which an
escheator's inquest would create.   Thus the act of
1548-9 against Sir William Sherrington, having stated it
was 'for the confirmation therfore of the same attaynder',
went on to declare that it was also 'for the more spedye
suretye of the King's Majesty touching the forfaiture and
actuall and reall possessyon' of all such castles, manors,
lands, tenements, and hereditaments, he held on the day of
his treason.   The act 29 Eliz. c. 1, passed in the parliament of 1586-7 against Lord Paget, Sir Francis Englefield, Francis Throckmorton, Anthony Babington, and
others, declared that their 'saide lawfull and juste con-

viccions and attaynders' 'maye be approved and confirmed'.
It added that all properties they had to their own use
were to be deemed vested in the actual and real possession
of the queen without any need for an inquisition as the
common law demanded. (114)   Acts which provided immediate
title for the king were not confined to the second half
of the sixteenth century.   There was one which forfeited
those estates which Sir Thomas More had conveyed to his
own use before he committed treason.   There was another
example passed by the parliament of 1495.   This referred
to an attainder act of 1485 which gave to Henry VII property whereof Richard III, or other to his use, was seised
in fee simple or tail for term of life.   It pointed out
that despite the long interval 'no office is yet found for
the king', and therefore it ordained that Henry was to
have the properties as if the office had been lawfully
found. (115)   It was such delays, probably caused by
doubt in the escheators' minds as to what fell within the
law of forfeiture and what without, that this type of attainder act was designed to obviate.

There were yet other reasons for the use of acts of
attainder in the Tudor period.   Two acts, the one which
attainted Katherine Howard and the one which condemned to
death Lord Thomas Howard for marrying Margaret Douglas,
were designed to contain within them general extensions to
the law of treason, as we have seen.   One other seems to
have awarded the penalties for treason against a man suspected but not yet convicted of that crime while adding,
because he had slain two servants of the marshal of the
royal household, a physical penalty (abscission of hands)
which was different from that decreed by the law. (116)
Acts of attainder were probably used also to convict
rebels who were still at large and for whose forfeiture to
be established by means of exaction and outlawry the crown
could not wait.   To do this at the earliest opportunity
was important, so that their friends and tenants knew the
danger they themselves would be in if they gave shelter or
support.   Furthermore, an attainder act gave uncommitted
men, if pressed to support an insurgent, an excuse for refusing. (117)   There was, however, no occasion in Tudor
times when, as had happened in the fifteenth century, an
act decreed the penalties of treason in suspension, so to
speak, in order to force a person suspected or indicted of
some lesser crime to appear in court to answer within a
specified period.   Yet another act was designed to provide for the conviction and forfeiture of the past and
future abettors and comforters of Thomas Fitzgerald, earl
of Kildare.   Although at first sight this seems like forfeiture in anticipation, it was hardly any more severe

than those fifteenth-century acts which decreed forfeiture on persons in flight. (118)

Another fifteenth-century legal convention concerning forfeiture for treason seems to have survived in memory rather than in actual process. This was the king's right to have as 'forfeiture of war' all lands, goods, and chattels, however held, of rebels who levied open war against him, and who never came before a court of common law. (119) A memorandum of the earl of Sussex of February 1570 put the question 'whether such as levy war against the crown do not *ipso facto* forfeit their lands and goods and whether the Prince is not lawfully entitled thereto without their attainder.' It is obvious that the writer expected an answer in the affirmative. The same point of view was expressed in another letter of the same time sent by Sir Thomas Gargrave to Cecil. The former said 'I think the law is that if any levy war in the realm against the Prince and die before attainder their lands and goods are forfeit.' (120) No royal legal advisers or judges ever affirmed these statements as correct, nor did the crown ever dare to seize lands of rebels in arms without some better title, but obviously the idea was borne in mind.

Arising, like the issue of 'forfeiture of war', at the time of the northern rebellion of 1569-70 was the question of the franchise and prerogatives of the bishop of Durham in respect of treason. The regalian rights of the bishop were stated in 1494 to extend not only to that bishopric as such, but also to the areas between the waters of the Tyne and Tees and 'in the place called Norhamshire and Badlyngtonshire'. In these regions he had 'forfeiture of war' in right of the cathedral church of St Cuthbert, Durham. Such right of forfeiture was long established, having been approved by the king and parliament in February 1327. (121) At Christmas 1569 the earl of Sussex, then commanding in the north, reported in a letter to Cecil that the forfeitures would be great; but he warned that all would go to the bishop. He suggested that either the queen should compound with the prelate for 'his royalties', or she should translate him. The queen took a third line of action. Within two months Attorney-General Gerard was asking the bishop's lawyers to show documentary evidence of *jura regalia* in respect of forfeiture of traitors, arguing that the act of 1352 had not allowed this privilege to continue. On 1 April 1570 Gerard wrote to Cecil from Durham to tell him that precedents had been shown for the bishop to have the forfeitures as in the rebellion in Henry VIII's reign, but that he was bringing back all the indictments of traitors and delivering them

to the king's bench.    It was there at Easter term the
same year that a decision was given in what must have been
a test case.    The judges decided that the bishop had possessed in previous centuries, despite the act of 1352,
proper rights to the lands which traitors, who committed
their offences within the liberty, held in fee simple.
Furthermore, because the act of 1534 (26 Hen. VIII c. 13)
remained 'unrepealed' in regard to what were called 'common law treasons', these rights continued to the present
time.    However, the judges held that the bishop did not
have the right to the traitors' fees tail. (122)    The
case was an interesting example of what must have been
judicial refusal to yield to royal pressure, yet, lest we
should be inclined to commend their independent spirit too
much, we should remember that it was an instance where
there must have been clear evidence of ancient user on the
part of the bishop of Durham.

      In addition to the question of regalian rights, the
church became involved in the issue of forfeiture for
treason through the monasteries.    Among Cromwell's
papers, in a draft which probably dates from 1533 entitled
'acts necessary this parliament', is a memorandum to the
effect that any bishop, dean, or abbot, convicted of high
treason was to forfeit the lands he held in right of his
corporation.    Since Cromwell at this time was much concerned with the Nun of Kent, her handlers, and her intended trial, it is possible the plan for an act concerning
forfeiture by high ecclesiastics was prompted as much by
that particular affair as by any consideration of monastic
suppression.    As it turned out, however, no abbot or
bishop was convicted of treason for his part in the scandal.    Elizabeth Barton and a number of monks and clergy
who had been her patrons were, as we have seen, not convicted in a court of common law but attainted in parliament. (123)    In its phraseology about forfeiture this act
appears to have served in turn as a precursor of the general treason act which followed soon after.    The act of
1534, although there were few words seeming to touch on
the matter, was of great importance in regard to forfeiture for treason by ecclesiastics.    A 'saving' clause
protected the rights of all persons, their heirs, and
their successors, except the convicted traitor and his
heirs and successors.    The word 'successor' was new to
treason legislation and must have been included to be
used, as 'heir' could not be, against monastic houses
whose abbot had been convicted of treason.    The first occasion on which the king used this law was in March 1537
when, after the suppression of the Pilgrimage of Grace,
John Paslew, abbot of Whalley, was convicted of treason

and his house's lands forfeited.    A little later it was
used in the cases of the abbots of Kirkstead, Barlings,
Jervaulx, and the prior of Bridlington, and when the dis-
solution of the monasteries was virtually complete it was
used against the heads and the houses of Lenton, Woburn,
Colchester, Reading, and Glastonbury.

Conviction of high treason meant in terms of forfeiture
not only loss of possessions on the part of the person
found guilty, but also the 'corrupting of his blood', that
is to say the disinheriting of his heirs.    Even the claim
of the victim's wife to dower, which was reckoned at one
third of her husband's lands excluding joint estates, was
generally not allowable in the period under review.    The
only time when this was not so was the years between the
first and second treason acts of Edward VI's reign.    The
statute 1 Edw. VI c. 12 stated quite categorically that
the wife of a man convicted of felony, murder, or any type
of treason, was to have her dower as if her husband was
not attainted, but section eleven of 5 & 6 Edw. VI c. 11,
in complete contrast, said the wives of traitors should
'in no wise be received to ask, challenge or demand dower
of any lands, tenements, hereditaments of any person so
attainted' while the attainder was in force. (124)    This
cõntinued to be the policy of the Tudor state even if the
act 5 Eliz. c. 1, which made treason out of refusing the
oath of supremacy a second time, and 5 Eliz. c. 11 and 18
Eliz. c. 1, both of which dealt with coin offences, excluded dower from forfeiture in regard to the particular
crimes they made into treason.

The fact that wives of convicted traitors lost their
dower and their right to challenge for it at law did not
mean, however, that the government was entirely mindless
of their plight, or that it implemented the provisions of
the treason laws in a manner which was completely rigid.
There are several references to wives being granted their
husbands' goods, movables, or something similar, in com-
pensation.    For example Sarah, the widow of Dr Lopez, and
her children, were granted the right, which the queen had
by his attainder, to Mountjoy's Inn in London with other
adjoining tenements and with goods and chattels up to the
value of £100.    In June 1536 Elizabeth Savage, lately the
wife of William Brereton, was granted all the goods, chattels, rents, fees, and annuities, belonging to her husband
at the time of his conviction. (125)    In June 1554 Jane,
the wife of Sir Thomas Wyatt, was given an annuity of 200
marks to alleviate her hard circumstances.    In March 1488
Henry VII 'in consideration of the poverty and wretched-
ness' of Joan, wife of the traitor John Lord Zouche, made
a grant to Sir John Dynham, Sir William Hody and two

others of an annuity of 100 marks, which they were to ad-
minister for the sustenance of Joan and her children. (126)    Concessions were made in regard to lands
far more rarely.    For the wife of a convicted traitor
to retain lands she possessed in her own right apart from
dower usually required a definite statement to that effect
in an act.    The act passed in the parliament of 1491,
which attainted of treason Sir Robert Chamberlain and
Richard White, excepted the lands whereof their wives were
seised in their own right or jointly with their husbands,
as well as any lands which were held to their own or to
their and their husbands' joint use.    Similarly the act
23 Hen. VIII c. 34, which attainted Rhys ap Griffyths,
contained the proviso that the lands held to the use of
his wife Katherine, or to the use of the longer liver of
the pair, as well as the lands of which she was seised
for term of life or for the life of the longer liver,
should be excepted.    Eleanor Stafford, duchess of Buckingham, was the beneficiary under an act (14 & 15 Hen.
VIII c. 22) specially designed to assign her for life in
recompense for her jointure use and her other claims on
her dead husband's property, certain premises decided on
by Cardinal Wolsey as mediator. (127)    Making provision
for dependants of convicted traitors was never standard
government policy;   luck and a connection with someone
near the king were all important.    Some of the concessions were the result of the monarch's taking a personal
interest in the case;   at other times they might derive
from the concern of a powerful minister.    Deserving the
greatest credit in this respect was probably Thomas Cromwell.    A memorandum of his, dating apparently from 1537
refers to the necessity 'for a boke to be made of the
wyves and poore children of those who have suffered to
thintent his majesty may extende his mercy to them for
their lyvinges ... and for debts.'    That this was not
mere humbug is shown by a letter he received in 1539 from
Margaret, Lady Bryan, thanking him for his kindness to her
daughter Lady Elizabeth Carew, wife of the attainted traitor Sir Nicholas Carew, who had recently been granted
lands in Sussex to the value of £120 to hold for
life. (128)

Forfeitures for treason went to the king, but they were
unlikely to stay in his possession for very long.    There
was frequently a line of supplicants willing to purchase
such property, some with what they considered to be a just
claim to the forfeited land, others with a claim on the
king's generosity.    The royal view was that forfeited
property should go, 'if we be so disposed', to those 'who
have truly served us', but the king was obviously willing

to listen carefully to petitioners who were able to support their request with an offer of hard cash.    A successful petition in 1522 by John Reskymer and Richard Antran to be restored to their inheritance as heirs of the attainted traitor Sir Henry Bodrugan, contained an offer of 1000 marks for the king and 500 for Cardinal Wolsey. (129)    At one time Henry VIIl kept books containing the names of those who were thought worthy to have grants, lands and fees which came into his hands.    Sometimes the pretence of reward for service and careful consideration of applicants virtually disappeared.    For example, in March 1570 Nicholas Bacon, keeper of the great seal, and others were commissioned to undertake the task of selling for ready money lands forfeited by those who had taken part in the recent revolt in northern parts. (130)

How soon forfeited lands could be granted away again depended on the manner in which they had originally come into the king's hands.    Whereas he might regrant them immediately if they had been acquired under an act of attainder, it was proper, because of the act 18 Hen. VI c. 6, to await the escheator's inquest if the traitors had suffered by process of the common law.    Another technical point of some relevance here concerned the reversal of attainder.    Normally an act of attainder could only be reversed in its entirety by a second act, this time one of restitution;  to regain lost possessions a pardon was not itself enough since usually it only 'enabled' the victim at law.    However, in 1504 a statute was passed empowering Henry VII to reverse attainder acts made in his reign by means of letters patent. (131)    This new power was put to considerable use by the king, but in 1509 the act died with him and Henry VIII did not pass similar legislation until 1523.    This later statute enabled the king to reverse by letters patent acts of attainder passed in the reigns of his father and Richard III.    It did not extend to the relatively few acts of his own reign. (132)    Neither Henry, at a later date, nor any subsequent Tudor monarch seems to have sought to acquire the power as Henry VII had possessed it.    One reason must have been that the treason statute of 1534 did away with much of the need for attainder acts, while another may have been that the crown feared to reverse attainder without the backing or force of an act of parliament which might palliate the wrath of dispossessed grantees.

Most would-be traitors, like any other sort of offender  when once they embarked on their criminal enterprises, must have had some hope that if things went awry they would be able to obtain pardon.    In essence there were

two types of pardon, the particular, or 'special', and
the general.   The former were granted by the crown in
response to requests made, either by the traitors themselves, or by their uninvolved friends, to the king directly.   The latter were obtained on specific occasions
when, by act of parliament or proclamation, pardons were
on offer for a fixed period.   If the pardon was promulgated by act, which was rare, any person might acquire one
who had the inclination to visit chancery and ask his name
be set down on one.   The beneficiary would pay only a few
shillings for its sealing, and sometimes even this was excused.   This type of pardon seems to have been offered as
an advert for royal generosity at a time of national cele-
bration, and the king was obviously prompted by the widespread demand.   Pardons issued by proclamation were, as
we shall see, even more easily obtained.   Although at
first sight we might tend to assume the king lost heavily
from the forfeitures he renounced through pardons, this
was not always the case.   In 1537 the king's council,
having decided that a general pardon would help to restore
'perfect tranquillity' after the suppression of the Pilgrimage of Grace, gave as its opinion that 'the benefit of
the seal' would countervail all losses. (133)
    Of the various types of 'special' pardons the first to
be noticed is that where the king admitted diminished res-
ponsibility on the part of the miscreant and decided to be
generous.   Thus in June 1569 a London draper John Bell
was pardoned his clipping of gold and silver coins because
of the fact he was 'of very simple nature', and furthermore only fifteen years of age.   In 1570 Sir William
Cecil, when determining how to do justice on the rebels
in the north, gave his approval to the reprieve from execution of one Henry Johnson, 'for his simplicity', and
John Markenfeld, 'for his youth'.   This pardoning Cecil
contrasted with that of four other rebels, whom 'we are
only moved to spare for the profit that might come to us
by their life'. (134)   Magnanimity might stretch to remarkable lengths.   There were even, at times of insurrection, examples of the king being moved to give a pardon by
such factors as the traitor having several children, or
having a reputation for honesty.
    Relatively few traitors could hope to obtain a special
pardon simply through the king's generosity, but other
ways were available.   One route to success was through a
third party.   Thus John Lord Grey, brother of the duke of
Suffolk, who was arraigned and convicted of treason in
June 1554, was granted a pardon, says Holinshed, through
the 'painfull travell and diligent sute of Lady Grey his
wife'.   In March 1541 Sir John Wallop was pardoned at the

intercession of Queen Katherine. (135)   It was quite
common for pardons to be recommended by the justices at
end of their sessions, and even by the attorney-general,
but this was usually for crimes less heinous than treason;
the perpetrators of coining offences might benefit but
other types of traitors only rarely.   When, at his trial,
John Charnock begged his master Sir Christopher Hatton,
the vice chamberlain, who was one of the justices, to get
the queen to pardon him, the latter replied, quite truthfully, that the offence treason was 'too high' for him to
be of any help. (136)
    More commonly the traitor who would be a successful
supplicant for pardon had to strike a bargain with the
king rather than beg his mercy.   Sometimes this could be
achieved by promising, or doing, the king some service or
duty.   In September 1500 Hugh Dumbylowe and two associates were granted pardons on the understanding that they
returned to England before Christmas and immediately after
entering the kingdom went before the king and took an oath
of fealty.   In May 1567 Richard Byngham was granted a
pardon provided that he should behave faithfully towards
the king in the future, keep the peace for seven years,
and that at the next four Michaelmases appear in person
before the keeper of the great seal.   In August 1506 a
pardon was issued to Thomas Kyllyngworth which provided
that when the king decided to have him examined on matters
concerning the royal majesty or the security of the realm,
he would 'clearly declare' everything about the treasons
committed with his consent. (137)   How men were clearly
aware that providing the king with useful information
could win them a pardon is shown by a letter dated December 1581 from the priest John Hart to Sir Francis Walsingham.   Hart, then a prisoner in the Tower, proposed to use
his intimacy with Dr Allen in order to discover 'all his
designs', and to elicit 'the very secrets of his whole
heart'; he did so 'being in hopes of pardon'.   Of course,
the initiative in regard to pardons was not always taken
by the traitor.   Holinshed states that to achieve the
betrayal of his confederates it was the council which ap-
proached Francis Throckmorton rather than the
reverse. (138)
    Quite the most frequent way of obtaining a 'special'
pardon was for the traitor, convicted or suspected, to
compound, that is to say to pay a fine.   Since the fine
varied from case to case this amounted to making an individual financial bargain with the king.   In the Middle
Ages the amount of the fine had been assessed, or
'afeered' as it was called, by juries composed of the suspected person's peers, but in the sixteenth century, in

the case of treason at least, it was left to royal officials.    Thus in 1498 a commission comprising Thomas
Harrys, king's chaplain, William Hatclyff, clerk of the
accounts of the household, and Roger Holand, was instructed to summon and examine all adherents of Perkin Warbeck
in Devon and Cornwall who as yet had not submitted to the
king's grace and obtained pardon and, if they were willing
to do this, to impose on them fines and ransoms.    In
March 1538 Roland Lee, bishop of Lichfield and president
of the council of the marches of Wales told Cromwell he
had empowered Sir John Porte and Edward Montague to assess
'good fines' in Shropshire on those gentlemen who had departed from their obedience. (139)    On 13 March 1570,
with orders to assess fines on all those in Durham, Yorkshire, Northumberland, Cumberland and Westmorland who had
been guilty of treason since 1 November 1569, was appointed a very high-powered commission comprising the earl of
Sussex, the bishops of Durham and Carlisle, the three war-
dens of the Scottish marches, the attorney-general, and
the solicitor-general.    In May 1601, in contrast, fines
were assessed against the earl of Rutland and the lords
Sandys, Monteagle and Cromwell, all supporters of Essex by
the privy council.    Those who appeared before royal servants empowered to assess fines were expected to 'submit'
themselves, though what that entailed exactly is obscure.
Very likely, when the question of their misdeeds was put
to them, there was extracted a verbal or written admission of guilt and perhaps also an oath of future loyalty.
However, there may have been cases where simply surrendering to authority and offering to pay any fine demanded was
considered acceptable.    All compounders were expected to
declare to the assessors the value of their property and
were warned apparently they should only have restitution
up to the amount they confessed to. (140)
    What determined the size of any one fine, and how soon
it must be paid, was quite complex.    It is true that this
was often left to the discretion of the assessors, yet it
is obvious they were guided by a number of general pre-
cepts.    The earl of Sussex and his fellow commissioners
were asked to consider how long those who submitted had
been in rebellion, whether they had stirred up others,
what 'burden' of wife and children they had, whether they
had rebelled before, and whether they had conformed to the
ecclesiastical law.    Those who had been tenants of the
crown, or held a royal office, were to be dealt with more
strictly than the rest.    In April 1570 Attorney-General
Gerard, one of this commission, told Cecil that many
rebels who appeared before them were very poor, having
been pillaged by soldiers and officers, and that therefore

they had been obliged to impose very small fines.   Cecil
was told by Sir Thomas Gargrave in June of the same year
that some insurgents were so poor they could not pay
before the harvest was in;   presumably allowance for this
was duly made. (141)   Giving an extension of time in
which to pay was a frequent concession on the government's
part and the practice was even extended to the rich.   It
has been argued that it was normal for an applicant 'to
enter into a recognizance for about a quarter more than
his assessed redemption, agreeing to pay the sum in specified instalments' while at the same time naming suitable
securities. (142)   In many instances the period allowed
for payment was an extended one, being perhaps as long as
ten years.   There were even arrangements whereby forfeited lands were returned on lease at a fixed rent, while
the erstwhile traitor paid a second fine in instalments to
secure them back in full ownership.   Evidence from the
reign of Mary suggests that most of these fines were eventually paid in full, and that cases of default were rare.

As we should expect, the size of fines varied enormously.   After the rebellion of Sir Thomas Wyatt rebels paid
between £1 and £5, at one end of the scale to tens of
thousands of pounds at the other.   The more prominent of
the supporters of Essex in 1601 were initially assessed
at from £40 to £30,000.   The latter sum was demanded of
the duke of Rutland, while the earl of Bedford was asked
for £20,000, Lord Sandys and Sir Henry Neville each for
£10,000, Lord Monteagle for £8,000 and Lord Cromwell for
£5,000;   but a month later Rutland's fine was mitigated by
£10,000 and those of the others were referred 'to the discretion of Mr. Attorney', which no doubt had a similar
effect. (143)   Sometimes the crown had no fixed sum in
mind but awaited offers from the miscreants and then told
them to bid higher.   Compounding by fine, as we might
expect, was never a right.   It might be allowed or it
might be refused to those who had taken part in a general
insurrection;   no general rule is apparent.   After the
discovery of a traitorous conspiracy it was usually refused.   It all depended on how the king decided to exercise his prerogative of mercy.   Should men prove stubborn
and not gladly accept the chance to pay a fine then, if
they had been indicted they were put on trial, and if they
had not they lost the major part of their lands and remained in prison until they changed their minds.

As for general pardons, most of those issued by act
were for felonies;   treasons were frequently excepted.
Sometimes the act went so far as to name particular
traitors in this respect.   General pardons embodied in

parliamentary acts which were specifically directed at traitors were few, but they did occur.   A good example was 3 & 4 Edw. VI c. 24, passed after a period of extended insurrection, which referred in its preface to last summer's 'inordynate dysobedience rebellyon and other wise', and stated that the king was replenished with mercy and pity and was giving the pardon to stir his loving subjects to future obedience. (144)   Those who took out pardons under such acts did not necessarily, at that time, stand convicted or even indicted.   Men who felt some guilt, or knew they were suspected, were wont to purchase one in anticipation of future difficulties.   In these cases there seems to have been no reason why the supplicant should make a submission and admit involvement.

The offering, to traitors who would submit, of a pardon by means of a proclamation was a more frequent phenomenon than the use of an act, and occurred regularly after rebellion.   It would often be followed by a moving spectacle at which the king awarded his mercy in person.   On 22 February 1554 some 400 of Wyatt's followers from Kent were led from the London prisons, bound together in pairs, and with halters about their necks, to the court at Westminster.   There, in the tiltyard, they knelt down in the mire and cried to the queen for mercy.   Queen Mary, 'lookinge owt at the gallerie by the gate', graciously gave her pardon.   There had been a similar event in May 1517.   Henry VIII, seated on a lofty platform, with Cardinal Wolsey and a number of lords in attendance, caused 400 of the May Day rioters to be brought before him. Each of the prisoners had a pair of beads in his hands, and in King street, Westminster, had been stripped to his shirt and a halter placed around his neck.   When all had assembled, Wolsey implored the king to pardon them, but Henry refused.   The cardinal then announced the king's reply to the miscreants, who thereupon fell on bended knee calling out 'mercy'.   Wolsey and the nobles present then repeated their request to the king, who eventually agreed. When Wolsey announced to the prisoners the generosity of the king each man took the halter from his neck and threw it in the air, 'and they jumped for extreme joy'.   It must have been, as the writer states, 'a very fine spectacle' and well arranged, being watched by an enormous number of bystanders. (145)   One interesting feature of the episode, which was noted by Grafton, was that the 400 original prisoners were suddenly joined before pardon was given 'by dyvers offenders which were not taken', but who had heard the king was inclined to mercy.   They had come 'well apparayled' to Westminster where they 'sodainlye

strypped them into their shirtes with halters and came in
among the prisoners willyngly to be partakers of the
kinges pardon'. (146)

Traitors who gained pardon for their offences in this
manner very probably, like those who hoped to benefit
from a general pardon promulgated by act of parliament,
had to visit chancery later on to acquire the actual document, though whether they had to pay for it is unclear.
It is important to notice that the granting of pardon by
act, or by the king in his own person, did not mean that
all processes against the offender ceased automatically.
If, as sometimes happened, the offender should subsequently be called into court to answer for his treason he must
not expect the justices to recognize immediately that he
was excused because of the general pardon.    By the end of
the century, at least, he must actually plead the pardon
since, as Coke remarked, general pardons had acquired so
many qualifications and exceptions 'in these days' that
the court was unable to take notice of them. (147)

One disturbing feature of the Tudor system of pardon is
the fact that even those who were tried and acquitted of
treason were sometimes forced into seeking them.    Lord
Dacre of the North, arraigned on 9 July 1534 for traitorously making treaties with the Scots, was acquitted.
Nevertheless he was reimprisoned, so Chapuys says, because
he refused to sign a schedule asking the king's pardon.
From the government's point of view this had the desired
effect, since Dacre soon acknowledged that he had kept
concealed two letters, one of which was from a Scotsman,
the king's enemy, and for this threw himself on the king's
forgiveness, offering £10,000 for his pardon.    The offer
was accepted, and it was arranged he should pay the fine
in instalments giving a bond of 10,000 marks as security
for this and for future good behaviour. (148)    Sir
Nicholas Throckmorton, acquitted of treason in April 1554,
was released only in January 1555, having been bound with
fellow prisoners in a recognizance 'to their good abear-
ing, ordre and fyne at pleasure' of £2,000.    However,
there seems to be no evidence that Throckmorton ever made
payment.    William Levenyng, accused and acquitted of
treason in 1537, seems to have been obliged to make a payment to protect himself from future proceedings against
him.    A deposition by John Thorpe of Birdsall, Yorkshire,
stated that at the Shrovetide sessions at York in 1537
Thomas Wentworth of Ganton asked him to point out Levenyng, saying that although he had been acquitted, charges
would be laid against him in the next sessions, and he
wished him to get the sheriff's favour.    As a result
Levenyng was induced to promise the sheriff either 20

marks, or £20, when his sheep were next sheared.   Whether this extortion was in fact some sort of fine and sanction- ed by the king, or simply a piece of local blackmail is not entirely clear, although the second alternative seems the more likely. (149)

The granting of pardon to anyone involved in treason was governed by a number of rules and precedents, but it is obvious that there was nevertheless a high degree of flexibility and that the king had more room to manoeuvre than in almost any other part of the legal process.   He granted pardons in considerable numbers but never with abandon.   It has been suggested that of 846 persons in- dicted of treason in the period 1532-40 96 were definitely pardoned and another 12 probably pardoned.   Of the 96, 55 were involved in the Lincolnshire rebellion of 1536-7, 29 had conspired the king's destruction and 9 had uttered treasonous words. (150)   In the setting of fines he could act in a particularly arbitrary manner, being able to impose them when the compounder was not yet convicted but only indicted, or even merely suspected.   Only where the suspect was a prime instigator of a traitorous conspiracy was the king unwilling to settle for the paying of a fine. The size of these fines varied not merely with the man's station and wealth but also according to the king's whim, his animosity, fear, or generosity, which in turn must have been affected by the advice of those magnates and courtiers who had his ear.   It was also left to the king to decide how payment of fines should be made.   The manner in which fines and recognizances were combined to- gether so that payment, and thus the return of posses- sions, was extended over a lengthy period seems to have been much favoured by the Tudors, even if it was not their invention.   It is worthy of note that in this period the royal prerogative of mercy in regard to treason was never challenged in parliament, nor reduced to a legal formula. The same is also true about the forfeiture of traitors' possessions.

Judicial process between judgment and execution, and governmental practices in regard to penalties inflicted, have tended to monopolize the attentions of historians concerned with treason and to draw the major part of their criticisms.   Since these were the end products of most accusations of treason, and because of the emotionalism which ritual death or physical punishment tends to arouse in the modern mind, it is natural this should be so. What must be remembered is that in many ways the Tudor monarchs proceeded along traditional lines.   The mode of execution for treason was that of previous centuries, and there seems to have been no effort made by them towards

the introduction of even greater cruelty as was done in
France, for example, by the ordinance of 1539.   England
acquired on the continent a reputation for 'great butchery', and being 'used to blood', but this was created, we
may suspect, as much by the numbers of men of rank and
education put to death in certain periods, and the public
nature of virtually all executions, as by the actual
manner of their suffering.   From the time of the Reformation Parliament Tudor policy was to use the execution of
traitors as an exercise in propaganda and the greatest
attention was given to its handling.   The victims were
persuaded to address the large crowds in attendance and
their words had to follow a certain pattern:   it was intended that they should include some form of confession.
There is little information to be gathered about gallows
speeches in the Middle Ages, but we may suspect that this
part of the execution was novel to the sixteenth century.
Certainly the appearance close by of witnesses ready to
contradict a speech which seemed unsatisfactory was an
innovation, as was the putting of questions by members of
the crowd and the presence of preachers.   The Tudor government overlooked almost nothing in execution management
and there can be little doubt it drew great benefit therefrom.   It was an age when men paid great attention to
words uttered just before dying, and if the state ensured
that those words, if not in praise of the prince or ex-
pressing abhorrence of the treason committed, were in no
way defiant or accusatory, it was reducing disloyalty in
the future.

   In their policy on forfeiture for treason the Tudors
did not differ much from their predecessors.   The matter
was never a controversial issue in the sixteenth century
as it had been in the fourteenth and fifteenth.   This may
have been because there was no coherent noble opposition,
but more likely because, once the treason act of 1534 had
been passed, the king's battle was basically won;   the
judges, we may note, managed to hold its provisions about
forfeiture to prevail even when in some years the law of
treason was reckoned to be totally enshrined in the statute of 1352.   In regard to dependants of executed traitors, the government showed it was capable of generosity,
though provision here was always *ad hoc* and *ex gratia* save
in the case of dower.   The rules, such as they were, concerning the award of pardons and the payment and the size
of fines allowed, since they were not governed by the
common law, much flexibility.   The Tudors used their prerogative here freely, which has tended to create an impression of inconsistency;   in fact they were no more so
than the Yorkist kings.   Governmental policy was usually

to make a good example of a small number of traitors as a
warning to those who might be inclined to disloyalty in
the future, but to pardon the rest.    Prime movers of a
traitorous conspiracy, those leading an armed force
against the prince in the field, and Jesuits and seminary
priests breaking the 'religious treason' laws in Elizabeth's reign, could expect little mercy, but for the rest
the possibility of achieving a pardon through service or
payment was a strong one.

# Appendix: Martial Law

Descriptions of Tudor insurrections make reference to a variety of what may be called quasi-legal usages which were employed by the crown in their suppression. Despite the importance of these usages and the manner in which they stand out quite clearly against the general backcloth of treason law administration they are still shrouded in mystery, having suffered almost total neglect from historians and lawyers. One very good reason for this omission is that such usages operated under the authority inherent in the rank of king, that is to say under his prerogative. They were mentioned in no medieval statute and hardly at all in the year books, and for that reason Tudor legal writers usually neglected to mention them, prerogative to the sixteenth-century lawyer being enshrined in the so-called act *de prerogitiva regis* which referred merely to the privileges of the king as feudal overlord, for example, in regard to alienation by tenants in chief, to wardship and to royal grants of land. Like the prerogatives of mercy and granting of titles, these usages in time of revolt had still not by the late sixteenth century been brought effectively within statute or common law even if Tudor men were coming to argue that all executive action must draw its authority from one or the other.

The history of one of these usages, martial law, deserves our particular attention. This is not the place to discuss the medieval antecedents at length, but an awareness of the chief developments in the fourteenth and fifteenth centuries is vital to a proper understanding of the matter. Under Edward I the offence of high treason was extended to take in the crime of levying war against the king. At about the same time there crystallized the procedure whereby, when the king by his own words 'reputed' rebels as traitors, the mere record of this served to convict them without the usual method of arraignment and ver-

dict of a jury.   By the reign of Edward III, despite,
perhaps, some efforts to extend it, this summary form of
justice had become restricted in use to the trying of insurgents captured waging open war against the king, such
war being defined as when the king displayed his banner
and suspended the sittings of his courts, thereby giving
formal notice that it was a time of hostilities.   Trials
of traitors taken in arms resulting in conviction 'on the
king's record' continued right through the fourteenth and
fifteenth centuries, although, probably because of chivalric conventions which developed at the time of the Hundred
Years War, they have tended to be identified by historians
as 'trials under the law of arms'. (1)   From the reign of
Edward II it became customary for the constable and the
marshal to preside over the commissions of notables which
held such treason trials, and because, also as a result of
the Hundred Years War, they developed jurisdiction over
cases involving ransoms, armorial bearings, and safe conducts, which were usually the privilege of the knightly
classes, their court was sometimes referred to as the
court of chivalry.   By the fifteenth century the law
under which they operated was sometimes referred to  not
as the 'law of arms' but as the 'laws and customs used
before the constable and the marshal'. (2)   Very noticeable is the fact that when the constable and the marshal
did summary justice in the field, or soon after the rebel
defeat, it was by report, nearly always on traitors of
rank, rarely the common soldier.   This may be because the
chroniclers were only interested in the shedding of noble
blood.   It is also possible that the officers of the constable and the marshal simply hanged in summary fashion
any rebel of lower rank without allowing him even the
modest form of trial given to his superiors.

     If this was not the case then the commission of 5 July
1497, whereby Sir John Digby, the marshal, and Sir Robert
Clifford were ordered to execute the office of the constable and marshal of England in regard to all insurgents
who had recently levied war in Devon, Cornwall, and elsewhere, was a novelty through its universality.   Nor was
the commission unique, since on 10 March 1500 Sir Thomas
Darcy was appointed to execute the offices of the constable and the marshal of England on all the adherents of
Michael Joseph and Perkin Warbeck, who should be captured. (3)   The latter commission has another importance.
By it the power to execute summary justice was vested in
one man, who was neither constable nor marshal.   Another
important development in the history of justice under the
law of arms at this time is to be found in the commission
of 1497 to Sir John Dynham, Sir John Digby, the king's

marshal, and others for the trial of James Tuchet, Lord
Audley.  Audley, although a leader of the recent Cornish
rising, was not tried for levying war but for conspiring
to levy war. (4)  This, even if it was traitorous behaviour under the act of 1352, which is unlikely, was treason
of a type not tried by the summary process since the early
fourteenth century. (5)  The law military was obviously
much to the taste of a king who had given, or was about to
give, a great deal in the way of summary powers of justice
over lesser offences to the justices of the peace.

From 1504, when the earl of Derby died, the constableship fell vacant save for the appointment of the duke of
Buckingham to the office for the purpose of Henry VIII's
coronation.  This meant that the court of chivalry, which
was the formal manifestation of the constable's authority, became dormant.  Thereafter the marshal continued to
hold a formal court, it is true, but this was not necessarily the same thing, being rather, so it has been suggested, a means of exercising jurisdiction over heralds
and the college of arms.  It became known as the court of
the earl-marshal. (6)  The dominance of the earl-marshal,
and his extended duties in matters to do with the law
military after the constableship became vacant, is probably reflected in the development of a new class of executive officer serving beneath him.  This was the provost-
marshal, who has been noticed as first being in existence
in the early years of Henry VIII's reign.  The inspiration for his creation may have been French:  Henry VIII
was probably imitating Francis I who re-established the
*prévôts* in France early in the sixteenth century, although
the English provost-marshal was at first unlike his French
counterpart in not having jurisdiction over civil offences
as well as military.  There seems little doubt that in
the English military forces, even before the time of Henry
VIII, there existed simultaneously not one but several
marshals or marshal's officers, and that they operated
courts within the section of the army to which they were
each attached. (7)  In the time of Edward I the justice
of the marshal seems to have been dispensed largely according to common law procedure.  Those who were accused
were allowed to make a plea, and if they said 'not guilty'
were tried by a jury.  The only difference from ordinary
criminal process was that the charges were sometimes based
not on the word of a jury of presentment, or an appeal,
but on the accusation of the marshal. (8)  There remains,
however, the possibility that this common law procedure
operated only if the accused was a member of the army, and
that against rebels taken in arms, whatever their class,
justice was as summary as that dealt out by sixteenth-century provost-marshals.

The relationship of summary military justice as operated in the later Middle Ages to the Tudor 'marshal law',
as it was usually spelt, is a matter of prime importance.
Early in October 1536 the duke of Norfolk was given the
title of 'high-marshal'.  It was a time when the army for
the suppression of the northern rebels was hardly in
being, and the intention of the crown was not so much to
maintain discipline among the troops as to execute summary
justice on captured insurgents. (9)  Such justice, according to contemporaries, was the 'marshal's law'.  It has
often been implied that this was a Tudor invention, orig-
inating perhaps in that very year (1536), but in fact it
was the same form of justice which had been dealt out in
the late medieval period under the law military and on the
king's record.  The phrases 'law marshall' or 'marshal
law' were simply the English form of the Norman-French
*leys et usages d'armes* and the Latin *leges et consuetu-
dines ... coram constabulario et marescallo*, albeit ones
which acknowledged the presiding authority of the marshal.
This is clearly demonstrated by a few words which Sir
Thomas More wrote in 1533, well before the insurrections
of the latter part of the decade.  He said he wished 'the
lawe were so that the iudges myght procede and put felons
to answere without endyghtmentes, as in treason is used in
thys realme by the law marshall uppon warre rered'. (10)
Who ordered the operation of martial law?  Until 1536
very likely only the king did, or the lieutenant entrusted
with the command of his army.  In 1536 and at times
thereafter were appointed lord-lieutenants with authority
in military matters over one or a number of counties:
these also had such authority.  A commission of 1585 gave
them power to execute against the king's enemies, traitors, and rebels, causing invasion, insurrection, riot or
unlawful assembly

> as necessity shall require by your discretion the law
> called the marshall law according to the law martial:
> and of such offenders apprehended or being brought in
> subjection, to save whom you shall think good to be
> saved, and to ... put to execution of death such and so
> many of them as you shall think meet by your said dis-
> cretion to be put to death.

To execute this commission each lord-lieutenant had at
least one provost-marshal.  There is nothing to suggest
that the latter ever possessed power to put martial law
into operation on his own authority, although he may have
possessed power to arrest anyone he suspected. (11)  As
the lord-lieutenant was a local substitute for the king,
and as his duties also included levying, arraying, and
leading men against enemies and rebels, there was no novel

principle arising, merely the proliferation of authorities, except perhaps in the abandonment of the custom of
displaying the king's banner as a sign of open war, and in
cases where the offenders were merely rioting or creating
unlawful assemblies. (12)

From about the middle of the sixteenth century the
categories of offence in regard to which martial law was
used became greatly extended.   Discharged soldiers,
rogues, and vagrants, many of whom had no connection with
the military life, whose chief fault was the threat to
public order posed by their lack of employment, became
justiciable under it.   So did those who broke down enclosures, destroyed parks, assembled illegally, rioted, or
created disorders in the Scottish marches.   There were
also embraced aliens whose native country was at that time
at war with England, those who obtained possession of
heretical and seditious books and failed to burn them,
those who gave assistance to pirates and those who brought
into the country papal bulls illegally. (13)   These cannot be said to have committed the original treason covered
by martial law, namely levying open war against the
prince.   It is also clear that in the suppression of any
insurrection there were executed by martial law, in addition to those who had been in the field against the forces
of the king, many who were merely sympathizers, and who
may not have ever given shelter or assistance to the rebel
fighting men. (14)   The scope of martial law had become
very wide.

Although there exist some brief descriptions of treason
trials under the law of arms from the later medieval
period we know very little of the procedure employed in
Tudor trials by martial law.   There is one report, from
1537, that the marshal, or a provost-marshal, should be
present, and that the king's attorney should prosecute. (15)   We can be sure that usually there was neither
grand jury nor petty jury employed.   Very likely the
trial took the form of a statement of the offence by the
marshal, a plea for judgment by the attorney, who might
put the case for the crown offering what evidence he had,
and then the giving of the verdict by the marshal. (16)
We do not know if the accused was given the opportunity to
make an answer to the charges.   In trials under the law
of arms in the fourteenth century requests to be allowed
to respond had been refused.   In 1598 the earl of Essex,
at that time earl-marshal, suggested there should be regular sessions of a 'marshal's court', whose procedure he
contrasted with dying *sans replique* at the hands of the
provost-marshal.   There is evidence that at the end of
the sixteenth century masterless men, discharged soldiers,

and rogues, who had been arrested by the provost-marshal, might be turned over to local constables, imprisoned, indicted, and delivered for trial at a special sessions held by the justices of the peace. (17)   In trials such as these procedure may well have been of the type usually practised in criminal cases under the common law.

We might imagine that the Tudor monarchs and their advisers employed martial law out of sheer necessity, that recurrent rebellion, threat of invasion and fearsome social problems forced them to a decision which they found very distasteful.   This was not the case.   In general they were very keen to use some harsher substitute for the common law whenever there was an excuse to do so, provided, that is, the rebels or rioters in question were not members of the nobility.   Bishop Roland Lee spoke for many judicial administrators when, on July 1538, he told Cromwell in regard to the state of the Welsh marches that 'Yf we should doo nothing but as the common lawe will then thinges so farr out of order wyll never be redressed'. No doubt on this occasion Lee had in mind the value of conciliar justice.   When on 19 February 1537 the duke of Norfolk wrote to the council from Carlisle about his suppression of the north, he emphasized that he was having to proceed continuously by martial law, since if he were to proceed 'by indictements' [the common law] many a great offender myght ... be found not giltie' by his peers. (18) Queen Elizabeth most definitely favoured the use of martial law.   Camden tells us that when in 1573 Sir John Hawkins was stabbed in the open street by Peter Burchet, who had mistaken him for Sir Christopher Hatton, the queen, very annoyed, commanded he should be executed by martial law.   She had to be told it could only be used 'in camps', or during 'turbulent times', and that elsewhere and in time of peace proceedings must be 'by forme of iudiciary processe'.   On 11 January 1570 she wrote to the earl of Sussex in the north to tell him she marvelled that she had heard of no execution by martial law, as was appointed for the 'meaner sorte that have been rebels' and commanded him to set about it. (19)   It is quite obvious from the Burchet case that the monarch had legal advisers who recognized the dangers inherent in the over-use, and illegal use, of martial law.   In September 1556 the earl of Sussex had the idea of using it against a number of 'shameful offenders that are discovered' in Sussex but the council told him that this would be unsatisfactory, and that they would be punished according to the laws of the realm.   One clear and influential opponent of the misuse of martial law was Sir Thomas Smith, who wrote that this law

hath beene sometime used within the Realme before any
open warre in sodden insurrections and rebellions, but
that not allowed of wise and grave men who in that
their judgement had consideration of the consequence
and example asmuch as of the present necessitie, es-
peciallie, when by anie meanes the punishment might
have beene doone by order of lawe.

He suggested that martial law was suitable for 'camps and
hosts', because in both there was 'no time for process
and pleading'. (20)

It is unlikely that martial law was used in the suppression of every rebellion in the Tudor period yet only
one exception suggests itself clearly, the revolt of the
earl of Essex in 1601.   On that occasion insurrection, if
such it can be called, was limited to a number of nobles,
gentry, and their servants who after an attempt to ride to
the court fortified themselves in Essex's London house.
There was no armed assistance offered them by men of lower
station either in London or elsewhere, although no doubt
it was hoped for.   Very likely the government felt there
was no need for such a drastic measure as martial law
since the rebellion was over almost as soon as it had
begun.   Admittedly in court Coke, then attorney-general,
told Essex that 'it was a great mercy of the queen's that
in *flagrante crimine* he was not, according to the martial
law, presently put to the sword' but this was probably
propaganda since the earl was tried by the common law as
seems to have always been intended. (21)   There remains
the possibility that the proclaiming of Essex as a traitor
in Cheapside and elsewhere on the day of the revolt was
reckoned to institute martial law in addition, and the
further argument can be advanced, although with little
conviction, that by the beginning of the seventeenth century martial law to operate at a time of rebellion did not
have to be proclaimed at all, just as it no longer had to
be preceded by the unfurling of the royal banner.   If
trial of Essex and his followers by martial law was legally acceptable, the queen and her advisers may have preferred to avoid it because of the high rank of many of the
accused.   Summary executions would have caused furore
among members of those classes, and also, they would have
deprived the crown of forfeiture of lands.

One further consideration concerns the class of the
victims.   It is evident that martial law was used almost
entirely against members of the lower classes.   Sussex
wrote to Cecil on 28 December 1569 that he intended going
to Durham 'to take order for such of the common people as
shalbe exequuted by the martiall lawe'.   The same policy
shows itself in a contemporaneous memorandum of Cecil.

He wrote that in every town or parish where the rebels had
found support there should be executions by martial law of
men who had no freehold or copyhold 'nor any substance of
land'.   Reports of executions suggest that this was the
policy put into effect. (22)   Men of some wealth, on the
other hand, were exempted.   Sussex told Cecil that he had
resolved 'not to exequute the martiall lawe against any
person that had inheritance or great welthe for that I
know the lawe in that case'.   The earl and Sir Ralph
Sadler, in a letter to the council of 1 January 1570, announced that, when they had executed a sufficient number
of rebels in Durham they would 'comitt to severall sure
prisons such of the principall offenders as have lands or
great wealth' so they might be 'tried by the lawes', meaning in this case the common law. (23)   The dividing line
between wealthy and poor seems, in the rebellion of 1569-
70 at least, to have been set at having lands of a yearly
value of £5 or not.   The reason for this difference in
treatment lay in the forfeiture of possessions which was
involved.   Under martial law, as by the medieval law of
arms, only the goods of the convicted man were forfeit to
the crown; under the common law lands were forfeited as
well.   If the king sought further forfeiture from a
person convicted by martial law an act of attainder in
parliament was essential.   Such an act was used to reach
the lands of Lord Audley in 1503, but thereafter the crown
avoided the necessity by never trying wealthy rebels under
martial law. (24)

# Notes

INTRODUCTION

1   J.F. Stephen, 'A History of the Criminal Law of England' (London, 1883), ii, 255-70.
2   Ibid., i, 319-26.
3   W.S. Holdsworth, 'A History of English Law' (London, 1923), iv, 493-500.
4   Ibid., viii, 310-19.
5   I.D. Thornley, Treason by Words in the Fifteenth Century, 'English Historical Review', xxxii (1917), 556-61
6   J.R. Tanner, 'Tudor Constitutional Documents A.D. 1485-1603 with an Historical Commentary' (Cambridge, 1922), 376-80.  Tanner made one very serious faux pas.  He said that the 1352 act did not punish conspiracy to compass the king's death.  In fact the phrase in the act 'compass or imagine' ('the death of our lord the king') meant just that.
7   Ibid., 422-8.
8   Unfortunately no statutes were given in full and the parts omitted were often quite important.  Furthermore, the summaries of the sections left out often lack crucial legal form.
9   S. Rezneck, The Trial of Treason in Tudor England, 'Essays in Honor of C.H. McIlwain' (Cambridge, Mass., 1936), 258-88.
10  Rezneck used a good variety of printed records, both historical and legal, from all periods.
11  There are some important details about the examination and punishment of traitors involved in the Wyatt and Dudley conspiracies of Mary's reign in D.M. Loades, 'Two Tudor Conspiracies' (Cambridge, 1965).
12  G.R. Elton, 'The Tudor Constitution. Documents and Commentary' (Cambridge, 1962), 80-1.

13  G.R. Elton, 'Policy and Police' (Cambridge, 1972)
    especially chapters 6 and 8.
14  Ibid., 314, 391, 393, 399.
15  The section of the 'charge' of 1538 (B.M. Add. MS
    48047 fos 63v-64) quoted on p. 46 of 'Policy and
    Police' is in fact based on these.

CHAPTER 1  THE SCOPE OF TREASON:  1

 1  On this point and medieval definition of treason as a
    whole see my 'The Law of Treason in England in the
    Later Middle Ages' (Cambridge, 1970), especially
    chapters 4 and 5.
 2  2 Hen. V c. 6.
 3  4 Hen. V c. 6;  2 Hen. VI c. 21.
 4  8 Hen. VI c. 6;  20 Hen. VI c. 2 'Rotuli Parliamentor-
    um' (ed.) J. Strachey et al. (London, 1767), v, 375.
 5  'Rot. Parl.', iv, 497a, v, 14b, 15, 17, 18a.
 6  J. Willis-Bund, 'A Selection of Cases from the State
    Trials' (Cambridge, 1879-82), i, 305n.
 7  J.R. Tanner, 'Tudor Constitutional Documents, 1485-
    1603' (Cambridge, 1922), 375-6.
 8  K.W.M. Pickthorn, 'Early Tudor Government, Henry
    VIII' (Cambridge, 1934), 158.
 9  'Essays in History and Political Theory in honor of
    Charles Howard McIlwain' (Cambridge, Mass., 1936),
    263, 268;  A.F. Pollard, 'The History of England from
    the Accession of Edward VI to the death of Elizabeth'
    (London, 1910), 129.
10  G.R. Elton, 'The Tudor Constitution, Documents and
    Commentary' (Cambridge, 1960), 59.
11  J.F. Stephen, 'A History of the Criminal Law of Eng-
    land' (London, 1883), ii, 256, 262-3;  J. Reeves, 'A
    History of the English Law' (ed.) W.F. Finlason
    (London, 1889), iii, 325.
12  PRO, SP1/93 fo. 52 ('Calendar of Letters and Papers,
    Foreign and Domestic Henry VIII' (eds) J.S. Brewer,
    J. Gairdner, R.H. Brodie (1862-1932) viii, no. 856).
    (Hereafter 'Letters and Papers'.)
13  Laws 'quiestoient si sanguinaires que en plusieurs
    parolles le plus souvent dictes par inadvertance et
    en bonne intention il avoid constitue crime de leze
    mageste':  'Correspondance Politique' (ed.) J.B.L.
    Kaulek (Paris, 1885), no. 231.
14  See G.R. Elton, 'Policy and Police' (Cambridge, 1972).
15  Simonds D'Ewes, 'A Compleat Journal of the Votes,
    Speeches and Debates both of the House of Lords and
    House of Commons throughout the whole reign of Queen
    Elizabeth' (London, 1708), 163, 340-1.

16  T. Starkey, 'A Dialogue between Reginald Pole and
    Thomas Lupset' (ed.), K.M. Burton (London, 1948),
    115, 177.
17  PRO, SP 1/93 fos 52-7 ('Letters and Papers',viii,856).
18  'State Trials' (ed.), W. Cobbett and T.B. Howell
    (London, 1809), i, 897.
19  PRO, SP 1/112 fo. 138 ('Letters and Papers',xi,1244).
20  By Sir John Mason:  'Calendar of State Papers,
    Foreign, Mary, 1553-8', 119;  F. Rose-Troup, 'The
    Western Rebellion of 1549' (London, 1913), 434.
21  3 Hen. VII c. 14;  'Rot. Parl.', vi, 402-3.
22  'The Anglica Historia of Polydore Vergil, 1485-1537'
    (ed.), D. Hay (Camden Society, lxxiv, 1950), 74.
23  W.A.J. Archbold, Sir William Stanley and Perkin War-
    beck, 'English Historical Review', xiv (1899), 530-4.
24  'Calendar of Patent Rolls, 1494-1509', 29;  R.L.
    Storey, 'The Reign of Henry VII' (London, 1968), 83.
25  'Rot. Parl.', vi, 503b.
26  A.F. Pollard, Tudor Gleanings. The De Facto act of
    Henry VII, 'Bulletin of the Institute of Historical
    Research', vii (1930), 12.   Perhaps the statute was
    interpreted also as meaning that those who did *not*
    attend the king would be guilty of treason.
        It is possible that Henry VII seized the estates of
    those who failed to appear at his side at Blackheath
    field in 1497 or to help in subduing  the rebels:
    'Cal. Pat. Rolls, 1494, 1509', 113.
27  'Statutes of the Realm'  (Record Commission, 1810-
    28) i, 367.
28  See, for example, PRO, KB 27/800 Rex m. 1 where the
    offence was an insurrection in London of July 1460.
29  'Year Books', 9 Edw. IV Pasch. pl. 2;  20 Edw. IV
    Trin. pl. 3.   For an interesting· interpretation of
    the de facto act to the effect that 'prince ... for
    the time being' meant simply the person who is king
    at any given time, see A.M. Honoré, Allegiance and
    the Usurper, 'Cambridge Law Journal', 25 (1967), 217.
    Certainly the phrases 'treasurer for the time being'
    and 'chancellor for the time being' are to be found in
    fourteenth- and fifteenth-century records.
30  Bellamy, 'Law of Treason', 64.
31  21 Ric. II cc. 3, 4.
32  'Year Books', 1 Hen. VII Mich. pl. 5.
33  R. Holinshed, 'Chronicles of England, Scotland and
    Ireland' (London, 1808), iii, 622.   The reference
    was to 2 Hen. V c. 6.
34  PRO, KB 27/476 Rex mm. 31, 31d and supplementary:
    'Rot. Parl.', iii, 75b.
35  See PRO, KB 27/507 Rex mm. 40-3 (printed in part by
    R. Bird in 'The Turbulent London of Richard II'
    (London, 1949, 137) and 'Stat. Realm.', ii, 89.

36   See A. Réville, 'Le Soulèvement des travailleurs
     d'Angleterre en 1381' (Paris, 1898), 177-8, 186;   and
     W.E. Flaherty, The Great Rebellion in Kent of 1381
     illustrated from the Public Records, 'Archaeologia
     Cantiana', iii (1860), 87, 89, 93.
37   R. Grafton, 'Chronicle at Large' (London, 1568),
     1023.   John Lincoln, a broker, was the real instiga-
     tor of the riots.   He persuaded Dr Beale, a canon of
     St Mary's Hospital, to preach a sermon against stran-
     gers on Easter Tuesday 1517.
38   J. Stow, 'Annales or a Generall Chronicle of England'
     (ed.), E. Howes (London, 1631), 524-5.
39   BM, Cleopatra MS F. vi, fo. 325;   BM Cottonian MS
     App. xlv-iii, fo. 5 ('Letters and Papers', iv, nos
     1323, 1324);   PRO, SP 1/34 fo. 209 ('Letters and
     Papers', iv, no. 1343).
40   PRO, KB 8/4 mm. 51, 55.
41   'The Anglica Historia of Polydore Vergil, 1485-1537',
     p. 74;   F. Bacon, 'History of the Reign of Henry VII'
     (ed.), J.R. Lumby (Cambridge, 1876), 123.
42   The act was 4 Hen. VII c. 18.   The declaration about
     sanctuaries is in 'Year Books' 1 Hen. VII Pasch. pl.
     15 and Trin. pl. 1.   For trials under the law of
     arms, see L.W. Vernon Harcourt, 'His Grace the Ste-
     ward and Trial of Peers' (London, 1907), 414-15, and
     'Cal. Patent Rolls, 1494-1509', 506.
43   As in the cases of Thomas Burdet and Dr John Stacey
     in May 1477;   PRO, KB 8/1 m. 9.
44   See 'The Great Chronicle of London' (ed.), A.H.
     Thomas and I.D. Thornley (London, 1938), 205-7.
     Markham's behaviour was still remembered in 1571;   a
     draft of the general treason act of 1571 (13 Eliz.
     c. 1) has, amongst many marginal notes, the comment
     'Gode sende many Markhams':   PRO, SP 12/185/38.
45   Henry VII seems to have tried to influence his judges
     in 1486 over the matter of sanctuary.   See C.H.
     Williams, The Rebellion of Humphrey Stafford in 1486,
     'English Historical Review', xliii (1928), 187.
46   BM Cleopatra MS E. iv, fo. 85 ('Letters and Papers',
     vii, no. 238);   'Letters and Papers', vi, no. 1445.
47   22 Hen. VIII c. 9.
48   'Letters and Papers', v, no. 120;   S.E. Lehmberg,
     'The Reformation Parliament', 1529-1536' (Cambridge,
     1970), 125.
49   'Rot. Parl.', v, 265a,
50   Ibid., iv, 260b.
51   PRO, SP 1/65 fos 87v-89.   On the relationship be-
     tween the various drafts see G.R. Elton, The Law of
     Treason in the Early Reformation, 'Historical Jour-
     nal', xi, 2 (1968), 213-19 which now supersedes the
     pioneer investigation of Isobel Thornley, The Treason

Legislation of Henry VIII, 1531-4, 'Transactions of the Royal Historical Society', 3rd series, XI (1917), 87-123.

52   'Letters and Papers', iv (iii), no. 6709/7.   James ap Griffyth may have been involved in the feud between Lord Ferrers and his own nephew Rhys ap Griffyths (see 'Y Cymmrodor', xvi (1909), 29-30) although a description of his being at the time of his apprehension 'a traitour and outlawe' ('Acts of the Privy Council' (ed.), J.R. Dasent (1890-1907), ii, 224) suggests a more serious offence.   There is a possibility that the bill was prompted not by misdeeds in Wales but others in the south-west.   One candidate is William Kendall of Cornwall ('Archaeologia', xxiii, 24-5). Another is the Marquis of Exeter, reported to be assembling men in Cornwall in 1531 ('Letters and Papers', xiii (ii) no. 804).

53   'Letters and Papers',iv (iii),no. 6659; PRO, SP 1/58 fos 49-51 ('Letters and Papers',iv(iii), no. 6619).

54   PRO, SP 2/Q fos 103-9.   It is quite possible that this bill was drafted at about the time of the trial at Michaelmas term 1531 in king's bench of Rhys ap Griffyths and his associates and with their offences in mind.   Rhys had plotted in August and September 1531 to mortgage his lands, fly to Scotland and persuade King James to invade England.   A confederate whose misdeeds figure in the indictment but who does not seem to have been arraigned was the James ap Griffyth ap Howell noted above:   PRO, KB 9/517/3. The government may have been made doubly nervous by talk of illegal assembly in Cornwall in summer 1531.

55   'Rot. Parl.', iii, 606b.

56   'Materials for a History of the Reign of Henry VII' (ed.), W. Campbell (Rolls Series, 1873-7), i, 512-13.

57   Bellamy, 'Law of Treason', 27.

58   The killing of Adam Walton, a royal messenger, in 1348 was held petty treason only, 'Year Books, Liver des Assises', 22 Edw. III, pl. 49.

59   Bellamy, 'Law of Treason', 191-5.

60   For example 14 & 15 Hen. VIII c. 21.

61   25 Hen. VIII c. 12; see 'Stat. Realm', iii, 446-51.

62   'Letters and Papers', viii, no. 48.

63   PRO, KB 9.72/14.

64   PRO, KB 8/1 m. 9.   It should perhaps be noted at this point that the Tudors made no effort to bring magic, sorcery, or witchcraft within the scope of the treason laws.

65   25 Hen. VIII c. 22.

66   BM Titus MS B.i,fo.417 ('Letters and Papers',vii,51).

67   'Rot. Parl.', vi, 455.   On the history of misprision see Bellamy, 'Law of Treason', 216-24.

68  PRO, SP 1/82 fos 266-7 ('Letters and Papers', vii, no. 298).
69  See Elton, Treason in the Early Reformation, 'Historical Journal', xi, 2 (1968), 223-6.
70  On the scope of high treason in France at this time see C.L. Von Bar et al., 'A History of Continental Criminal Law' (London, 1916), 281-5.
71  Bellamy, 'Law of Treason', pp. 89-90, 122n.
72  'Year Books', 19 Hen. VI Mich. pl. 103.
73  Ibid., 13 Hen. VIII Easter pl. 1.
74  'Rot. Parl.', v, 375.
75  Thus the indictment against Francis Philipps and his confederates in 1524 ran '... mortem et destructionem dicti domini Regis ... felonice et proditorie imaginati et compassi fuerunt ... et ad eandem intencionem perimplendum adtunc et ibidem felonice et proditorie imaginati et compassi fuerunt guerram versus ipsum dominum Regem in hoc regno suo': PRO, KB 9/492/216.   See also PRO, KB 8/1 m. 9, KB 8/2 m. 4, and KB 8/5 m. 28.
76  PRO, KB 27/564 Rex m. 12.   The offender was John Sperhauk.   He had repeated the words of a tailor's wife that the earl of March was the rightful king, not Henry IV.
77  Elton, Treason in the Early Reformation, 'Historical Journal', xi, 2 (1968), 227-8.
78  However,the manner in which Bishop Fisher was willing, on the advice of his brother Robert (MP for Rochester), to base his court strategy on the word suggests he expected to touch on a tender point and gain support at large: PRO, SP 1/93 fo. 52 ('Letters and Papers', vii, no. 856);   BM Cleopatra MS E. vi, fo. 169 ('Letters and Papers', viii, no. 858); 'State Papers, Henry VIII' (Record Commission, 1830), I (ii), 431-2.
79  'Stat. Realm', iii, 471-4.
80  PRO, KB 8/5 m. 28.   Also appearing in indictments in the earlier part of Henry VIII's reign were phrases like 'by precogitated malice and diabolical instigation': PRO, KB 9/492/216.
81  For example J. Duncan M. Derrett, The Trial of Sir Thomas More, 'English Historical Review', lxxix (1964), 456.
82  The antecedent was the draft of a new treason act, probably dating from late 1530, which included as an offence the act of withdrawing contemptuously, after summons to appear before the king, to any of his castles and maintaining resistance there: PRO, SP 1/65 fos 87v-89.
83  The indictment of Griffyths is to be found in PRO, KB 9/517/3.   See above, note 54.

84   PRO, KB 8/6 m. 10.

85   'Letters and Papers', vi, no. 1528.

86   The protection section of this clause (iv) of the act
     covered the rights of everyone save actual traitors
     and their heirs and successors.   As Elton has noted
     (Treason in the Early Reformation, 'Historical Jour-
     nal', xi, 2 (1968), 234) the inclusion of the last
     word, which seems to have been novel, allowed the
     king to acquire by forfeiture the property of a mon-
     astery whose abbot had been convicted of high trea-
     son.

87   In August 1535 Cromwell instructed Sir John Wallop to
     tell the French king that the laws on treason had
     been devised 'by grete and mature advise' and were by
     no means novel being 'of grete antiquyti and many
     yeres passed ... made and executed within this
     realme':   PRO, SP 1/95 fo. 159 ('Letters and Papers',
     ix, no. 157).   The context was the conviction of
     More and Fisher, and the laws were presumably the act
     of supremacy and its penal statute the act of trea-
     son (26 Hen. VIII c. 13).

88   PRO, KB 8/7/3 m. 7.

89   28 Hen. VIII c. 10.

90   28 Hen. VIII c. 24.

91   This act did not supersede the second act of succes-
     sion.

92   33 Hen. VIII c. 23.

93   These provisions were the general part of an attain-
     der act convicting Katherine Howard of treason.   See
     below p. 41.

94   PRO, KB 8/9 mm. 18, 21.

95   J.G. Bellamy, Justice under the Yorkist Kings, 'Amer-
     ican Journal of Legal History', 9, 2 (1965), 150;
     G.R. Elton, Henry VIII's Act of Proclamations, 'Eng-
     lish Historical Review', lxxv (1960), 209.

96   Thus in 1535 Robert Feron and John Hale were accused
     under the first succession act and quite possibly the
     treason act of 1533-4 as well (PRO, KB 8/7/1 m. 10).
     Fisher and More were indicted under that part of the
     Henrician treason act which enforced the act of sup-
     remacy (PRO, KB 8/7/2 m. 9 and KB 8/7/3 m. 7) as were
     the priors of three Carthusian houses (PRO, KB 8/7/1
     m. 11) and Lords Darcy and Hussey, despite in the
     last case some talk of conspiring or abetting the
     levying of war (PRO, KB 8/10/2 mm. 12, 13, 17).   The
     crimes of Sir Edward Neville, Sir Geoffrey Pole,
     Henry, Lord Montacute, and the marquis of Exeter,
     seem to have been dealt with under the 1352 treason
     act as well as under the one of 1534 (PRO, KB 8/11/1
     mm. 13, 19, 21;   KB 8/11/2 mm. 18, 21, 22, 26, 27).

97   PRO, KB 8/14 mm. 9, 11, 12.
98   PRO, KB 8/9 mm. 18, 21; E.W. Ives, Faction at the
     Court of Henry VIII: The Fall of Anne Boleyn, 'His-
     tory', 57 (1972), 187-8 quoting BM Hargrave MS f.
     187v.
99   PRO, KB 8/13/1 mm. 20, 21.
100  The only instance of procedure similar to this had
     been in 1423 when the victim had been Sir John Mor-
     timer who contested the Lancastrian title to the
     throne.  See 'Year Books of Henry VI, 1 Henry VI,
     1422' (ed.), C.H. Williams (Selden Society, 1933),
     xxiv-xxvii.
101  'Journal of the House of Lords' (London, 1846), i,
     171, 174-5.
102  G. Burnet, 'The History of the Reformation of the
     Church of England' (Oxford, 1865), iv, 415-23.   See
     also G.R. Elton, Thomas Cromwell's Decline and Fall,
     'Cambridge Historical Journal', x (1951), 177-83.
103  PRO, KB 27/564 Rex m. 12 and 'Eulogium Historiarum'
     (ed.), F.S. Haydon (R.S., 1863), iii, 390.   The
     friar was accused of imagining the king's death as
     was Stanley.
104  It appears the bill of attainder was not accepted by
     the commons from the lords without alterations.
     They may have virtually rewritten it 'Journal of the
     Lords', i, 149.
105  C. Wriothesley, 'A Chronicle of England' (ed.), W.D.
     Hamilton (C.S., New Series, xi, 1875), i, 120;
     Stow, 'Annales', 580b.
106  Burnet, 'History of the Reformation', iv, 415-23.
107  PRO, SP 1/83 fo. 12 ('Letters and Papers', vii, no.
     377).
108  See G.R. Elton, 'The Tudor Constitution' (Cambridge,
     1962), 59n.   The discovery was by Professor J.R.
     Lander.
109  Wriothesley, 'Chronicle of England', i, 60.
110  'English Reports', Brooks New Cases, 183-4.
111  'Year Books', 2 Henry IV, Trin. pl. 25.
112  'Letters and Papers', v, no. 105;  'Correspondance
     politique', 215.
113  G.R. Elton, 'Reform and Renewal' (Cambridge, 1973),
     p. 148;  Lehmberg, 'Reformation Parliament', 125;
     Elton, 'Policy and Police', 267.
114  'Letters and Papers', vi, no. 1460.
115  BM Titus B. i, fo. 440 ('Letters and Papers', xii
     (i), no. 1106).   Another, dated June 1535, runs
     'Item, to advise the kyng of the orderyng of Master
     Fisher and to showe hym of the Indenture whiche I
     have delyveryd to the Solicitour': BM Titus MS B. i,
     fo. 474 ('Letters and Papers', viii, no. 892).

116  Elton, Treason in the Early Reformation, 'Historical Journal', xi, 2 (1968), 230, 232.
117  Elton, 'Policy and Police', 387.
118  Ibid., 82.
119  'Stat. Realm', ii, 59
120  Ibid., iv (i), 240, 366-7.
121  See for example PRO Assizes 35/21/7, 22/10, 28/1, 32/2, 34/2, 36/2.

CHAPTER 2  THE SCOPE OF TREASON:  2

1  'Statutes of the Realm' (Record Commission, 1810-28), iv, 18-19.
2  'Henrici de Bracton de Legibus et Consuetudinibus Angliae' (ed.), G.E. Woodbine (New Haven, 1915-42), ii, 335.
3  See G.R. Elton, The Good Duke, 'Historical Journal', xii, 4 (1969), 704-5;  M.L. Bush, The Lisle-Seymour Land Disputes, ibid., ix, 3 (1966), 274;  M.L. Bush, 'The Government Policy of Protector Somerset' (London, 1975), 145.
4  For example the Cornish rebels in 1548 (PRO, KB 8/15 mm. 1, 2, 13, 14), Robert Ket in 1549 (PRO, KB 8/17 mm. 5, 6, 7, 8), and Thomas Bonham, Thomas Watts and William Turner in 1549 (PRO, KB 8/17(2) mm. 2, 3). Robert Bell and John Patchyn seem to have been tried under both the act of 1352 and that of 1547 (PRO, KB 8/17(1) mm. 2, 3).  So were Thomas Clokke, Robert Smythe and James Wilkyns, who were among those who assembled at Mousehold Heath (Norfolk Records Office, Norfolk Quarter Sessions, Indictments, 3 Edw. VI, nos 132, 133).
5  PRO, KB 8/19 mm. 12, 23, 26, 27.  Somerset's indictment was also based on the act 3 & 4 Edw. VI c. 5 whereby it was treason to assemble men intending to murder or imprison a privy councillor, or if they numbered more than forty to stay together for more than two hours while intending to commit a traitorous act.  Somehow the court, which was that of the lord high steward, managed to acquit Somerset of treason. It seems to have preferred to find him guilty of felony under clause three of the act, which referred to bringing men together for a riot by a malicious artifice.  The report of the trial also says that the peers of the jury concluded that Somerset simply conspired to imprison the duke of Northumberland. This ought to have been treason but Northumberland said no practice against himself should be reputed

treason.    Then, after 'great difference of opinion
they all acquitted him of treason' and judgment was
given he should be hanged, 'State Trials' (ed.), W.
Ccbbett and T.B. Howell (London, 1809), i, 521.

6   2 & 3 Edw. VI c. 18.    In the house of lords the
judges declared the offences to be manifest treason:
when the bill reached the lower house the lawyers
there declared similarly.    For the political background to the chargessee W.K. Jordan, 'Edward VI:
The Young King' (London, 1968), 372-7.

7   'Journals of the House of Commons (London, 1803), i,
20.    William Cook was in fact a civilian.    Gosnold
and Caryll had been among the 'students of law' who
complained in 1547 about the lord chancellor delegat-
ing his responsibilities to four civilians.    With
Cook and Stanford they also served from February 1552
on the commission to reform the canon law:   see
Jordan, 'Edward VI: The Young King', 71n and 'The
Chronicle and Political Papers of Edward VI' (ed.),
W.K. Jordan (London, 1966), 110-11.

8   A.F. Pollard, 'History of England from the Accession
of Edward VI to the death of Elizabeth' (London,
1910), 66.

9   P.L. Hughes and J.F. Larkin, 'Tudor Royal Proclamations' (New Haven, 1964-9), i, no. 336;   G.R. Elton,
Government by Edict, 'Historical Journal', viii, 2
(1965), 271;   'State Trials', i, 527-8.

10   The trials before the lord high steward are in PRO,
KB 8/21 mm. 19, 20, 23, 24:   those before commissioners of oyer and terminer in PRO, KB 8/22 mm. 24, 25.

11   PRO, KB 8/23 mm. 11, 12.

12   PRO, KB 8/23 m. 11.

13   PRO, KB 8/25 mm. 5, 6.    Robert Dudley was convicted
but pardoned.    Although he was put on trial only in
January 1554, Robert Dudley had been under arrest
from the previous July.    The first Marian treason
act, although decreeing a return to the statute of
1352 and thereby removing 'compassing to deprive the
king of his crown and royal dignity' from the list of
treasons, excepted the cases of those arrested before
30 September 1553 ('Stat. Realm', iv, 198).

14   At his trial Sir Thomas Palmer pleaded not guilty,
saying he had never borne arms against the queen.
The judges asked 'Can ye denye but that ye were
there?'    'No' said Sir Thomas.    'Then can it not be
that ye are culpable', said the judges ('The Chronicle of Queen Jane and of two years of Queen Mary'
(ed.), J.G. Nichols (C.S., xlviii, 1850), 18).

15   PRO, KB 8/29 m. 13.

16   'Compassing to levy war' appeared in the indictments
     of Francis Philipps in 1524 (PRO, KB 9/492/2/6) and
     of Lord Darcy and his allies in May 1537 (PRO, KB
     8/10/2 m. 17).   On the first occasion it was as an
     example of compassing the king's death, and on the
     second of compassing to deprive the king of his royal
     dignity, which was treason under the act of 1534 (26
     Hen. VIII c. 13).   In 1554 it was being held as
     treason in its own right.
17   PRO, KB 8/26 mm. 32, 33.
18   'State Trials', i, 887.   The account of the trial
     was probably compiled by Throckmorton himself at the
     beginning of Elizabeth's reign, although it must have
     been based on notes made at the time.
19   Ibid., i, 889.
20   See J. Bellamy, 'Law of Treason' (Cambridge, 1970),
     101.
21   'State Trials', i, 890-1.
22   'English Reports', Brooks New Cases, 183-4, Dalison,
     14.
23   'State Trials', i, 897.   There exists the possibil-
     ity that Throckmorton illicitly received legal advice
     in some way.   'The Legend of Sir Nicholas Throckmor-
     ton' refers to 'the mann whoe lent me lawe of late.
     To save my life and putt himself in danger'.   'The
     Legend of Sir Nicholas Throckmorton' (ed.), J.G.
     Nichols (Roxburgh Club, 1874), 33.
24   1 & 2 Ph. & M. c. 10.
25   As in the second general treason act of Edward VI,
     concealment of treason was to be misprision of trea-
     son: 'Stat. Realm', iv, 257.
26   I have omitted the act 1 & 2 Ph. & M. c. 3, which
     provided punishment for writings that maliciously
     slandered the king and queen or encouraged rebellion
     yet were not quite within the 1352 act.
27   'English Reports', 2 Dyer 107b.   A similar overrid-
     ing of a Marian act, in this case 1 & 2 Ph. & M. c.
     10 is to be found in a case in king's bench in Trin-
     ity term 1556, where the judges and king's serjeants
     gave as their opinion that treason committed outside
     the realm was triable under 35 Hen. VIII c. 2 (2 Dyer
     132a).   The issue, however, was basically procedu-
     ral.
28   PRO, KB 8/33 m. 6;   KB 8/34 mm. 14, 15;   KB 8/35 mm.
     7, 8.   There was one doubtful case at this time but
     not enough is known to arrive at a firm conclusion.
     William Featherstone, who in 1555 claimed to be Ed-
     ward VI and had been whipped for it, was the next
     year executed for treason for saying he had seen

Edward alive and had spoken to him (R. Holinshed,
'Chronicles of England, Scotland and Ireland' (London, 1808), iv, 75.

29  1 & 2 Ph. & M. c. 11.

30  The need for sanctions against forgers of Mary's sign
manual was brought into prominence by such a crime on
the part of William Hackney, who in December 1553 had
forged a bill granting him an annuity of 40 marks for
life and had signed it 'Marye the Quene'.   He was
found guilty of high treason nevertheless (PRO, KB
8/24 mm. 7, 8).

31  PRO, KB 8/37 mm. 7, 8.

32  'English Reports', 2 Dyer 144b;   Brooks New Cases,
183-4.

33  J.E. Neale, The Elizabethan Acts of Supremacy and
Uniformity, 'English Historical Review', lxv (1950),
315.

34  PRO, KB 8/38 m. 7.

35  PRO, KB 8/40 m. 11.

36  13 Eliz. c. 1.

37  Dr Storey's offences and legal position were argued
by the judges in the king's bench at Hilary term
1571.   It was decided that a subject conspiring beyond the seas the invasion of England, even if the
design was not executed, was guilty of treason for
compassing the prince's death.   The judges also decided that sending or procuring the sending of money
to rebels abroad against whom there was a proclamation of enmity was high treason;   so was helping to
distribute papal money to rebels abroad ('English
Reports', 3 Dyer 298b).

38  There had been discussion among the judges in the
king's bench at Hilary term 1570 as to whether those
who committed treason under 26 Hen. VIII c. 13 and
5 & 6 Edw. VI c. 11 and then fled to Scotland could
be outlawed for it.   The decision, remarkably
enough, was that they could.   This is further proof
of certain aspects of repealed treason acts being
held by the judges as still operative ('English Reports', 3 Dyer 287b).

39  'English Reports', 3 Dyer 288b, 289a.   The case concerned the prerogatives of the bishop of Durham.

40  M. Hale, 'Historia Placitorum Coronae:  the History
of the Pleas of the Crown' (ed.), Sollom Emlyn (London, 1736), i, 257.

41  13 Eliz. c. 16.   Of the earls and their followers
some had been arraigned and convicted but others had
only been outlawed or stood merely indicted.   It is
worthy of note that, despite the attainder act, the

queen soon felt she had failed to secure the forfeiture of all the rebels' possessions and thus there
was an act in the parliamentary session of 1576 (18
Eliz. c. 4), which tried to destroy the effect of
secret conveyances made before the rebellion by in-
sisting that those claiming land under conveyances
made within the last eighteen months should produce
the relevant deed for enrolment in the exchequer and
offer evidence of its bona fide nature.

42  J.E. Neale, 'Elizabeth I and her Parliaments, 1559-
1581' (London, 1953), 225-33.

43  D'Ewes, 'Journal of the Lords and Commons', 162-5;
Hoker's Journal of the House of Commons in 1571
(ed.), J.B. Davidson, 'Reports and Transactions of
the Devonshire Association', xi (1879), 490.

44  There is little evidence of misgivings in the country
at large.  However, a contemporary opinion on the
statute by Alexander Fissher reflected concern over
traitorous prophecies which were not the subject of
an indictment until considerable time had elapsed
(PRO, SP 12/185/38).  No doubt he felt that the rule
allowing six months between misdeed and indictment
was too generous.

45  PRO, KB 8/42 m. 11.

46  'State Trials', i, 971.

47  PRO, KB 8/43 m. 8.

48  There was included an interesting and novel proviso
that conviction for treason under this act was not to
result in the corruption of blood, the disinheriting
of any heir, or the forfeiture of dower ('Stat.
Realm', iv, 407).

49  'Narratives of the Reformation' (ed.), J.G. Nichols
(C.S., lxxvii, 1859), 180-1;  PRO, SP 15/21/111.

50  BM Cotton MS Caligula, B VIII fos 240-6;  Neale,
'Elizabeth I and her Parliaments, 1559-1581', 282-3.

51  W. Camden, 'Annals or the History of the most renow-
ned and victorious princess Elizabeth, late queen of
England' (London, 1635), 197.  In the 1560s some
penal statutes had also lain dormant.

52  J. Morris, 'The Troubles of Our Catholic Forefathers'
(London, 1872), i, 71-4.  It is possible although
unlikely that Thomas Woodhouse, who had been arrested
in 1561 but arraigned only in April 1573, was indicted under the act 13 Eliz. c. 2.  The indictment has
not yet been found ('Lives of the English Martyrs'
(ed.), B. Camm (London, 1905), First Series, ii,
197).

53  Sherwood's indictment is in PRO, KB 27/1264 Rex m. 3.
His and Nelson's statements about the queen being a

heretic or schismatic would not have been made in
speech at large but in answer to questions put to
them when in custody ('Lives of the English Martyrs',
First Series, ii, 226-7, 238, 240, 246).

54  The indictment seems to have been drawn up in court
immediately prior to the arraignment and following
certain questions of a conditional nature put to the
suspect by the judge, who in this case was Fleetwood
recorder of London ('Lives of the English Martyrs',
First Series, ii, 256, 262-3); J. Bridgewater 'Concertatio Ecclesiae Catholicae in Anglia' (Treves,
1588), 78-9). The same device had been used with
Nelson and Sherwood.

55  PRO, KB 27/1279 Rex mm. 2, 2d, 3, 3d.

56  PRO, KB 27/1292 Rex m. 4.

57  Apart from Hanse there seems to have been only one
priest who was accused of reconciling men with Rome
and seducing them from their allegiance. This was
William Hart, who was also indicted of bringing to
the realm writings from the see of Rome (Bridgewater,
'Concertatio', 108-9).

58  English Reports, Savile 3-4. How it should deal,
under the 1581 act, with laity suspected of receiving
Jesuits and seminarists who refused to answer on
oath at their examination also caused much governmental concern. The conference of judges soon after
the 1581 act could not decide whether they should be
punished in star chamber or by indictment in the
king's bench. The acts of 1571 were almost as unsatisfactory as that of 1581 in this respect. The
Jesuits and seminarists had concocted a method of
answering which made indication of guilt difficult to
obtain. They offered obedience to the queen generally but would not say if they would withdraw it if
the pope so commanded (Holinshed, 'Chronicles', iv,
513). Examiners often resorted to one final question: 'Quas igitur partes sequi velles si Pontifex
aut alius quispiam eius authoritate fretus bellum
Reginae inferret?' (Bridgewater, 'Concertatio',
163b).

59  On the proclamation of 1 April 1582 see F.A. Youngs
Jr, Definitions of Treason in an Elizabethan Proclamation, 'Historical Journal', xiv, 4 (1971), 682-9,
and Hughes and Larkin, 'Tudor Royal Proclamations',
ii, no. 660.

60  'Select Cases in the Exchequer Chamber II' (ed.),
M. Hemmant (Seldon Soc., 64, 1948), 134-5; PRO, KB
8/49 mm. 13, 14; KB 8/48 m. 20; Hughes and Larkin,
'Tudor Royal Proclamations', ii, no. 683. It is

worth noting that in 1534 it was necessary to pass a
statute which made a traitor of anyone who had, or
should in future, comfort, abet or adhere to Thomas
Fitzgerald, earl of Kildare, who had levied war
against the king (26 Hen. VIII c. 25).

61  For example Ralph Crockett, Edward James, Francis
Edwardes and John Oven were convicted under the act
at a sessions of oyer and terminer at Chichester, 30
September 1588 ('Lives of the English Martyrs' (ed.),
E.H. Burton and J.H. Pollen (London, 1914), Second
Series, i, 480-1).   John Pibush was convicted under
it in July 1585, William Freeman in August 1595 and
John Jones in July 1598 ('Unpublished Documents relating to the English Martyrs, 1584-1603' (ed.),
J.H. Pollen (Catholic Record Society, v, 1908), 339,
353, 368).   By the end of the reign it seems the
government was only enforcing the act periodically
(see Hughes and Larkin, 'Tudor Royal Proclamations',
iii, no. 254).   It is of some interest that the
crown seems to have experienced difficulties in the
framing of indictments under this act and that ten
years later it sought and gained from the judges a
confirmation that an indictment did not need inter
alia to state where the accused had been made a
Jesuit or priest so long as it mentioned he was born
within the realm and was in fact a Jesuit or priest
by the 'pretended' authority of the see of Rome
(English Reports, Popham 93).

62  Hughes and Larkin, 'Tudor Royal Proclamations', iii,
nos 93, 94;  PRO, SP 12/217/1.   The latter is an
account of the trial of Crockett, James, Edwardes and
Oven where Bowyer was one of the justices.   The argument that offences under a later treason act were
also justiciable under the act of 1352 had first been
propounded at the trial of Norfolk in 1572 (see
above, p. 65).

63  PRO, SP 12/217/1.

64  The indictments were often framed in such a way that
it was impossible to be sure if they were based on
one or a number of sixteenth-century acts, or on the
statute of 1352 as well.   Sometimes, when the indictment seemed to have been drawn only under a sixteenth-century act, the prosectuion would argue, and
the judges would support their claim, that an offence
like seeking to deprive the queen of her title meant
seeking her death and was thus within the act of
1352.

65  PRO, KB 8/45 mm. 9, 10;  KB 8/46 mm. 3, 4;  KB 8/47
mm. 10, 11;  KB 8/50 mm. 6, 7;  KB 8/54 mm. 3, 4;
KB 8/55 mm. 5, 6.

66  PRO, KB 8/48 mm. 16, 17, 20;  KB 8/49 mm. 13, 14;
    KB 8/51 mm. 8, 9;  KB 8/52 mm. 15, 16, 17, 18, 19;
    KB 8/56 mm. 14, 15, 18, 19.
67  'State Trials', i, 1148.
68  Holinshed, 'Chronicles', iv, 543;  'State Trials',
    i, 1253.
69  J. Stow, 'Annales or a Generall Chronicle of England'
    (ed.), E. Howes (London, 1631), 769a, 770a; 'English
    Reports' 2 Anderson, 4-5.
70  PRO, SP 12/253/48.
71  PRO, KB 8/53 mm. 12, 13, 14, 15.
72  PRO, SP 12/261/10 ('Cal. State Papers, Domestic,
    1595-7', 316).
73  E. Coke, 'The Third Part of the Institutes of the
    Laws of England' (London, 1797), 10.   Coke referred
    to the insurgents as going from town to town general-
    ly to cast down enclosures.
       All the judges and barons of the exchequer met at
    Serjeants' Inn on 15 April 1597 to consider the
    matter.   One opinion vented was that rebellion had
    always been treason at common law, based apparently
    on the argument that 'rebellion is all the war a sub-
    ject can make against the king'.   Eventually they
    endeavoured to make a clear distinction between fel-
    onious assemblies, as in the act 1 M. st. 2 c. 12,
    and traitorous rebellion.   They decided the univer-
    sality of the designs of the participants, for
    example an intent to overthrow all enclosures or
    churches rather than just one or two, made for trea-
    son ('English Reports', Popham 122-3).
74  'English Reports', 2 Anderson 4-5.
75  'State Trials', i, 1421.
76  PRO, KB 8/56 mm. 18, 19.
77  'State Trials', i, 1421.   In regard to 'armed peti-
    tions' see also PRO, SP 1/117 fo. 18 ('Calendar of
    Letters and Papers, Foreign and Domestic, Henry VIII'
    (ed.), J.S. Brewer, J. Gairdner, R.H. Brodie (1862-
    1932), xii, no. 666).
78  'State Trials', i, 1420-1.
79  Ibid., i, 1438.
80  Ibid., i, 1419.   For the history of term 'lese-
    majesty' see Bellamy, 'Law of Treason', 7 et passim.
    It had appeared momentarily in the act attainting
    Thomas Cromwell and in a pardon of 1547.
       Yelverton was copying, albeit unknowingly and in
    regard to different offences, the attempts of the
    lawyers of Edward III who tried unsuccessfully to
    smuggle 'accroaching the royal power' into the common
    law.

81  Something like it was to be found in Edward VI's
    reign and 'subverting the realm' was a common phrase
    in medieval treason indictments.   Also common from
    about 1570 was the phrase 'disturbing the tranquil-
    lity of the realm' (see PRO, SP 12/253/48 and KB 8/53
    mm. 12, 13, 14, 15).

82  Coke at one point said that 'it was a great mercy of
    the queen that *in flagrante crimine* he [Essex] was
    not according to the martial law, presently put to
    the sword' ('State Trials', i, 1435).

83  There seems at times in the later sixteenth century
    to have been a reluctance to check legal precedents,
    and one cannot escape the suspicion that other min-
    isters as well as Attorney-General Coke may have
    taken it as a statement of policy that to search for
    them might be construed at large as showing doubt in
    the correctness of the procedure used, MSS Hatfield
    33/3 ('Calendar of the Manuscripts of the Marquis of
    Salisbury' (Historical Manuscripts Commission,
    1883- ), v, 256).

84  The failure of the nobility to protest forcibly
    against the general 'attack on their power' by Henry
    VIII has been noticed in C.S.L. Davies, A New Life
    of Henry VIII, 'History', liv (1969), 46.


CHAPTER 3  APPREHENSION, EXAMINATION AND INDICTMENT

1  'Henrici de Bracton, De Legibus et Consuetudinibus
   Angliae', ii, 335;  'Britton' (ed.), F.M. Nichols
   (Oxford, 1865), i, 99; 'Fleta, II' (ed.), H.G.
   Richardson and G.O. Sayles (Selden Society, lxxii,
   1953), 57.

2  'Rotuli Parliamentorum' (ed.), J. Strachey et al.
   (London, 1767), iv, 65-6.   However, in January 1597
   Attorney-General Coke stopped the indicting of Roger
   Symons, one of the Oxfordshire insurgents, on the
   grounds that he never used speech of consent save to
   understand and reveal the treason: MSS Hatfield
   38/12 ('Cal. MSS Salisbury', vii, 50).

3  G.R. Elton, 'Policy and Police' (Cambridge, 1972),
   331.

4  PRO, SP 1/85 fo. 2 ('Calendar of Letters and Papers,
   Foreign and Domestic, Henry VIII' (ed.), J.S. Brewer,
   J. Gairdner and R.H. Brodie, vii, no. 902);  PRO, SP
   1/84 fo. 130 ('Letters and Papers', vii, no. 779);
   PRO, SP 1/131 fo. 168 ('Letters and Papers', xiii
   (i), no. 801).   Justices of the peace did, however,
   have power to examine when the offence was the counterfeiting, filing, or washing of coin.

5   PRO, SP 1/65 fos 90-1.
6   T. Starkey, 'Dialogue between Reginald Pole and
    Thomas Lupset' (ed.), K.M. Burton (London, 1948),
    116.
7   'Letters and Papers', vi, no. 541.
8   The exceptions were in regard to those who under a
    proclamation of 17 May 1550 told the king about pro-
    jected rebellion and those who under others of 1 July
    1570 and 12 October 1584 gave information about the
    dispersal of slanderous and traitorous books.    In
    the first instance informers were to receive £20, in
    the second and third 'large rewards' and half of the
    forfeitures incurred:  P.L. Hughes and J.F. Larkin
    'Tudor Royal Proclamations' (New Haven, 1964-9), i,
    no. 358, ii, nos 577, 672.
9   PRO, SP 12/151/23 ('Cal. State Papers, Domestic,
    1581-90', p. 36).    For details of four of the spies
    employed by Walsingham between 1581-90 to track down
    priests see C. Read, 'Mr. Secretary Walsingham and
    the Policy of Queen Elizabeth' (Oxford, 1925), ii,
    322-38.
10  PRO, SP 12/156/17 ('Cal. State Papers, Domestic,
    1581-90', 78).
11  MSS Hatfield 71/69 ('Cal. MSS Salisbury', ix, 237);
    PRO, SP 12/248/94, 95 ('Cal. State Papers, Domestic,
    1591-4', 498);  PRO, SP 12/150/80 ('Cal. State
    Papers, Domestic, 1581-90', 32).
12  PRO, SP 12/243/51, 71 ('Cal. State Papers, Domestic,
    1591-4', 283, 288);  'Lives of the English Martyrs'
    (ed.), B. Camm (London, 1905), First Series, ii, 571-
    2n.
13  C.H. Williams, The Rebellion of Humphrey Stafford in
    1486, 'English Historical Review', xliii (1928), 182.
14  PRO, SP 1/129 fo. 201 ('Letters and Papers', xiii
    (i), no. 416).
15  'Calendar of State Papers relating to Scotland and
    Mary, Queen of Scots, 1547-1603', ix, 27;  PRO, SP
    12/192/22 ('Cal. State Papers, Domestic, 1581-90',
    344).
16  PRO, SP 1/166 fo. 29 ('Letters and Papers', xvi, no.
    875);  'Acts of the Privy Council' (ed.), J.R.
    Dasent (1890-1907), xii, 345, 353.
17  PRO, SP 12/172/111, 113 ('Cal. State Papers, Domes-
    tic, 1581-90', 198-9).
18  PRO, SP 1/93 fo. 63 ('Letters and Papers', viii, no.
    859);  PRO, SP 1/121 fo. 61 ('Letters and Papers',
    xii (ii), no. 43).
19  PRO, SP 1/79 fos 75, 97 ('Letters and Papers', vi,
    nos 1149, 1169).

20    Thus in 1580 a government spy, Sledd, persuaded a
      constable in London to pursue the seminary priest
      Robert Johnson.    The constable, when it seemed as
      though Johnson might excape, called out to bystanders
      to stop the traitor, which they did (see R. Simpson,
      'Edmund Campion, a biography' (London, 1867), 128).
21    PRO, SP 12/256/5 ('Cal. State Papers, Domestic, 1595-
      7', 159).
22    'Acts of the Privy Council', x, 122.
23    PRO, SP 15/15/139 ('Cal. State Papers, Domestic, Ad-
      denda 1566-79', 172).
24    E. Perlin, 'Description des royaulmes d'Angleterre et
      d'Escossa ... par 1558' (London, 1775), 27.
25    'Calendar of Letters, Despatches, and State Papers,
      relating to the negotiations between England and
      Spain' (ed.), M.A.S. Hume, viii, no. 365.    'Thence
      traytor like I'm brought through every streete' says
      Sir Nicholas Throckmorton in the 'Legend of Sir Nich-
      olas Throckmorton', 31.
26    35 Hen. VIII c. 2.
27    'English Reports', 2 Dyer 129a.
28    'Foedera' (ed.), T. Rymer (The Hague, 1740), V, pt
      iv, 168.
29    'Letters and Papers' iv (ii), no. 4511;  BM Add. MS
      28585 fo. 200 ('Letters and Papers', v, no. 354).
30    'Letters and Papers', xv, no. 189;  ibid., no. 161.
31    PRO, SP 1/160 fos 196-7 ('Letters and Papers', xv,
      no. 793);  'State Papers, Henry VIII', viii, 219.
32    'Letters and Papers', xv, no. 175.
33    Ibid., xvi, no. 612.    Henry told his ambassador Sir
      Ralph Sadler to ask for the surrender of these under
      either the 1502 treaty or the 'agreement' about
      border treasons (ibid., xv, no. 136).
34    Ibid., xvi, no. 766.
35    'State Papers, Henry VIII', viii, 316, 343.
36    Ibid., viii, 367;  'Letters and Papers', xv, no.
      1017.
37    PRO, SP 1/163 fos 230-2 ('Letters and Papers', xvi,
      no. 240);  'State Papers, Henry VIII', viii, 511.
      In March 1536 Henry VIII asked Laurence Stayber,
      'eques auratus' of Nurnburg, to intercept and send to
      England an English subject James Griffiths, whom he
      described as being of law birth and guilty of trea-
      son, robbery, manslaughter and sacrilege, and cur-
      rently on his way to Italy ('Letters and Papers',
      xvi, no. 529).
38    'State Papers, Henry VIII', viii, 344.
39    Three young merchants involved in the capture, Roger
      Ramsden, Martin Bragge and Simon Jewkes were reported

on 11 September 1570 to be soliciting payment of
their expenses:  PRO, SP 12/73/64;   74/26;   73/24
('Cal. State Papers, Domestic, 1547-80', 392, 395,
389).

40   PRO, SP 1/177 fo. 177 ('Letters and Papers', xviii
(i), no. 505).

41   The phrase was Thomas Cromwell's.   He was explaining
for the benefit of Francis I why English traitors
would not be banished, a policy only altered in 1585:
PRO, SP 1/95 fo. 160-1 ('Letters and Papers', ix, no.
157).   The same argument obviously applied to fugitives.

42   PRO, SP 1/179 fo. 91 ('Letters and Papers', xviii
(i), no. 754).

43   See for example, ('Letters and Papers', xv, no. 136)
and 'Foedera', V, pt, iv, 168.

44   See in general I.D. Thornley, The Destruction of
Sanctuary in 'Tudor Studies ... presented to A.F.
Pollard' (ed.), R.W. Seton Watson (London, 1924),
182-207.

45   The sanctuary men of St Martin's-le-Grand frequently
went on criminal enterprises into the city of
London (see ibid., 186).

46   'Year Books', 1 Hen. VII, Pasch. pl. 15;   Trin. pl.
1.

47   See, for example, 'Materials for a History of the
Reign of Henry VII (ed.), W. Campbell (R.S., 1873),
i, 49.

48   In 1487 two traitors were taken from the liberty of
Hexham;   in 1494 four men guilty of 'sedition' were
taken from St Martin's-le-Grand;   in 1495 two, who
were 'appeched of treson', were sent by the sheriff
of the bishopric of Durham to the sheriff of Yorkshire (see Thornley, 'Tudor Studies', 199).

49   PRO, KB 9/475/2.

50   The case appears in 'English Reports', Keilway, 186,
though Cowley is erroneously given the christian name
Walter.   There is no comment on the refusal to plead
and the judgment of the justices.

51   Thus the London Counters held some of the supporters
of Lambert Simnel in 1493-4 ('Chronicles of London'
(ed.), C.L. Kingsford (Oxford, 1905), 198-9) and some
of those involved in the May Day riots in 1517 (Hall,
'Chronicle' (London, 1809), 589).   In 1488 it was
decided that treason suspects should go to Newgate
rather than Ludgate ('Calendar of Letter-Books of the
City of London, Letter-Book L' (ed.), R.R. Sharpe
(London, 1912), 250) and this seems to have been
carried out.   A number of adherents of Perkin War-

beck were to be found there in 1495 ('The Great
Chronicle of London' (ed.), A.H. Thomas and I.D.
Thornley (London, 1938), 259; 'Chronicles of
London', 206).   The Fleet was used for the leaders
of the Suffolk insurrection of 1525 (Hall, 'Chron-
icle', 700).

52  'Lives of the English Martyrs' (ed.), E.H. Burton
    and J.H. Pollen (London, 1914), Second Series, i,
    119.

53  'State Trials' (ed.), W. Cobbett and T.B. Howell
    (London, 1809), i, 387, 1253.

54  'Narratives of the Reformation' (ed.), J.G. Nichols
    (G.S. lxxvii, 1859), 207.

55  'Unpublished Documents relating to the English Mar-
    tyrs' (ed.), J.H. Pollen (Catholic Record Society,
    v, 1908), 94-5, 81-2;   'The Rambler', New Series, x
    (1858), 210.

56  For a list of Jesuits and seminary priests in London
    gaols in 1596 with the names of their apprehenders
    and the date of committal see MSS Hatfield 43/41
    ('Cal. MSS Salisbury', vi, 311-13).   Royal ignorance
    about prisoners in the Tower is revealed in 'Select
    Cases in the Court of King's Bench, Edward III'
    (ed.), G.O. Sayles (Selden Society, lxxxii, 1965),
    73.

57  PRO, SP 12/261/69 ('Cal. State Papers, Domestic,
    1595-7', 335).

58  For a bitter complaint about prolonged imprisonment
    before trial see the letter of the priest Thomas
    Wright of 20 January 1598 to Secretary Cecil.
    Wright, who was in the Gatehouse, had been 'closed
    within four walls and buried alive' for eighteen
    weeks without examination or sentence.   He asked to
    be tried 'and if by law I deserve death let me
    rather die once, than every day die a new death':
    PRO, SP 12/266/23 ('Cal. State Papers, Domestic,
    1598-1601', 10).

59  Wright asked also to be allowed 'that liberty of
    prison which is granted to common prisoners and not
    lie thus rotting in a corner' (ibid.).

60  PRO, SP 12/73/30 ('Cal. State Papers, Domestic, 1547-
    80', 390);   PRO, SP 1/168 fos 120-1 ('Letters and
    Papers', xvi, no. 1433).

61  'State Trials', i, 1126.

62  See Nicholas Sanders, 'De Origine et Progressu Schis-
    matis Anglicani' (Ingolstadt, 1587) for the 'Diary of
    the Tower' compiled by John Hart;   D. Jardine, 'Read-
    ing on the use of torture in the criminal law of
    England' (London, 1837), 26, appendix 79;   R. Challo-

ner, 'Memoirs of Missionary Priests' (ed.), J.H.
Pollen (London, 1924), 139;  W. Allen, 'A briefe
historie of the glorious martyrdom of xii reverend
priests' (ed.), J.H. Pollen (London, 1908), xix.

63  'Unpublished Documents relating to the English Martyrs', 327.    The reference was in a letter of 31
August 1588 to Father General Claudio Aquaviva.

64  'Diary of the Tower', 27 March 1581, 14 August 1582;
'Unpublished Documents relating to the English Mar-
tyrs', 327;  R. Persons, 'De Persecutione Anglicana'
(Ingolstadt, 1582), 52

65  Thus Thomas Barnes was in irons for the first ten
days after apprehension:  PRO, SP 12/269/67 ('Cal.
State Papers, Domestic, 1598-1601', 144).

66  See 'Lives of the English Martyrs', Second Series, i,
68, 74, 313.

67  J. Bridgewater, 'Concertatio Ecclesiae Catholicae in
Anglia' (Treves, 1588), 157b.

68  R. Simpson, The Life and Martyrdom of Mr Richard
White, Schoolmaster, 'The Rambler', N.S., iii (1860),
236.

69  BM Harleian MS 530 fo. 54 ('Letters and Papers',
viii, no. 895);  'Letters and Papers', viii, no. 846.
John Rastell says seventeen days (N. Harpsfield, 'The
Life and Death of Sr. Thomas Moore' (ed.), E.V.
Hitchcock and R.W. Chambers, E.E.T.S., O.S., 186
(1932), 235.

70  PRO, SP 12/73/18 ('Cal. State Papers, Domestic, 1547-
80', 389);  'The Rambler', N.S. iii (1860), 239.

71  'Lives of the English Martyrs', Second Series, i, 10-
11;  'Narratives of the Reformation', 207, 203.

72  J.H. Pollen, 'Acts of the English Martyrs' (London,
1891), 311.

73  In the smaller provincial gaols a treason suspect
might have considerably more freedom.    There is reference to Richard White standing at the door of the
gaol in his irons with his infant child in his arms
('The Rambler', N.S., iii (1860), 241).    At Winches-
ter Edward Kenyon, committed as a traitor, never had
any irons put on him, dined with the deputy keeper,
and frequently visited the man's wife.    He lived in
the parlour by the gaol door.    He was able to escape
while Thomas Garnett, the under-keeper, was away
drinking in the town with two other prisoners:  PRO,
SP 12/273/23 ('Cal. State Papers, 1598-1601', 338-9).

74  PRO, SP 12/73/53 ('Cal. State Papers, Domestic, 1547-
80', 391).

75  PRO, KB 8/2 m. 5.

76  PRO, SP 12/168/21 ('Cal. State Papers, Domestic,

1581-90', 160;  PRO, SP 1/93 fos 54-9 ('Letters and Papers', viii, no. 856).

77   'State Trials', i, 1027.

78   'Lives of the English Martyrs', Second Series, i, 42, 433.

79   'Acts of the Privy Council', iv, 257, 344;  PRO, SP 12/281/67 ('Cal. State Papers, Domestic, 1601-3 and Addenda', 89).

80   'State Trials', i, 388, 872, 967.

81   PRO, SP 15/15/139 ('Cal. State Papers, Domestic, Addenda, 1566-79', 172).

82   R. Holinshed, 'Chronicles of England, Scotland and Ireland' (London, 1808), iv, 512;  'Diary of the Tower', 27 March 1581.

83   'Diary of the Tower', 15-16, 19 December 1580;  Challoner, 'Memoirs of Missionary Priests', 31.

84   J. Morris, 'The Troubles of our Catholic Forefathers related by Themselves' (London, 1872-7), i, 27; 'Lives of the English Martyrs', First Series, i, 260-4.

85   'Unpublished Documents relating to the English Martyrs', 23-4;  'Lives of the English Martyrs', Second Series, i, 119.

86   Bridgewater, 'Concertatio', 151.

87   'Miscellanea', Catholic Record Society, iii (1906), 27, 28.

88   BM Titus B. i, fo. 155 ('Letters and Papers', xii (ii), no. 181).   In More's case the charges were not apparently paid for a period of three months.

89   'Diary of the Tower', 15 January 1581, 26 January 1581, 5 February 1581.

90   'The Rambler', N.S., iii (1860), 238.

91   Allen, 'Briefe historie', 15.

92   Bridgewater, 'Concertatio', 133.

93   'Unpublished Documents relating to the English Martyrs', 81;  Bridgewater, 'Concertatio', 166.

94   PRO, KB 8/2 m. 4.

95   MSS Hatfield 55/96 ('Cal. MSS Salisbury', vii, 417); J. Morris, 'The Life of Father John Gerard' (London, 1881), 286-8;  PRO, SP 12/273/23 ('Cal. State Papers, Domestic, 1598-1601', 339);  Challoner, 'Memoirs of Missionary Priests', 143.

96   'Cal. MSS Salisbury', iv, 428;  Persons, 'De Persecutione', 52;  C. Wriothesley, 'A Chronicle of England' (ed.),W.D. Hamilton (C.S.,New Series, xi,1875),i, 46.

97   'The Chronicle of Queen Jane and of two years of Queen Mary' (ed.), J.G. Nichols (C.S., xlviii, 1850), 76.   J. Stow, 'Annales or a Generall Chronicle of England' (ed.), E. Howes (London, 1631), 706-7.

98   'Unpublished Documents relating to the English Martyrs', 46.   Few suspect traitors died in gaol except

in the 1530s;   PRO E 36/153 fos 1, 2 ('Letters and
Papers', vii, no. 1607) shows 32 deaths among 143 imprisoned friars about 1534.   If the suspect was of
prime importance positive steps might be taken to
safeguard his health.   For example, in August 1570
the duke of Norfolk was moved out of the Tower, when
there was a fear of plague, to his house at the
London Charterhouse:   PRO, SP 12/73/5 ('Cal. State
Papers, Domestic, 1547-80', 387).

99   PRO, SP 1/83 fo. 263 ('Letters and Papers', vii, no.
630);   'Acts of the Privy Council', vii, 83.

100   Stow, 'Annales', 580;   'Lives of the English Martyrs', First Series, i, 474-5.

101   On examination in general see my 'Crime and Public
Order in England in the later Middle Ages' (London
and Toronto, 1973), 136-9.

102   It is possible that these processes were instituted
in a systematic way in Mary's reign under the statutes 1 & 2 Ph. & M. c. 13 and 2 & 3 Ph. & M. c. 10
(see J.H. Langbein, 'Prosecuting Crime in the Renais-
sance' (Cambridge, Mass., 1974), 1);   in fact they
were common early in the century.

103   PRO, SP 1/78 fo. 119 ('Letters and Papers', vi, no.
967);   PRO, SP 12/197/21 ('Cal. State Papers, Domestic, 1581-90', 381);   PRO E 36/119 fos 27-32 ('Letters and Papers', xii (i), no. 201).

104   'Acts of the Privy Council', ii, 256.   Seymour was,
however, eventually attainted by act of parliament
and not tried in open court.

105   'State Trials', i, 1274.

106   'Letters and Papers', xiii (i), no. 904.

107   PRO E 36/119 fo. 21 ('Letters and Papers', xii (i),
no. 201);   'The Correspondence of Sir Thomas More'
(ed.), E.F. Rogers (London, 1947), no. 214;   PRO, SP
1/78 fo. 119 ('Letters and Papers', vi, no. 967).

108   PRO, SP 1/116 fos 81-2 ('Letters and Papers', xii
(i), no. 467);   PRO E 36/119 fos 72, 99-120 ('Letters
and Papers', xii (i), nos 481, 901).

109   Commissions of oyer and terminer for the trial of
suspect traitors frequently referred to them as being
certified as vehemently suspect by three of the privy
council who had examined them (see PRO, KB 8/15 m.
21;   KB 8/16 m. 7;   KB 8/17 m. 12;   KB 8/17 m. 9;
and KB 8/33 m. 9.

110   PRO, SP 12/197/21 ('Cal. State Papers, Domestic,
1581-90', 381);   'Acts of the Privy Council', xi, 32.

111   PRO, SP 1/114 fo. 86 ('Letters and Papers', xii (i),
no. 69).

112   See 'Unpublished Documents relating to the English
Martyrs', 85-6.

113   Bridgewater, 'Concertatio', 140.

114  Ibid., 159;  'Unpublished Documents relating to the
     English Martyrs', 160.   Sometimes the language of
     the answers given by catholic suspects was tailored
     so as not to irritate the magistrates (see ibid.,
     325).   Edmund Campion and his fellows, arraigned in
     1584, were said to have answered 'sophisticallie,
     deceiptfullie and traitorouslie, restraining their
     confession of allegiance onelie to the permissive
     forme of the pope's toleration' (Holinshed, 'Chron-
     icles', iv, 513).
115  PRO, SP 12/217/1:  the examinations had also been
     used as the basis for the indictments;  'State Tri-
     als', i, 1419.
116  PRO, SP 1/138 fos 123-30 ('Letters and Papers', xiii
     (ii), no. 804);  PRO, SP 12/269/32 ('Cal. State
     Papers, Domestic, 1598-1601', 140).
117  MSS Hatfield 6/15 ('Cal. MSS Salisbury', i, 522);
     'Unpublished Documents relating to the English Mar-
     tyrs', 85;  PRO, E36/119/99-120 ('Letters and
     Papers', xii (i), no. 901);  PRO, SP 1/118 fos 92-7
     ('Letters and Papers', xii (i), no. 946);  BM Titus
     MS B. i, fo. 70 ('Letters and Papers', xiii (ii),
     no. 968).
118  PRO, SP 1/138 fo. 16 ('Letters and Papers', xiii
     (ii), no. 695);  PRO, SP 12/278/87 ('Cal. State
     Papers, Domestic, 1598-1601', 579).
119  J. Fortescue, 'De Laudibus Legum Angliae' (ed.), S.B.
     Chrimes (Cambridge, 1942), 65.
120  E. Coke, 'The Third Institute of the Laws of England'
     (London, 1797), 34-5.
121  'The Register of William Greenfield, Pt. V' (ed.),
     A. Hamilton Thompson (Surtees Society, cliii, 1938),
     xxxiii-xl;  'The chronicle of Walter of Guisborough'
     (ed.), H. Rothwell (Camden Soc., lxxxix, 1957), 392.
122  'Letters and Papers illustrative of the Wars of the
     English in France' (ed.), J. Stevenson (R.S., 1864),
     II, ii, 789-90;  Stow, 'Annales', 420.
123  See the biography of Sir Thomas Wyatt the elder in
     the 'Dictionary of National Biography'.
124  T. Smith, 'De Republica Anglorum' (ed.), L. Alston
     (Cambridge, 1906), 105.
125  Jardine, 'Reading on the use of torture ...', 73-103.
126  PRO, SP 1/78 fos 26, 84 ('Letters and Papers', vi,
     nos 887, 934).
127  See PRO, SP 1/176 fo. 137 ('Letters and Papers',
     xviii (i), no. 277) for an example of Henry VIII per-
     sonally ordering the use of torture.
          There is one Henrician reference to racking in the
     Tower which dates from the time when Wolsey's influ-

ence was paramount (Elton, 'Policy and Police', 313)
and there is the likelihood that the rack was used
during the early years of the reign in the English
continental possessions (see 'Letters and Papers',
ii (i), no. 1254 and ii (ii), no. 2789).   Also, in
1523, one John Marche asserted he had only confessed
to treason 'ne pro veritatis exploracione ad torturas
committeretur (see P. Heath, The Treason of Geoffrey
Blythe, Bishop of Coventry and Lichfield 1503-31,
'Bulletin of the Institute of Historical Research',
xlii (1969), 108).   It is worthy of note that there
is one instance where a suspect seems to have been
tortured at Cromwell's house in Stepney (Elton,
'Policy and Police', 145n).

128   See 'Acts of the Privy Council', vi, 130 (riot), vii,
367 (murder), v, 202 (horse stealing) and J. Foxe,
'Acts and Monuments' (ed.), G. Townsend and S.R.
Cattley (London, 1837-41), v, 547, 699 (heresy).

129   'Letters and Papers', vii, no. 384.

130   'Acts of the Privy Council', xi, 157-8;   'Cal. State
Papers, Domestic, Addenda, 1566-79', 172.

131   'Unpublished Documents relating to the English Martyrs', 83;   Allen, 'Briefe historie', 48.

132   'State Trials', i, 1009, 1256.

133   'Acts of the Privy Council', vii, 373, viii, 319.

134   Holinshed, 'Chronicles', iv, 514.   See also C. Read,
'William Cecil and Elizabethan Public Relations',
in 'Elizabethan Government and Society' (ed.), S.T.
Bindoff, J. Hurstfield and C.H. Williams (London,
1961), 37.

135   W.D. Cooper, Further particulars of Thomas Norton and
of state proceedings in matters of religion in the
years 1581 and 1582, 'Archaeologia', xxxvi (1855),
115;   'Narratives of the Reformation', 188.
     The rack and brake are both depicted in Foxe's cut
showing the torturing of Cuthbert Simpson in 1557,
and the rack by itself appears in the first edition
of the Italian translation of Allen's 'Briefe historie' (Macerata, 1583).   Lingard states that
     the rack was a large open frame of oak raised
     three feet from the ground.   The prisoner was
     laid under it on his back on the floor;   his
     wrists and ankles were attached by cords to two
     rollers at the ends of the frame;   these were
     moved by levers in opposite directions till the
     body rose to a level with the frame.   Questions
     were then put;   and if the answers did not prove
     satisfactory the sufferer was stretched more and
     more till the bones started from their sockets

(J. Lingard, 'History of England' (Dublin, 1888), vi, 688).

136  Jardine, 'Reading on the use of torture ...', 14; R.D. Melville, The use and forms of judicial torture in England and Scotland, 'Scottish Historical Review', ii (1905), 224-48.

137  'Narratives of the Reformation', 188-9.

138  M. Tanner, 'Societas Jesu usque ad sanguinis et vitae profusionem militans' (Prague, 1675), 18.

139  'Narratives of the Reformation', 188-9; 'Lives of the English Martyrs', First Series, ii, 507, 550.

140  Lingard, 'History of England', vi, 688-9.  See also J. Morris, 'The Life of Father John Gerard' (London, 1881), 241.

141  'Unpublished Documents relating to the English Martyrs', 210;  Morris, 'The Life of Father John Gerard', 241.

142  'The Rambler', N.S., iii (1860), 246.

143  'Unpublished Documents relating to the English Martyrs', 212.   Jardine, quoting 'Acts of the Privy Council', xxii, 39-40, argued that the first mention of manacles was on 25 October 1591 and suggested that perhaps they had been captured from the Armada (Jardine, 'Reading on the use of torture ...', 37).

144  See 'Acts of the Privy Council', xxiv, 56, 222; xxvi, 374, 457.   By 1590 the Bridewell seems also to have contained a rack:  see the council's letter of 18 April 1590 to Justice Younge (ibid., xix, 69-70).

145  Ibid., xxvii, 38;  Morris, 'The Life of Father John Gerard', 240-7;  'Unpublished Documents relating to the English Martyrs', 212;  'Acts of the Privy Council', xviii, 338-78;  PRO, SP 12/230/104 ('Cal. State Papers, Domestic, 1581-90', 650).

146  'Lives of the English Martyrs', First Series, ii, 570.

147  BM Add. MS 32,651 fo. 93 ('Letters and Papers', xviii (i), no. 884).   A torture similar to that ordered on Brewer and Shepherdson was inflicted in April 1583 on Dermot O'Hurley, archbishop of Armagh.   On Burghley's instructions he had his feet toasted before a fire.   See R. Bagwell, 'Ireland under the Tudors' (London, 1963), iii, 118n.   Most interestingly there is a report that the 'shoe torture' was the invention of Thomas More when he was chancellor.   He used it on poachers ('Letters and Papers', x, no. 587).

148  'Unpublished Documents relating to the English Martyrs', 327.

149  When the circumstances warranted it and a suspect was captured far from London the council might order a local magnate to examine using 'some kinde of torture' (see 'Acts of the Privy Council', vii, 222; vi, 130).

150    The lieutenant of the Tower, when present, seems to
       have had the authority to commence and cease the
       racking as is shown by the case (one of heresy) of
       Anne Askew (Foxe, 'Acts and Monuments', v, 547).
151    The names of those appointed to examine suspects by
       torture are to be found in 'Acts of the Privy Coun-
       cil', iii-xxx.
152    MSS Hatfield 158/28 ('Cal. MSS Salisbury', i, 525);
       W. Camden, 'Annals or the History of the most renow-
       ned and victorious princess Elizabeth, late queen of
       England' (London, 1635), 254;  Cooper, 'Archaeolo-
       gia', xxxvi (1855), 116.
153    'Unpublished Documents relating to the English Mar-
       tyrs', 212, 329-30.
154    MSS Hatfield 34/67 ('Cal. MSS Salisbury', v, 353-4);
       Challoner, 'Memoirs of Missionary priests', 186, 224.
155    'Narratives of the Reformation', 44.
156    Holinshed, 'Chronicles', iv, 512, 537-8.
157    Allen, 'Briefe historie', 17, 49.
158    PRO, SP 12/249/114 ('Cal. State Papers, Domestic,
       1591-4', 550);  'State Trials', i, 1059.
159    PRO, SP 12/249/114 ('Cal. State Papers, Domestic,
       1591-4', 550);  PRO, SP 12/247/97 ('Cal. State
       Papers, Domestic, 1591-4', 444);  see also MSS Hat-
       field 34/67 ('Cal. MSS Salisbury', i, 85;  v, 353-4).
160    'Unpublished Documents relating to the English Mar-
       tyrs', 335;  Morris, 'The Life of Father John
       Gerard', 233.    Instructions to those in charge might
       be to rack 'at their discretion' or 'as often as they
       see cause':  'Acts of the Privy Council', xv, 51;
       xiv, 271.
161    Holinshed, 'Chronicles', iv, 172.
162    Cooper, 'Archaeologia', xxxvi (1855), 116.   Some-
       times the torture warrant actually contained the
       words 'there are vehement presumptions he is guilty'
       (see 'Acts of the Privy Council', xiii, 172).   Often
       there seem to have been confessions by associates
       which already incriminated the man to be tortured.
163    Cooper, 'Archaeologia', xxxvi (1855), 116;  Holin-
       shed, 'Chronicles', iv, 513-14.
164    Cooper, 'Archaeologia', xxxvi (1855), 116.
165    'State Trials', i, 1121.
166    Cooper, 'Archaeologia', xxxvi (1855), 115;  'Unpub-
       lished Documents relating to the English Martyrs',
       212.    There was complaint also by those ordered to
       perform the racking.   In September 1571 Sir Thomas
       Smith and Dr Thomas Wilson asked to be excused using
       the rack:  MSS Hatfield 158/28 ('Cal. MSS Salisbury',
       i, 525).
167    Camden, 'Annals', p. 262.
168    'Acts of the Privy Council', viii, 94.

169  Some treasons, like seditious words, which were
     thought to be of no great consequence, might be dealt
     with first of all by ordering a further investiga-
     tion.   If this showed the suspect was guilty there
     might well follow the imposition of some form of cor-
     poral punishment like the pillory under the council's
     authority.   See 'Letters and Papers', xx (i), no.
     1281, which shows John George was to have his ears
     nailed, and 'Acts of the Privy Council', vii, 71,
     where Sir Henry Doyle and Christopher Goldingham were
     ordered, if they believed the accusers were honest
     men of credit, to put Ralph Backhouse, a parish
     priest, on the pillory at Ipswich and to cut off one
     of his ears before subsequently committing him to
     gaol.
170  'State Trials', i, 510-12.
171  W. Lambarde, 'Eirenarcha' (London, 1619), 43.
172  For very large oyer and terminer treason commissions
     see 'Cal. Pat. Rolls, 1494-1509', 30, 33.   For some
     which were very small see PRO, KB 8/10/2 m. 23 and
     KB 8/10/1 m. 11.
173  PRO, KB 8/7/3 m. 10.
174  'State Trials', i, 1238-9.
175  'State Trials', i, 1168;   'State Papers relating to
     Scotland', ix, no. 92.
176  BM Harleian MS 283 fo. 204 ('Letters and Papers',
     xiii (i), no. 680).
177  'State Papers relating to Scotland', ix, no. 298.
178  R. Bagwell, 'Ireland under the Tudors', iii, 121;
     Bellamy, 'Crime and Public Order', 128-31.
179  Holinshed, 'Chronicles', iv, 509.
180  See PRO, E36/120 fo. 94 ('Letters and Papers', xii
     (ii), no. 918).   The accuser/informer John Peterson
     was proven fraudulent by bringing those he had accu-
     sed face to face with him.   He failed to identify
     them.
181  'Statutes of the Realm' (Record Commission, 1810-28),
     iv (i), 842;   PRO, SP 15/13/43 ('Cal. State Papers,
     Domestic, Addenda, 1566-79', 22);   'Stat. Realm', iv
     (ii), 616;   cf. PRO, SP 2/Q fos 103-9 and 'Stat.
     Realm', iii, 508-9.   Elton has been concerned to em-
     phasize that in the period 1532-40 there were no
     monetary rewards for treason informers (whom he pre-
     fers to call 'delators') (Elton, 'Policy and Police',
     329).
182  BM Caligula B. i, fo. 319 ('Letters and Papers', xii
     (i), no. 1156);   Elton, 'Policy and Police', 387.
183  See Bellamy, 'The Law of Treason in England in the
     Later Middle Ages' (Cambridge, 1970), 138-9 and
     'Crime and Public Order', 122-3.

184 For example, PRO, KB 9/492/216.
185 See, for example, PRO, KB 8/10/2 m. 13.
186 Smith, 'De Republica', 87.
187 PRO, SP 1/123 fo. 46 ('Letters and Papers', xii (ii),
    no. 303).
188 Brooks New Cases, 50-2.
189 In a case occurring in 1595 a single confession by a
    fellow prisoner was sufficient to indict William
    Freeman ('Unpublished Documents relating to the Eng-
    lish Martyrs', 353).
190 PRO, SP 1/120 fo. 26 ('Letters and Papers', xii (i),
    no. 1172).
191 BM Caligula B. i, fo. 319 ('Letters and Papers', xii
    (i), no. 1156).
192 PRO, SP 1/134 fo. 205 ('Letters and Papers', xiii
    (i), no. 1411).   Elton suggests there were thirty-
    seven refusals to indict in treason cases in the
    period 1532-40 ('Policy and Police', 387).
193 PRO, KB 27/1176 Rex m. 3.
194 BM Titus MS.B. i, fo. 474 ('Letters and Papers',
    viii, no. 892).   It is usually very difficult to
    decide whether the decision to prosecute a suspected
    traitor in the courts had been made by the monarch
    himself, by his chief minister, by his attorney-
    general, or by a majority of the council.
195 Especially in the mid-1530s (see PRO, KB 8/7/2, and
    KB 8/7/3).
196 Bellamy, 'Law of Treason', 105.
197 See above pp. 55-6.
198 PRO, KB 27/1292 Rex m. 4;   'Unpublished Documents re-
    lating to the English Martyrs', 51.
199 PRO, SP 1/92 fo. 120 ('Letters and Papers', viii, no.
    616).
200 PRO, KB 8/7/1 m. 11.
201 MSS Hatfield 65/40 ('Cal. MSS Salisbury', viii, 421).


CHAPTER 4   TRIAL

1 There were no treason trials held before the council,
  as had occurred on one occasion in the fourteenth
  century.   The nearest thing was the trial there on
  20 November 1581 of Lord Vaux, Sir Thomas Tresham,
  Sir William Catesby, and two other catholics on the
  grounds that they had received Edmund Campion in
  their houses and on 17 May 1586 of the earl of Arundel for the 'contemptes' of receiving Jesuits and
  seminary priests.   The crime in the former case
  could not be treason since at that time Campion was

not an attainted traitor.  The accused were eventually punished with imprisonment and fines for refusing to swear an oath that they would answer interrogatories administered to them truthfully.  The
episode illustrates very well how ineffective conciliar proceedings might be at times and why no treason
trials were staged under them:  see BM
Harleian MS 859 fos 44-51 (printed by R. Simpson
under the title of A Morning at the Star-Chamber in
'The Rambler', N.S. vii (1857), 15-37).

2  For example, tried in Westminster Hall were the earl
of Warwick in 1499 (PRO, KB 8/2 m. 1), the duke of
Buckingham in 1521 (KB 8/5 m. 1), Sir Thomas Wyatt in
1554 (KB 8/27 m. 1), the duke of Norfolk in 1571 (KB
8/42 m. 1), Dr William Parry in 1584 (KB 8/46 m. 1),
Anthony Babington and his fellow conspirators in 1586
(KB 8/48 m. 24), Sir John Perrot in 1592 (KB 8/50 m.
1) and the earl of Essex in 1600 (KB 8/56 m. 1).  At
the London Guildhall were arraigned Edmund Dudley in
1509 (KB 8/4 m. 55), Dr Mackerell in 1537 (KB 8/10 m.
1), Thomas Culpeper and Francis Derham in 1541 (KB
8/13/1 m. 1), the earl of Surrey in 1547 (KB 8/14 m.
1), Lady Jane Grey in 1553 (KB 8/23 m. 1), Sir Nicholas Throckmorton in 1554 (KB 8/29 m. 1), John Somervyle in 1583 (KB 8/45 m. 1), and Dr Lopez in 1594
(KB 8/52 m. 10).

3  Except in Wales.

4  The act may have resulted from difficulties encountered in trying in London Sir Thomas Culpeper and
Francis Derham, whose alleged offences were committed
in Yorkshire, Surrey and Kent (PRO, KB 8/13/1 mm. 20,
21).

5  'English Reports', 3 Dyer 286b.  Another report con-
nects the incident with the trial of the would-be
reginacide John Somervyle (1 Anderson 106).

6  See for example 'Calendar of Letters and Papers, Foreign and Domestic, Henry VIII' (ed.), J.S. Brewer, J.
Gairdner, R.H. Brodie (1862-1932), vii, no. 973.

7  T. Smith, 'De Republica Anglorum' (ed.), L. Alston
(Cambridge, 1906), 101.

8  'Letters and Papers', x, no. 908.

9  'State Trials' (ed.) W. Cobbett and T.B. Howell
(London, 1809), i, 958;  'Unpublished Documents relating to the English Martyrs 1584-1603' (ed.), J.H.
Pollen (Catholic Record Society, v, 1908), 355.
Security at the trial and escorting the prisoner from
gaol and back again was a considerable problem:  see
Burghley's notes calculating the number of men necessary for duty at Norfolk's trial:  'Cal. MSS Salisbury', ii. 3.

10  PRO, SP 15/27/107 ('Cal. State Papers, Domestic, Addenda, 1580-1625', 71-2).
11  PRO, SP 1/131 no. 142 ('Letters and Papers', xiii (i), no. 783).
12  PRO, SP 12/217/1 ('Cal. State Papers, Domestic, 1581-90', 549).
13  'Cal. State Papers relating to Scotland and Mary, Queen of Scots, 1547-1603', ix, no. 78.
14  PRO, SP 15/27/107 ('Cal. State Papers, Domestic, Addenda, 1580-1625', 71-2).
15  'Letters and Papers', xvi, no. 1401.
16  Allen, 'Brief historie', 18-19.
17  BM Add. MS 8715 fo. 252 ('Letters and Papers', x, no. 956);  'Correspondance Politique' (ed.), J.B.L. Kaulek (Paris, 1885), no. 380.
18  For example, see 'State Papers, Henry VIII', i, 726-7.
19  E. Hall, 'Chronicle' (London, 1809), 815.
20  C. Wriothesley, 'A Chronicle of England' (ed.). W.D. Hamilton (C.S. New Series, xi, 1875), ii, 63.
21  W. Allen, 'A briefe historie of the glorious martyrdom of xii reverend priests' (ed.), J.H. Pollen (London, 1908), 18-19.
22  'Unpublished Documents relating to the English Martyrs', 120;  D. Jardine, 'Criminal Trials' (London, 1832-5), i, 271.
23  'State Trials', i, 1407.
24  Smith, 'De Republica', 96-7.    See also J.S. Cockburn, 'A History of English Assizes, 1558-1714' (Cambridge, 1972), 67-9.
25  MSS Hatfield 87/107 ('Cal. MSS Salisbury', x, 284); 'State Trials', i, 1045-6, 1091.
26  Ibid., i, 965, 1091.
27  'Unpublished Documents relating to the English Martyrs', 335;   J. Morris, 'The Troubles of our Catholic Forefathers' (London, 1872), i, 70.
28  Jardine, 'Criminal Trials', i, 143.
29  'The Rambler', N.S., iii (1860), 367.    If the trial was at the assizes suspects of all types of crimes would first appear before the justices together. Then a small number would be selected for immediate trial and the rest remanded to gaol (Smith, 'De Republica', 96).
30  J. Duncan M. Derrett, Neglected Versions of the Contemporary Account of the Trial of Sir Thomas More, 'Bulletin of the Institute of Historical Research', xxxiii (1960), 215.
31  See Morris, 'The Troubles of our Catholic Forefathers', i, 71-3.

In one case it appears that a particular charge in the indictment was not read out but shown in writing to the accused. Chapuys said that one offence alleged against Lord Rochford in 1536 was that his sister, Anne Boleyn, had told his wife that the king 'nestoit habile en cas de soy copuler avec femme et quil navoit ne vertu ne puissance'. He was warned not to repeat it out loud but did so none the less ('Letters and Papers', x, no. 908).

32   'State Trials', i, 870, 1044.
33   Ibid., i, 1043;  R. Holinshed, 'Chronicles of England, Scotland and Ireland' (London, 1808), iv, 28.
34   Jardine, 'Criminal Trials', i, 147.
35   Smith, 'De Republica', 98.
36   PRO, KB 8/7/1 mm. 3, 4.
37   PRO, KB 8/31 m. 3;  KB 8/10/3 m. 4.
38   Smith, 'De Republica', 97.

In the case of Dr Storey in 1571 the justices, on his refusal to plead gave him a book to read 'wherein he might see what they might do to him'. Whether this was a threat of *peine forte et dure*, or merely a description of how traitors should be executed, we cannot tell. Judgment and sentence followed immediately ('State Trials', i, 1091).

39   PRO, KB 9/475/2.  It is, of course, quite possible the sheriff used force or deprivation of food to try to make him change his mind.  It was not unknown in the seventeenth century for prisoners' thumbs to be tied together with whipcord for this purpose (see J. Bellamy, 'Crime and Public Order in England in the Later Middle Ages' (London and Toronto, 1973, 141).
40   'The Rambler', N.S., iii (1860), 367.
41   'State Trials', i, 1070;  'Lives of the English Martyrs' (ed.), E.H. Burton and J.H. Pollen (London, 1914), Second Series, i, 513.
42   By the act 33 Hen. VIII c. 23.
43   J. Fortescue, 'De Laudibus Legum Anglie' (ed.), S.B. Chrimes (Cambridge, 1942), 65;  PRO, KB 8/29 m. 10.
44   'State Trials', i, 1318, 1278.
45   Ibid., i, 1335, 521;  'The Chronicle of Queen Jane and of two years of Queen Mary' (ed.), J.G. Nichols (C.S., xlviii, 1850), 17.
46   'State Trials', i, 871.
47   Morris, 'The Troubles of our Catholic Forefathers', i, 74.
48   Smith, 'De Republica', 97;  'Narratives of the Reformation' (ed.), J.G. Nichols (C.S., lxxvii, 1859), 207.
49   'State Trials', i, 1318.  The crown was not expecting the laying of formal charges, merely information.

50　'Year Books', 9 Edw. IV Pasch. pl. 4: 'Et nota qe le
　　defendant en endictment de felony n'avera counsel
　　vers le Roy s'il ne soit matter en ley: Mes en
　　appeal auter est'. In this case a woman had brought
　　a bill of appeal against those who had mainperned
　　some men convicted of felony.

51　BM Harleian MS 78 fo. 7 ('Letters and Papers', xvi,
　　no. 641); R. Persons, 'The Jesuits Memorial for the
　　Intended Reformation of England under their first
　　Popish Prince' (London, 1690), 249.

52　Jardine, 'Criminal Trials', i, 144-5; 'State Tri-
　　als', i, 1277, 1291.

53　Holinshed, 'Chronicles', iv, 541; 'Acts of the Privy
　　Council' (ed.), J.R. Dasent (1890-1907), vii, 90;
　　Jardine, 'Criminal Trials', i, 145. Jardine argued
　　that perhaps it might have been permissible to send
　　legal advice to prisoners awaiting trial by letter.

54　E. Coke, 'The Third Part of the Institutes of the
　　Laws of England' (London, 1797), 136-7; Williams,
　　The Rebellion of Humphrey Stafford in 1486, 'English
　　Historical Review', xliii (1928), 187.

55　Coke, 'Third Part of the Institutes', 137; W. Stan-
　　ford, 'Les Plees del Coron' (London, 1557), 152.

56　BM Harleian MS 78 fo. 7 ('Letters and Papers', xvi,
　　no. 641). In 1541 Sir Thomas Wyatt the elder, con-
　　structing an anticipatory defence while in gaol,
　　wrote that he wished he had had time to read the in-
　　dictment and to write down his response, 'but it may
　　not be, therfor I must answer directly to the accusa-
　　tion which wilbe hard for me to remember'. He ex-
　　pected the length and the reasoning of the indictment
　　might well deceive the jury and 'amaze' him. The
　　difficulty of doing without a copy of the indictment
　　was not confined to those accused of treason. John
　　Udall, tried for felony in 1590 is reckoned only to
　　have managed to obtain a copy of his indictment at
　　Easter term 1592 ('State Trials', i, 1315).

57　N. Harpsfield, 'The Life and Death of Sr. Thomas
　　Moore' (ed.) E.V. Hitchcock and R.W. Chambers,
　　E.E.T.S., O.S., 186 (1932), 258-9; 'State Trials',
　　i, 1143.

58　'State Trials', i, 1325; J. Bellamy, 'The Law of
　　Treason in England in The Later Middle Ages' (Cam-
　　bridge, 1970), 168-9.

59　PRO, SP 1/116 fos 85-6, 92-8 ('Letters and Papers',
　　xii (i), nos 469, 479); 'Cal. State Papers relating
　　to Scotland', ix, no. 89.

60　Year Books, 1 Hen. VII Trin. pl. 1.

61　See for example BM Titus MS B. i, fo. 440 ('Letters

and Papers', xii (i), no. 1106).    We should expect
evidence to have been referred to the king's attorney
and solicitor for a report as to whether there was a
chance of a successful prosecution, but Cromwell,
perhaps because of his legal training, was not inclined to let things follow this course (compare
'Acts of the Privy Council', i, 116).

62  PRO, SP 12/278/96 ('Cal. State Papers, Domestic,
1598-1601', 585).

63  'Cal. State Papers relating to Scotland', ix, no. 63.

64  As, for example, in the cases of Sir Thomas More and
Bishop Fisher where Cromwell and Audley were on the
commission (PRO, KB 8/7/2 m. 14 and KB 8/7/3 m. 10).
However, Cromwell does not seem to have taken his
place on the bench at More's trial ('State Trials',
i, 387).

65  For example, 'Cal State. Papers relating to Scotland', ix, no. 65.

66  'State Trials', i, 871, 875, 1051, 1327, 999, 1015;
Jardine, 'Criminal Trials', i, 142-3.

67  'State Trials', i, 1318, 1051-3.

68  Ibid., i, 1318;  PRO, SP 12/217/1 ('Cal. State
Papers, Domestic, 1581-90', 549).

69  Jardine, 'Criminal Trials', i, 322; 'State Trials',
i, 1317.

70  Morris, 'The Troubles of our Catholic Forefathers',
i, 73;  'State Trials', i, 879.
    Attorney-General Coke, at the trial of Sir Chris-
topher Blunt,  introduced the earl of Essex's post-
trial confessions, but it was admitted they should
not count as evidence (ibid., i, 1430-1).

71  Ibid., i, 889.

72  Hall, 'Chronicle', 623;  PRO, SP 1/82 fos 85-6
('Letters and Papers', vii, no. 72).

73  'State Trials', i, 979-85;  Morris, 'The Troubles of
our Catholic Forefathers', i, 73-7.

74  'State Trials', i, 872;  Jardine, 'Criminal Trials',
i, 150.

75  'The Rambler', N.S., iii (1860), 370.

76  'State Trials', i, 1443, 1318, 1053.

77  'Ibid.', i, 873-4, 882-3.   On the practice of reading out mere sections of answers to examinations see
H.W.R. Lillie, The English Martyrs and English Criminal Law, II, 'The Clergy Review', xiii (1937), 307-
8.

78  'State Trials', i, 877, 1147, 886.

79  Year Books, 13 Hen. VIII Pasch. pl. 1;  G.R. Elton,
'Policy and Police' (Cambridge, 1972), 319;  'State
Trials', i, 1260.

80   'State Trials', i, 888-97.
81   See Bellamy, 'Crime and Public Order', 147-8;   For-
      tescue, 'De Laudibus Legum Anglie', 77.
82   W. Roper, 'The Lyfe of Sir Thomas Moore, knighte'
      (ed.), E.V. Hitchcock (Early English Text Society,
      no. 197), 87-91;   'State Trials', i, 401.
83   PRO, SP 1/124 fo. 199 ('Letters and Papers', xii
      (ii), no. 667);   PRO, E36/143 fo. 27 ('Letters and
      Papers', xiv (ii), no. 494).
84   PRO, SP 1/117 fos 133-7 ('Letters and Papers', xii
      (i), no. 731).
85   'Statutes of the Realm' (Record Commission 1810-28),
      iii, 897, 961.   In August 1540 Marillac told Francis
      I that by a new statute, if two witnesses would swear
      before the king's council that they had heard someone
      speak against the king's edicts on obedience and the
      articles on religion, they would suffer death without
      further process:   'Correspondance Politique', no.
      241.   There is some evidence that the government
      tried to supplement indictments under the 'six arti-
      cles' statute by adding charges after the inquest had
      found a 'true bill'.   The case is mentioned in ano-
      ther context in Elton, 'Policy and Police', 133.
86   Brooks New Cases, 50-2.
87   The only treason act specifically dealing with spoken
      words which omitted provision for witnesses at in-
      dictment was 1 & 2 Ph. & M. c. 9, which made it trea-
      son for prayers to be offered that if the queen did
      not change her religious views she should die.   How-
      ever, since by 'prayers' the drafters meant 'communal
      prayers', there were bound to be plenty of witnesses.
88   'State Trials', i, 492, 520-1.
89   Jardine, 'Criminal Trials', i, 167-8.
90   Ibid., i, 1146-8, 1253, 1257.
91   L.M. Hill, The Two-Witness Rule in English Treason
      Trials:   Some Comments on the Emergence of Procedural
      Law, 'American Journal of Legal History', 12 (1968),
      111.
92   BM MS 39 (printed in E. Edwards, 'The Life of Sir
      Walter Raleigh' (London, 1868, i, 387-435;   see es-
      pecially i, 407-11).   Raleigh's indictment was simi-
      lar in many ways to Norfolk's in 1571.   Thus it
      might also have been held to have been based on the
      1352 act, although like the duke's there were in fact
      some charges stemming from the statute 13 Eliz. c. 1
      (PRO, KB 8/58 mm. 14, 15).
93   'State Trials', i, 1257, 1330.
94   Ibid., i, 883-4;   1 Dyer 99b-100a.
95   Coke, 'Third Part of the Institutes', 25;   'State

Trials', i, 1257, ii, 20.    See also Jardine, 'Criminal Trials', i, 427 and J.H. Wigmore, The History of
the Hearsay Rule, 'Harvard Law Review', xvii (7),
440-4.

96    Elton, 'Policy and Police', 320 (referring to PRO,
St. Ch. 2/24/163; 'State Trials', i, 1007, 1009.
There can be no denying that many of the witnesses
used by the crown at treason trials later in the century, especially where Jesuits and seminary priests
were concerned, were government spies and officials
whose job it was to bring them to justice.

97    See above, p. 153.

98    'State Trials', i, 1319-20, 1328, 1330.

99    Ibid., i, 1257-8.

100   'The Rambler', N.S., iii (1860), 368-9.

101   'State Trials', i, 878.

102   Ibid., i, 1281, 993, 885, 887-8.
There is no evidence of any prisoner being cut off
by the bench while he had something left to say.
Throckmorton, furthermore, interjected comments and
replies at will.

103   Jardine, 'Criminal Trials', i, 170.

104   'State Trials', i, 1050-1, 1064-5, 1066-7, 1070-1.

105   See for example ibid., i, 1143-54.

106   Ibid., i, 1130, 1108-9;  Jardine, 'Criminal Trials',
i, 254.   Parry offered to read out the confession
himself.

107   'State Trials', i, 861-4.   Wyatt might, of course,
have launched a tirade against the queen, but the
court seems to have been sure he would not.

108   BM Harleian MS 78 fo. 7 ('Letters and Papers', xvi,
no. 641);  'State Trials', i, 1289, 401.

109   'State Trials', i, 897, 1326.

110   Ibid., i, 1070-1.

111   However, in his final few words to the jurors,
Throckmorton spoke about 'how grievous and horrible
the shedding of innocents' blood is in the sight of
Almighty God', and how not only his own life, but
also the destruction of his posterity rested on their
judgment (ibid., i, 898).

112   2 Hen. V st. 2 c. 3;  PRO, KB 8/4 m. 55.

113   Holinshed, 'Chronicles', iii, 623.   The justices
gave as their justification the act 11 Hen. VII c.
21, whereby the qualification was required in London
in personal actions where damages might be more than
40 marks.

114   Wriothesley, 'Chronicle of England', i, 177;  PRO, SP
1/130 fo. 63 ('Letters and Papers', xii (i), no.
519).

115   PRO, KB 8/5 m. 30;   KB 8/19 m. 7.
116   PRO, KB 8/9 mm. 7-13;   KB 8/10/2 m. 7.
117   PRO, KB 27/559 rex m. 4;   KB 8/7/2 m. 5.
118   BM Add. MS 32651 fo. 269 ('Letters and Papers',
      xviii (ii), no. 74);   'State Trials', i, 871.
119   25 Edw. III st. 5 c. 3;   PRO, SP 1/120 fo. 26
      ('Letters and Papers', xii (i), no. 1172;   BM Add.
      MS 32651 fo. 269 ('Letters and Papers', xviii (ii),
      no. 74).
120   PRO, SP 15/4/34 ('Cal. State Papers, Domestic, 1601-
      3 and Addenda', 423);   Morris, 'The Troubles of our
      Catholic Forefathers', iii, 94.
121   Allen, 'Briefe historie', 18.
122   Smith, 'De Republica', 100-1;   'The diary of Henry
      Machyn citizen and Merchant Taylor of London, from
      1550 to 1563' (ed.), J.G. Nichols (Camden Series,
      xlii, 1848), 15.
123   'State Trials', i, 1267;   ii, 13.
124   Ibid., i, 1289, 1265;   Jardine, 'Criminal Trials', i,
      361-2.
125   Morris, 'The Troubles of our Catholic Forefathers',
      i, 88-9;   'The Rambler', N.S., iii (1860), 371.
126   'Unpublished Documents relating to the English Mar-
      tyrs', 335;   'State Trials', i, 1446, 1326, 1258.
127   'State Trials', i, 402, 898-9;   PRO, SP 1/117 fos
      133-7 ('Letters and Papers', xii (i), no. 731).
128   Morris, 'The Troubles of our Catholic Forefathers',
      i, 89;   'State Trials', i, 899.
         The justices at Sir Nicholas Throckmorton's trial
      were so startled by the acquittal that they apparent-
      ly asked for the verdict not only from the foreman
      but from the other jurors as well.   Having received
      the same answer they then asked the jurors if they
      had 'considered substantially the whole evidence in
      sort as it was declared and recited', and added, in a
      minatory manner, 'the matter doth touch the queen's
      highness and yourselves also, take good heed what you
      do'.   The jury was apparently unmoved (ibid.).
129   Jardine, 'Criminal Trials', i, 227;   'State Trials',
      i, 1258, 897;   Stanford, 'Les Plees del Coron', 184a.
130   Smith, 'De Republica', 109;   BM Harleian MS 78 fo. 7
      ('Letters and Papers, xvi, no. 641).
131   PRO, KB 9/390 mm. 84, 97d;   KB 9/475/2;   KB 8/6 m. 5;
      KB 8/19 m. 5;   KB 8/38 m. 4;   Elton, 'Policy and
      Police', 387:   unfortunately the total of those ar-
      raigned in this period is not given.
132   BM Harleian MS 78 fo. 7 ('Letters and Papers', xvi,
      no. 641);   Smith, 'De Republica', 109.
133   For example 'Acts of the Privy Council', i, 122, v,

222, vi, 382 and PRO, SP 1/231 fo. 126 ('Letters and Papers, Addenda', I (i), no. 70).   There do not seem to have been any instances of a jury reversing its verdict in a treason case although this did happen in ordinary assize court criminal business:   see J.S. Cockburn, 'A History of English Assizes 1558-1714' (Cambridge, 1972), 123.

134   'State Trials', i, 899-902.
135   Smith, 'De Republica', 109.
136   PRO, SP 15/3/78 ('Cal. State Papers, Domestic, 1601-3 and Addenda', 407-9).
137   Morris, 'The Troubles of our Catholic Forefathers', iii, 90-2.
138   'State Trials', i, 1327, 1329-30, 1328;   Holinshed, 'Chronicles', iv, 578.
139   Jardine, 'Criminal Trials', i, 228;   'State Trials', i, 864, 1258, 1264.
140   'State Trials', i, 1154-5;   Holinshed, 'Chronicles', iv, 4.
141   Jardine, 'Criminal Trials', i, 364.
142   'State Trials', i, 392-3;   Roper, 'Lyfe of Moore', 92-5.
143   'State Trials', i, 1328, 1301, 1299.
144   Ibid., i, 1071-2, 402.
145   In the parliamentary session of April-May 1540 an act was passed attainting of treason Richard Fetherstone, Dr Thomas Abel, Dr Edward Powell, William Horne, Laurence Cooke (prior of White Friars, Doncaster) and Margaret Tyrell.   The first four were held to have traitorously adhered to the bishop of Rome, the king's enemy, and refused to accept the king as supreme head of the realm, as well as perpetrating other treasons to the destruction of the king's person and disherison of the realm.   Cooke was stated to have adhered to Roger Aske, and Margaret Tyrell to have traitorously refused allegiance to Prince Edward ('Letters and Papers', xv, no. 498).
146   Persons, 'Jesuit's Memorial', 249-51.   The point that the transmarine catholics were lacking in expertise in the common law is made in T.H. Clancy, 'Papist Pamphleteers' (Chicago, 1964), 119.
147   Persons, 'Jesuit's Memorial', 250;   'Unpublished Documents relating to the English Martyrs', 356.
148   'State Trials', i, 870.
149   'Narratives of the Reformation', 199.
150   'State Trials', i, 900, 1328, 1069-70.

CHAPTER 5   TO THE GALLOWS AND AFTER

1   'Unpublished Documents relating to the English Mar-
    tyrs' (ed.), J.H. Pollen (Catholic Record Society, v,
    1908), 337;   J. Stow, 'Annales or a Generall Chron-
    icle of England' (ed.), E. Howes (London, 1631),
    793a;   'State Trials' (ed.), W. Cobbett and T.B.
    Howell (London, 1809), i, 1259.
2   See, for example, C. Wriothesley, 'A Chronicle of
    England' (ed.), W.D. Hamilton (C.S. New Series, xi,
    1875), i, 119, BM Arundel MS 152 fo. 294 ('Calendar
    of Letters and Papers, Foreign and Domestic, Henry
    VIII' (ed.) J.S. Brewer, J. Gairdner, R.H. Brodie
    (1862-1932), viii (i), no. 659), 'Letters and
    Papers', xvii, no. 63;   PRO, KB 8/13 mm. 1-9.
3   'Lives of the English Martyrs' (ed.), B. Camm
    (London, 1905), First Series, ii, 197;   (ed.), E.H.
    Burton and J.H. Pollen (London, 1914), Second Series,
    i, 198.
4   W. Allen, 'A briefe historie of the glorious martyr-
    dom of xii reverend priests' (ed.), J.H. Pollen
    (London, 1908), 50;   'The Rambler', N.S., iii (1860),
    375.
5   R. Holinshed, 'Chronicles of England, Scotland and
    Ireland' (London, 1808), iv, 510.
6   'Letters and Papers', xiii, no. 1024.
7   PRO, SP 11/8/53.   Anne Askew was racked after con-
    viction but her offence was heresy:   J. Foxe, 'Acts
    and Monuments' (ed.), G. Townsend and S.R. Cattley
    (London, 1837-41), v, 547;   Wriothesley, 'Chronicle
    of England', i, 168.
8   PRO, SP 15/21/51 ('Cal. State Papers, Domestic, Ad-
    denda, 1566-79', 399);   PRO, SP 12/278/104 ('Cal.
    State Papers, Domestic, 1598-1601', 588).
9   Wriothesley, 'Chronicle of England', ii, 86, 100,
    101;   PRO, SP 12/118/27 ('Cal. State Papers, Domes-
    tic, 1547-80', 566).
10  A rare example of the awarding of punishment by the
    pillory in a treason trial in the queen's bench oc-
    curred on 2 March 1571 when Timothy Penredd was ar-
    raigned for forging the seal of that court (PRO, KB
    8/41 m. 20).
        A physical punishment which seems to have been
    wholly a Tudor invention was the abscission of a hand
    for an additional offence like murder just before the
    prisoner was executed for treason or heresy:   'Stat-
    utes of the Realm' (Record Commission, 1810-28), iii,
    629-30 (27 Hen. VIII c. 59).
11  'The diary of Henry Machyn citizen and Merchant

Taylor of London, from 1550 to 1563 (ed.), J.G.
Nichols (C.S. xlii, 1848), 34;  Wriothesley, 'Chronicles of England', ii, 129.

12  'Acts of the Privy Council' (ed.), J.R. Dasent (1890-
1907), iv, 70;  PRO, SP 1/127 fo. 133 ('Letters and
Papers', xii (ii), no. 1256).

13  'Acts of the Privy Council', v, 27;  iv, 332.

14  PRO, SP 12/176/9 ('Cal. State Papers, Domestic, 1581-
90', 223);  PRO, SP 12/246/82 ('Cal. State Papers,
Domestic, 1591-4', 404).

15  Holinshed, 'Chronicles', iv, 554-6.

16  PRO, SP 12/246/82 ('Cal. State Papers, Domestic,
1591-4', 404);  'Recusant Documents from the Elles-
mere Manuscripts' (ed.), A.G. Petti (Catholic Record
Society, 60, 1968), 22-3;  P.L. Hughes and J.F.
Larkin, 'Tudor Royal Proclamations' (New Haven, 1964-
9), iii, no. 817.

17  Hall, 'Chronicle' (London, 1809), 806;  'Letters and
Papers', vi, no. 1460.

18  Wriothesley, 'Chronicle of England', i, 148;  Foxe,
'Acts and Monuments', v, 528.

19  F. Pollock and F.W. Maitland, 'The History of English
Law before the time of Edward I' (Cambridge, 1895),
ii, 500.

20  Richard White was placed on a 'stade', not a hurdle
('The Rambler',N.S.,iii (1860), 377; 'Unpublished
Documents relating to the English Martyrs', 337-8.

21  Allen, 'Briefe historie', plate 5.   There were occasions towards the end of the sixteenth century when
the victims were taken part or all of the way in a
cart ('Lives of the English Martyrs', Second Series,
i, 365, 413, 529).
       It was suggested by J.H. Pollen that the route
from the Tower to Tyburn was by way of Tower St,
Cheapside, Newgate, Snow Hill, High Holborn, St
Giles, and Oxford St (Allen, 'Brief historie', xv).

22  R. Simpson, 'Edmund Campion, a biography' (London,
1867), 317-18;  'Lives of the English Martyrs',
Second Series, i, 269;  J. Morris, 'The Troubles of
our Catholic Forefathers' (London, 1872-7), i, 98.

23  A breefe and true report of the Execution of certaine
Traytours at Tiborne the xxviii and xxx dayes of
Maye, 1582.   Gathered by A.M. who was there present,
(ed.),'Downside Review', x (1891), 224-5.   In one
case of July 1585 the minister of St Andrews, Holborn, harangued on the need to repent traitors en
route for Tyburn as they passed his church wall:
'The Life and End of T. Awfield and T. Webley, Trai-
tours' (London, 1585), n.p.

24  'State Trials', i, 1083;  'Unpublished Documents relating to the English Martyrs', 326.

25   'Cal. State Papers relating to Scotland and Mary,
     Queen of Scots 1547-1603', ix, no. 328.   For the
     arrangements for Mary's execution see 'Cal. MSS
     Salisbury', iii, 216-17.
26   'State Trials', i, 404, 595.   Mary, Queen of Scots,
     was told she was to die on the morrow and the warrant
     read out to her ('State Trials', i, 1207);   Essex was
     informed after supper the evening before the chosen
     day (PRO, SP 12/278/111 ('Cal. State Papers, Domes-
     tic, 1598-1601', 591).
27   'Acts of the Privy Council', iii, 476, 483;   ii, 262-
     3;   MSS Hatfield, 85/71 ('Cal. MSS Salisbury', xi,
     112).
28   'Acts of the Privy Council', x, 224;   R.N. Worth,
     'Calendar of the Plymouth Municipal Records' (Ply-
     mouth, 1893), 115.
29   Hall, 'Chronicle', 825;   'Acts of the Privy Council',
     i, 117;   'The diary of Henry Machyn', 142;   PRO, KB
     8/53 m. 3.
30   'Acts of the Privy Council', xiv, 57-8.   Justices
     sometimes omitted to designate the place of execu-
     tion:   for example PRO, KB 8/48 mm. 23, 28, 33, 43,
     49.
31   'Unpublished Documents relating to the English Mar-
     tyrs', 327;   'The diary of Henry Machyn', 55;   'State
     Trials', i, 1092.
32   Holinshed, 'Chronicles', iv, 267;   'Cal. State Papers
     relating to Scotland', ix, nos 270, 300.
33   PRO, SP 1/103 fo. 312 ('Letters and Papers', x, no.
     902);   'State Trials', i, 406;   G. Whetstone ('The
     Censure of a Loyall Subject' (London, 1587)) tells us
     that for the execution of fourteen traitors in 1587
     the scaffold area was railed off to keep back horse-
     men.
34   'The diary of Henry Machyn', 42;   'Unpublished Docu-
     ments relating to the English Martyrs', 327;   'Let-
     ters and Papers', x, nos 908, 911, 918.
35   'Letters and Papers', viii, no. 666.   Chapuys re-
     ported the rumour that the king himself wanted to
     watch the butchery, and might even have attended the
     executions in disguise.
36   Stow, 'Annales', 742a;   PRO, SP 12/278/114 ('Cal.
     State Papers, Domestic, 1601-3 and Addenda', 595).
37   When Thomas Mountayne, in gaol at Cambridge, was told
     to prepare hi  elf for immediate execution the gaoler
     volunteered the information that the prison yard was
     full of people come to view the spectacle, some from
     as far away as Lincoln ('Narratives of the Reforma-
     tion' (ed.), J.G. Nichols (C.S. lxxvii, 1859), 203;
     'Cal. State Papers relating to Scotland', ix, no.
     26).

38   See 'Cal. State Papers relating to Scotland', ix,
     no. 266;   'State Trials', i, 1087.
39   'Cal. State Papers relating to Scotland', ix, no. 32;
     'Unpublished Documents relating to the English Mar-
     tyrs', 327.    It was a rare occasion when an intel-
     ligent member of the crowd left a notable execution
     not knowing why the victim had been condemned, but it
     did occur.    Edward Hall states that at the execution
     of Barnes, Garard and Jerome (for heresy) in 1540 he
     asked the London sheriffs why they had been convicted
     and was answered they could not tell (Hall, 'Chron-
     icle', 84).
40   PRO, SP 12/278/111 ('Cal. State Papers, Domestic,
     1598-1601', 591-2);   W. Roper, 'The Lyfe of Sir
     Thomas Moore, knighte' (ed.), E.V. Hitchcock (Early
     English Text Society, no. 197), 101.
41   Foxe, 'Acts and Monuments', vi, 544-5;   'Cal. State
     Papers relating to Scotland', ix, no. 26.
42   'Unpublished Documents relating to the English Mar-
     tyrs', 358-9.    The 'minister of the Towne' argued
     with Robert Southwell at his execution over the
     decrees of the Council of Trent (ibid., 336).
43   'Cal. State Papers relating to Scotland', ix, no. 26;
     no. 266;   'Unpublished Documents relating to the Eng-
     lish Martyrs', 336.
44   PRO, SP 1/132 fo. 134 ('Letters and Papers', xiii
     (i), no. 1024);   'Lives of the English Martyrs',
     Second Series, i, 516.
45   Holinshed, 'Chronicles', iv, 493;   'Lives of the Eng-
     lish Martyrs', First Series, ii, 497.    At the execu-
     tion of John Weldon in 1588 a preacher, making ref-
     erence to the church councils of the fourth and fifth
     centuries, tried to demonstrate that the pope had not
     always been acknowledged as head of the church ('A
     True Report of the inditement, arraignment of J.
     Weldon, W. Hartley and R. Sutton' (London, 1588).
46   'Cal. State Papers relating to Scotland', ix, no. 26;
     'Unpublished Documents relating to the English Mar-
     tyrs', 207.
47   Holinshed, 'Chronicles', iv, 489, 491-2;   'Lives of
     the English Martyrs', First Series, ii, 488.
48   PRO, SP 12/279/25 ('Cal. State Papers, Domestic,
     1601-3, and Addenda', 14).
49   'State Trials', i, 1094, 1414-15, 1359.
50   'Cal. State Papers relating to Scotland', ix, nos 25,
     32.    A monk of Glastonbury, John Oynyon, who was
     adamant in his denial until the rope was around his
     neck, then said he had offended the king 'in such
     sort of treason that it was not expedient to tell

thereof' (PRO, SP 1/155 fo. 169 ('Letters and
Papers', xiv (ii), no. 613)).

51  'A Chronicle of Queen Jane and of two years of Queen
    Mary' (ed), J.G. Nichols (C.S., xlviii, 1850), 56;
    'Cal. State Papers relating to Scotland', ix, no. 26.

52  'Chronicle of Queen Jane', 22;  Foxe, 'Acts and Monu-
    ments', vi, 545.

53  Hall, 'Chronicle', 624;  'Cal. State Papers relating
    to Scotland', ix, no. 32.

54  Hall, 'Chronicle', 839;  'Cal. State Papers relating
    to Scotland', ix, no. 26;  'State Trials', i, 1093.

55  PRO, SP 15/3/78 ('Cal. State Papers, Domestic, 1601-3
    and Addenda', 407-9);  E. Herbert, 'History of Eng-
    land under Henry VIII' (London, 1870), 650.

56  'State Trials', i, 523;  PRO, KB 8/46 mm. 3, 4;  J.
    Strype, 'Annals of the Reformation' (Oxford, 1824),
    III (i), 363.

57  Simpson, 'Campion', 451;  Holinshed, 'Chronicles',
    iv, 489;  'Unpublished Documents relating to the Eng-
    lish Martyrs', 358.

58  W. Camden, 'Annals or the History of the most renow-
    ned and victorious princess Elizabeth, late queen of
    England' (London, 1635), 403;  Stow, 'Annales', 764a;
    'Cal. State Papers relating to Scotland', ix, no. 26.

59  'Cal. State Papers relating to Scotland', ix, no. 26;
    'State Trials', i, 1414, 1088.   In one or two cases
    the prisoner received a reply immediately.   The dean
    of Westminster, who was on the scaffold at the execu-
    tions of the duke of Suffolk and Sir Thomas Wyatt in
    1554, told both, when they requested the queen's for-
    giveness, that her majesty had forgiven them already
    'Chronicle of Queen Jane', 64, 74.

60  'Cal. State Papers relating to Scotland', ix, no. 26;
    'State Trials', i, 405;  'Unpublished Documents rela-
    ting to the English Martyrs', 358.

61  'State Trials', i, 1414;  'Unpublished Documents re-
    lating to the English Martyrs', 358-9.

62  PRO, SP 15/21/46 ('Cal. State Papers, Domestic, Ad-
    denda 1566-79', 397-8);  PRO, SP 12/217/1 ('Cal.
    State Papers, Domestic, 1581-90', 549).

63  'Lives of the English Martyrs', Second Series, i,
    467, 383;  'The Rambler', N.S., iii (1860), 379.

64  'State Trials', i, 1159;  'Cal. State Papers relating
    to Scotland', ix, no. 26.

65  'State Trials', i, 1160;  'Chronicle of Queen Jane',
    73.

66  'Cal. State Papers relating to Scotland', ix, no. 26;
    'State Trials', i, 1094.

67  L.B. Smith, English Treason Trials and Confessions in

the Sixteenth Century, 'Journal of the History of
Ideas', xv (1954), 476.   This was the first piece of
historical writing to assess critically the content
of condemned traitors' gallows speeches.

68   It was suspected at the time that the two were connected ('Original Letters relating to the English
Reformation' (ed.), H. Robinson (Parker Soc. 1846),
203.

69   'Chronicle of Queen Jane', 25;   'Letters and Papers',
viii (i), no. 948.

70   Hall, 'Chronicle', 826;   N. Sanders, 'De Visibili
Monarchia Ecclesiae' (Louvain, 1571), 732;   Holinshed, 'Chronicles', iv, 493;   'Lives of the English
Martyrs', First Series, ii, 455-7, 469-70, 488-9,
496-8.

71   Wriothesley, 'Chronicle of England', i, 27-8, 162.

72   'State Trials', i, 1158;   'Unpublished Documents relating to the English Martyrs', 78;   PRO, SP 12/217/1
('Cal. State Papers, Domestic, 1581-90', 549).

73   PRO, SP 1/103 fo. 312 ('Letters and Papers', x, no.
902);   'Letters and Papers', x, no. 965;   PRO, SP
12/278/111 ('Cal. State Papers, Domestic, 1598-
1601', 591).

74   Wriothesley, 'Chronicle of England', i, 85;   'Unpublished Documents relating to the English Martyrs',
288, 293.

75   J. Bridgewater, 'Concertatio Ecclesiae Catholicae in
Anglia' (Treves, 1588), 142b;   'The Rambler', N.S.,
iii (1860), 379.

76   PRO, SP 15/21/46 ('Cal. State Papers, Domestic, Addenda 1566-79', 398);   'Unpublished Documents relating to the English Martyrs', 359.

77   'Lives of the English Martyrs', First Series, ii,
557;   'The Rambler', N.S., iii (1860), 379.

78   See 'The Rambler', N.S., iii (1860), 379.

79   See H. Foley, 'Records of the English Province of the
Society of Jesus' (London, 1875-83), iii, 734.

80   Allen, 'Briefe historie', 62, 69, 96;   'The Rambler',
N.S., iii (1860), 380.

81   'The Rambler', N.S., iii (1860), 380;   Morris, 'The
Troubles of our Catholic Forefathers', i, 99;
Camden, 'Annals', 403.

82   'Unpublished Documents relating to the English Martyrs', 208.

83   'The Rambler', N.S., iii (1860), 380;   'Unpublished
Documents relating to the English Martyrs', 207.

84   Wriothesley, 'Chronicle of England', i, 115;   'State
Trials', ii, 884;   'Recueil des Croniques ... par
Jehan de Waurin (ed.), W. Hardy (R.S., 1864-91), ii,
42.

85   'The Rambler', N.S., iii (1860), 380;   'Unpublished
     Documents relating to the English Martyrs', 288.
86   'Epistolarum Reginaldi Poli' (ed.), Cardinal Quirini
     (Brixen, 1744), i, 98-9.
87   'Unpublished Documents relating to the English Mar-
     tyrs', 292;   Holinshed, 'Chronicles', iv, 260.
88   'Unpublished Documents relating to the English Mar-
     tyrs', 207, 359;   'The Rambler', N.S., iii (1860),
     380;   'State Trials', i, 1088.
89   PRO, SP 15/21/46 ('Cal. State Papers, Domestic, Ad-
     denda, 1566-79', 398);   see also 'State Trials', i,
     1034.
90   PRO, SP 12/278/112 ('Cal. State Papers, Domestic,
     1598-1601', 592);   'State Trials', i, 1035, 1208;
     'Cal. State Papers relating to Scotland', ix, no.
     267;   Sir Thomas More however was told by the lieu-
     tenant of the Tower not to wear his best apparel
     (Roper, 'Lyfe of Moore', 102).
91   PRO, SP 12/278/112 ('Cal. State Papers, Domestic,
     1598-1601', 594);   'Letters and Papers', x, no. 911.
92   'Chronicle of Queen Jane', 58;   'Cal. State Papers
     relating to Scotland', ix, no. 300.
93   PRO, SP 15/21/47 ('Cal. State Papers, Domestic, Ad-
     denda 1566-79', 398-9);   'Letters and Papers', x, no.
     911;   'Chronicle of Queen Jane', 58;   'Cal. State
     Papers relating to Scotland', ix, no. 300.
94   PRO, SP 12/278/112 ('Cal. State Papers, Domestic,
     1598-1601', 594);   PRO, SP 15/21/46 ('Cal. State
     Papers, Domestic, 1566-79', 398).   Katherine Howard
     practised putting her head on a block whilst still
     in prison, 'Cal. State Papers, Spain', vi (i), no.
     232.
95   PRO, SP 12/278/112 ('Cal. State Papers, Domestic,
     1598-1601', 594).
96   PRO, SP 15/21/46 ('Cal. State Papers, Domestic, Ad-
     denda 1566-79', 398);   'Cal. State Papers relating to
     Scotland', ix, no. 300.
97   'Cal. State Papers relating to Scotland', ix, no.
     267;   'Cal. State Papers, Spain', vi (i), no. 166.
98   PRO, KB 8/9 m. 13;   KB 8/23 m. 5.   John Spelman
     tells us that the justices 'murmured' at the judgment
     against Queen Anne, for such a judgment in the dis-
     junctive had not been seen:   E.W. Ives, Faction at
     the Court of Henry VIII: The Fall of Anne Boleyn,
     'History', 57 (1972), 187.
100  Wriothesley, 'Chronicle of England', i, 80;   ii, 30;
     'State Papers, Henry VIII', v, 93.
101  'State Trials', i, 1086;   'The diary of Henry
     Machyn', 59-60.   One of the few occasions when trai-

tors' bodies were buried at the place of execution
was in May 1582, when the remains of the priests
Lawrence Richardson and William Filby and of the
Jesuit Thomas Cottam were thus interred because, according to one report, it was feared that the popu-
lace might object to seeing so many limbs set up over
the London gates ('Lives of the English Martyrs',
First Series, ii, 499).

102  'State Trials', i, 421, 396;  'Lives of the English
     Martyrs', First Series, ii, 181;  'Letters and
     Papers', x, no. 911;  'Cal. State Papers, Spain',
     vi, (i), no. 232.

103  'Cal. State Papers relating to Scotland', ix, no.
     266;  E.H. Harbison, 'Rival Ambassadors at the Court
     of Queen Mary' (Princeton, 1940), 138;  Bridgewater,
     'Concertatio', 110a.

104  Bridgewater, 'Concertatio', 119b;  'Unpublished Docu-
     ments relating to the English Martyrs', 327.

105  Holinshed, 'Chronicles', iv, 504;  Wriothesley,
     'Chronicle of England', i, 115.   Pity was likely to
     be engendered in the minds of the watchers by the
     victim's high social station according to Whetstone
     ('Censure of a Loyall Subject').

106  Holinshed, 'Chronicles', iv, 494-5;  iii, 793-4.

107  'Correspondance Politique' (ed.), J.B.L. Kaulek
     (Paris, 1885), no. 393.   The one exception concern-
     ing the displaying of trepidation was John Felton,
     who was described as at one point 'quivering and
     shaking with fear' ('State Trials', i, 1087).

108  J.E. Neale, 'Elizabeth I and her Parliaments 1584-
     1601' (London, 1953), 49;  'State Trials', i, 1160-2;
     'Lives of the English Martyrs', Second Series, i,
     371, 467, 472, 520, 530, 535, 548;  'Unpublished
     Documents relating to the English Martyrs', 186.

109  See above chapters 1 and 2.   One other type of for-
     feiture I have omitted altogether.   Any nobleman who
     was a knight of the garter would probably forfeit his
     membership of that order.   He might be degraded
     therefrom at any time after he had been proclaimed a
     traitor.   'Cal. State Papers, Domestic 1547-80',
     348;  'State Trials', i, 298.

110  'English Reports', 2 Dyer 107b;  3 Dyer 288b and
     289a.   Henry IV early in his reign had tried to
     claim without attainder act the forfeiture of the
     fees tail of those who had been killed in battle
     against him.   He discovered that such an act had
     become a necessity.

111  For the chronology and circumstances of Henry VIII's
     attainder acts see S.E. Lehmberg, Parliamentary At-

tainder in the Reign of Henry VIII, 'Historical
Journal', xviii, 4 (1975), 703-24.

112   'State Trials', xiii, 537;   'Journals of the House of
Commons' (London, 1803), i, 9;   'Acts of the Privy
Council', ii, 260;   'Letters and Papers', xvii, no.
124.

There seems to have been an unsuccessful move to
bring Seymour before the commons.   Instead there was
an offer that if the lower house needed further evidence certain peers would bring it down:  W.K.
Jordan, 'Edward VI: The Young King' (London, 1968),
380.

113   13 Eliz. c. 16.   There was one act of attainder (it
was against Sir Francis Englefield), which had as its
purpose to enact that the several attainders already
standing against him 'be good and effectual in law'
('Stat. Realm', iv (ii), 850).   Englefield and his
counsel were summoned before the house of lords, told
to set down in writing why the act should not pass
and then to show certain deeds of conveyance to the
judges and queens learned counsel at a meeting at
Serjeants' Inn:  Simonds D'Ewes, 'A Compleat Journal
of The Votes, Speeches and Debates both of the House
of Lords and House of Commons throughout the whole
reign of Queen Elizabeth' (London, 1708), 462.

114   2 & 3 Edw. VI c. 17;   'Stat. Realm', iv (ii), 766.

115   27 Hen. VIII c. 58;   11 Hen. VII c. 28.

116   33 Hen. VIII c. 21;   28 Hen. VIII c. 24;   27 Hen.
VIII c. 59.

117   PRO, SP 15/17/68, 10 ('Cal. State Papers, Domestic,
Addenda, 1566-79', 222).   In 1486 Humphrey Stafford
in order to attract supporters publicly announced
that King Henry had pardoned him of his former attainder producing forged letters patent to that
effect.   C.H. Williams, The Rebellion of Humphrey
Stafford in 1486, 'English Historical Review', xliii
(1928), 183.

118   See J. Bellamy, 'The Law of Treason in England in the
Later Middle Ages' (Cambridge, 1970), 188-9;   26 Hen.
VIII c. 25:  the comforters and abettors, who were
not named, were given the chance to escape attaint by
submitting before 16 December 1536.

119   See Bellamy, 'Law of Treason', 81, 90, 184, 194, 204.
For how levying open war was defined by convention in
the later medieval period see M.H. Keen, Treason Trials under the Law of Arms, 'Transactions of the Royal
Historical Society', 5th Series, xii (1962), 94-6.

120   PRO, SP 15/17/80, 95 ('Cal. State Papers, Domestic,
Addenda, 1566-79', 228, 236).

121   'Cal. Patent Rolls, 1485-94', 473;   'Cal. Close
      Rolls, 1327-30', 55.
122   PRO, SP 15/15/125, 17/100, 18/26 ('Cal. State Papers,
      Domestic, Addenda, 1566-79', 166, 238, 267);   3 Dyer
      288b, 289a.
123   BM Titus MS B. i, fo. 446 ('Letters and Papers', vi,
      no. 1381);   'Stat. Realm', iii, 450.   The clerics
      who were attainted lost 'all suche benefices and
      spiritual promocions' as they enjoyed at the time
      their treason was committed.
124   'Stat. Realm', iv (i), 146.
125   PRO, SP 12/251/50 ('Cal. State Papers, Domestic,
      1595-7', 15);   'Letters and Papers', x, no. 1256/52.
      However Lady Savage met with some difficulty in get-
      ting the grant enforced:   see E.W. Ives, Court and
      County Palatine in the reign of Henry VIII: The
      Career of William Brereton of Malpas, 'Historic Soc-
      iety of Lancashire and Cheshire' (1972), 34.
126   D.M. Loades, 'Two Tudor Conspiracies' (Cambridge,
      1965), 122;   'Materials for a History of Henry VII'
      (ed.), W. Campbell (Rolls Series, 1873-7), ii, 286;
      J.R. Lander, Attainder and Forfeiture, 1453-1509,
      'Historical Journal', iv, 2 (1961), 141.
127   7 Hen. VII c. 23;   'Stat. Realm', ii, 415-16;   iii,
      267.
128   BM Titus MS B. i, fo. 450 ('Letters and Papers', xii
      (i), no. 1315);   PRO, SP 1/156 fo. 147 ('Letters and
      Papers', xiv (ii), appendix, no. 9).
129   'State Papers, Henry VIII', i, 537;   PRO, SP 1/233
      fo. 189 ('Letters and Papers, Addenda', i (i), no.
      361).
130   'Letters and Papers', xii (i), no. 1315;   'Cal.
      Patent Rolls, 1569-72', 197.
131   'English Reports', 2 Dyer 146a;   19 Hen. VII c. 27:
      the reason given for passing this act was to speed
      the answering of petitions, since parliament was
      nearly finished.
132   See 'Cal. Patent Rolls, 1494-1509', 374, 454, for
      examples of pardons under the powers granted by the
      1504 act;   14 & 15 Hen. VIII c. 21 ('Stat. Realm',
      iii, 259).   On Henry VIII's acts of restitution in
      general see Lehmberg, Parliamentary Attainder', His-
      torical Journal', xviii (1975), 699-70.
133   Hughes and Larkin, 'Tudor Royal Proclamations', i,
      246-7, 256-8, 425-7;   PRO, E36/119 fo. 93 ('Letters
      and Papers', xi, no. 1224);   PRO, SP 1/121 fo. 203
      ('Letters and Papers', xii (ii), no. 177).
134   'Cal. Patent Rolls, 1566-9', 363;   PRO, SP 15/18/21
      ('Cal. State Papers, Domestic, Addenda, 1566-79',
      266).

135 Holinshed, 'Chronicles', iv, 56; 'Letters and Papers', xvi, no. 678/41.
136 See PRO, SP 12/266/30, 270/118, 273/25 ('Cal. State Papers, Domestic, 1598-1601', 13-14, 199, 341); 'State Trials', i, 1155.
137 'Cal. Patent Rolls, 1494-1509', 218; '1566-9', 63-4; '1494-1509', 468.
138 PRO, SP 12/150/80 'Cal. State Papers, Domestic, 1581-90', 32); Holinshed, 'Chronicles', iv, 537.
139 'Cal. Patent Rolls, 1494-1509', 159; PRO, SP 1/130 fo. 64 ('Letters and Papers', xiii (i), no. 519).
140 PRO, SP 15/18/7 ('Cal. State Papers, Domestic, Addenda, 1566-79', 251-2); PRO, SP 12/281/67 ('Cal. State Papers, Domestic, 1601-3 and Addenda', 38).
141 PRO, SP 15/18/7, 26, 75 ('Cal. State Papers, Domestic, Addenda, 1566-79', 251-2, 267, 303).
142 Loades, 'Two Tudor Conspiracies', 120-1.
143 Ibid., 117, 125; PRO, SP 12/279/106, 281/67 ('Cal. State Papers, Domestic, 1601-3 and Addenda', 50, 88-9); MSS Hatfield 85/76 ('Cal. MSS Salisbury', xii, 72).
144 'Stat. Realm', iii, 809-11; iv, 125.
145 'The diary of Henry Machyn', 56; Wriothesley, 'Chronicle of England', ii, 113; 'Letters and Papers', ii (ii), no. 3259.
146 Grafton, 'Chronicle', 1025.
147 E. Coke, 'The Third Part of the Institutes of the Laws of England' (London, 1797), 234.
148 PRO, KB 8/6 mm. 1-5; 'Letters and Papers', vii, no. 1013; PRO, SP 1/Fol. Q (14) ('Letters and Papers', vii, no. 1270).
149 'Acts of the Privy Council', v, 90; PRO, SP 1/132 fo. 88 ('Letters and Papers', xiii (i), no. 970).
150 G.R. Elton, 'Policy and Police' (Cambridge, 1972), 387.

## APPENDIX MARTIAL LAW

1 J. Bellamy, 'The Law of Treason in England in The Later Middle Ages' (Cambridge, 1970), 41-58. For the 'law of arms' see M.H. Keen, Treason Trials under the Law of Arms, 'Transactions of the Royal Historical Society', 5th Series, xii (1962), 85-103.
2 'Year Books', 37 Hen. VI Pasch. pl. 8; Vernon Harcourt, 'His Grace the Steward and Trial of Peers' (London, 1907), 415.
3 'Cal. Patent Rolls, 1494-1509', 115, 202.
4 Ibid., 115; Vernon Harcourt, 'His Grace the

Steward', 414.    In the sixteenth century, as had
happened on occasion in the fifteenth, noble traitors
accused of conspiring treason were usually tried
under the common law before the lord high steward and
a jury of magnates.

5   Henry VII seems to have fallen into the same error as
the advisers of Queen Mary, namely believing that to
conspire to levy war was treason by the act of 1352
(see above pp. 55-6).

6   G.D. Squibb, 'The High Court of Chivalry' (Oxford,
1958), 30-1, 39.    Even in July 1495 there was a commission issued to the 'king's marshal' Sir John Digby
commanding him to cite before him, and pronounce sentence on, the king's adversaries, aliens, and strangers ('Cal. Patent Rolls, 1494-1509', 34).    The last
case of treason heard before the constable was probably that of Thomas Tyrell (May 1502), whose offences
had been committed at Guisnes near Calais (ibid.,
506).

7   L. Boynton, The Tudor Provost-Marshal, 'English Historical Review', lxxvii (1962), 438-9.

The 'book of statutes and ordinances at Berwick',
a copy of which is to be found in the state papers of
Henry VIII, was perhaps compiled at the time of the
reorganization of that fortress by Henry VII.    There
is reference to a marshal and a marshal's court
there; PRO, SP 1/170 fo. 145 ('Calendar of Letters
and Papers, Foreign and Domestic, Henry VIII', (ed.),
J.S. Brewer, J. Gairdner, R.H. Brodie (1862-1932),
xvii, no. 343).    Calais had its own high-marshal,
deputy high-marshal, and under-marshal ('Statutes of
the Realm' (Record Commission, 1810-28), iii, 634,
637, 639).

8   PRO, E39/93/15 m. 5.

9   PRO, SP 1/107 fo. 38 ('Letters and Papers', xi, no.
579).    By January 1537 a provost-marshal named Hart-
well was attaching men in Lincoln and taking them to
London:  PRO, E36/119/2 ('Letters and Papers', xii
(i), no. 70).

10  See 'The Workes of Sir Thomas More, Knyght' (ed.),
W. Roper (London, 1557), 990.

11  G.W. Prothero, 'Statutes and Constitutional Documents, 1558-1625' (Oxford, 1906), 154-6;  G. Scott
Thomson, 'Lords Lieutenants in the Sixteenth Century' (London, 1923), Appendix B, 149-50.

12  Cf. PRO, SP 1/116 fos 95-6, 108 ('Letters and Paper
Papers', xii (i), nos 479, 498).

13  Boynton, The Tudor Provost-Marshal, 442-5;  P.L.
Hughes and J.F. Larkin, 'Tudor Royal Proclamations'

(New Haven, 1964-9), i, nos 341, 342, iii, no. 699;
PRO, SP 15/3/20 ('Cal. State Papers, Domestic, 1601-3
and Addenda', 394-5).

14    Brooks New Cases, 185; PRO, SP 15/15/132 ('Cal.
State Papers, Domestic, Addenda, 1566-79', 169).

15    PRO, SP 1/116 fo. 108 ('Letters and Papers, xii (i),
no. 498).

16    Norfolk, in March 1537, intended to use common law
indictments as evidence in trials under martial law:
PRO, SP 1/116 fo. 236 ('Letters and Papers', xii (i),
no. 615).

17    Boynton, The Tudor Provost-Marshal, 446, 449-50.

18    PRO, SP 1/134 fo. 205, 1/116 fo. 83 ('Letters and
Papers', xiii (i), no. 1411, xii (i), no. 468).

19    W. Camden, 'Annals or the History of the most renown-
ed and victorious princess Elizabeth, late queen of
England' (London, 1635), 174; PRO, SP 15/17/17
('Cal. State Papers, Domestic, Addenda, 1566-79',
188).

20    'Acts of the Privy Council' (ed.), J.R. Dasent (1890-
1907), v, 349; T. Smith, 'De Republica Anglorum'
(ed.), L. Alston (Cambridge, 1906), 59.

21    'State Trials' (ed.), W. Cobbett and T.B. Howell
(London, 1809), i, 1435.

22    PRO, SP 15/15/132, and 139, SP 15/17/14 ('Cal. State
Papers, Domestic, Addenda, 1566-79', 169, 172, 186).

23    PRO, SP 15/15/132, SP 15/17/2 ('Cal. State Papers,
Domestic, Addenda, 1566-79', 169, 175).

24    PRO, SP 15/17/80 ('Cal. State Papers, Domestic, Addenda, 1566-79', 228); 'Rotuli Parliamentorum'
(ed.), J. Strachey et al. (London, 1767), vi, 544.
There were, of course, good reasons why in certain
circumstances insurgents convicted under the common
law should be attainted by act of parliament: see
for example the case of the earl and countess of
Northumberland, the earl of Westmorland, a knight,
and 41 esquires and gentlemen, in 1571 ('Stat.
Realm', iv (i), 549).

# Index

**DATE DUE**

| | | | |
|---|---|---|---|
| | | | |
| | | | |
| | | | |
| | | | |
| | | | |
| | | | |
| | | | |
| | | | |